RACE AND MULTIRACIALITY IN BRAZIL AND THE UNITED STATES

RACE AND MULTIRACIALITY IN BRAZIL AND THE UNITED STATES

CONVERGING PATHS?

G. REGINALD DANIEL

the pennsylvania state university press
university park, pennsylvania

Library of Congress Cataloging-in-Publication Data

Daniel, G. Reginald, 1949–
    Race and multiraciality in Brazil and the United States :
    converging paths? / G. Reginald Daniel.

      p.   cm.
Includes bibliographical references and index.
ISBN 978-0-271-02883-5 (cloth : alk. paper)
ISBN 978-0-271-03288-7 (paper : alk. paper)

1. Brazil—Race relations.
2. United States—Race relations.
I. Title.

F2659.A1D36 2006
305.800981—dc22
2006002712

Second printing, 2007

The Pennsylvania State University Press is a member of
the Association of American University Presses.

It is the policy of The Pennsylvania State University Press
to use acid-free paper. This book is printed on Natures
Natural, containing 50% post-consumer waste, and meets
the minimum requirements of American National Standard
for Information Sciences—Permanence of Paper for Printed
Library Material, ANSI Z39.48–1992.

CONTENTS

On December 2, 1955, my first-grade teacher began class by saying, "Yesterday, in Montgomery, Alabama, a colored women, Mrs. Rosa Parks, was arrested for refusing to let a white passenger have her seat on the bus. It's time we colored people stood up for our rights!" The question of "rights" went over my head, and I was especially confused by the phrase "we colored people." I knew that everyone was "colored." Some people were brown. Others were pink (which I knew to be a blend of red and white) or beige or tan (which were blends of varying degrees of brown and white). I remember how excited I was that year when Crayola came out with a box of crayons that included pink, beige, tan, and so on, although I was somewhat perplexed by the flesh crayon. It was similar to tan, but I knew that everyone was not "flesh"-colored. Nevertheless, I was happy to see my own tan color among the crayons. Up to that time, crayon boxes included only the basic colors. Consequently, I could not get pink, beige, or tan, except when I did watercolors and had access to white paint to blend with red or brown. Just to get a clarification, I raised my hand and asked who "colored" people were. "Everyone in this school!" she said quite startled. "What color are they?" I asked. "We're brown! We're Negroes!" I had seen brown people. (In fact, there were many at my school.) I also knew that my own tan-colored skin tone was part brown. However, I had never heard of the color "Negro" before, much less come across it among my crayons or paints. Consequently, this whole discussion left me quite confused.

At the end of class, my teacher gave me a note to take home to my mother instructing her to have a long talk with me about being Negro and about seg-regation. (Many years later, my mother told me that she had avoided this topic because she did not want me to develop a sense of inferiority.) She now tried to explain the absurdity of segregated schools, water fountains, public parks, theaters, restaurants, hospitals, funeral homes, cemeteries, and so on. She agreed that our family was "tan," rather than "brown." (There were some pink and beige family members, however, who I later discovered were not pink or beige at all but looked "white." I had never seen anyone the color of the white crayon, or blackboard chalk.) My mother went on to explain how we came to be "tan" Negroes, throwing in details about African slavery, about our Irish, English, French, American Indian, Asian Indian, and possibly German-Jewish ancestry. She concluded by saying that although we were a blend of many things and, thus, only part-Negro, we were still members of the Negro race, which was another word for colored people. This struck me as being somewhat illogical, so I said, "But Mommy, when you mix brown and white, you don't get brown or white, you get tan." She told me it was not the same with people. Outwardly I acquiesced but could not understand how I could have East Indian and African and Native American and several European backgrounds and be Negro. How could you take one part of my whole background, the African part, and then get rid of all the rest? "That's stupid," I thought. "That doesn't make any sense. One plus one equals two, not one."

I shelved the entire issue until 1965 when I stumbled upon Era Bell Thompson's *Ebony* magazine article "Does Amalgamation Work in Brazil?" which discussed Brazilian race relations. As I browsed through the article, my eyes fell upon a passage that spoke of these mysterious creatures called "mulattoes." They were the products of racial blending between Africans, Europeans—primarily Portuguese— and Native Americans and were intermediate to these groups. "Just like me! . . . Just Like Tabitha on *Bewitched*; like Mr. Spock on *Star Trek!* . . . Like twilight, that zone between day and night that we all pass through at dusk and dawn." From that point on the classroom became not merely an academic arena but also a platform for self-discovery, transformation, and personal liberation, albeit most often under the mocking and disapproving scrutiny of my peers and superiors.

I wanted to gain insight into why multiracial individuals of partial African American descent were prevented from embracing their other racial backgrounds in the United States. I discovered part of an answer in a social code called the "one-drop rule of hypodescent," which held that the offspring of interracial unions were to be defined as African American, regardless of the racial background of their other parent. And not only the children of interracial unions but, in fact, anyone who had any traceable African descent, anyone with "one drop of African blood," was designated as black. Accordingly, the one-drop rule supported a binary racial project that renders racial identification as either black or white.

The dominant whites used the one-drop rule to justify legal prohibitions against interracial sexual relations, and especially interracial marriage, in order to preserve white racial and cultural "purity." The rule also conveniently exempted white landowners (particularly slaveholders) from the legal obligation of passing on inheritance and other benefits of paternity to their multiracial offspring. Moreover, the rule helped maintain white racial privilege by supporting legal and informal barriers to equality in most aspects of life. The one-drop rule did not become a normative part of the legal apparatus in the United States until the early twentieth century (circa 1915) but gained currency as the informal or "commonsense" definition of blackness over the course of the seventeenth and eighteenth centuries. This was increasingly the case during the nineteenth century and definitively so by the 1920s.

The one-drop rule has become such an accepted part of the Anglo–North American fabric that most individuals, except perhaps African Americans, are unaware that it is unique to the United States. Rules of hypodescent have been applied to the first-generation offspring of European Americans and Americans of color (Native Americans, Asian Americans, Latinas/os, and so on). Successive generations of individuals whose lineage has included a background of color, along with European ancestry, however, have been treated with greater flexibility. These individuals have not invariably been designated exclusively, or even partially, as members of that group of color if the background is less than one-fourth of their lineage. Furthermore, self-identification with that background has been more a matter of choice. This flexibility has not been extended to individuals of African American and European American descent. The one-drop rule has not only precluded any choice in self-identification but also ensured that African American ancestry is passed on in perpetuity. All future offspring are socially designated as black. Most individuals in the United States never question the rule's logic, and thus reinforce, if only unwittingly, blackness and whiteness as mutually exclusive, if not hierarchical, categories of experience.

Through my research in Brazil and the United States I discovered that Brazilian race relations, like those in the rest of Latin America, have displayed more pervasive miscegenation than the United States. More important, this racial blending has been validated in a ternary racial project that differentiates the population into whites (*brancos*), multiracial individuals (*pardos* in official contexts; *mulatto* in everyday parlance), and blacks (*pretos*). Moreover, blackness and whiteness in Brazil represent extremes on a continuum where physical appearance (in conjunction with class and culture), rather than ancestry, has come to determine one's racial identity and status in the social hierarchy. This has led to fluid racial/cultural markers and an absence of legalized barriers to equality, which in turn has given rise to the belief that Brazil is a racial democracy.

By virtue of this dynamic, select multiracial individuals have been allowed token vertical socioeconomic mobility into the bourgeoisie through an informal window of opportunity that historian Carl Degler calls the "mulatto escape hatch." Degler does not imply that the masses of mulattoes gain access carte blanche to the prestigious ranks of whites because they are mulatto (as opposed to black). Indeed, the social positioning of individuals designated as "multiracial," although intermediate in the Brazilian racial hierarchy, is collectively speaking closer to blacks than to whites. Rather, Degler argues that the escape hatch is an informal social mechanism by which a few "visibly" multiracial individuals, for reasons of talent, culture, or education, have been granted situational whiteness in accordance with their phenotypical and cultural approximation to the dominant whites. In its broadest sense, however, the escape hatch and the accompanying ideology of racial "whitening" through miscegenation have made it possible over time for millions of individuals whose ancestry has included African forebears, but who are phenotypically white, or near-white, to become self-identified and socially designated as white. The social construction of whiteness—as well as the extension of white racial privilege—is more inclusive in Brazil than the United States, where the one-drop rule can transform into black an individual who appears otherwise white.

The issues surrounding racial categories and identities in Brazil and the United States are by no means limited to the experience of individuals of predominantly African and European descent. Nevertheless, there are several reasons for focusing on the multiracial phenomenon as it relates to the social construction of blackness. First, the history of African slavery and the unique legacy of attitudes and policies that have crystallized around individuals of African descent in both Brazil and the United States make a comparative analysis particularly meaningful. Second, although U.S. law has been preoccupied with race in general, the specificity of blackness in U.S. jurisprudence, combined with the post–civil rights eradication of formal expressions of racism in the United States and the dismantling of the racial democracy ideology in Brazil, makes a comparative historical examination meaningful, particularly as it relates to the multiracial progeny of black-white unions.

Furthermore, the black-white paradigm, as well as Brazil's and the United States's historic treatment of individuals of African descent, has been the touchstone for their treatment of all racialized "Others." Despite its limitations in application to those racial "Others," the black-white paradigm has provided the larger context in which their experiences have been grounded. Therefore, unless otherwise indicated, the words "mulatto" (Forbes 1988, 131–50),[1] "multiracial," and

1. In popular thought, "mulatto" is said to have evolved from the Portuguese word *mulo* (mule) as an epithet. The mulatto, as the offspring of a black and a white, was imagined to be degenerate and at least low in fertility, if not actually sterile, like its barnyard counterpart. That said, some linguists have argued that as a legacy of the Islamic occupation of the Iberian Peninsula, the Arabic word used to refer to individuals of African/Arab descent—*muwallad*—may have evolved into the Portuguese

"biracial" are used interchangeably in this book to refer to individuals of predominantly black and white backgrounds, although other backgrounds—particularly Native American—may be included in their lineage. "Black" generally refers only to individuals who are considered to be completely (or at least predominantly) African, African American, or African Brazilian. However, the term is sometimes used as a synonym for "African Brazilian," "African American," "African-descent Brazilian," and "African-descent American," which encompass both "black" and "multiracial" individuals.

Given that genetic, archaeological, and linguistic evidence indicates that the first human communities evolved in Central Africa millennia ago, everyone in the Americas is in some sense an African-descent American. Between 90,000 and 180,000 years ago, populations from Africa spread throughout Africa, Asia, Europe, and the Pacific; perhaps as early as 30,000 years ago but at least as recently as 15,000 years ago they migrated to the Americas. As they adapted to various environments they evolved into geographical aggregates of populations displaying differences in various bodily features. Some of the externally visible features—skin color, hair, and facial morphology—are commonly referred to as "racial traits." These physical differences (phenotypes) reflect some of the differences in genetic information (genotypes) that are transmitted through one's ancestors. So there are human populations that, taken as aggregates, exhibit higher incidences of particular geno-phenotypical traits than do other human populations, taken as aggregates.

Nevertheless, despite such commonly observed differences, all members of the species *homo sapiens sapiens* share 99.9 percent of their genes. If geno-phenotypical diversity of racial traits is a biological fact, the boundaries delineating geno-phenotypical subgroupings are not discrete or fixed entities. These boundaries have always been eroded by contact—through migration, trade, and war—that has inevitably set into motion a countertrend toward "racial entropy." Over time racial entropy levels out absolute differences by diffusing common genetic information—and ultimately common phenotypical traits—throughout the general population if no forces intervene to prevent this process. Consequently, the 0.1 percent of the genetic information that determines phenotypical traits associated with racial differentiation is itself the product of millennia of genetic "blending" (Henig 2004; Tobias 1972, 19–43). Thus, although we recognize certain phenotypical traits as marking off population aggregates as different from one another, in fact, a "multiracial" lineage is the norm rather than the exception. Indeed, if

word *mulato* to refer to Afro-Europeans (or Eurafricans). The word "mulatto" can be used with derogatory connotations; yet it is more often used simply as a designation for individuals of African and European backgrounds.

we trace a person's lineage back over the generations, the number of ancestors, as well as the myriad possibilities in terms of their "racial" composition, is staggering (Forbes 1990, 37–38).

Generally speaking, the smaller the proportion of any given ancestry the more probable it is that the number of genes inherited from that ancestry is also proportionately smaller. Yet genes are randomly distributed in individuals and having one or more West African ancestors does not guarantee that an individual will inherit genetic information from those forebears or exhibit discernible West African phenotypical traits (Davis 1991, 19–23). Indeed, individuals may be of partial African ancestry and also inherit genetic material from those ancestors, yet appear completely European American. This "illusion" of complete "whiteness" is attributable to the fact that the human visual system is unable to perceive information at the genetic level (except by technological means) where we could possibly see DNA inherited from both African and European ancestors. Yet the U.S. one-drop rule, which uses ancestry as the criterion in arriving at racial designations, has designated as black all individuals of any traceable West African ancestry irrespective of one's geno-phenotype (Davis 1991, 19–23).

The biological concept of race attempts to explain differences in human populations, but racial boundaries are illusory. Phenotypical traits are not transmitted in genetic clusters but vary independently, which has led some people to assert there is no such thing as race. They view race as an unfortunate legacy of the past five hundred years of human history and recommend we discard the concept altogether. Those who hold a social constructionist position argue that race has a social reality, even if the concept has no scientific basis. They point out that race has been a powerful force in Western thought and behavior, one embedded in the structure of social institutions. Even people who maintain that race is an illusion recognize the social reality of race and cannot avoid using the term even as they deny its existence (Omi and Winant 1994, 54–55; Smedley 1993, 18–21).

Like the larger educated community, scholars have reached no consensus on the definition of race, although they agree that the concept should be regarded as a neutral classificatory term. One could argue that we do not need to dispense with the concept of race but should consider race as one of many differentiating categories, like sex and gender or class, that influence human experience. Rather than reject the concept, we should transcend essentialized notions of race and deal more forthrightly with racism and racial inequality, which have less to do with race than with the abuses committed in the name of race.

Any attempt to use the term "race" in an objective, scientific, and neutral manner is nevertheless undermined by unavoidable contradiction. Despite its supposed neutrality as a biological concept, race has been (and continues to be) inextricably intertwined with a society's distribution of wealth, power, privilege, and prestige, and therefore with inequality. In the U.S. national consciousness, race has generally had priority over class, sex, gender, age, and religion as an indicator of social and economic inequality. Race has often served to disguise, or deflect attention from, other types of social division (for example, when poor white farmers in the post-Reconstruction South were encouraged to identify with wealthy white planters rather than with poor black farmers, with whom they had more in common economically). The concept of racial difference has created a chasm of social distance expressed explicitly and implicitly in all kinds of social intercourse. It is this social construction of race, not the biological concept, which has had such a deleterious effect on the social order in the United States and elsewhere.

The social sciences seek to explain the sociopolitical reality of race apart from its use as a concept in the biological sciences. Accordingly, racial formation theory challenges the position that race is an illusion, that race is something that we can and should move beyond. It also rejects the position that race is an "objective reality" but acknowledges its existence as a social construction. The concept of race is based on biological characteristics, but the selection of particular human features for purposes of racial signification has changed over time and is necessarily a sociohistorical process. This process groups different geno-phenotypical features for social and ideological, not scientific, purposes (Omi and Winant 1994, 55–60).

By recognizing race as a construction, racial formation theory makes it possible to analyze how a society determines racial meanings and assigns racial identities. At any given moment in space and time many interpretations of race exist in the form of "racial projects." Every racial project is a discursive or cultural initiative. This involves an interpretation, representation, or explanation of racial dynamics by means of identity politics in order to rescue racial identities from their distortion and erasure by the dominant society. At the same time, each racial project is a political initiative. Its goal is to organize and redistribute resources, a process in which the state is often called upon to play a significant role.

From the very beginning, the state in Brazil and the United States has exercised power not only in the politics of racial exclusion (and inclusion) but also in enforcing racial definition, classification, and identification. For much of its history, the racial state in both countries has been characterized by not democracy and reform but rather despotism and tyranny. Under normal conditions the racial status quo has gone undisturbed for extended periods of time because state institutions have effectively and systematically marginalized legal and political challenges to the prevailing racial order. Indeed, only since the last half of the twentieth century has there been the necessary political space and conceptual flexibility about race in Brazil and the United States to secure and reformulate racial meanings, forge an oppositional racial ideology, and constitute alternative racial institutions (Omi and Winant 1994, 77–91).

Although state institutions organize and enforce the racial politics of everyday life, the centrality of race to state institutions and policies varies over time. Indeed, race becomes a political issue only when a critical mass of individuals view state institutions as enforcing an unjust racial order. Consequently, the racial policies of the state and opposition to them alternate between periods of virtual stasis and rapid change, between eras of relative passivity and of massive mobilization. In one context, the majority of people may understand race uncritically and define it on the basis of simple "common sense." Racial identities would be reproduced by their own "naturalness" and "taken-for-grantedness" in the daily life of the society. Racial contestation would be limited to a few marginalized racial projects at most. In another context, race might be highly politicized and the site of significant social mobilization. Here we would expect a high degree of contestation in the form of a national debate about race and a great deal of popular uncertainty about its significance in everyday life.

In sum, the racial state and its institutions are the site of collective demands both for egalitarian reforms and for the enforcement of existing inegalitarian privileges. Yet rather than serve one coordinated racial objective, state institutions often work at cross-purposes, a condition of institutional competition and conflict within the state that is only exacerbated when the social changes set in motion by oppositional projects threaten to disrupt the racial equilibrium. The need to establish a new equilibrium thus becomes paramount and is achieved through a process of conflict and compromise between the racial state and racially based opposition (Omi and Winant 1994, 77–91).

ACKNOWLEDGMENTS

Neither time nor space allow me to acknowledge the support I received from hundreds of individuals who helped bring this book to fruition. Maria P.P. Root, Paul R. Spickard, Teresa K. Williams-Leon, Ludwig (Larry) and Francis Lauherhass, Nina Moss, the Huber family (Dona Maria, Valburga, and Teresa), and Vera de Araujo-Shellard provided personal and professional encouragement, which made it possible to carry on in the face of seemingly insurmountable obstacles and against overwhelming odds. This manuscript would not have been possible without the editorial assistance provided by Josef Castañeda-Liles and Chris Bickel. Stephen Small, Edward Telles, and Howard Winant provided invaluable feedback that helped refine my analysis. Connie McNeely and David Estrin helped tighten up the manuscript without sacrificing my ideas. Sheila Gardette, José Garcia, Monique Vogelsang, Tarik Sadowski, Maiya Evans, Paulo de Luz Moreira and Nicholas (Nick) Hall are outstanding research assistants who helped track down material in the United States and Brazil. Marcelo Paixão, professor of the Instituto de Economia at the Federal University of Rio de Janeiro, provided critical assistance in collecting recent data in Brazil. My research also benefited from the collections at the Center for Afro-Asiatic Studies, Biblioteca Nacional, Academia Brasileira de Letras—all in Rio de Janeiro—and Lily Library at Indiana University in Bloomington. Miki Goral and Norma Corral, who are the backbones of the Reference Department at the UCLA Research Library, and Sylvia Curtis, UCSB Black Studies Librarian, left no stone unturned and went several extra miles to acquire critical sources. I am also indebted to Jiro Ochoa at University Postal Shipping and Copies, as well as Grafikart Copy Shop, for their technical support in completing this project.

My thanks to the Fulbright-Hays Commission for a grant to do research in Brazil, and the University of California, Santa Barbara, for awarding me both an Academic Senate grant to do archival research in the United States and a Faculty Career Development Award, which gave me the time I needed to complete the manuscript. However, completion of this project would not have been possible without a generous grant from the K & F Baxter Family Foundation. I owe a special debt to my colleagues and the staff in the Center for African American Studies and the Latin American Center at UCLA, as well as the Department of Sociology and Center for Black Studies Research at UCSB.

A special thanks to the many individuals I have met at support groups and at conferences on the topic of intermarriage and multiracial identity, whose sentiments and experiences I have tried to capture in this book. Also, I am eternally grateful to Nadia Kim, Julie Silvers, Shadi Alai, and the many other students in my classes who have had faith in my vision and me when others have not.

Sandy Thatcher of Pennsylvania State University Press is an exemplary editor. I am grateful to him, the copyeditor, and the readers recruited by the Press.

Santa Barbara, California
February 2006

INTRODUCTION

Since Carl Degler published his pivotal comparative historical research on race relations in Brazil and the United States (*Neither Black nor White*, 1971), several scholars have compared the gradual demise of Brazil's ideology of racial democracy and the dismantling of Jim Crow segregation in the United States.[1] There are also several comparative historical analyses of state-defined racial categories as these relate to the multiracial movement in the United States and the black movement in Brazil that emerged in the late 1970s.[2]

In this book I build on this research as well as examine broader racial dynamics as they relate to the multiracial phenomenon. Part I ("The Historical Foundation") argues that the historical trajectories of the seemingly divergent racial orders in Brazil and the United States have much in common.

Chapter 1 traces the origin of Eurocentrism, as well as its companions white racism and white supremacy, which are the foundation of the Brazilian and U.S. racial orders.

Chapter 2 examines the history of Brazil's ternary racial project, the mulatto escape hatch, and the associated "whitening through miscegenation" ideology, along with the absence of legalized barriers to racial equality. These phenomena led to the notion that class and cultural rather than racial signifiers determine social stratification in Brazil. More important, they earned Brazil the reputation as a racial democracy, an image popularized by anthropologist Gilberto Freyre in his monumental studies of Brazilian race relations: *The Masters and the Slaves* (1933), *The Mansions and the Shanties* (1936), and *Order and Progress* (1959).

---

1. See Skidmore 1993, Sundiata 1987, Winant 1994, Penha-Lopes 1996, and Daniel 2000.
2. See Daniel 2000 and Nobles 2000.

Chapter 3 highlights racial projects during the nineteenth and early twentieth centuries that challenged the ternary racial project, the mulatto escape hatch, and whitening ideology. These included projects formulated by individuals such as Luís Gama and Lima Barreto, who spoke out against racial oppression. Collective strategies involved the Black Guard (Guarda Negra), the Brazilian Black Front (Frente Negra Brasileira), and the Black Experimental Theater (O Teatro Experimental do Negro), which sought to unify blacks and mulattoes in the struggle for African Brazilian rights. In order to accomplish this aim these organizations and others like them deployed binary racial projects similar to those in the United States. Yet racial pluralism was generally viewed as a temporary tactic in the struggle for racial equality. The goal was to fulfill Brazil's ideology of racial democracy by integrating blacks and mulattoes into the social order as equals, rather than maintaining African Brazilians as a distinct group.

Chapter 4 maps out the historical development of the U.S. one-drop rule and the binary racial project. It also analyzes the informal and formal practices sanctioning the unequal treatment of African-descent Americans in most aspects of social life.

Chapter 5 focuses on racial projects that historically contested the binary racial project and the one-drop rule. Individual projects have included "passing." Collective strategies have included the formation of blue-vein societies, Louisiana Creoles of color, and triracial isolates, which created alternative third identities (or ternary racial projects) in a manner similar to Brazil. Yet these tactics were inegalitarian and maintained the racial hierarchy.

Part II ("Converging Paths") analyzes the changes in Brazilian and U.S. race relations beginning in the 1950s and 1960s that led to the gradual erosion of the racial democracy ideology in Brazil and the dismantling of legalized racial segregation in the United States. I argue that by the late 1970s race relations in these two countries began to converge, particularly in terms of the multiracial phenomenon.

Chapter 6 examines the U.S. racial order that emerged in the 1950s and 1960s with the dismantling of Jim Crow segregation, the implementation of civil rights legislation and affirmative action initiatives, and the removal of the last laws against racial intermarriage (*Loving v. Virginia*). After the 1967 *Loving* decision, social relations became comparatively more fluid, the rate of interracial marriage rose, and many interracial couples began raising their offspring to embrace a "multiracial" identity. By 1979, interracial couples in Berkeley, California, founded I-Pride (Interracial/Intercultural Pride) to demand that the Berkeley Board of Education include a multiracial identifier on public school forms.

Although previous work on the one-drop rule existed, only beginning in the late 1980s did there emerge ground-breaking research on the "new" multiracial identity generally, and more specifically, the implications of the one-drop rule on a multiracial identification, premier examples being Paul R. Spickard's *Mixed Blood* (1989) and Maria P.P. Root's *Racially Mixed People in America* (1992) and *The Multiracial Experience* (1996).[3] This new multiracial identity seeks to resist the one-drop rule and the binary racial project, as did previous racial strategies (passing, blue-vein societies, triracial isolates, Louisiana Creoles of color). Yet it differs from those tactics in that it is egalitarian and challenges racial hierarchy.

Chapter 7 looks at Brazil's racial democracy ideology in terms of research on Brazilian race relations conducted in the 1950s and 1960s. This research indicated that the more phenotypically African the individual, the lower he or she was in the social order in terms of education, occupation, and income despite the lack of legal barriers to equality. Notwithstanding the contradiction between the reality of race relations and the ideology of racial democracy, these findings, along with research conducted in the early 1970s by U.S. scholars indicated that Brazil exhibits fluid racial markers.[4] However, during the two decades of military rule (1964–85) Brazilian scholars were largely prohibited from discussing the problem of racial inequality by a government invested in claiming that no such problem existed.

The gradual return of civilian rule in the 1970s set the stage for a revitalized black movement. Activists argued that racial inequality, apart from class, was a main factor in social stratification. A new generation of Brazilian social scientists (most of whom are white) bolstered these claims by providing a rigorous analysis of official data on health, income, and education (see, for example, Silva 1978 and Hasenbalg 1979). Further analyses since the 1980s support these findings.[5]

The racial mobilization beginning in the 1970s generated a more radical critique of the ternary racial project, mulatto escape hatch, and whitening ideology. New modes of political organization and confrontation, as well as new conceptions of racial identity and definitions of the state's role in promoting and achieving equality, were debated and contested in the political sphere. In order to forge a politicized racial identity the black movement sought to sensitize individuals to the notion of African ancestry in a manner similar to African American identity in the United States. Accordingly, they deployed a racial discourse that replaced the color terms *preto* and *pardo* with the racial term *negro* (African Brazilian). In addition, the public and political debate increasingly focused on the importance of race in determining social inequality.

3. See also Hall 1980, Wardle 1987, Zack 1994 and 1995, Funderburg 1994, J. M. Spencer 1997, R. Spencer 1999, Azoulay 1997, Korgen 1998, Kilson 2000, Dalmage 2000, Brown 2000, Kreb 2000, Wallace 2001, Rockquemore and Brunsma 2001, Daniel 2002, Winters and DeBose 2003, Renn 2004, and Brunsma 2006.
4. See Degler 1972 and Skidmore 1974.
5. See Fontaine 1981, Andrews 1991, Hanchard 1994 and 1999, Marx 1995, Twine 1997, Reichmann 1999, Davis 1999, Johnson and Crook 1999, Hamilton et al. 2001, Sheriff 2001, Winant 2001, Sansone 2002, Dávila 2003, and Telles 2004.

By the 1990s, the debate surrounding multiraciality in Brazil and the United States increasingly centered on the collection of official data on race. These developments, which have been explored in previous analyses (see, for example, Daniel 2000 and Nobles 2000), further support the argument that Brazilian and U.S. race relations are converging.

In Chapter 8, I discuss the growth of the multiracial movement since the founding of I-Pride, particularly the campaign to bring about changes in official racial classification to make possible a "multiracial" identification. I also analyze the public and political debate, which more and more includes discussions about the declining importance of race as a factor influencing social stratification since the dismantling of legalized segregation (see, for example, Wilson 1980 and Sowell 1984).[6] I also discuss how many have begun to question the need for affirmative action and other directives aimed at tracking and eradicating patterns of racial discrimination, which they claim no longer exist, despite extensive research pointing to pervasive, if largely informal, racial barriers to equality. These trends indicate the United States is moving toward a ternary racial project, as well as increasingly informal expressions of racism accompanied by a racial democracy ideology, which have typified Brazil (see, for example, Hacker 1992, Feagin and Sikes 1994, and Bonilla-Silva 2001 and 2003).[7]

Chapter 9 explores the growth of the black movement in Brazil since the founding of the Unified Black Movement (O Movimento Negro Unificado, MNU), particularly the campaign to replace the terms *pardo* and *preto* with the term *negro* on the census. One of the goals of the movement is to persuade blacks, and particularly multiracial-identified individuals, to view themselves as part of an African Brazilian constituency. In addition, activists reject the notion that Brazil is a racially and culturally integrated, or a whiter, nation. Rather, they consider it to be composed of differentiated and mutually respectful, if not mutually exclusive, African Brazilian and European Brazilian racial/cultural pluralities.

Earlier strategies (of, for example, the Black Guard, the Black Front, and the Black Experimental Theater) generally viewed group pluralism as a temporary tactic to mobilize against social inequities—and ultimately to fulfill the racial democracy ideology. The contemporary black movement considers pluralism a strategy for dismantling the racial democracy ideology. In addition, they are working to achieve a more equitable redistribution along racial and class lines through the implementation of affirmative action. These trends indicate that

---

6. See also D'Souza 1996a and 2002 and Thernstrom and Thernstrom 1997 and 2002.

7. See also Feagin 2000, Boston 1988, Small 1994, Oliver and Shapiro 1995, and Steinhorn and Diggs-Brown 1999.

Brazil is moving in the direction of a binary racial project, as well as a rethinking of public policy to attack racial inequality, in a manner similar to the United States.

In the epilogue, I assess the multiracial and black movements as they relate to several questions. For example, what impact might changes in traditional racial categories and boundaries have on the social construction of "whiteness" and "blackness" in Brazil and the United States? Also, to what extent might the deconstruction of these categories help dismantle or maintain racist ideology and racial privilege?

I examine race and multiraciality in Brazil and the United States as part of the ongoing sociohistorical process of racial formation as outlined by sociologists Michael Omi and Howard Winant in *Racial Formation in the United States from the 1960s to 1990s* (1994). My data are drawn from various sources, including secondary literature, along with data obtained from academic journals, the popular print media—particularly newspapers, magazines, and the internet—television and radio, as well as from the U.S. Congressional Hearings on Racial Census Categories, U.S. *Federal Register* reports, Brazilian and U.S. census data tabulations, which are available through the Statistical Information Office and Bureau of the Census in the United States and the Instituto Brasileiro de Geografía e Estadística in Brazil (Brazilian Institute of Geography and Statistics, IBGE). My data are also taken from analyses of written correspondence by activists as well as from observations of public behavior in Brazil and the United States as it relates to the topic of racial identity and race relations. In particular, I have relied on data collected through observation of the public behavior of students at the University of California at Los Angeles, Santa Barbara, and Santa Cruz, and that of individuals in attendance at support group meetings and conferences on the subject of multiracial identity, as well as data obtained through observation as a member of the advisory board of the Association of MultiEthnic Americans (AMEA) and former advisory board member of Project RACE (Reclassify All Children Equally, 1992–97). These two organizations have sought to revise the collection of official racial and ethnic data to make possible a multiracial identification.

Finally, my analysis builds on my essay "Multiracial Identity in Brazil and the United States," in *We Are a People: Narrative and Multiplicity in Constructing Ethnic Identity,* edited by Jeffrey Burroughs and Paul R. Spickard. Earlier versions of this research appeared in my paper "Converging Paths: Race Relations in Brazil and the United States," which I presented at the Winter Colloquium Series, Center for African American Studies, University of California, Los Angeles, in 1989. Other versions were presented at the Seventeenth International Congress on Latin American Studies in Los Angeles in 1992 and the "Conference on Ethnicity and Multiethnicity: The Construction and Deconstruction of Identity" at Brigham

Young University, in Laie, Hawaii, in 1996. Finally, sections of my analysis of multiraciality in the United States (Chapters 1, 4, 5, 6, and 8 and the epilogue) borrow heavily from my book *More Than Black? Multiracial Identity and the New Racial Order* and from the essay I coauthored with Josef Castañeda-Liles, "Race, Multiraciality, and the Neoconservative Agenda," which appears in *Mixed Messages: Multiracial Identities in the "Color-Blind" Era*, edited by David Brunsma.

part one THE HISTORICAL FOUNDATION

one EUROCENTRISM

Racial Formation and the Master Racial Project

The Emergence of European Domination: The Origin of the Dichotomous Racial Hierarchy

Race is a modern concept. It was born in the late fifteenth- and early sixteenth-century colonial expansion of the Western European nation-states—specifically Spain, Portugal, Italy, France, Germany, Holland, Denmark, and England. Expansion, conquest, exploitation, and enslavement had characterized the previous several thousand years of human history, but these phenomena were not supported by ideologies or social systems based on race. However, increased competitiveness among the nation-states of Europe; the cultural and phenotypic differences between Europeans and the populations of the Americas, Asia, the Pacific Islands, and Africa; and the relative ease with which the Europeans were able to dominate those populations influenced European perceptions of all non-Europeans. This in turn laid the foundation for the formation of the concept of race, which justified both the conquest and a unique form of slavery. Although racial formations differed in detail among the various colonizing powers, none of the populations that came under European domination contributed to the creation of the racial classification system imposed upon them, even as they inherited and internalized it (Smedley 1993, 14–16; Wilson 1996, 37–47).

A corollary to the rise of European nation-states to global dominion was a Eurocentric worldview. Eurocentrism emerged during the Renaissance in the fifteenth century, matured during the Enlightenment in the late eighteenth century, and has been a dominant mode of consciousness in Western civilization ever since. It is a peculiarly narcissistic view of Europe as a self-contained entity and as the transcendental nexus of all particular histories, by virtue of its unprecedented accomplishments in materialist rationalism, science, and technology, and the extremes to which it thus progressed into the outer reaches of "modernity." European accomplishments in these realms enabled the exploration of remote areas of the globe and exploitation of resources, including human beings, found there. The colonization of these areas, although it was a complicated process fraught with conflicting aims and motives (and not without its European dissenters), brought European nation-states to a position of global preeminence and turned fledgling nation-states into commanding imperial powers that could dominate non-Europeans. The ruling classes of Western Europe, in their progressive evolution toward "enlightenment," tended to see the process of conquest and colonization as a contest between "civilization" and "barbarism."

The epistemological underpinnings of the Eurocentric paradigm, and ultimately the entire modern worldview, originated in what sociologist Pitirim Sorokin called the sensate sociocultural mode. This paradigm supports the belief that the external world has a logical order, which is the interplay of calculable forces, discernible rules, and measurable bodies—the empirical, rational perspective on nature. Mechanical principles were seen to govern the movement of the planets, the changes on earth, and the structure of the smallest insects. Once grasped, these laws could also be manipulated for human gain. This materialist-rationalist conception represented a fundamental reorientation toward the cosmos and was a radical shift away from what Sorokin called the ideational sociocultural mode, which had prevailed during the medieval era. During that period spiritual and metaphysical beliefs gave rise to the conviction that the structure of the universe was divinely ordained and that the religious authority of the church prevailed over natural knowledge (Sorokin 1957, 15, 226–30, 272–75).

By medieval reckonings, the physical world had a moral plan, and all bodies, from the smallest particle up through humanity and beyond to the heavens and God, had their fixed and "natural" place in a hierarchy. It was understood that changes undergone by bodies on earth were parallel to and controlled by movements in the heavens. Although the heavenly bodies were considered to be of a "higher" order than terrestrial ones in this Great Chain of Being, all creation was linked. In social terms this meant that the individual cooperated with his or her neighbors and obeyed God's representatives, who in descending order were the pope, the monarch, and the lord of the manor. Security in this world and everlasting life in the world to come depended on faithfully playing one's assigned role in the grand hierarchy (Goldstein 1980, 191–98; Hoogvelt 1978, 41; Mazlish 1989, 24–26, 32; Rifkin 1991, 15).

In this medieval worldview there could be no distinction between, or dichotomization of, physical events, truths, and spiritual experiences. Indeed, the underlying principles of the Great Chain of Being have more in common with what philosopher and integral psychologist Ken Wilber has defined as holarchy than with hierarchy. Differential function, responsibility, and rank are not necessarily equivalent to differential value and worth. In other words, in the Great Chain of Being all developmental processes, from matter to life to mind, occur via holarchies, or orders of increasing holism or wholeness. Wholes then become parts of new wholes, each of which transcends and includes its predecessor. The whole is greater than the sum of its parts; the whole is at a higher or greater or deeper level of organization than the parts alone (Wilber 1996, 38–51).

By contrast, the Renaissance worldview—embodied in the sensate mode— was based on an almost sacred "law of the excluded middle" that supported an "either/or" paradigm of dichotomous hierarchical ranking of differences. Accordingly, the spiritual or metaphysical universe and the world of natural phenomena were viewed as mutually exclusive, if not antagonistic, phenomena. The natural environment until then had been experienced as an organic unity of spirit and matter. It was now viewed as a composite of lifeless material bodies, acted upon by immaterial forces and energies. In the Renaissance worldview taken to its logical conclusion, the natural world was not an "inspirited" domain with which humans felt a sacred kinship but a secular terrain subject to objective laws, which were discoverable by logical deduction and empirical observation (Amin 1989, 79–81; Hoogvelt 1978, 41–42). The humanity that knew and worked to discover these laws was a dematerialized mind distinct from the body and the rest of the objective world it observed.

In this context technology itself not only received new emphasis but also gained preeminence over other types of mentation and cultural expression. This shift was accompanied by the further detachment of human beings (creatures of reason and intellect) from nature (that which God controlled), although it was man who had been provided with reason in order to serve as God's steward of the earth's resources and make the fullest use of nature's gifts. Nature, along with woman (as well as human traits such as feeling and intuition, which were deemed more reflective of the female value sphere), was to be dominated and rendered submissive to the rational will of man (and, indirectly, God) (Berman 1989, 111–12; Easlea 1980, 201, 216–18, 241–42; Little 1989, 3–5; Mazlish 1989, 3–9, 12–14; Riencourt 1974, 262–63).

The growth of Western science and technology, which was catalytic in the rise of sensate sociocultural dominance, was the result of a combination of factors. The relatively even distribution of rainfall in Western Europe throughout the year meant that extreme periods of dryness and flooding were infrequent and precluded the need for complex irrigation systems. This in turn diminished the need for political rule to sustain economic prosperity. European farmers' herds were spared tropical diseases, and once livestock were built up and farmers developed the technology to plow the heavy soils, agricultural improvements followed. As a result, European farmers could produce relatively large agricultural surpluses, which led to an increase in urban populations and the rise of new cities. Moreover, a secure and growing urban merchant tradition and a multiplicity of political units and classes fighting with each other for supremacy—feudal lords, centralizing kings, and the church—thwarted political unity and provided leeway for commerce and independent urban life. Urban merchants could bargain for considerably greater freedom and self-government than elsewhere, which in turn provided more room and greater reward for independent thinkers. In no region outside Western Europe was this combination of circumstances more favorable for the development of an autonomous urban tradition whose practitioners were allowed to pursue their work unhampered. Rationalism, science, and a new kind of philosophical speculation flourished, and the sensate mode became deeply rooted (Chirot 1994, 66–67).

The paradigmatic shift to the sensate mode in Western consciousness, having separated the physical from the moral world, led to a decline in the church's authority and the disintegration of the relationship between church and state. The Protestants of the Anglo-Germanic cities of Northern Europe pushed this rationalization furthest and eventually broke with the Church of Rome.

In subsequent social changes the merchant class replaced the nobility and hereditary monarchies with the principles of liberal democracy. This was the ultimate political expression of the sensate mode, as was Protestantism its religious expression and the capitalist mode of organization its economic expression. Yet capitalism was to take acquisitive property-based individualism and freedom in the marketplace to unprecedented extremes. The capitalist orientation involves the investment of capital in the production of commodities for the market, while profits are created through extracting surplus from labor by having laborers work longer hours than is necessary for their own subsistence. Consequently, capitalism more often than not undermines the egalitarian principles of democracy and becomes a mechanism for the exploitation of the weak by the powerful in both the economic and political domains (Morrison 1995, 6–16; Ritzer 2000, 6–7).

Nevertheless, the new modes of production and exchange unleashed by capitalist dynamics provided the foundation for less constrained social relations and restrictive political institutions than those which had prevailed under medieval feudalism. Indeed, the sense of mutual obligation and the influence of the church and religious belief had helped to prevent, for the most part, the kind of resistance and revolt that began to characterize Western culture (a result of the Renaissance concept of individualism) and eventually became a license for the unbridled pursuit of freedom (particularly in the marketplace) that has plagued human society ever since. That said, medieval Europe was every bit as unfair, brutal, and bloody as any other period in human history (until the modern era).

The feudal order began to weaken in the thirteenth century, after the Crusades and the discovery of new markets in China following the journeys of Marco Polo. By the end of the fifteenth century, the feudal laws of mutual obligation were being replaced by commercial or fiduciary relations originating in the new money economy and mercantile classes. Moreover, merchants, bankers, and manufacturers were no longer tied to local markets but were free to make the entire world their domain. Everything that could be sold on the market for profit became a commodity. The desire for profit was not, however, merely a reflection of the long-standing human desire to have the most or to take the most from others. Rather, the pursuit of profit was a new passion in which the goal was the insatiable accumulation of the medium of exchange. This process of accumulating wealth was an abstract pursuit in which the passion for the process of accumulation replaced the passion for the object of desire. Everything, including human life, was subordinated to the quest to extract value, exchange commodities, and accumulate wealth (Wilson 1996, 41–47).

Europeans and "Others": Establishing the Dichotomous Racial Hierarchy

In the European worldview before the Renaissance (and its companion piece, the Reformation), the ideational and sensate modes were more reciprocal than antithetical, complementary rather than opposed. It should not be assumed, however, that the schism between the two modes, and their various sociocultural embodiments, had never existed before.[1] The increasing dominance of the sensate over the ideational mode in the West made a first major inroad at the height of Greco-Roman Hellenism. Whereas science for the early Greeks had been mainly a theoretical pursuit, the Hellenistic world put theory into practice. The major areas of development were utilitarian, with concrete advances in medicine and engineering, for example, rather than speculation in biology or physics (Robinson 1983, 111–13, 118; Sorokin 1957, 15, 226–30; Warger 1977, 1–14).

From the fall of the Roman Empire through the end of the first millennium the remnants of Greco-Roman knowledge in the West were smothered beneath the ideational shroud of Christianity. Yet Byzantine thinkers in Eastern Europe and Islamic and Jewish scholars in the Afro-Eurasian world preserved this ancient Hellenistic learning—as well as the learning from India, China, and the

---

1. Ever since humanity crossed the threshold of city or "civilized" life, all humans to some extent have been confronted with the embodiments of the schism between the sensate and ideational modes. The balance between the two modes that prevails in a given period may be viewed as its defining characteristic.

Far East. Indeed, the incorporation of Hellenistic heritage by Byzantine civilization was so thorough that Hellenism and Christianity were in dialogue on common concerns (Robinson 1983, 111–13, 118). At that time Muslim forces still kept Western Europe relatively cut off from contact with urban centers in the Afro-Eurasian world. Later, while Western Europe was still recuperating from its "Dark Ages," a flourishing cultural exchange existed among the civilizations of not only Eastern Europe and parts of the Near East and the Far East but also West Africa as far south as the Senegal and Niger Rivers to North Africa and southern Europe (Islamic Spain, Portugal, and Sicily) (Foner 1975, 36–47; Goldstein 1980, 45–58).[2]

Western European knowledge of populations beyond the eastern fringes of the European peninsula decreased dramatically during this period because of the decline of urban centers in Western Europe, the geographical isolation of Western Europeans from other centers of civilization, and the Islamic colonization of the Mediterranean. The ancient civilizations of Asia and Africa became the stuff of legends. As knowledge became increasingly a monastic preserve, secular knowledge and renderings of the non-European world declined significantly. This was due to the felt need to interpret history in accordance with the ecclesiastical perceptions of divine revelation and will. With the evolution of Christian ideology into the dominant worldview it was considered sufficient to know that humanity was divisible into a dichotomous hierarchy: the forces of Light or Good, personified by Europeans, and the forces of Darkness or Evil, represented for the time being by the rest of humanity. Thus, it was European Christianity, distorted by isolation, and to some extent intertwined with and buttressed by notions of European superiority, that shaped medieval knowledge and understanding of the world (Robinson 1983, 110–11).

If Christian Europe viewed itself as morally superior to the darker-skinned Muslim infidels of the Afro-Eurasian world, it also displayed an uncomfortable awareness of its own technical, material, and cultural "inferiority" to Islamic civilization. This sentiment pervaded much of Western European consciousness until the rediscovery of Eastern Christianity and Hellenistic thought in the West—ironically through trade and other contacts with the Islamic world—gave birth to medieval Christian scholasticism. Considering that Western consciousness was dominated by the ideational mode until the eleventh century, this ancient

2. Other evidence, which continues to be largely dismissed, suggests that prior to the Renaissance, civilizations in West Africa had empirical knowledge of the Americas, particularly the Meso-American area. This information may have been responsible for Portugal's "accidental" discovery of the New World, considering that southern Portugal had intimate contact with the latest navigational, cartographic, astronomical, and geographic knowledge available through Islamic civilization with which parts of West Africa were closely linked (Foner 1975, 34–47, 95, 101–2; Drake 1987, 312; Sertima 1976, 19–107, 180–231).

Greco-Roman Hellenism was necessarily rediscovered through the "mediation of the Islamic metaphysical construct" (Amin 1989, 71–76). In addition, it is no accident that medieval Christian scholasticism evolved beginning in the twelfth century in regions in close contact with the Islamic world: the Iberian Peninsula and Sicily (Goldstein 1980, 92–96). It was only later, however, that the West learned that Greco-Roman Hellenism was preceded by Classical Greece, whose very existence was largely unknown until that time.

Medieval scholasticism represented a fragile synthesis of ideational and sensate mentalities as expressed, respectively, in the form of Christian faith and Aristotelian empiricism. It originated in the need to reconcile the realities of a burgeoning economic prosperity of the physical world with the metaphysical tradition of medieval consciousness, which displayed a greater preoccupation with "otherworldly" concerns and frowned on, or at least displayed a notable lack of interest in, those of this world. By giving birth to a new world largely freed from the domination of metaphysics, medieval scholasticism laid the intellectual foundation for the Renaissance, the Reformation, and thus the "rebirth" of the West (represented in the seventeenth-century personages of Descartes and Newton). This sensate ideal blossomed in the eighteenth century during the Enlightenment. The rise to dominance of the sensate ideal and the consequent meteoric ascent of secularism, materialism, scientific rationalism, technology, and the ideology of property-based individualism catapulted Europe onto the stage of modernity by freeing it from the comparatively more ideational and communalistic values and constraints of the past. These social forces in turn served as the basis for Europe's presumption of superiority and its justification of the secular and religious colonization of non-Europeans. Colonization was construed as a beneficial "civilizing" influence as well as a way to enrich the various emerging European nation-states (Amin 1989, 71–76; Sorokin 1957, 268–75; Stromberg 1975, 4, 10, 14–16).

By the fifteenth century, the drive to accumulate wealth had reached the point where Western culture was coming to view the entire world, including the human beings living in it, as objects to be used to create that wealth, or obstacles to be disposed of if they stood in the way of acquiring it. This view informed the conquest of the Americas, the extermination of Native Americans, the African slave trade, and the rise of plantation slavery in the New World. These developments composed the Eurocentric master racial project from which all other modern racial projects originate. Racialized thinking matured during the eighteenth and nineteenth centuries and received new impetus in the last third of the nineteenth century, when the European powers scrambled madly to divide up Africa.

Never before had the opportunity for seemingly unlimited wealth and resources been so great as during Europe's imperialist expansion. The conquest of the Americas was of particular importance. The New World exceeded the wildest dreams of European explorers and merchants seeking new venues for trade. But the New World—like Africa, Asia, and the Pacific Islands—contained not only natural resources to exploit but human populations as well, populations that were phenotypically and culturally different from themselves. These differences challenged European understandings of the origins of the human species and raised the disturbing question as to whether these strange peoples could even be considered part of the same human family. Perhaps the differences of these "Others" could justify their exploitation and even enslavement. Given the scope of the European onslaught—the Europeans' advantages in military technology, their religious conviction of their own righteousness, and their lust for new goods and new markets—the division between a "civilized" world of white European culture and a "primitive" world of red, black, and brown "savages," seemed "natural" (Omi and Winant 1994, 61–62).

The breaking of the "oceanic seal" separating the Old and the New Worlds, which began with the European "discovery" of the Americas, was paralleled by a break with the previous "proto-racial awareness" by which Europe had contemplated "Others" (Omi and Winant 1994, 61–62). The conquest of the Americas was not simply an epochal event; it also marked the beginning of modern racial awareness. This consciousness was first expressed in religious terms, then in political and scientific ones, as a rationale for the exploitation, appropriation, domination, and dehumanization of people of color.

The Eurocentric concept of race, and its corollaries white racism and white supremacy, is not just a form of ethnocentrism—that has existed in almost every society. It is more extreme than racial and cultural chauvinism because it has given rise to a more systematic, comprehensive, integrated, and reciprocal set of ideological beliefs. All of the major European philosophies, social theories, and literary traditions of the modern age have been implicated in this process. Even the antagonism that medieval Europe displayed toward the two most significant non-Christian "Others"—the Muslim and Jewish populations—cannot be considered more than a "dress rehearsal" for racial formation. Despite the chauvinism and atrocities of, for example, the Crusades, these hostilities were universally interpreted in religious terms even when they had racial metaphors (Smedley 1993, 14, 18; Omi and Winant 1994, 61–62).

The initial primary distinction Christian Europeans made between themselves and Muslims in terms of superiority versus inferiority was a "natural" outgrowth of the distinction between believers and nonbelievers of any faith. However, this phenomenon was exacerbated by the fact that substantial portions of Christian territory in southwestern Europe were under the control of African Muslims. Thus, the distinction based on religious differences was amplified to ideological warfare that accompanied the actual physical warfare, which took place during the Crusades and the Christian "reconquest" of southern Spain, Portugal, and Sicily from Islam. Throughout this period, the enslavement of Africans in Europe was not uncommon. It occurred through enslavement of African Muslims by European Christians (and vice-versa) who were captured in battle. The Catholic Church, in the course of "just wars" against the "Muslim infidels," sanctified this long-held tradition of enslaving enemies captured in warfare.[3]

Portugal regained complete control of southern Iberia from Muslim forces in 1250, approximately 250 years before Spain completed its *reconquista* in 1492. In 1415 the Portuguese invaded and occupied Islamic areas in Northwest Africa. They also maintained the practice of enslaving Muslim prisoners of war. The populations that Europeans encountered as they progressed further down the West African coast in the fifteenth century were not Muslim; however, they were not Christian either. That, combined with their apparent ignorance of the Bible as the sacred text of the one true faith, confirmed their inferiority in European eyes and justified their enslavement. Indeed, it implied their predestination to slavery, since the body cannot be free when the soul has not been set free by the faith. However, this did not necessarily imply the manumission of African slaves once they converted. Portuguese merchants did not see these captives as the church did. They realized that they could enrich themselves by capturing Africans and selling them as slaves (Davis 1967, 186; Devisse and Mollat 1979, 154–60; Little 1989, 6–7).

Spain, initially through Islamic and then Portuguese intermediaries, followed suit. African slaves on the Iberian Peninsula were used primarily as domestic servants and artisanal labor in urban areas. They were not used extensively in agricultural labor, with the exceptions of sugar plantations in the Algarve, Madeira, and the Azores Islands (Portugal), as well as the Canary Islands (Spain). This was primarily because African slaves were more expensive than local unpaid serf and peasant labor. As the Portuguese continued down the coast of Africa capturing (and trading for) slaves, they maintained the "just war" rationale, no matter how

---

3. Eurocentrism has obscured the West's indebtedness to this Asian, Near Eastern, not to mention North and West African, influence that is often concealed in the term "Moor." The latter in and of itself simply refers to the inhabitants of Mauritania (present-day Morocco). It became associated in the European mind with the invading Islamic forces that entered the Iberian Peninsula from North Africa. Many of these individuals were in fact Moors and a substantial number were culturally Arab, if not from the Arabian Peninsula. European historians have often obscured, sometimes deliberately, the fact that many of these so-called Moors or Arabs, like their more distant Egyptian neighbors, were phenotypically Africoid or Eurafricoid and largely a racial and cultural blend of European, Asian, and African ancestries and heritages (Foner 1975, 85–86, 88).

loosely it was interpreted, as a justification for the enslavement of West Africans. As they began requiring ever-larger quantities of slave labor, particularly for their offshore African sugar-plantation islands of Cabo Verde and São Tomé—and eventually in the Americas—the "just war" rationale for African enslavement became increasingly inadequate. Yet the powerful mercantilists in Lisbon (and their financiers in the Northern Italian city-states and the Low Countries) had become too dependent on the massive profits of the sugar/slave trade to give up everything so easily. Therefore, a new rationale for the enslavement of Africans was necessary (Little 1989, 6–7; Saunders 1982, 94–97).

Western Europeans and West Africans began their encounter in the fifteenth century as different but equal in terms of sociocultural development. Indeed, the urban centers of Africa and Europe had more in common with each other than either did with the rural areas of their own countrysides. Although they were comparatively less technologically "advanced" than Renaissance Western Europe—particularly in terms of military technology—coastal West Africans lived in densely populated and highly organized agrarian communities. Consequently, they could not be overwhelmed by armies or by masses of European colonists spreading through their lands. In fact, had it not been for Muslims folding back on West African soil after their defeat in Europe—a major factor in the sacking, breakdown, and physical destruction of medieval West African civilizations such as Ghana, Gao, and Songhay—Africans might have been an even more formidable force to be reckoned with. Yet faced with the brutality of retreating Islamic forces, large portions of those populations had fled, and cities, built mainly of timber and clay and abandoned for the jungle inhabited by less urbanized populations, were left to crumble (Davis 1967, 181–82; Gann and Duignan 1972, 256–59; Foner 1975, 34–47, 100–101; Sertima 1976, 19–107, 180–231).

West African contact with Europeans was confined to small groups of professional traders and missionaries clustered in vulnerable forts along the coast and subject to the rules and restrictions of a well-developed commercial system. When the chieftain of a semi-feudal society sold Africans to a European trader, he was following a practice long established with Islamic markets to meet the demand for domestic slaves, particularly women to fill harems, and eunuchs to tend the latter. Neither African chieftains nor local traders, however, envisioned that the colonization of the Americas would transform the nature of this trade into the deportation of millions of their kin. The influx of European goods, particularly firearms, further disrupted the equilibrium of West African societies that already had been weakened by the Muslims. To Europe, particularly the ruling elite, improved technology brought power and wealth. To Africa, particularly the masses, it brought only a more efficient means of capturing slaves for the New World market.

Furthermore, the religious and political power structure of West Africa was corrupted by the slave system. Priests who had traditionally imposed heavy fines on individuals who had offended an oracle found it more profitable to cite and justify an increasing number of offenses and demand payment in slaves, who could then be sold to European traders for profit (although the profits that accrued to West African elites was a pittance compared to the wealth amassed by their West European counterparts). Communities bound by religious allegiances and loyalty to ones' kin increasingly began to treat each other as commodities (whatever the overt pretext) that could be traded to the Europeans for, among other things, guns (Davis 1967, 180–82; Foner 1975, 35, 93).

If the religious and political power structure of West Africa was complicit in justifying the transatlantic slave trade, the Judeo-Christian explanation for the blackening and banishing of Noah's son Ham and his offspring provided its most extreme rationalization. This "curse of Ham" began as an innocuous anecdote: Noah cursed Ham's son for Ham seeing Noah naked while he was drunk, condemning him and his progeny to be servants of servants (Genesis 9:20–25). The descendants of the son of Ham, according to theological interpretations, were the inhabitants of Africa, including the Egyptians, who at the time the myth began to circulate had fallen from their pinnacle of power. The curse, ordained by God as an eternal punishment for Ham's disobedience, was said to be the curse of blackness, which in turn was the badge of slavery, although nothing in the biblical passage states or even implies this (Allahar 1993, 39–55; Sanders 1969, 521–32; Sertima 1976, 108–10; Williams 1990, 75–76).[4]

The symbology of blackness was intensified when Europeans observed that Africans pursued an "uncivilized" (or premodern) way of life in which the ideational and sensate worlds were seen not as antithetical but as complementary opposites. Even worse, to European minds, Africans went about in states of nakedness and semi-nakedness and had no apparent sense of modesty about their bodies. The Africans' nakedness, their sexual mores, and above all their blackness set them off as a profoundly distinct form of humanity from the Europeans, if they were even human at all. The discovery of anthropoid apes in Africa did nothing to diminish this suspicion. Whatever was forbidden and horrifying was characterized as black and could be projected onto the African, and if African skin was not absolutely black, it was close enough. God (or nature) had conveniently seen to it that Africans came to represent blackness, darkness, and the unconscious, which would become the "nuclear fantasy" (Kovel 1970, 14–20, 62–64), or nightmare, of

---

4. This myth did not originate in the Bible, as some contemporary theologians thought. Rather, it drew its inspiration from an arbitrary interpretation of the biblical story of Ham, which appears in the Talmud, a collection of Jewish oral traditions, in the sixth century C.E.

its polar opposite—the whiteness, lightness, and rational consciousness personified by Europeans (Davis 1967, 186; Drake 1987, 1:31, 62–75; Jordan 1968, 248, 253).

With the growing need for cheap plantation labor in the Americas, the notion of the black Hamite as slave gradually became an accepted part of the secular justification for African enslavement. Although some form of color prejudice against blacks had existed in various places since antiquity, it had never been institutionalized in a system of racialized slavery, nor had it been justified by an elaborate racialized ideology of white superiority and black inferiority. More-over, slavery had never been a permanent condition, only a temporary status; slaves in other cultures were generally granted their freedom after serving an allotted time. Nor had color (or phenotype) been a crucial factor in determining an individual's social location (Wilson 1996, 37–40).

Beginning in the sixteenth century, however, black Africans bore the ancestral stigma of Ham's curse, which served the economic, political, and religious interests of white Europeans. The biblical sanction dispelled moral concerns about the economic exploitation of blacks but kept Africans within the human family, which had the advantage of keeping Christian cosmology intact as recounted in Genesis. But European slavers did not simply own the body of the black slave. They went further, reducing the slave to a body without a mind. By objectifying black slaves, European slavers made them quantifiable and more easily absorbed into a rising world of productive exchange. Slaves were chattel (from the Middle English for *property,* derived from the medieval Latin for *cattle*), and thus were reduced to beasts of burden, and in certain key respects to inanimate matter (Kovel 1970, 16–19; Sanders 1969, 524).

In its progressive evolution toward enlightenment and thus modernity, Western Europe deemed anything that recalled humanity's primal and premodern origins as a threat to the rational world that had been so painstakingly created. Thus, it was an act of humanity to remove black Africans from their harsh world of sin and darkness. Blacks were better off in Christian lands, even as slaves, than living like beasts in Africa. With this view of servitude as a reciprocal relationship between loving master and quiescent slave (instituted by God for the better ordering of a sinful world), bondage appeared to balance natural freedom and worldly fate, human authority and the equality of all individuals under the supreme rule of God.

Yet the church did not actually intend to baptize blacks and instruct them in the faith. This might have awakened them to the contradiction between Chris-tianity's egalitarian tenets and the church's endorsement of the practice of slavery. Rather, the church only wished to instill in blacks the Christian precepts of patience, obedience, and humility. This would make it possible for masters to rule by love rather than by force, irrespective of the mounting empirical cruelties of slavery that eclipsed this ideal. Nevertheless, the ideal of the contented slave in a benevolent Christian society, the remoteness of Africa, and the fact that as the slave trade progressed larger numbers of slaves were taken from the truly "uncivilized" bush societies of forest regions behind the coastal cities made it easier to disassociate African servitude from the act of enslavement and justify an institution vital to the economy of Europe and the Americas. In the end, the decision to enslave Africans had the dual benefit of profiting both the spiritually minded church fathers in search of lost souls and the more enterprising colonists in search of cheap labor (Davis 1967, 186).

From White Racism to White Supremacy: Consolidating the Dichotomous Racial Hierarchy

The rise and expansion of African slavery during the Renaissance and Enlighten-ment to meet the increasing demand for cheap labor caused European and European American thinkers to become concerned with distancing the origins of Western civilization from any association with individuals of African descent. Consequently, these thinkers sought to prove that Africans were a different, subhuman species by replacing the doctrine of monogenesis with the theory of polygenesis in explaining human origins. In keeping with the book of Genesis, the doctrine of monogenesis supported the belief that all individuals are equally human, if not equal in stature and ability, and constitute one species; the effects of climate and environment explain "racial" differences. According to the doctrine of polygenesis, all individuals are not equally human, for there are at least two species of humanity, if not several, differing intrinsically, and the species comprised by persons of African descent is separate, different, and inferior (Sanders 1969, 521–32; Young 1994, 160–65; 1995, 118–41).

Egypt became central to this debate because it not only is located in Africa but also has a history of contact with Europe and Asia. Egypt, after all, had given rise to one of the earliest recorded civilizations. According to Martin Bernal's "Ancient Model," beginning around 1500 B.C.E., Egyptians and Phoenicians colonized Greece and "civilized" the "primitive" indigenous population. This view was derived from the writings of Greek philosophers—particularly Herodotus and Deodorus—who based their accounts largely on the oral traditions of Egyptian priests. With the concomitant expansion of African slavery, however, the idea that Greek civilization could have been the result of the blending of Europeans, Africans, and Semites became increasingly unpalatable. Eighteenth- and nineteenth-century Romantic nationalists and racists replaced the Ancient Model of Greek history with what Bernal calls the "Aryan Model" (the currently accepted version of Greek history) (Bernal 1987, 1:1–2, 29).[5] These scholars discarded the accounts of the Egyptian basis of Greek civilization as fanciful notions, as out of place in serious history as Greek myths of sirens and centaurs.

The notion of the Greek ancestry of Western Europe—which underlies the Eurocentric paradigm—thus performed an essential function in the assertions of Europe's superiority over Africans and "Others." Greece became the source of rational philosophy and a prefiguration of the triumph of reason that characterized Enlightenment thought (the sensate mode). But in order to incorporate Greece fully into Western Europe's lineage, the differences between Greece and the ancient Afro-Asian world had to be accentuated. And in order to support the ancestral connection with the Greeks—who were highly "civilized" at a time when most Western Europeans were still "barbarians"—it became necessary to emphasize, if not invent, commonalities between the Greeks and modern Europeans. Those who supported this historical revisionism resolved the contradiction between anecdotal accounts of Egyptian colonization and their more scientific chronicles by treating those accounts as exceptional departures from otherwise rational Greek thought, as products of "Egyptomania" (Bernal 1987, 1:1–2, 29). This delusion supposedly served the nationalist pride of both Egyptian priests and Greek thinkers by linking the latter with the impressive accomplishments of the former (Amin 1989, 77, 90–92; Robinson 1983, 108; Slater 1994, 101–3).[6]

The interpretation of the history of Christianity, itself a long and complicated process, suffered a similar fate. Christianity was Afro-Eurasian in origin, that is to say, it emerged in the complex racial/cultural crucible encompassing the region extending from Egypt into Eastern Europe, Africa, and Asia. Yet Christianity's history has been rendered in such a way as to imbue it with particular and exclusive virtues that made it possible to become part of the basis of Europeaness and the principal factor for the maintenance of European cultural unity. In fact, the West has so completely emphasized Christianity's European origins and erased the Afro-Asian context from which it emerged that in vernacular culture, as well

5. Bernal's Revised Ancient Model accepts the invasions from the north by Indo-Europeans but also supports the stories of Egyptian and Phoenician colonization of Greece set out in the Ancient Model, though he sees them as beginning somewhat earlier, in the first half of the second millennium B.C.E.

6. Some scholars argue that, beginning with the pre-Christian seventh century on Egyptian law, science, art, architecture, religion, and philosophy had a dramatic impact on Greek civilization as well as vice versa (Robinson 1983, 108). Others acknowledge Egyptian influence on Greece and vice versa but continue to challenge the accuracy of the claims of Egyptian colonization. This scholarship also rejects the accounts passed on orally to Greek thinkers by Egyptian priests, claiming that Greek philosophers such as Plato and Aristotle studied in Egypt (Lefkowitz 1996, 53–90, 134–54). Yet even this more modest version of Egyptian influence on Greece, if not actual colonization, has not been the most common rendering of the relationship between the two civilizations.

as in official religious iconography, the Holy Family is presented as blue-eyed and blond. Greek Hellenism and Christianity were not only severed from the milieu in which they unfolded but also employed to account for the superiority of the West—"the Occident"—and its conquest of the globe. A vision of Africa, the Near East, and the more distant Far East was constructed on these same racialized and dichotomous premises and resulted in the creation of the artificial, antithetical construct of the (Afro-) "Orient" (Amin 1989, 89–100; Slater 1994, 101–3).

The discovery of the antiquity of Egyptian civilization during Napoleon's expedition into North Africa in the early nineteenth century, which raised the possibility that Africans could have contributed significantly to Egypt's development, represented a major obstacle to the claim that Africans were inferior to Europeans. European scholars in the nineteenth century may have felt certain that Greek civilization was self-generated and owed nothing to Egypt. They could not, however, convincingly argue the inherent and permanent biological inferiority of African-descent individuals as long as Egypt remained an African civilization. Christian theologians began to argue, therefore, that Noah had cursed only Canaan, the son of Ham, and his progeny, which included all black (sub-Saharan) Africans and their descendents. Another son, Mizraim, had not been cursed and was the progenitor of the gifted, dark-skinned white (or "Caucasian") Egyptians, the creators of one of the earliest recorded civilizations. Consequently, a population that was Afro-Eurasian in ancestry—and in many respects predominantly African in origin—was given a berth among the Aryan races, not in first class, but in the section reserved for whites of questionable ancestry. The creation of two lineages—a servile, cursed Africoid branch and a gifted, blessed Caucasoid branch—neatly resolved the problem of the Hamitic curse and allowed the Christian conscience to rest peacefully (Drake 1987, 1:132–37; Sanders 1969, 521–32).

Throughout the nineteenth century the scientific establishment of Europe and the United States tried to prove that the Egyptians were and had always been white. They did not deny that blacks were numerous in Egypt, but they argued that their social position had not changed significantly from ancient times to the present—Egyptian blacks had always been servants and slaves, whereas Egyptian kings, priests, and military had always been white. Thus, Egypt served as an ancient historical precedent for a white society with black slaves, which justified the "natural" place of blacks in the modern era. Researchers used this evidence not only to support claims that the races were permanently different and mutually antagonistic but also to advance policies that would maintain their permanent separation in the social order. That the contemporary Egyptian population was clearly made up of a blend of Arabs, Africans, and Afro-Arabs did not disprove the "Caucasian thesis," they argued. It only explained Egypt's long decline. Aryans alone created Egyptian civilization, and the subsequent blending of the races debased it, bringing about its degeneration, infertility, barbarism, and ultimately its fall (Sertima 1976, 108–10; Young 1994, 163–68).

These arguments were supported and justified by the founders of U.S. anthropology Josiah Nott, George Gliddon, and Samuel G. Morton. From the 1840s onward these men and others presented their claims as scientific truth and were instrumental in promoting the Anglo North American ideology of race in Europe and the United States (Gossett 1963, 54–83). Their sentiments were the clearest indication of the gradual broadening of the ideology of white racism, which had been used to support African enslavement and the systematic subordination of blacks after slavery. Now, however, this ideology was expanded to include notions of white supremacy, which were grounded in "scientific" arguments perpetuating the fiction of the genetic superiority of Europeans and the genetic inferiority of Africans in order to preserve white privilege.

Racial oppression was, therefore, grounded in exploitive economic relations and was sanctioned by the state. Eurocentric values permeated the major institutions of society by structuring how individuals thought about race. The social and political activities of the dominant class played a major role in the construction of Eurocentric culture. Eurocentric racial formation is based on particular assumptions about human difference, but it is not a unified set of ideas. It evolved under the influence of "the material conditions, the cultural and naturalistic knowledge, as well as the motivations, objectives, and levels of consciousness and comprehension of those individuals who formulated the concept of race and first imposed racial classifications on the human species" (Smedley 1993, 14). As a cultural initiative the concept of race had no basis in natural science but was the culmination of popular beliefs about human differences. Beginning in the mid- to late eighteenth century, however, the concept of race was embraced by naturalists and other learned individuals who gave it credence and legitimacy as a product of scientific investigation concurrently with the decline of the authority of the Old Testament as history. In this intellectual climate, "race" came to designate a biologically defined group.

Racial formation not only underpinned a social order that divided the world's peoples into biologically discrete and exclusive groups; it also became a way of categorizing what were already conceived as inherently unequal populations. More important, racial formation supported the notion that these groups were by nature unequal and could be ranked on a continuum of superiority and inferiority. The concept of race became so widely used that it began to replace other classificatory terms. Indeed, had the concept of race never been invented, it is likely that people would have continued to be identified by their own name for themselves or by other categorizing terms such as "people," "group," "society," and "nation," or by labels derived from the geographic region or locales they inhabited (Smedley 1993, 25–29).

Racist ideology was so universal and infinitely expandable that by the nineteenth century all human groups of "varying degrees of biological and/or cultural diversity could be subsumed arbitrarily into some 'racial' category, depending upon the objectives of those establishing the classifications" (Smedley 1993, 27). Once structured in the form of a dichotomous hierarchy of inequality, different racial pluralities became socially meaningful wherever the term was used and to whatever groups it could be applied. By borrowing the methods of animal classification from Linnaeus and Curvier and transferring them to Darwin, Gobineau, and Renan, nineteenth-century European savants contended that the genetic variants of the human species called races inherited innate characteristics that transcended social evolution. "Races" were thus conceived as "naturally" immutable and heritable status categories linked to visible physical markers. Racial formation not only served to justify the dominance of certain socioeconomic classes or ethnic elements but also became a new dimension of social differentiation that superseded socioeconomic class (Amin 1989, 94–97; Banton 1979, 17; Bernal 1987, 1:31–33; Smedley 1993, 14–18).

The meaning of race is, therefore, neither fixed in the physical characteristics of differing populations nor is it a unitary phenomenon. It is, rather, a synthesis of various elements originating in popular beliefs. When combined, these generated a new way of viewing human differences that served as the basis for the authority of the scientific orientation. As the authority of the scientific orientation waxed and that of the Old Testament as history waned, people increasingly relied on a more systematic and scientific understanding of the natural order (Banton 1979, 17).

Races, which were formed by the landscape and climate of their homelands, retained permanent and pure essences, even though they took on new forms in each era. History became the biography of races and consisted of the triumph of strong and vital populations over weak and feeble ones. Victors were seen as more advanced than and thus superior to the vanquished. It was self-evident that the greatest race in world history was the European or Aryan one. It alone had and always would have the capacity to conquer all other peoples and create advanced and dynamic civilizations. European identity, constructed to distinguish it from the identity of "Others," led necessarily to a ranking among Europeans themselves based on their closeness to or distance from the Western European ideal (Amin 1989, 94–97; Bernal 1987, 1:31–33).

Racial formation reached maturity as the European nation-states reached positions of global economic, military, political, and cultural domination in the eighteenth and nineteenth centuries. Racialized thinking thus justified not only African slavery but also the conquest, dispossession, and control of all non-European "Others." During the second half of the nineteenth and early part of the twentieth centuries it culminated in and was mobilized to justify the burst of imperialist expansion in Africa, Asia, and the Pacific (Tiffin 1990, vii–xvi; Williams and Chrisman 1994, 1–19; Young 1994, 160–65).[7] It also served as the foundational justification for the Anglo North American annexation and incorporation of Mexican territory into the United States, the expansion into the Philippines and the Pacific, and the extension of influence into Latin America and the Caribbean through the implementation of "free trade" hegemony or Monroe Doctrine-style military interventions (Shohat and Stam 1994, 40).

From its inception race was a product of popular beliefs about human differences that evolved from the sixteenth through the nineteenth centuries. By the early decades of the nineteenth century, the concept of race generally contained several ideological ingredients—beliefs, values, and assumptions generally unrelated to empirical facts—that served to guide individual and collective behavior. The first and most basic ingredient of "race" was the universal classification of human groups as discrete, mutually exclusive biotic pluralities. Racial classifications were based not on objective variations in culture but on subjective and arbitrary judgments that reflected superficial assessments of phenotypic and behavioral variations. A second ingredient was an inegalitarian ethos that ranked these biotic pluralities hierarchically, with white Aryan Europeans at the top of the pyramid (Smedley 1993, 27–29).

A third ingredient was the belief that physical characteristics reflected behavioral, intellectual, temperamental, moral, and other qualities. It followed that the culture of any given "race" was a reflection of its biophysical form. A fourth ingredient was the notion that biophysical characteristics, behavioral attributes and capabilities, and social status were inheritable. Finally, and perhaps most important of all, was the belief that each race was created by God or nature as unique and distinct from all others. Imputed differences could never be altered, bridged, or transcended. Christians saw racial inequalities as divinely ordained, and the secular-minded rationalized them as the product of natural laws. "Scientific" inquiry confirmed inequalities between the races in a way that supported Europeans' conviction of their own superiority. The state ultimately gave this structural inequality official sanction. White racism and white supremacy were institutionalized as systematic components of social structure (Smedley 1993, 27–29).

---

7. Colonialism was a specific phase in the history of Western imperialism, although the latter is frequently limited to the period between 1870 and 1914. At that time conquest of territory became linked to a systematic search for markets and an expansionist exportation of capital. In a broader sense this included the expansion of the First World capitalist mode of production and mass culture, as well as the concomitant destruction of pre- or noncapitalist forms of social organization (Shohat and Stam 1994, 1–54).

two THE BRAZILIAN PATH

The Ternary Racial Project

Neither Black Nor White: The Origin of the Ternary Racial Project

The Brazilian racial order, like other racial orders in the Americas, originated in the Eurocentric paradigm. Consequently, blackness and whiteness represent the negative and positive designations, respectively, in a dichotomous hierarchy premised on the "law of the excluded middle" and grounded in African and European racial and cultural differences. In comparison with racial formation in the United States, Latin American racial formation, particularly in places like Brazil, has been characterized by a more attenuated dichotomization of blackness and whiteness—and thus a more mitigated implementation of the "law of the excluded middle." This is reflected in the region's extensive miscegenation and the validation of this blending by the implementation of a ternary racial project that differentiates the population into whites, multiracial individuals, and blacks. Moreover, blackness and whiteness are merely extremes on a continuum where physical appearance, in conjunction with class and cultural (rather than exclusively racial) signifiers, has come to determine one's identity and status in the social hierarchy. This, in turn, has led to fluid racial/cultural markers and been accompanied by the absence of legalized barriers to equality in both the public and private spheres.

Brazil's supposedly more equitable ternary racial project was popularized by anthropologist Gilberto Freyre and attributed largely to the exceptional racial altruism on the part of the Portuguese colonizers. However, Freyre's argument was more romantic than realistic. Indeed, the quantity and quality of miscegenation and the social differentiation of multiracial individuals from whites and blacks were primarily motivated by self-interest. These appear to have been influenced less by the varying national and cultural origins of the colonizing Europeans than by social conditions that prevailed in the Americas, particularly the ratios of European men to women and whites to blacks (Bender 1978, 33–41).

In Brazil, and other areas of Latin America—including areas of "Latin" North America such as the lower Mississippi Valley, the Gulf Coast, and South Carolina—the early colonizing Europeans were mostly single adult males, either bachelors, widowers, or married men who arrived without wives (Bender 1978, 33–41).[1] In Brazil, this was exacerbated by the fact that at the time of colonization in the early 1500s, Portugal had a population of only about one million, and was able to send only four hundred settlers. This was compounded by the Portuguese Crown's restrictions on immigration from other parts of Europe to Brazil. Moreover, immigrants found Brazil's dyewood, parrots, and hostile Native Americans, along with the intractable tropical environment, less appealing than, for example, the riches of India. Consequently, the Crown found it difficult to get immigrants to settle in Brazil, despite expanding its penal code to make some two hundred crimes punishable by exile to that locale (Coon 1965, 70–72; Schwartz 1987b, 21).

Although there are no reliable national data on the racial composition of the Brazilian population prior to 1872, the number of whites in Brazil remained small throughout the colonial period. As late as the seventeenth century, whites were predominantly European by birth. By 1600 they represented about one-third of the population. By 1798, estimates indicate that whites numbered 1,000,000, slaves 1,500,000, Free Coloreds 225,000, and Native Americans 250,000 out of a total population of almost 3 million (Alden 1963 173–205; Burns 1970, 103; Marcílio 1984, 37–63). African slaves were the primary source of labor and composed a large portion, if not the majority, of the population in the coastal lowlands. In some areas, slaves outnumbered Europeans by fifteen to one. Even in many urban centers, almost half of the colonial population had some degree of African ancestry (Bender 1978, 33–41).

Africans supplemented, or replaced, the Native American labor force, slave or otherwise, which had been decimated by overwork, physical abuse, and the constraints of sedentary life, whether on the plantations or the cloistered confines of the missions. Old World diseases had even more of a devastating impact, slaughtering millions of Native Americans. Also, many Native Americans resisted enslavement, as well as encroachment on their lands, by escaping into

---

1. In Brazil, the southern provinces of Santa Catarina and Rio Grande do Sul were the exception to this pattern. The Crown organized the immigration of families from the Azores and Madeira to that region as part of its policy to protect strategically important and peripheral areas. Accordingly, family enterprises based on small holdings and involved in food production, either for subsistence or internal consumer demands, prevailed over slave labor and plantation agriculture for the export market (Degler 1972, 230; Prado 1969, 95–96).

the interior. Africans were somewhat easier to control because their lack of familiarity with the American terrain made successful escape into the interior comparatively more difficult, if not less likely to be attempted. Furthermore, Africans were from the Old World and had greater resistance to European diseases. Consequently, they were a cheaper and comparatively more reliable source of urban and agricultural labor.

The preponderance of Africans in the slave-holding regions of the coastal lowlands, in conjunction with the shortage of European women, gave rise to permissive attitudes toward miscegenation between white men and women of African descent, as had been the case with attitudes toward liaisons with Native American women. There were legal barriers to interracial marriages during most of the colonial period and strong social prejudice against them afterward. Yet limited opportunities for the numerical self-perpetuation of the white family led to the informal legitimization of the interracial family. In practice, fleeting extra-marital relations, extended concubinage, common-law unions, and marriages involving European men and women of color became the norm and were approved, if not encouraged, by the prevailing unwritten moral code, as well as by the church and the Crown (Bender 1978, 42–45; Karasch 1987, 294; Lockhart and Schwartz 1987, 389).

In the later colonial period, laws were passed explicitly encouraging marriages of whites with Native Americans and *mamelucos* (multiracial individuals of European and Native American descent) in order to increase the frontier population and assimilate the indigenous population. Although marriages between whites and individuals of African descent were excluded from these provisions, by the early nineteenth century, the colonial laws that discriminated against African Brazilians, including those forbidding interracial marriage, were overturned. Yet there remained an informal social stigma attached to interracial marriages with individuals of African descent. There was also formidable social prejudice against even informal unions between black or mulatto men and white women, whereas informal relationships between European Brazilian males of all social classes and women of color continued to be widespread (Degler 1971, 213, 214, 226–38; Karasch 1975, 375).

During the colonial period, most multiracial individuals were *mamelucos.* When the Native American population began to die by the thousands, colonists increasingly imported African slaves (although as late as the 1580s, Native Americans still made up two-thirds of the slave labor force). After 1600, when the transition to African labor was complete in most regions, there was a significant increase in the numbers of multiracial individuals of African and European or African, European, and Native American descent (*mulatos*)—and to a lesser extent, individuals of

African and Native American descent, or *cafusos* (Lockhart and Schwartz 1987, 197–200; Poppino 1961, 55–58).[2]

As slaves, these multiracial individuals worked in the sugar and coffee plantations, the gold mines, and urban centers alongside enslaved blacks. Yet they were often assigned prestigious and exacting tasks as artisans and domestics that were less physically demanding, required greater skill, and symbolized greater personal worth. Some of these tasks also gave them more intimate exposure to, and therefore greater knowledge of, the social and cultural values of the dominant whites. Mulatto offspring of white masters and slave concubines were frequently reared in the master's house, where many learned to read and write. The scarcity of white women not only mitigated opposition from the legal wife but also enhanced the likelihood that these offspring would be the recipients of socially tolerated demonstrations of affection, as well as economic and educational protection. Some were even provided with formal educations, either locally thorough public institutions or private tutors, or in Europe, if their white fathers were of ample financial means. In exceptional cases, they were bequeathed large inheritances.

This social differentiation of mulattoes from both whites and blacks, along with the preferential liberation of the mulatto offspring and slave mistresses (as opposed to self-purchase), gave these individuals greater opportunities to enter the free classes early in the colonial period, as compared to blacks. By dint of these advantages, mulattoes developed into a group with greater potential for vertical social mobility early in the colonial period and long before the official abolition of Native American slavery in 1758 and African slavery in 1888. Large numbers, if not the majority, of mulattoes in colonial Brazil remained enslaved, and many blacks were free (Berlin 1974, 177–81; Lockhart and Schwartz 1987, 217, 266, 269; Russell-Wood 1972, 94, 116). Yet mulattoes were disproportionately represented among Free Coloreds, as compared to their numbers among slaves, throughout the Americas, and particularly in Brazil. Moreover, where a considerable portion of the progenitors were white elite males, a sizable sector of prosperous and prestigious individuals within the Free Colored population developed (Hoetink 1973, 23).

Data indicate that by the late eighteenth century, free people of color had increased in both absolute numbers and as a percentage of the total population. Consequently, they represented a significant portion of the free classes in virtually

---

2. *Cafusos* were less common because Africans and Native Americans had limited intimate and lasting contact after the early phase of colonization and slavery. Exceptions to this trend were the *quilombo* settlements of runaway slaves scattered throughout the interior, where unions (especially in the Northeast) between African men and Native American women were facilitated by the shortage of African women (Prado 1969, 121–22).

every region of Brazil (Klein 1986, 227–28, 230). In addition, the increase in the number of free multiracial individuals over the black slave population was, in part, due to continued manumissions and self-purchase. More important, however, was natural increase caused by the larger ratio of females to males among the free multiracial population, as compared to the ratio among the predominantly black population of slaves. By the early nineteenth century, multiracial individuals were the fastest growing segment of the free population. Moreover, in areas with major concentrations of Free Coloreds—the Northeast, Minas Gerais, and Rio de Janeiro—mulattoes reached parity with whites and in some cases (e.g., Pernambuco, Bahia, Minas) outnumbered them. By midcentury, their numbers had increased significantly over the black slave population, despite some 1,350,000 Africans who were brought in between 1831 and 1850 (Burdick 1992b, 37, 40–42; Cohen and Greene 1972, 1–23; Klein 1972, 309–34; 1986, 227–28, 230, 309–34; Russell-Wood 1972, 84–133).

Data from the first systematic national census conducted in 1872 confirm this trend. Color was not as politically significant as it would become on some subsequent censuses, and the terminology employed was primarily recognized as subcategories of the larger division between slave and free. The terms *branco, preto,* and *pardo* referred to color, whereas *caboclo* generally signified ethnicity (or origin), encompassing the Native American or indigenous population and their descendants. *Pardo* was applied to individuals descended from both *pretos* (blacks) and *brancos* (whites) (Nobles 2000, 89; Piza and Rosemberg 1999, 40–41). According to census data, the Brazilian population consisted of 3,787,289 *brancos* (38.1 percent), 1,954,543 *pretos* (19.7 percent), and 4,188,737 *pardos* (42.2 percent). (The number of *caboclos* was miniscule, totaling 386,955.) Of the 8.5 million free inhabitants, the 4.2 million *pardos* and *pretos* outnumbered the 3.8 million *brancos* and the 1.5 million slaves. Also, the 3.3 million *pardos* outnumbered the 921,150 *pretos* among the Free Coloreds and almost equaled the number of *brancos* (Brookshaw 1986, 314, 315, 318–19; Klein 1986, 223; 1972, 313–15, 320–22).

The Escape Hatch: White Domination and the Illusion of Racial Inclusion

When the slave population in Brazil (and elsewhere in the Americas) was relatively large and the Free Colored and white populations were relatively small, Free Coloreds filled interstitial economic roles, because of a shortage of European labor and for which the use of slave labor was generally considered less practical. These circumstances provided mulattoes, who were a majority of Free Coloreds, with opportunities to become plantation overseers or farmers who worked small parcels of land that supplied nearby sugar plantations with food. Others migrated to Salvador, São Luís, and Rio de Janeiro, where they became self-employed artisans and merchants. Women worked as domestics, midwives, seamstresses, skilled cooks, and hairdressers, men as shoemakers, tailors, carpenters, butchers, street merchants, barber-surgeons, small tavern and shop keepers, sailors, stevedores, and the like. Throughout the Americas, Free Coloreds frequently competed with cheaper slave labor in many of these same capacities. Yet in Brazil they dominated most of the skilled crafts and trades and artisanal categories of labor. In addition, by the eve of abolition in 1888 mulattoes outnumbered blacks by as much as four to one in these areas of employment (Burdick 1972, 50; 1992b, 40–42; Cohen and Greene 1972, 1–2; Degler 1971, 227, 229, 230; Harris 1964, 79–94; Klein 1986, 227–28, 230; 1972, 318; Lockhart and Schwartz 1987, 237; Russell-Wood 1972, 84–133, 309–34).

Because of the shortage of whites, Free Coloreds also performed a critical role in the civilian militia. Throughout the colonial period, the European monarchs in Portugal often viewed the Free Colored militia as a means of expanding the frontier. They also secured Portugal's territorial borders in that region against foreign interlopers and attacks by Native Americans, while also providing a military brake on the ambitions of independence-minded whites (Berlin 1974, 111). Given the large number of mulattoes among Free Coloreds, whites also viewed them as natural allies against the black slave majority. So reliable were Free Coloreds that Brazilian slaveholders used the Free Colored militias to suppress slave uprisings, as well as to catch and return fugitive slaves. The incorporation of Free Coloreds into the security apparatus of the colonial state, however, contributed as much to their own circumscribed status as to the super-ordinate position of whites. Free Colored militia could hardly have hoped to overthrow whites and simultaneously hold slaves in their place. Any attempt at revolt would have brought them into opposition to the Crown as well as the colonial government, resulting in severe reprisals in the event of defeat (Berlin 1974, 5–6, 112; Klein 1972, 309–34; Russell-Wood 1972, 84–133).

Although Free Coloreds were often allowed to serve as notaries and clerks, and engage in service occupations, they were generally barred from holding public office or rising beyond a certain level in the clergy or governmental bureaucracy, and experienced limitations on educational attainment. Some Free Colored urban artisans, long before abolition, advanced from their favored positions in the artisanal and skilled trades into the arts, letters, and liberal professions (including medicine, engineering, law, and the civil service). However, they did not achieve this through competition in the open market. Rather, their vertical mobility was generally facilitated through the support of patrons in the white elite, who always controlled their advancement. Moreover, most Free Colored subsistence farmers depended on large slaveholders for land rights, credit, and protection (Burdick 1992b, 40–42; Costa 1985, 239–43).

Not surprisingly, Free Coloreds feared that the end of slavery would threaten their social position. They typically remained silent on the question of slavery, were generally reluctant to fight against it, and eschewed all forms of alliance with slaves. Free Coloreds were also silent on the question of racism, which held them in a position of second-class citizenship during slavery, and would hold the African Brazilian masses at the bottom of the social hierarchy long after abolition. Free Coloreds, therefore, were valuable allies in preserving the social and political status quo. Yet some of them were among the first to raise issues of personal liberty and protest social injustices against blacks and mulattoes. Consequently, their seeming loyalty and tendency to shun alliances with slaves says as much about their own anomalous position and the precarious circumstances in which most of them lived as it does about their corruptibility, or commitment and acquiescence to the racial order (Berlin 1974, 111, 214–15; Cohen and Greene 1972, 1–23; Hoetink 1973, 108; Klein 1972, 84–133; 1986, 232; Russell-Wood 1972, 309–34).

Both the Crown and colonists in Brazil, and other areas of Latin America by extension, provided some protection of Free Colored rights. Yet these conciliatory attitudes varied from region to region and changed over time. Rarely was complete de jure or de facto equality possible. The prevailing assumption among the European Brazilian elite was that Free Coloreds were, because of their African ancestry, unworthy of the privileges normally accorded to free persons. Free mulattoes ranked above free blacks, and as free people of color, occupied a status intermediate to masters and slaves. In the minds of whites, however, they were often thought of as being part of one inferior slave class. Even in the most tolerant regions of Latin America, such as Brazil, free mulattoes remained in the less privileged socioeconomic sectors, always being closer to the third-class status of blacks than to the first-class status of whites.

Yet whites in colonial Spanish and Portuguese America extended a remarkable degree of social acceptance to light mulattoes, despite the social stigma attached to African ancestry and the various restrictions that were put into place as their numbers increased. Consequently, the mulatto escape hatch allowed a select few multiracial individuals, for reasons of talent, culture, or education, to be granted token vertical socioeconomic mobility and with it the rank of situational whiteness. However, not being white, yet aspiring to be treated as first-class citizens, multiracial individuals at any time could be treated as "inferiors" by even the most socially and culturally "inferior" whites. Consequently, the mulatto escape hatch could easily become a trap door to the bottom of society (Cohen and Greene 1972, 16–17; Degler 1971, 167–70, 213–16, 223–32; Freyre 1963a, 354–430;

Hoetink 1973, 13, 25–45, 100; Klein 1972, 309–34; Pierson 1967, 165–76; Russell-Wood 1972, 84–133). Contrary to André João Antonil's famous eighteenth-century statement characterizing Brazil as an "inferno for blacks, a purgatory for whites, and a paradise for mulattoes" (Antonil 1711, 124), mulattoes were stranded in a purgatorial "no man's land" just beyond the infernal conditions of African Brazilian slaves, yet still outside the "gates of paradise" set ajar for *mamelucos* but open only for whites.

The paradoxical nature of the ternary racial project in both its comparatively more liberal Southwestern European (Portuguese and Spanish America) and somewhat more restrictive Northwestern European (British, Danish, Dutch, French South America, and the Caribbean) variants ensured that multiracial individuals were stigmatized for every feature they shared with blacks and rewarded for every degree of approximation to the European psychosomatic norm.[3] By granting multiracial individuals an intermediate status, European Brazilians allayed their discontent, held their resentment in check, and won their loyalty, without undermining white domination (Burdick 1992b, 40–42; Cohen and Greene 1972, 1–23; Hoetink 1973, 108; Klein 1972, 309–34; Russell-Wood 1972, 84–133).

Consequently, Free Coloreds pressed not for drastic social change but instead for improvements in their own social status. This can be seen in the voices of protest in the mulatto press of the early 1830s, the colored brotherhoods, and the colored militia during the eighteenth century. The process of abolition sealed this racial contract and enabled whites to continue relying on mulatto support long after slavery ended. As long as blacks were retained in the least remunerative sectors of the secondary labor force, mulattoes willingly settled for token integration into the skilled trades, the petite bourgeoisie, intelligentsia, and primary labor force (Burdick 1992b, 40–42, 37; Cohen and Greene 1972, 12, 17; Klein 1972, 328; 1986, 232–33; Russell-Wood 1972, 123, 125).

From White Domination to White Hegemony: Maintaining Racial Privilege

Considering the "questionable" social origins (Schwartz 1987a, 28) of many Portuguese immigrants and the frequency of sexual liaisons or marriages between the early European settlers and Native Americans (and later Africans) among even the wealthiest Brazilian families, it was suspected that all colonial-born

---

3. Hartimus Hoetink defines "somatic norm image" as the cluster of phenotypical (and ancestral) traits, particularly skin color, which racial/ethnic groups accept as the ideal for that group. However, somatic (external) characteristics of a cultural and economic nature (e.g., speech, mannerisms, attire,

whites were of multiracial descent. These factors helped increase the colonial elite's sensitivity to social hierarchies based on color and desire for the insignia of noble birth. They continually sought grants of nobility, knighthoods, pensions, membership in the military orders, and other symbols of nobility. Yet the Portuguese crown was not forthcoming in this regard. The Crown created no titled nobility in Brazil prior to the arrival of the Portuguese Court in 1808. Because the colonists lacked the traditional credentials of noble status, they sought to demonstrate their status in other ways. This included maintaining an aristocratic lifestyle on a landed estate, keeping numerous slaves, displaying liberal and patriarchal attitudes, and indulging a penchant for personal justice. Eventually, commissions in the militia and other such social honors served as substitutes for noble status. Yet as late as the 1790s, exactly when traditional concepts of nobility were being challenged in Portugal, the colonial elite in Brazil increasingly sought ways of obtaining the rank of nobility, which they considered to be a true reflection of their social position in colonial society (Schwartz 1987a, 28–30).

The lack of credentials provided by the emblems of noble birth nurtured a sense of insecurity among the Brazilian elite. In the eighteenth century, they sought to compensate for this deficiency by creating genealogical histories. Accordingly, the commoner origins of the great planter lineages could be overlooked the longer the family had been in Brazil. Consequently, these families became "noble by antiquity." Any connection with a noble house in Portugal was invoked to give the impression of nobility. As a last resort, families could be considered at least "honorable," or "free of stain." If Native American ancestry in the genealogy could not be ignored, it was acknowledged with the justification that "alliances of the soil" between Portuguese men and Native American women were common among the most prominent families in Brazil, and did not diminish the respect with which these houses were held. Moreover, nobility could be conferred on the family lineage by designating these Native American women as "princesses" (Schwartz 1987a, 29).

The romanticization of Brazil's indigenous population (and indigenous ancestry) was made possible by the fact that the Native American threat to continued Brazilian territorial expansion had been sufficiently neutralized by disease and the ravages of colonization (Brookshaw 1988, 1–11; Haberly 1983, 10–14; Hemming 1987, 466–81).

---

occupation, income, and so on) and psychological (internal) factors, such as beliefs, ideals, values, and attitudes, are also taken into consideration, which I define as the "psychosomatic" norm image. When one group has the power to establish its psychosomatic norm image as the dominant one in a given society, social inequities arise as the result of inter- and intragroup prejudice and discrimination directed against individuals and groups that diverge from that norm (Hoetink 1973, 197–98, 200, 201; 1967, 88–89, 122).

African ancestry, on the other hand, was a source of shame, which was exacerbated by the presence of millions of slaves. Moreover, the existence of African and Portuguese centers of cultural reference, in which the demographic significance was heavily tilted in favor of a black majority, meant that African culture not only helped shape the evolving contours of an African Brazilian culture but also influenced the European core culture. This sociocultural interplay between Africa and Europe served as the basis for a significant egalitarian cultural integration in perceptions of time, aesthetics, ecstatic religious experience, an understanding of the godhead, and ideas of the afterlife. Much African Brazilian cultural expression, particularly music, dance, language, the culinary arts, holiday celebrations, visual traditions, architectural styles, habits of work, and medical knowledge, was incorporated into Brazilian national culture. Even the distinctive linguistic features of Brazilian Portuguese are a creolization of West African (along with Native American) and sixteenth- and seventeenth-century Portuguese speech patterns (Freyre 1963b, 278–476; Mendonça 1973, 42–94).

The politically dominant Portuguese in Brazil did not force Africans to learn Portuguese, use European tools, or eat foods prepared in the European manner. Even with the transfer of the Portuguese Court to Rio de Janeiro in 1808, the memories of European life were already losing their meaning to each new generation of Portuguese in the Americas. Indeed, by the eve of independence in 1822, individuals of European descent were coming to view themselves less as Europeans, and more as Brazilians. However, the first- and second-hand accounts of Africa never really lost their significance to new generations of African Brazilians. The black majority included a large number of *boçal* (African-born) slaves well into the nineteenth century. African Brazilian culture remained strongly African—particularly in areas with large concentrations of slaves—even after several centuries of enslavement. It was only after the official abolition of the slave trade in 1850 that *crioulos* (creole or Brazilian-born) became the sole source for replenishing both the slave and free African Brazilian population. Previously, ethnocultural differences representing various African origins were significant status and identity markers, particularly in areas with large African populations. During the second half of the nineteenth century, these were gradually replaced with forms of ethnoracial and ethnocultural identification as African Brazilian (Butler 1998, 52–58).

Egalitarian cultural integration, however, did not result in equitable treatment in either the primary (interpersonal) or secondary structural (educational, political, and socioeconomic) arenas. Nevertheless, a significant amount of Brazilian culture, as well as the racial physiognomy of the Brazilian people, is in varying degrees a blend of both Africa and Europe. During much of the early colonial period, many European Brazilians may have been unaware of their own transformation in this process, but they became painfully aware of this fact by the end of the colonial period, and increasingly over the course of the nineteenth century. Some of these attitudes were reflective of toxins indigenous to Brazil's own racial ecology. We cannot, however, ignore how Brazil was saturated during the nineteenth and early twentieth centuries with the ideas of European and Anglo North American thinkers such as Lapouge, Gobineau, Nott, Glidden, and Morton, who expounded upon the genetic, psychological, and cultural inferiority of individuals of color (particularly individuals of African descent) as well as the evils of miscegenation (Fernandes 1969, 1–54; Knight 1974, 84–93; Marx 1998, 163–64; Skidmore 1974, 48–69; Torres 1969, 87–89, 317).

In order to understand the seriousness of this paranoia about invisible blackness, often referred to as "cryptomelanism" (Mathews 1974, 318), we need only examine the second national census conducted in 1890. The data indicate that just over half (56 percent) of Brazil's approximately 14,000,000 inhabitants were African Brazilians. While there had been a decrease in the numbers of *pardos* (which was replaced with term *mestiço* on the census) from 42 to 41 percent and *pretos* from 20 to 15 percent, and an increase in the numbers of *brancos* from 38 to 44 percent since the 1872 census, African Brazilians still outnumbered whites (Conselho Nacional de Estatísticas 1961, 201; Skidmore 1974, 44–45; Nascimento 1979, 78). In addition, not even the most phenotypically and culturally European individuals of the elite could be certain their genealogy was free of the stigma of African ancestry. Thus, by the latter half of the nineteenth century, the majority of Brazilians were de facto *mulato claro* (clear [light]-skinned mulatto), or *claramente mulato* (clearly mulatto) in terms of culture, ancestry, or phenotype (Coutinho 1989, 8–12). In fact, according to Freyre, in portraits of the period, "the retoucher's art was taxed to the utmost to transform the least Caucasian features into perfectly Aryan ones . . . and to provide rosy complexions for those . . . whose pigmentation was suspiciously suggestive of the tar brush" (Freyre 1970, 201).

If, according to the scientific racism dominant in this period, miscegenation and cultural blending were the disease, whitening through miscegenation and the Europeanization of Brazilian culture was the Brazilian elite's prescription for a cure. In order to achieve this goal, the Brazilian state encouraged the immigration of Europeans, particularly those of Germanic origin, and passed waves of legislation restricting the immigration of blacks. Consequently, the growth in the number of whites in Brazil was due more to massive European immigration than to whitening through miscegenation (Skidmore 1974, 44–46). Although this influx of European immigrants prompted increased concern statistically with the various national origins represented in the Brazilian population, officials continued to display a conspicuous preoccupation with race (Piza and Rosemberg 1999, 39, 41). In the early twentieth century, Brazilian newspapers expressed alarm at the suggestion that North American blacks be encouraged to immigrate. Such immigration, wrote one journalist, would undermine the numerical disappearance of African Brazilians (Burdick 1992b, 41). Moreover, a massive campaign was mounted to eradicate African Brazilian culture. This included dance forms such as samba and religious expression such as *candomblé*, in which Africans had disguised the worship of African deities behind a show of devotion to Catholic saints and religious icons. This campaign was also directed at *capoeira* (a martial art emphasizing attacks with the feet from a handstand position).[4] These grassroots countercultural expressions celebrated African Brazilian communal solidarity—particularly during Carnival—in response to the elite culture of the largely European Brazilian bourgeoisie (Butler 1998, 167, 187–88, 201–7).

In addition, there was a tendency for many individuals to seek a spouse more apparently European in values, beliefs, and physical appearance than themselves and a feverish desire to import and assimilate any and everything from ideas to cultural artifacts that tasted of Europe, and by extension, the United States (Spitzer 1989, 104–5). Moreover, the racial state (and the Brazilian elite) envisioned the legacy of informal inegalitarian pluralism (column f in Figure 1) as the final solution that eventually would eliminate the "black peril" through the laissez-faire genocide of sharply lower levels of education and higher rates of poverty, malnutrition, disease, and infant mortality (Domingues 2004, 270; Haberly 1972, 30–46).

Brazil's history of widespread miscegenation since colonial times and the conspicuous absence of explicit legal barriers to racial equality since the abolition of slavery should not, therefore, obscure either the European descent and European manner of the ruling elite or how they have discriminated, overtly and covertly, against the African Brazilian masses to keep them in a subordinate status. Furthermore, even though miscegenation and the mulatto escape hatch had made the line between black and white imprecise at best, the resulting racial and cultural blending were not part of a project of egalitarian integration (column a of Figure 1) (Ortiz 1947, ix–xi). There has not been, as Freyre argued, a random integration of European, African, and by extension, Native American traits, in which equal value was attached to each through a reciprocal process of "café-au-lait universalism" or "metaracial brunettism" (Nascimento 1979, 72). Rather, it had been a contest between unequal participants manipulated by the ruling elite in order to purge Brazilian culture of its inferior African (and Native American) traits by assimilating them until they have disappeared (column b of Figure 1). Nevertheless, Brazilian popular culture and the physiognomy of the

4. It is believed that *capoeira* originated with African slaves taken from Angola (Almeida 1986, 1–30; Butler 1998, 186–89).

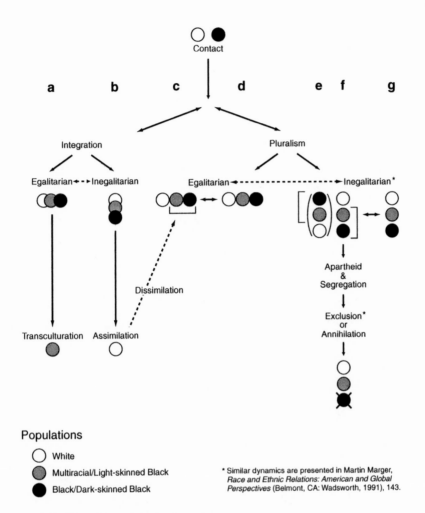

Fig. 1   Pluralist and integrationist dynamics.

Brazilian people remain strongly indebted to and influenced by the African component, despite attempts by the elite to ignore, disguise, and erase its presence (Nascimento 1979, 74–80; Skidmore 1974, 64–77).

These two types of integration are predicated on different assumptions and have different ends. *Egalitarian integration* does not assume that any particular culture or people is more valuable than any other and seeks a population that is phenotypically and culturally a blend of all its antecedents. *Inegalitarian integration* assigns value to one tradition and one people and seeks the elimination of all others through assimilation.

The Post-Abolition Racial Order: From Racial Dictatorship to Racial Democracy

From the introduction of slavery in Brazil, the planter aristocracy controlled national social and political life. The abolition of African slavery (1888), the overthrow of the monarchy (1889), and the subsequent establishment of the Republic (1890) shifted the sugar-coffee economy from slave to paid labor and fostered urban expansion and industrialization. In this social transformation, an overwhelmingly white urban bourgeoisie replaced the white landowning and slave-holding elite as the dominant sector of society. Meanwhile, the former African Brazilian slave masses assumed the role of rural and urban workers.[5] In the late 1880s and 1890s, as well as the first two decades of the twentieth century, immigrants from Italy, Germany, Portugal, and Spain were brought in to replace (and displace) African Brazilians in the labor force, particularly in southern Brazil. As a result of the preferential hiring of European immigrants over African Brazilians, the latter were concentrated in the most underpaid and intermittent types of employment. Many became vagrants, beggars, prostitutes, or thieves.

On the whole, Brazil's post-slavery social and racial physiognomy merely took on a new expression, making small modifications with respect to race and social location. The uppermost levels of society continued to be overwhelmingly European Brazilian, even with the transfer of wealth, power, privilege, and prestige from the aristocracy to the bourgeoisie. The lowest levels remained overwhelmingly African Brazilian and disproportionately black. Nevertheless, the urban bourgeoisie differentiated itself from the landowning aristocracy as new specialists and professionals. This class of individuals replaced the old hereditary social values with meritocratic ones. Despite existing social inequities, these increased opportunities for vertical social mobility made it possible for some African Brazilians (particularly mulattoes, who had reached the half-way mark in the cleansing or bleaching process) to gain entry into the middle class—the petite bourgeoisie and intelligentsia (Bender 1978, 43; Costa 1985, 239–43).

Still, mulattoes remained closer to blacks in status than to whites. Nevertheless, a brief examination of the names and photographs of prominent African Brazilians in politics, the arts, and other professions reveals that the same hierarchy that guaranteed European Brazilians an advantage over African Brazilians assured that those few African Brazilians who were the beneficiaries of the meritocracy were largely mulattoes rather than blacks. Moreover, mulattoes had so internalized the ideology of whitening (*embranquecimento*) in their collective consciousness

---

5. I am using the terms "workers," "working class," and "laborers" in the broader sense of proletariat.

that many did not acknowledge their African ancestry. The concept of blackness was so irreconcilable with social advancement that virtually any degree of achievement or prominence was enough to grant an individual white status. There have historically been a number of individuals of known African Brazilian ancestry in high public office, including one president—Nilo Peçanha (Thompson 1965, 32).[6] Yet these individuals did not refer to themselves, and were not referred to, as *negro*, and some cases, even as *mulato* (Butler 1998, 51; Fernandes 1969, 1–130; Toplin 1981, 45–50).[7]

Extensive miscegenation and the escape hatch, by blurring the line between whites and blacks, helped diminish any collective problem in post-slavery Brazil stemming from race per se and fueled the racial democracy ideology that would become dominant in the twentieth century. More important, they have served to maintain European Brazilian dominance and control by creating the illusion that social prejudice and discrimination were based not on ascribed characteristics such as race but rather on acquired economic and cultural characteristics that can be altered by individual merit and achievement. In reality, first-class citizenship has been awarded according to one's economic standing and approximation to European phenotypical and cultural traits.[8] The social articulation of race had become somewhat subordinate to class, but it was not, in fact, submerged by it (Hasenbalg 1985, 25–41; Silva 1985, 42–55). Consequently, the socioeconomic polarization between haves and have-nots has generally mirrored the racial divide between white and black.

The ternary racial project has ensured that African Brazilians are denied the privileges of whites. However, the mulatto escape hatch has brought with it the expectation, if not the actual achievement, of social advantages on the part of multiracial individuals. More important, it has imbued them with a psychological edge in the pursuit of those opportunities not available to individuals considered light-skinned blacks in the United States. This supposedly benevolent gesture actually served as a form of social control that has retarded, if not prevented, political mobilization along racial lines. It has achieved this by encouraging multi-racial individuals to view blacks as a separate class of social outcasts with whom they have little common cause. This in turn guarantees that a significant number of individuals most likely to possess the cultural, intellectual, and social capital to

6. Then vice-president Nilo Peçanha assumed the presidency on June 15, 1909, after the death of President Afonso Pena and governed until November 15, 1910.

7. Lecture given by Abdias do Nascimento at the University of California, Los Angeles, in 1975.

8. The escape hatch allows vertical mobility primarily based on phenotypical characteristics. Yet behavior, attitude, and economic status also play a role. Consequently, a few exceptional blacks (such as soccer legend Pelé) have gained vertical mobility in accordance with their socioeconomic and sociocultural approximation to the dominant whites.

serve as mouthpieces in the struggle for African Brazilian rights are neutralized, or co-opted into silence.

Rio de Janeiro and the States Northward

The comparatively more liberal attitudes associated with the mulatto escape hatch have been the dominant trend in the states from Rio de Janeiro northward. The racial order established in the colonial period remained relatively intact, despite shifting demographics caused by changes in the economy. In addition, whites in the less privileged socioeconomic sectors of society functioned as interstitial labor and lived in conditions similar to many Free Coloreds. However, the more fluid racial order generally inhibited these whites from developing any sense of "racial competition" with Free Coloreds, even as the latter increased in number and in some provinces became a majority during the eighteenth century (Hoetink 1973, 8–37; Mattoso 1986, 182, 191–92).

The state of Bahia, specifically the city of Salvador, is particularly representative of this pattern. Individuals of African descent were always a majority in Salvador and remained so during the fifty years after the abolition of slavery. In 1890, Bahia's population was almost 2 million, which made it the second-largest state in the nation. The population of the city of Salvador was 174,412 (9 percent of Bahia's population), which made it more than twice the size of São Paulo (64,934). European immigration, which swelled the population of São Paulo in the late nineteenth and early twentieth centuries, had a negligible affect on Salvador. People of color—*preto, caboclo,* and *mestiço*—remained in the majority; the 107,250 *pretos* and *mestiços* made up 61.4 percent of the city's population (Butler 1998, 133–34; Mattoso 1986, 181, 191–93).

During slavery, nativity as either Brazilian- or African-born, along with slave or free status, were important stratifiers among Salvador's African Brazilian population. The large African-born population was itself composed of many "nations" (*nações*) of different ethnocultural backgrounds originating in Africa. The African-born population was further stratified in terms of the degree of acculturation. The *ladino,* who was familiar with Portuguese language and Brazilian customs, had more status than the *boçal* (Butler 1998, 52–54, 140–41; Mattoso 1986, 92).

Former slaves, whether African- or Brazilian-born, had the option of either remaining in Bahia or emigrating to Africa. Most freed slaves chose to stay in Bahia. Yet throughout the nineteenth century emigration to Africa, although expensive, was a feasible alternative, given Salvador's close commercial ties with and geographical proximity to the West African coast. Indeed, voluntary emigration to Africa over the course of the nineteenth century helped tilt the demographic balance in favor of Brazilian-born individuals (Boadi-Siaw 1982, 292; Butler 1998, 141, 142). Meanwhile, African-born individuals who remained in Bahia after their manumission not only considered Brazilians of all colors as outsiders but also formed their own brotherhoods (or mutual aid societies). Sometimes these organizations were based on a specific African nativity and generally excluded Brazilians. To some extent both African- and Brazilian-born blacks necessarily formed their own societies because they were excluded from white and mulatto brotherhoods. That said, several black brotherhoods welcomed individuals from all racial backgrounds. None excluded women, although some prohibited them from holding office. White brotherhoods excluded all but racially "pure" European Brazilians; mulatto brotherhoods often welcomed whites but excluded blacks (Butler 1998, 53, 147–50; Mattoso 1986, 192–93; Nishida 1998, 329–48; Russell-Wood 1972, 122–25).

Of course, since the early colonial period, Africans and African Brazilians had created their own brotherhoods under the sponsorship of the Roman Catholic Church. By encouraging individuals of African descent to identify with the religion of the ruling class, whites envisioned these brotherhoods as a form of social control. However, these organizations became more than replications of their European Brazilian counterparts; they transformed into independent African Brazilian social and political organizations. African Brazilian brotherhoods shared many characteristics with West African cults dedicated to a particular patron spirit and preserved some of the characteristics of West African secret fraternal societies. In West Africa, these organizations dominated in the commercial centers and social and political life outside family structures. Many brotherhoods worked publicly to improve the conditions of African Brazilians. Others functioned as militant social and political organizations that promoted slave rebellions, organized slave escapes, and maintained access to fugitive slave settlements. Under the cover of religion these organizations engaged in "illegal" resistance to slavery that often involved terrorism and violence. In the nineteenth century, both types of organizations inevitably became involved in the abolitionist movement (Luna 1976, 213; Trochim 1988, 287–88).

These organizations also provided an opportunity for the formation of African Brazilian religious institutions such as *candomblé*. Membership in *candomblé*, carnival groups, and *capoeira* schools was not restricted to individuals of any specific background. Nevertheless, they derived directly from African traditions and were predominantly African Brazilian in membership. The role of *candomblé* is especially important, because African-derived religious expression served as the basis for the formation of pan-African and African Brazilian identity. Furthermore, between 1888 and 1938 *candomblé* and "African" Carnival clubs were the most visible sites of African Brazilian resistance to attempts by the ruling elite to stifle African Brazilian cultural expression. In fact, merely participating in African-derived cultural manifestations was an act of resistance to the dominant European Brazilian culture (Butler 1998, 133, 141, 167, 187–88, 201–9).

During the early nineteenth century, when African-born individuals constituted the majority of Salvador's population, African ethnicity based upon "nation" was a primary form of self-identification. Between 1851 and 1870 an intraethnic "African" (or pan-African) and African Brazilian identity gradually replaced individual ethno-national identities. This is attributable to the decline in the number of new African arrivals after the termination of the slave trade at midcentury. Other factors contributing to this decline were natural decrease and the back-to-Africa movement, which reached its zenith between 1835 and the 1870s. "Nation" came to be broadly defined as Africa, although specific subnationalities were recognized as secondary identifications. This was particularly true after the 1835 slave revolt, when "Africans" generically became the objects of public hostility and retaliation. Moreover, the increase in the numbers of Brazilian-born blacks (*crioulos*) was pivotal in reshaping the contours of racial identity and growth of African Brazilian institutions in the decade following abolition. This population included an intermediate group of Brazilian-born offspring of Africans who retained some connection with the world of their African ancestors, but whose experience was forged in the Americas (Butler 1998, 53, 54).

Over the course of the nineteenth century, racial identities were transformed as the African Brazilian population in Salvador shifted from a majority of African slaves to a majority of Brazilian-born free people of color. Also, between 1871 and 1888, Brazilian-born mulattoes outnumbered blacks for the first time. The term *preto* replaced the concept of "nation" and became an all-encompassing designation that included blacks of various African backgrounds. The distinction between Brazilian- and African-born was no longer salient, although individuals typically distinguished themselves as either black or mulatto (Butler 1998, 53, 58, 141).

Whether black or multiracial, being visibly of African descent was synonymous with social inferiority, and darker individuals who retained many African and African Brazilian cultural traits ranked significantly below lighter-skinned individuals who were conversant with the dominant European Brazilian culture. Furthermore, in Salvador there was the long-standing tradition of circumventing obtrusive racial regulations by ensuring that multiracial individuals would be considered legally white in official documents when necessary (e.g., the appointment of mulattoes to high government office).[9] Consequently, the line between

9. For example, during the colonial era ordinations of African-Brazilian priests were forbidden. Yet there were a number of mulatto and black priests in Salvador. The Society of Jesus supposedly barred entry to African-Brazilians but included among its most renowned members Father Antonio Vieira, the grandson of a mulatto woman. Vieira was an ardent defender of Native Americans, a

black and white in Bahia was illusory and even gave rise to the interesting designations *branco da terra* or *branco da Bahia*. These terms, which translate literally
as "home-grown white" and "Bahian white," refer to individuals who display
some African phenotypical traits (or at least have known African ancestry), but
who are regarded as whites in Bahia (Butler 1998, 53–54; Degler 1971, 103, 140,
196–99; Mattoso 1986, 191; Pierson 1967, 139).

Late nineteenth- and early twentieth-century residential patterns in Salvador
reflected this more fluid racial order. Although some racial clusters were discernible,
statistics indicate that there were no racially distinct enclaves. Socioeconomic
status appears to have been the key factor in spatial distribution. Although the
public sphere was integrated, blacks and mulattoes did not make significant
gains in the secondary structural sphere as lawyers, physicians, or politicians,
which remained the preserve of whites. They were largely retained in the same
types of jobs they had held during the nineteenth century as slaves or free people
of color. Women worked as domestics, sometimes specializing as seamstresses,
laundresses, or cooks, which provided them with better opportunities for self-
employment. Other African Brazilian women worked as itinerant vendors, or in
markets and small shops. Men held occupations mainly in skilled trades and
manual labor (Butler 1998, 134–40).

São Paulo and the States Southward

The markers delineating blacks from whites, and more specifically mulattoes from
whites, in the states from São Paulo southward were far more restrictive than they
were in the region encompassing Rio de Janeiro and the states northward. The
south has no expressions that correspond to "home-grown white." In the São
Paulo region, the primary distinction in statistical indicators, as well as perceptions of race, is between whites and African Brazilians, not whites, mulattoes, and
blacks. Although mulattoes are somewhat more privileged than blacks, the racial
order is much closer to a binary racial project. Consequently, the terms "mulatto"
and "black" take on the meaning of something akin to "light-skinned" and "dark-
skinned" African Brazilians (Andrews 1991, 249–54).

Some of the differences in the racial order in the São Paulo region and further
southward are attributable to the large numbers of whites. For example, in 1797
whites were 56 percent of the São Paulo population. However, they became an
even greater majority by the end of the nineteenth century, reaching 63 percent
in 1890 and 84 percent in 1940, largely because of massive European immigration

---

prolific writer, and a religious leader whose influence in seventeenth-century Portugal as well as
Brazil was immense (Mattoso 1986, 191).

(Andrews 1991, 247; Domingues 2004, 188). Yet well into the eighteenth century, São Paulo province was a unique combination of Native Americans, *mamelucos*, and whites, in which the population balance was heavily tilted in favor of a Native American majority, which was the primary source of labor, either as slaves or settled villagers (Luna and Klein 2003, 11–13).

African Brazilian slaves played an important role in the São Paulo economy as far back as the early colonial period. But as late as the eighteenth century they were few in number and mostly Brazilian-born. Yet increasing state and church opposition to Native American slavery, combined with the expanding economy in São Paulo, not only made it possible to purchase African slaves, but after 1700 also led to the gradual replacement of Native Americans with Africans as slaves (Butler 1998, 68; Luna and Klein 2003, 11–19). The termination of Native American slavery by the middle of the eighteenth century led to a dramatic increase in numbers of African Brazilian slaves. Further expansion of the São Paulo economy over the course of the nineteenth century, principally in the areas of export agriculture (e.g., sugar and coffee), furthered this growth in the slave population, which was based heavily on the importation of predominantly African-born individuals. By midcentury these individuals were the overwhelming majority of the slave-labor force (Luna and Klein 2003, 22, 133–37, 156).

The formal cessation of the Atlantic slave trade to Brazil in 1850 meant that by the 1860s and 1870s the vast majority of African Brazilian slaves were native-born. Consequently, they had become a major source of labor when commercial coffee agriculture finally dominated the São Paulo economy in the late nineteenth century (Andrews 1991, 37).[10] By 1872, São Paulo province's slave population reached some 157,000, making it the third-largest slave-holding state in the nation, after Mina Gerais and Rio de Janeiro (Andrews 1991, 26–27; Luna and Klein 2003, 77). During the same period 3,828 slaves constituted one-third of the capital's African Brazilian population. The 31,385 *pardos* and *pretos* made up 37 percent of the population but only 14 percent of *pardos* were slaves as compared to 58 percent of *pretos*. By 1886, only 593 (1.2 percent) slaves lived in the capital, with the majority (95 percent) located in the province's agricultural zones (Butler 1998, 68–69).

Meanwhile, the free population of color in the city of São Paulo grew considerably just before abolition. Whites generally treated the predominantly mulatto class of Free Coloreds little differently from blacks. They did circumvent laws and were willing to define less rigorously the interstices distinguishing *mamelucos* from free mulattoes where it served their interests. Indeed there were

---

10. In 1831, Brazil signed a treaty with Great Britain ending the Atlantic slave trade. However, actual slave importations did not cease until 1853, despite British diplomatic pressure and the intervention of British warships in several Brazilian ports between 1849 and 1850 (Andrews 1991, 32–33).

probably few whites that were not themselves actually *mamelucos*. Official policy and social convention more often than not treated *mamelucos* as whites, whereas all African Brazilians in the region were rejected as inferior beings (Hemming 1987, 6; Luna and Klein 2003, 158–79; Mattoso 1986, 193, 195, 203–4; Morse 1974, 10; Poppino 1961, 55–58; Prado 1969, 116; Russell-Wood 1972, 93).

After the abolition of slavery blacks and mulattoes were pushed to the margins of society, where they were sharply differentiated from whites in terms of color and occupation. They lacked the support necessary for social and economic advancement. Progress was slow and subject to reversals, thus perpetuating conditions that were little better than during slavery. In a sense, their plight worsened. With the disappearance of slavery, so disappeared slaveholders, who if only for practical reasons had made certain that their slaves had food and shelter. After emancipation, there was no attempt to divide the plantations, provide the freedmen and freedwomen with land, or consider their educational needs. Moreover, the recently freed African Brazilians (*libertos*) were now responsible for their own livelihoods but had little, if any, preparation for integration as wage earners in the new economy. Under these circumstances, many remained on rural estates in the service of and dependent on their former masters for employment as domestics and servants. In the areas of slowest growth, where labor was scarce, manumitted slaves continued to work on plantations with few changes (Andrews 1991, 51–52; Butler 1998, 45, 69; Fernandes 1969, 17; Mattoso 1986, 180–81, 193; Taylor 1978, 26–27; Toplin 1981, 45–50).

During this same period, an increasing number of European Brazilian intellectuals began blaming blacks and mulattoes for Brazil's lack of progress. Freedmen and freedwomen, with limited education or capital, were considered incapable of adapting to the new economic order. Negative stereotypes about Brazilian workers, particularly African Brazilians, as genetically "inferior," culturally "backward," and socially "degenerate," informed national labor policy, thus further undermining their already weakened bargaining power (Andrews 1991, 48; Butler 1998, 71; Domingues 2004, 23; Taylor 1978, 27).

The racial state encouraged European immigration not only to hasten racial and cultural whitening but also to remove African Brazilians as competitors in the labor force. To further this policy of "ethnic cleansing," Brazil passed an immigration law in 1907 prohibiting black immigration and limiting Asian immigrants to an annual rate of 3 percent of the current Asian population. (In the early decades of the twentieth century, Japanese immigrants began arriving to work on the coffee plantations.) Moreover, state policy deliberately undercut African Brazilian workers' leverage in negotiating salaries and working conditions by subsidizing this flood of "docile" European immigrants. In addition to keeping wages artificially low and weakening a labor movement committed to racial equality and interracial solidarity, the policy enabled employers to impose negative sanctions against those workers who drove the hardest bargains—they could use or threaten to use other workers as a reserve labor force of strikebreakers. Initially, the workers who drove the hardest bargains were former slaves. European immigrants and their descendants were willing to work under horrible conditions and for even lower wages after the abolition of slavery. In the agricultural colonies where labor was abundant, European immigrants quickly replaced freedmen and freedwomen who left the plantations, displacing those who might have sought these avenues of employment (Andrews 1991, 54–85; Domingues 2004, 23, 67–71 104–6; Hasenbalg 1999, 61–62; Mattoso 1986, 180–81; Skidmore 1974, 137, 142–43, 193–97; Taylor 1978, 27).[11]

In response to these dynamics, blacks and mulattoes migrated in droves from the São Paulo interior and neighboring states to the capital and other urban centers. The cities not only held out the promise of improving their economic and educational status but also offered them an opportunity to escape the agricultural occupations that were linked with slavery. There is evidence that some individuals attempted to establish private businesses. Many hoped for employment in the expanding industrial sector in the cities of the southern states of Rio de Janeiro, Rio Grande do Sul, and especially São Paulo. The primary industries were textiles, clothing, food processing, pharmaceuticals, and chemicals. In 1907, São Paulo supplied 16 percent of the nation's total industrial production; by 1915 production had grown to nearly 31 percent. This expanding industrial sector was largely an outgrowth of the profound transformation of the Paulista economy brought on by commercial coffee production. By the mid-nineteenth century, coffee had become São Paulo's leading export. Between 1890 and 1920, the booming coffee economy not only thrust São Paulo's agrarian entrepreneurs into leadership roles in the national economy but also transformed the capital into Latin America's foremost modern industrial metropolis (Butler 1998, 69–78, 132).

The growing industrial sector attracted not only African Brazilian migrants but also European immigrants. By 1940, blacks and mulattoes comprised 12.6 percent of the population of the capital. Yet African Brazilian migration to the city of São Paulo—despite its size and significance—was a trickle compared to

---

11. Among the European arrivals, the largest number was from Italy, followed by Portugal and Spain, with Germany as a distant fourth. There were also immigrants from regions outside Europe (such as Syria, Lebanon, China, and Japan). These latter groups were outside the black-white dichotomy that has historically underpinned the Brazilian racial order; consequently, they had to carve out spaces for themselves that were largely unscripted. Some sought to achieve integration into the Brazilian racial order as close as possible to whiteness and its privileges. Others formed pluralistic enclaves that sought to maintain distinct societies, or maintained identities as "hyphenated" Brazilians through various combinations of both of these trends (Lesser 1999, 1–12, 168–73).

European immigration. An important point of contrast between São Paulo and Salvador was the unmistakable presence of European immigration in the former and its noticeable absence in the latter. European immigrants not only replaced and displaced African Brazilians in agriculture, as well as in the modest urban occupations they traditionally held, but also were given preferential hiring in all the expanding opportunities in industry. Foreign workers, many of whom were women and the Brazilian-born children of immigrants, dominated São Paulo's textiles, which was the city's principal industry. In 1894, foreigners in the city of São Paulo outnumbered Brazilians in domestic work, manufacturing, crafts, transportation, and commerce. They also functioned as important entrepreneurs in the growth technologies of industry, transportation, and utilities (Andrews 1991, 60–85; Butler 1998, 69–78, 135; Taylor 1978, 26).[12]

This racial discrimination in favor of European immigrants and against African Brazilian migrants made fulfillment of the city's seeming promise difficult, if not impossible, for the latter. Consequently, most African Brazilian migrants became low-wage day laborers who were retained on the periphery as the underemployed and unemployed (or relegated to the informal economy), whereas impoverished but white-skinned European immigrants and their descendants experienced considerable social mobility. African Brazilians found work (when they could) in domestic and other types of service positions or occasional work (Andrews 1991, 60–85; Butler 1998, 74–78; Taylor 1978, 28).

These changing racial demographics in the post-abolition period had an impact not only on São Paulo's political economy but also on the formation of African Brazilian collective identity. Historian Kim Butler found that in São Paulo, where African Brazilians were comparatively fewer in number, there were many unique African-derived cultural forms. In addition, African-born slaves were the majority of the African Brazilian population by mid-century at a time when their numbers were decreasing in Salvador. That said, African culture and ethnocultural distinctions based on African nations (nações), were less salient as the basis of collective identity in São Paulo. In Salvador, the significance of African culture continued to hold greater sway (though not as much as previously). This is attributable to the fact that African Brazilians were a majority, and African culture was more diverse, pervasive, and enduring, even as the numbers of the African-born population decreased. In São Paulo, the experience of racial blackness and the stigma associated with it was the overriding tie that not only bound African Brazilians together but also separated them from the white majority (Butler 1998, 57–58).

12. By 1940 Italians, Syrians, and Portuguese held a monopoly on 44 percent of the capital earned in industrial enterprises (Butler 1998, 70).

Distinctions in terms of origin that held any relevance in São Paulo were largely based upon the Brazilian cities and towns from which individuals had migrated. Butler argues that the experience of migration, which forged a link between the metropolis and the interior, ultimately served as the basis for the creation of a new sense of community and became a defining characteristic of São Paulo's African Brazilian neighborhoods and collectives. The most vocal of these collectives were the social clubs, political advocacy groups, and newspaper cooperatives. African Brazilian religious institutions, which were central to slave life prior to the city's expansion, continued to play a key role. During slavery, the lay Catholic brotherhoods sought to help enslaved members purchase their freedom, though limited resources generally made this difficult. After the abolition of slavery, these associations more typically assisted their members with loans and burial expenses. Yet the membership of the brotherhoods still tended to follow color lines. Some associations, such as the brotherhood at the Igreja da Boa Morte, were limited to mulattoes; the memberships of the brotherhoods of Santa Efigenia, São Bento, São Francisco, and São Benedito were black (Butler 1998, 56–59, 75, 78–87).

New types of African Brazilian collectives emerged from neighborhood-based social groups organized around events such as excursions, picnics, dances, and Carnival. The samba world, in particular, served as an important basis for collective identity. This included the highly structured Carnival associations, as well as informal and spontaneous gatherings where acquaintances and friends met on a regular basis at house parties and nightclubs. These samba spaces were even more closed to outsiders and gave rise to the modern samba schools or *escolas de samba*. Finally, soccer was another major vehicle in the formation of collective identity, although neighborhood soccer clubs were fluid in terms of membership and open to players of all backgrounds (Butler 1998, 79–80, 87).

African Brazilians lived clustered around the city in enclaves, which helped facilitate the formation of these pluralistic cultural spaces. One factor influencing this residential concentration was geographical proximity to family and friends. Consequently, social ties to a hometown in the interior linked the urban enclaves that sprang up around the city. In a pattern similar to that of European immigrant communities, these African Brazilian migrant networks helped new arrivals settle in with hometown family and friends who assisted in finding housing and employment. Indeed, the *porões* (storage basements) and *cortiços* (tenements) where African Brazilians lived were so overcrowded that the larger of these became miniature communities in which mutual assistance was essential. Public services such as water and electricity were inadequate in the densely populated and largely segregated African Brazilian neighborhoods (Butler 1998, 56–59, 74–77).

Butler found that another factor influencing the development of these African Brazilian enclaves was convenience and practicality. Specifically, African Brazilians in service occupations required easy access to the whites that employed them. Consequently, African Brazilian residential patterns were generally characterized by "proximity to whites" (although not residential integration with them) as well by "the availability of low-cost housing" (Butler 1998, 76). Yet for many African Brazilians, residential proximity to whites probably did not originate in the fact that the latter employed the former. Rather, it was because numerous immigrant families rented out backyards and basements to African Brazilian borders. Finally, these residential patterns were also to some extent the result of racial discrimination. European immigrants were more readily integrated as equals into the dominant European Brazilian society and culture, whereas color differences, along with socioeconomic status, set African Brazilians apart from and subordinated them to their white counterparts. These factors made it relatively easy to form and maintain separate "white" and "black" racial identities, especially in comparison to Salvador (Butler 1998, 57, 70, 74–77; Domingues 2004, 132–83).

Urban centers in the southeast, such as Porto Alegre, São Paulo, and Rio de Janeiro, also included upwardly mobile African Brazilians who formed a prominent elite. The number of individuals in the Afro-Paulista bourgeoisie was a small fraction of African Brazilian society that composed 8–15 percent of the population of São Paulo and other southern cities (Domingues 2004, 208–11; Taylor 1978, 28). This elite sector consisted of many ex-slaves who had been domestic servants before abolition. Many were literate, although only 3 percent of blacks and 2 percent of mulattoes in São Paulo had finished primary education as compared to 92 percent of whites (Butler 1998, 67, 77). Those with some education or who maintained connections with white patrons were able to secure better employment than the majority of African Brazilians. They worked as lower-level civil service employees, as well as clerks, office assistants, messengers, or door attendants. Yet even those who were able to attend school had limited financial resources to spend on the necessary supplies and clothes. Consequently, they were very self-conscious about their marginal socioeconomic status. Many responded by distancing themselves as much as possible from the African Brazilian masses. Still others participated in cultural activities and supported social agitation that challenged the racial order and fought for African Brazilian rights (Taylor 1978, 28).

three THE BRAZILIAN PATH
LESS TRAVELED
Contesting the Ternary Racial Project

Off the Beaten Path: Luís Gama and Lima Barreto

Multiracial individuals in Brazil have historically sought to maximize whatever social rewards accompany their partial European ancestry, typically refraining from speaking out on questions of racial inequality. Most of the Free Colored political elite avoided taking a public stand against slavery before the abolition campaign gained popular momentum in the 1870s. Some, such as Baron de Contegipe, strongly opposed abolition (Burdick 1992b, 40–42). Others, however, broke the code of silence and publicly fought for African Brazilian rights. One such individual was lawyer-journalist-poet Luís Gonzaga de Pinto da Gama (1830–82). Gama's African-born mother, Luisa Mahin, eventually gained her freedom and was reportedly involved with several slave uprisings in Bahia during the early nineteenth century. Her fate afterward is unknown. His father was a Bahian aristocrat of Portuguese descent who drank and gambled excessively. After his mother disappeared, Gama's father sold him into slavery to pay off a gambling debt. Gama gained his freedom by running away after he secretly obtained documents proving his enslavement was illegal. He eventually secured employment as a clerk in a police department and devoted his free time to writing poems for newspaper publication (Brookshaw 1986, 192–94; Kennedy 1974, 255–57; Sayers 1956, 105–7; L. Silva 1989, 59–69).

In 1859, Gama's book *Primeiras Trovas Burlescas* (First Burlesque Ballads) catapulted him into prominence in São Paulo. The most widely read poem is "Quem Sou Eu?" (Who am I?), frequently called "A Bodarrada" (The Herd of Goats). In it Gama lashes out against the snobbery perpetuated by Brazil's whitening ideology. He argues that because of centuries of miscegenation all Brazilians, from the most noble to the most plebian, are *bodes*, "goats," a derogatory reference to mulattoes. Having won acclaim as a poet, Gama dedicated the rest of his life to the abolition of slavery in Brazil, and his work helped kindle the abolitionist movement. Gama fought slavery in the radical press, the courtroom, and in underground organizations working for the flight of slaves from plantations—for which he was imprisoned several times (Kennedy 1974, 259–60; L. Silva 1989, 59–69).

Although he had no formal legal training, Gama learned the rudiments of law while working as a clerk in a law office. Eventually, he developed a vast knowledge of jurisprudence. Gama presented clever, eloquent defenses that profoundly impacted the Brazilian political and judiciary systems, gaining freedom for hundreds of slaves through the courts. He even dared to decree: "According to the Law, any crime committed by a slave against his master is justifiable . . . any slave who kills his master, does so in self-defense" (Kennedy 1974, 257, 262). The 1871 Lei do Ventre Livre (Law of the Free Womb), which ordered the manumission of children born to slave mothers, as well as all slaves currently belonging to the state, intensified Gama's desire for complete abolition.[1]

Yet, as a result of Gama's radical views, a schism developed in the abolitionist movement. One faction, represented by Gama and his followers, envisioned African Brazilian participation not only in the struggle for abolition but also in efforts to replace the monarchy with a democratic government. The other faction, represented by the aristocracy, wanted to maintain the monarchy and exclude African Brazilians from the abolitionist campaign. They feared that African Brazilians would infuse the campaign with a radicalism that would lead to the demise of the regime and the aristocracy's position of national leadership (Kennedy 1974, 263–67; L. Silva 1989, 59–69).

Gama's position on these and other slavery-related issues, along with his numerous successes in the courtroom, not only made him unpopular among slaveholders and high-ranking government officials but also led to threats on his life. However, he continued his campaign, ultimately becoming disillusioned with and contesting the very political movement he helped incite because of its unwillingness to support either the absolute and immediate end to slavery or the end of the monarchy. In 1873, Gama protested when the Brazilian Republican Party, which he helped to found, drafted a manifesto proposing the gradual emancipation of slaves with indemnification to slave owners. Gama had believed

---

1. The Lei do Ventre Livre proved to be less effective than advocates had hoped. If the slave owner refused to accept the state's indemnity payment for a child at age eight, they still had the option of retaining the "freeborn" child in the status of a de facto slave until the child reached the age of twenty-one. This 1871 statute was part of Brazil's gradualist approach to the abolition of slavery. It was followed in 1885 by the Lei do Sexegéssima (The Sexagenerian Law), which unconditionally freed all slaves over sixty-five, while conditionally freeing those between sixty and sixty-five, who had to render three more years of service to their masters (Butler 1998, 7; Skidmore 1974, 16–17).

that as an advocate of complete democracy, the party would automatically support the immediate abolition of slavery. He had not considered that many Republicans were themselves large plantation owners who depended on slave labor.

By the late 1870s, slave owners experienced a rude awakening when the abolitionist movement gained nationwide momentum. Abolitionist propaganda dominated the press; clandestine organizations that helped slaves escape from plantations and prevented their recapture grew in number. As the military became more sympathetic and refused to chase runaway slaves, slave owners found themselves helpless to prevent the general flight of slaves from their plantations. Thus, they began to free their slaves voluntarily. However, Gama did not live to see the official abolition of slavery, which took place on May 13, 1888, six years after his death (Andrews 1991, 34–42; Kennedy 1974, 265–66).

Considering the reprisals Gama suffered for his activities, it is not surprising that few multiracial individuals in late nineteenth-century and early twentieth-century Brazil followed his lead (Flory 1977, 199–224; Kennedy 1974, 255–67). Also, considering that literary life in Brazil had traditionally been elitist, African Brazilian writers in particular succeeded only to the extent that their work mirrored the European Brazilian literary canon. This required avoiding the controversial topic of racism, which explains in part why there is no extensive body of literature by African Brazilians that reflects the harsh life of blacks and mulattoes.[2]

Afonso Herniques de Lima Barreto (1881–1922) is perhaps the lone successor to the tradition of racial protest exemplified by Gama. Lima Barreto was born into the petite bourgeoisie of suburban Rio but had to care for a mentally ill father and struggled with poverty most of his life. He worked as a civil servant and pursued a career as a journalist. However, Lima Barreto had difficulty getting published because he spoke out openly, and often caustically, on controversial contemporary issues. Thus, he never secured the support of patrons in the white elite critical to social advancement (Brookshaw 1986, 193–99; Nunes 1979, 1–9).

Lima Barreto was the first African Brazilian prose fiction writer who refused to toe the "racial comportment line" (Brookshaw 1986, 194). He openly discussed the topic of racism from an African Brazilian point of view, reflecting the life of black and mulatto inhabitants of late nineteenth- and early twentieth-century suburban Rio. This is particularly evident in his novels *Clara dos Anjos* (Clara of the Angels), *Recordações do Escrivão Isaías Caminha* (Memoirs of the Scribe Isaías Caminha), and *Vida e Morte de M. J. Gonzanga de Sá* (The Life and Death

---

2. For a discussion of the controversy surrounding multiracial author Joaquim Maria Machado de Assis, Brazil's foremost writer of the late nineteenth and early twentieth centuries, see G. Reginald Daniel, *Racial Identity and the Brazilian Author: The Life and Writings of Machado de Assis* (Lewiston, N.Y.: Edwin Mellen Press, 2007).

of M. J. Gonzaga de Sá). Lima Barreto directed his harshest criticism at Brazil's ruling elite, which was obsessed with pursuing material wealth and whiteness while discriminating against blacks and mulattoes. He sought comfort in his own multiracial background, which he viewed as the foundation of Brazil's past, present, and future.

As an author, Lima Barreto symbolized a blend of the past, present, and future in other ways. Living at the turn of the twentieth century, he was the most important writer of the transitional period between realism-naturalism and modernism in Brazilian literature, commonly referred to as "premodernism." Indeed, the social consciousness of Lima Barreto's novels anticipates that of the novelists of social realism who emerged in the 1930s and 1940s. Moreover, he rejected what he considered the previous era's rarified, artificial, and sterile Parnassian classicism, which was supported by purist Portuguese grammarians. Instead, he sought to forge a language more closely reflecting Brazilian speech patterns, a vision that prefigured the objectives of the modernists of the 1920s (Brookshaw 1986, 193–99; Nunes 1979, 1–9).

An Uncharted Path: The Black Guard, Black Modernism, the Black Front, and the Black Experimental Theater

The struggle to end slavery in Brazil reached its peak as slave owners themselves rushed to free their slaves and take some credit for the "great humanitarian act" of emancipation (Trochim 1988, 285). Yet it was the grassroots organizing among African Brazilians that helped slaves flee the plantations in the 1880s that dealt slavery the final blow (Andrews 1991, 46). And it was African Brazilians who proposed significant social and economic reforms in the post-abolition period (Trochim 1988, 285). Mulatto engineer André Rebouças, for example, played a key role in formulating a program for "rural democracy" and the distribution of land among the *libertos* (freed men and women), which was adopted by many abolitionist organizations. Another mulatto, newspaper editor and activist José do Patrocínio, publicized Rebouças's ideas in his popular daily *A Cidade do Rio* (The City of Rio) and in public meetings. The propaganda campaign launched by these men, along with growing public opposition to slavery and the strong abolitionist sentiment of Princess Isabel (acting as Regent or head of state while Emperor Dom Pedro II was in Europe) finally prompted the government to enact legislation to end slavery. On May 13, 1888 the General Assembly under the leadership of Prime Minister João Alfredo Correio de Oliveira passed Law No. 3353, known as the Golden Law (Lei Áurea) abolishing slavery, which was signed by the Princess Regent (Conrad 1972, 157; Trochim 1988, 286).

Disrupting the Racial Order

A prominent organization, the Guarda Negra (Black Guard) sought to ensure that social and economic reform remained on the post-abolition Brazilian political agenda. Shortly after abolition in May 1888, the members of a recreational club (the Inhabitants of the Moon) in Rio de Janeiro founded the Black Guard. This secret society sought to overcome the invidious distinctions that had divided blacks and mulattoes and prevented traditional organizations (e.g., "brother-hoods") from promoting African Brazilian racial solidarity. The Black Guard was composed exclusively of African Brazilians. However, José do Patrocínio (1853–1905)—who is believed to have been the organization's mastermind and certainly its informal mentor—encouraged the Black Guard and similar organizations to join forces with white-dominated abolitionist groups (Andrews 1991, 44–45; Trochim 1988, 286–88). Patrocínio's strategy was to unite all abolitionist groups with the larger reform movement in order to fight attempts by reactionary planters and politicians to impose new systems of "forced labor, harsh vagrancy laws, and forced military recruitment" to control the *libertos* (Trochim 1988, 290).

In addition, African Brazilians had calculated interests in opposing the Republican cause, which was supported by the pro-slavery sectors of the planter class. The latter were bitter because the monarchy had capitulated to the abolitionist movement and feared that it would support further liberal reforms. Consequently, the Black Guard identified the Republicans as enemies. Instead, they supported the monarchist cause, particularly the João Alfredo Conservative party cabinet in power in 1888, which seemed prepared to implement a new progressive order based on social and economic reforms. Patrocínio was himself closely associated with the Conservative party government and a sympathizer of the monarchy. Moreover, Clarindo de Almeida, official leader of the Guard, was also employed by the government. This provided the Guard with a liaison to reformist elements in the European Brazilian elite, and to the highest councils of the Brazilian government. The Guard and similar organizations generally followed Patrocínio in idolizing Princess Isabel as the *Redentora* (Redemptress) for signing abolition into law. Though Patrocínio could have easily presented elaborate economic arguments for reforms (e.g., land redistribution), he apparently believed the African Brazilian masses would respond more fervently to the princess as symbolizing their freedom and the regime that seemed committed to further reforms. Indeed, many *libertos* viewed Isabel in this manner (Andrews 1991, 44–45; Trochim 1988, 289–91).

Although the Black Guard was urban in origin, it appealed to rural workers and gave rise to a number of informally affiliated groups in several Brazilian provinces. The organization's membership was drawn mostly from ordinary *libertos* but also attracted less reputable elements, including a number of local *capoeiristas.*[3] Despite this factor, the police responded to the development of the Guard with restraint, perhaps acting on orders from higher up. This led some opponents to accuse this group of being a tool of the monarchy and their supporters. However, since the Guard was a secret society, it is impossible to find evidence that would clarify the nature of its relationship with the government (Trochim 1988, 288–93).

The Guard, reflecting an attitude common among former slaves, resorted to violence to express its frustration over the lack of opportunity for economic and social advancement. In fact, some sources have described the Guard as a paramilitary organization. For example, between December 1888 and July 1889, the Black Guard was formally involved in several riots and public disruptions of Republican gatherings in Rio de Janeiro. These phenomena reportedly inspired similar disturbances among African Brazilians in the plantation zones and in provincial urban centers as well—São Paulo, Minas Gerais, and Espírito Santo. However, there is little evidence that these disturbances were directly linked to the Black Guard. Patrocínio and members of the organization tried to represent this social unrest as part of the African Brazilian struggle for inclusion in the political process. They argued that the Guard was simply protecting African Brazilian rights against the assaults of racist Republicans. Yet the Black Guard's use of violence undermined its legitimacy even among the most sympathetic white abolitionists (Andrews 1991, 44–45; Trochim 1988, 294–98).

White abolitionists were at least sympathetic to African Brazilian political participation and expressed solidarity with the organization's goal of defeating the Republicans, whom they characterized as "enslavers of the free" (Trochim 1988, 294). Meanwhile, the Republicans "conjured up images of race war, of civil war, and extremist dictatorship" (295). Judging from the less partisan press, one can deduce that many Brazilians rejected any notion that African Brazilians could mobilize politically on their own. The Black Guard was viewed as a group of simple-minded African Brazilians manipulated by the João Alfredo government and Princess Isabel to destroy the planter class for their own political purposes. This view was shared by the powerful rural landowners, as well as by contemporary observers and later historians.

As the confrontations between former slaves and Republicans became more violent, the public view of these disturbances took on explicitly racial overtones.

---

3. Frustrated by their lack of prospects for social and economic advancement, many *libertos* who migrated to the cities after the abolition of slavery joined or formed *capoeira* gangs—particularly in Rio de Janeiro. In the transition to the Republic, these gangs, adept in both unarmed combat and the use of clubs and blade weapons, became associated with criminal or antigovernment activities and were used by both monarchists and republicans to harass their opponents and disrupt their rallies. *Capoeira* was finally outlawed in 1892 (Almeida 1986, 1–30; Bueno 1996; Butler 1998, 186–89).

Some African Brazilians began to repudiate the Black Guard to allay fears of a race war. The public activities of the Black Guard subsided and eventually ceased altogether when the Republicans and the army took control of the government in November 1889. The Black Guard thus lost its ability to deploy violence as an effective tool and a rallying point in the reformist monarchy. In addition, the social and economic reforms advocated by abolitionists were lost in the political reorganization that took place with the declaration of the republic. These circumstances left a legacy of antipathy toward the formation of explicitly political African Brazilian organizations (Trochim 1988, 298–300).

Race Thinking and the Remaking of "Nation"

In the period between 1889 and 1914, the great majority of the Brazilian intelligentsia undoubtedly supported the belief in whitening through miscegenation. Others, including some German immigrants residing in the southern states, sought to segregate themselves from native Brazilians. This is not to suggest, however, that all members of the Brazilian elite espoused this ideology. Some thinkers openly sought a more "authentic" national identity, believing they could devise a workable social order reflecting Brazil's uniqueness. This confidence can be partly attributed to the fact that race was no longer considered *prima facie* the most important determinant of historical development and did not necessarily preclude Brazil's future as a great nation. Consequently, Brazil's hitherto supposed racial (and cultural) liabilities were now transformed into assets (Skidmore 1974, 64–77, 78, 98, 176–79, 207–8).

This new thinking among Brazilian intellectuals, which led to the remaking of Brazil's national identity and the interrogation, if not complete rejection, of Eurocentric discourse in the post–World War I era, reflected a larger international trend. Many thinkers across the globe viewed the carnage of World War I as a failure of Western civilization itself, a sentiment captured by Oswald Spengler in *Decline of the West*. Intellect and reason, and their sensate cultural embodiments in science and technology, were seemingly turning humanity not only away from the ideational domain but also against life itself. Furthermore, the new psychoanalytical theories of Freud questioned bourgeois Christian morality. European civilization (and civilization generally) was, according to Freud, founded on the repression of instinct, which was the primary cause for the high incidence of mental dis-ease (Brookshaw 1986, 85–88).

These and similar ideas led to an ironic about-face on the part of many early twentieth-century Western thinkers. They sought to recapture all that had been discarded and marginalized in humanity's progressive ascent onto the citadel of intellect and reason that had accompanied Europe's rise to global dominion. A questioning of "white" Christian morality, which represented white as good and black as evil, led to a new "cult of the primitive." In the arts, this avant-garde sought to break away from the rigid classical canons in Western art. Stylized forms of African sculpture, in particular, directly influenced the Cubist Movement. African American musical forms such as blues and jazz became increasingly popular in Europe. This "Black Modernism," combined with the influence of Freud, Jung, and existentialist philosophers, symbolized liberation from the shackles of reason and intellect. Yet it was not the validation of blacks per se but rather the allure of the "black" forces of the subconscious that captured their interest. This was fundamentally a "positive" rearticulation of an older "negative" stereotype wherein blacks were seen as a physical embodiment of humanity's forbidden and subconscious desires (Brookshaw 1986, 85–88).

The influences of this primitivist cult culminated in the "Negritude" movement of the 1930s and 1940s in Europe, Africa, and the Americas. These ideas stimulated a fascination with African and African American life among the white intelligentsia in the United States, who used blackness as a tool in rebelling against the artificial restraint of Puritan morality. African American artists and thinkers during the 1920s and 1930s, in the Harlem Renaissance, were themselves influenced by the cult of the primitive. This is equally true of the contemporary culturally nationalistic movements in Latin America, based on Native Americans in Mexico and the Andean countries, and on blacks in other parts of Latin America and the Caribbean. Though the primitivist trend originated in and was sanctioned by prevailing fashion in Europe, avant-garde movements in the Americas had unique local origins and traits of their own. These forces had been unleashed in the early 1900s, and lay the groundwork for utilizing the "native" element for political or artistic purposes in the 1920s and 1930s (Davis 1999, 56–60).

In Brazil, the school of Parnassian poets, who stressed "correct form," maintained their grip on the Brazilian Academy of Letters in Rio de Janeiro at a time when revolutionary aesthetic movements that rejected formalistic literature were gaining momentum in Europe. Before the war, the Italian writer Filippo Marinetti, along with others, spearheaded an attack on prevailing European grammatical and literary canons. Symbolizing their rupture with the past, these iconoclasts called themselves futurists. They glorified and sought to give artistic expression to the tempo of twentieth-century life and the fluidity of contemporary technology.

Yet most of Brazil remained unaffected by the futurists' concerns. The exception was the city of São Paulo, where a booming coffee economy helped finance the modernization of commercial agriculture and the beginnings of modern industrialization. Although less cosmopolitan than Rio de Janeiro, São Paulo was nevertheless Brazil's most vibrant economic hub. Consequently, an expanding urban middle class produced an artistic intelligentsia that first absorbed modernist ideas from

Europe and ultimately toppled the rigid standards of their counterparts in Rio de Janeiro (Brookshaw 1986, 85–116; Skidmore 1974, 176–78).

Though Brazilian modernism began as an attempt by younger writers to introduce the latest European trends to Brazil, they eventually sought to capture new, more original Brazilian subject matter. The modernists of São Paulo not only introduced surrealism and other avant-garde techniques but also incorporated Native American and African Brazilian subject matter into the Brazilian arts. These trends culminated in the Week of Modern Art, a series of "festivals" of painting, sculpture, literature, and music that were held in the Municipal Theater of São Paulo in February 1922 (Brookshaw 1986, 5–116; Skidmore 1974, 176–78).

The revolution that was transforming artistic sensibilities in São Paulo extended to all the major states and was linked in varying degrees to São Paulo and Rio de Janeiro (although the Regionalist Movement in the Northeast had strong local roots of its own). Yet modernist writers in the Southeast, unlike those in the Northeast, were inspired only incidentally by African Brazilian themes. They generally considered Amazonian myths of colonial São Paulo to be more compelling sources of inspiration. The modernist cult of "indigenism," much as the Negritude movement, called for a rejection of the Western intellect and a return to a natural, atavistic world that the repressive culture of Europe had forced into the subconscious. It was less concerned about the exploitation or extermination faced by Native Americans. Rather, the European Brazilian intelligentsia, like its counterparts in other Western countries, extolled Native Americans and African Brazilians as symbols of a zest for life and artistic freedom in its struggle against the sterile intellectualism of its own culture and the general social values of the established bourgeoisie.

Nevertheless, Native Americans were viewed as contributors, both culturally and racially, to the formation of the Brazilian national identity. In contrast, it was primarily African Brazilians' cultural, rather than racial (phenotypical), assets that were deemed most useful. Notwithstanding the greater prominence of the African Brazilian in the modernist currents of the Northeast, mulattoes, rather than blacks, were generally viewed as playing a role in Brazil's racial blending by ultimately being bleached of their racial (though not cultural) blackness. At its best, this modernist vision sought full integration of all the various cultural, but not the various racial, elements of the country in the formation of a Brazilian national identity (Brookshaw 1986, 99, 106–8).

The Art of Black Racial Politics

Another consequence of the seismic economic and social changes in São Paulo and the states southward between 1888 and 1920 was the growth of the African

Brazilian press, and the formation of the Brazilian Black Front (Frente Negra Brasileira). The Black Front was the only national African Brazilian civil rights organization to emerge in the post-abolition era, and Brazil's first and only race-based political party. The *Clarim da Alvorada* (Clarion of the Dawn), one of the earliest African Brazilian newspapers, worked closely with the Black Front. Founded in January 1924 by Jaime d'Aguiar, the *Clarim* published articles attacking racial discrimination in São Paulo and the Southeast. In order to promote racial unity, the newspaper launched a campaign to bring about a shift from the traditional distinction between blacks and mulattoes based on color to a racial identity as African Brazilian, or *negro*. During slavery, the term *negro* was derogatory and almost synonymous with slave. Many early twentieth-century African Brazilian newspapers used the term *homens de cor* (colored) on their mastheads. Others completely avoided racial references. In their initial stage, journals such as *Clarim* and *Progresso* used *preto*. Yet in 1928 *Clarim* became one of the first news-papers to use *negro* on its masthead in a manner similar to U.S. constructions of African American identity. In addition, the *Clarim* kept readers informed of U.S. legislative developments relating to African Americans (Butler 1998, 57–58, 88–112; Davis 1999, 182; Taylor 1978, 28–39, 57).

On September 16 and October 12, 1931, Arlindo Viega dos Santos, a migrant from Bahia and a part-time journalist who frequently contributed to the African Brazilian press, held public meetings for black and multiracial individuals to discuss the creation of a new, explicitly political, national African Brazilian organization, which was christened the Frente Negra Brasileira. Viega was selected general president, a position he held until 1934. The Black Front proposed the moral, intellectual, and artistic uplift of African Brazilians. It also expressed a desire to extend social, economic, and legal aid to African Brazilian workers through the creation of cooperative societies, as well as technical and scientific schools. The organization established an elementary school and sponsored adult education courses focusing on literacy skills and vocational training. It also organized a medical clinic that provided dental and medical care at reduced rates or no cost to patients. The Front's legal department assisted members involved in disputes with landlords or employers. Furthermore, it provided mutual aid benefits and established a credit union as part of its "buy your own home" campaign. This campaign appears to have been somewhat successful, judging from observations of African Brazilians moving into newer sections of the city of São Paulo (Andrews 1991, 147–56; Butler 1998, 113–15; Davis 1999, 182–92; Pinto 1996, 45–59; Taylor 1978, 26).

The main leadership of the Front's Directorate was composed of blacks and mulattoes from the bourgeoisie. The organization gained support from many intellectuals, as well as from the small African Brazilian professional class. Yet a substantial part of the general membership was from the working class (Andrews 1991, 149–50; Barbosa 1998, 12). Women were important constituents of the Front, as evidenced by the creation of the Departamento Feminino da Frente Negra Brasileira (Women's Department of the Brazilian Black Front). This entity spoke out against sexual discrimination, harassment, and exploitation of African Brazilian women, many of whom worked as domestics, as store clerks, and in the growing manufacturing and transportation industry (Barbosa 1998, 37–38).

Frentenegrinos, as Front members were called, recruited potential members and supporters from both urban residential areas and the countryside. The exact size of the membership is difficult to determine. By 1933 the organization is estimated as having 4,000 members (although at one point the Front boasted of 100,000 to 200,000 members). Regardless, the organization expanded rapidly to the states of Minas Gerais, Espírito Santo, Bahia, Rio de Janeiro, and Rio Grande do Sul. Between 1931 and 1937, at least nineteen autonomous regional or local clubs and associations were organized that recognized the Front as the parent body and espoused similar goals. Several groups in the northeastern states of Pernambuco and Bahia were created to protect African-inspired cultural traditions from ethno-cidal campaigns. Some began research projects with the support of scholars to study African Brazilian culture and its influence on Brazilian society (Butler 1998, 113–17; Davis 1999, 183, 187; Pinto 1996, 45–59; Taylor 1978, 26–32).

The economic hardships of the Great Depression undoubtedly convinced many to support the Black Front. Perhaps even more important were the political changes precipitated by the Revolution of 1930. Workers, the urban middle class, and junior army officers disillusioned by corruption in the military combined to overthrow the dominant landed interests of the Old Republic (1889–1930) and swept populist Getúlio Vargas to power. Vargas, a former governor of Rio Grande do Sul, and unsuccessful opposition presidential candidate in the 1930 election, was installed by a military junta as the head of state of a provisional government, which lasted until 1934. He was elected constitutional president by Congress and governed in that position until 1937. In 1937 he engineered a coup with the assistance of the military, established the Estado Novo (New State), and ruled as dictator until 1945. Many individuals feared Vargas would stage another coup before the 1945 elections. Consequently, members of the military staged their own coup and forced Vargas to resign. Later, Vargas returned to power as constitutional president elected by popular vote (1951–54) (Andrews 1991, 148; Burns 1970, 290).

Vargas was a shrewd politician who understood the importance of gaining mass support without simultaneously antagonizing the elite. Although his regime was repressive, it was not brutal. Indeed, he promulgated many decrees assuring the masses he was an ally. Vargas also incorporated the growing urbanized masses into national political life. His overall relationship with the masses was paternalistic and charismatic, and reflected the contradictions characteristic of populism. The Brazilian masses, which formed an ever-growing urban proletariat, gradually became more politically conscious and optimistic, in part because of Vargas's rise to power. The growth of this population was attributable to economic expansion brought about by increasing industrialization in the 1930s. This gave rise to a demand for labor in the major urban centers throughout Brazil, particularly in the South. This demand, along with rural poverty (particularly in the Northeast) furthered massive migration to urban centers. It was also instrumental in the general urbanization of what had previously been a largely rural African Brazilian population, as well as the attendant growth of *favelas* (shantytowns) in all the major cities (Andrews 1991, 148; Butler 1998, 112, 188; Davis 1999, 80–83; Marx 1998, 170–72; Winant 2001, 222–24).

African Brazilians and others whose concerns had been ignored by the Republic's fraudulent democracy welcomed the Vargas "revolution." Vargas kept the promises he made to his African Brazilian supporters, although he generally framed his appeals in class rather than racial terms that focused on the masses of workers. For example, Vargas created a new Ministry of Labor and instructed officials to implement reforms to improve the status of Brazilian workers. In 1931, the Law of the Nationalization of Labor was implemented to "defend the Brazilian worker from competition from immigrants" by requiring enterprises to maintain at least a two-thirds Brazilian-born workforce. Vargas also took measures to decrease immigration quotas and openly criticized the formation of "cysts of foreign influence" in Brazil (Andrews 1991, 147).

This change in state policy was in part the culmination of events and practices dating back to the early part of the twentieth century. On the one hand, there was a significant reduction in the flow of European immigrants during World War I. On the other hand, by the 1920s, European immigrants and their descendents had proved to be less compliant than Brazilians expected. They become increasingly aggressive and effective in the pursuit of their interests and better working conditions through unionization and strikes. Correspondingly, Brazilian officials reexamined their labor preference policy (Andrews 1991, 85–87). By the 1930s state policy was reconfigured to end the preferential hiring of Europeans and gradually reintegrate native Brazilians into the industrial work force. Employment in the factories of São Paulo and other urban centers, in turn, provided a channel of vertical mobility for African Brazilian workers through trade unionism. Yet African Brazilians were typically treated as "second tier" workers earning less than those in white-dominated first-tier jobs, and were paid less than their white counterparts in the same jobs (Andrews 1991, 66–69, 105–21; Winant 2001, 225). Nevertheless, the African Brazilian masses acclaimed Vargas as "father of the poor" and supported him until his death in 1954. They also sought to take advantage of the political opening created by the Vargas revolution and destruction of the rabidly anti-black Republican regime.

Accordingly, the Black Front concluded that blacks and mulattoes could constitute a strong pressure group to lobby for changes in public policy and the Brazilian social order. Yet it felt that African Brazilians were not educationally or psychologically prepared for competitive industrial society. Thus, the organization would train African Brazilians to compete with whites as equals and to defend their political rights (Butler 1998, 120; Fernandes 1969, 187–233; Taylor 1978, 29–30). The Front espoused integration through reform but argued that African Brazilians would join forces with whites only after the way had been prepared for the transition to egalitarian integration (although Viega dos Santos's rhetoric at times seemed to be refracted through an inegalitarian, or assimilationist, lens that implicitly endorsed the ideology of whitening).

The organization's motto "separate now to unite later" (Butler 1998, 120) was more a call for egalitarian pluralism, that is to say, unity and action within the African Brazilian community, than a protest against whites. Ultimately, the Front looked forward to the day when race no longer served as the basis for meaningful distinctions in the Brazilian social order. Yet after 1931 the Front was one of the first entities to deploy the word *negro* with militant connotations. Its official newspaper, *A Voz da Raça* (The Voice of the Race), spoke out against racial discrimination in Brazil with the statement, "Color prejudice, in Brazil, is something only we African Brazilians [*negros*] can feel." This banner ran across the masthead for three years. One masthead admonished its readers, "*NEGRO não te envergonhes de ser negro!*" (African Brazilians, do not be ashamed to be black!) (57).

The Black Front utilized two major tactics to achieve its objectives. First, the organization sought to lobby on issues involving racial discrimination. Second, it attempted to elect some of its members or sympathizers to the national Chamber of Deputies in hopes of gaining recognition, which would lead to political and economic concessions. The organization achieved real, if limited, results by focusing attention on industrial or commercial establishments (e.g., public skating rinks and parks, the state police force) that discriminated against African Brazilians (Butler 1998, 118). Initially, Black Front leaders visited the managers or owners of these establishments and requested a policy change. If this strategy was unsuccessful, Front members or sympathetic local European Brazilians wrote newspaper articles exposing the facility's policies. In many instances, this negative publicity forced establishments to cease their overtly discriminatory practices. If this tactic failed, the Front resorted to more "direct" action, usually in the form of "sit-ins," similar to those used during the U.S. civil rights movement in the early 1940s and particularly in the late 1950s and early 1960s. The Front's militia would enter and occupy the facility until the management reversed its policy. After a few incidents, many businesses and public accommodations changed their policies to avoid further confrontations (Andrews 1991, 150–51; Barbosa 1998, 52–54; Davis 1999, 184; Fernandes 1969, 187–233; Taylor 1978, 31; Pinto 1996, 45–59).

Meanwhile, the Front's tactics in the political sphere were largely failures. The Black Front promised to participate in the election of representatives, especially those who were strictly "Brazilian." However, literacy was a requirement for voting, and most Front members were nonliterate. Furthermore, African Brazilians who were enfranchised did not always vote for Black Front candidates. Internal divisions, in combination with the small size of the African Brazilian vote, prevented the Front from becoming a significant political agent. The Front does not appear to have elected any candidates during its seven-year existence, and initially experienced difficulty registering as a political party. Moreover, Viega dos Santos's controversial leadership style, which was similar to Vargas's populist-like authoritarianism and influenced by the extant national commitment to "order and progress" (with an emphasis on the former), was marked by a paternalistic attitude toward the masses. He remarked that the lack of education and family values among African Brazilians contributed to their lack of integration into the social order. Furthermore, Viega supported the need for a strong head of state in the form of a monarchy, an anachronistic stance that would eventually lead to his departure from the Front (Andrews 1991, 150; Barbosa 1998, 90; Davis 1999, 184–85; Taylor 1978, 30).

Yet Viega's call for racial pride, unity, and discipline among blacks and mulattoes, coupled with national pride and patriotism, had a more enduring impact. The Black Front condemned what it considered "crassly materialistic and amoral" (Taylor 1978, 30) policies and values that accompanied industrialization and served international ends. It correctly viewed industrialization and large-scale European immigration as factors leading to the demographic and economic decline of African Brazilians, as well as the increase in anti-black prejudice. The Front's leaders recommended the Vargas regime "close the doors of Brazil [to foreigners] for twenty years or more" (Andrews 1991, 153) so that African Brazilians could regain their rightful position in society. Accordingly, the Black Front urged the destruction of foreign political influences and the "nationalization" of all commerce (Taylor 1978, 30).

This anti-immigrant sentiment was not unique to the Front. It was part of a larger national trend in response to the Republic's efforts to remake Brazil in the image of Europe. Through European immigration, the Brazilian elite had sought to transform Brazil into a "tropical Belle Époque" patterned after Paris and London. Instead, the nation was inundated by peasants and laborers from southern and eastern Europe, who, to the planters' horror, proved to be just as "illiterate, unwashed, crime-ridden, and averse to honest labor" (Andrews 1991, 152) as Brazil's own racially blended population. Even worse, they were more radical politically. Consequently, when Brazil's fascist-inspired Integralist movement emerged in São Paulo in 1932, anti-immigrant sentiment formed one of the movement's dominant themes (152, 153).

The Front characterized itself as a counterforce to the Integralists, who they believed would divide and destroy Brazil with their racist assumptions if they came to power. However, both the Front and Integralist movements displayed not only anti-immigrant sentiments but also an authoritarian ideology and practice that borrowed heavily from European fascism, despite espousing a general rejection of foreign political philosophies. Viega was critical of Brazil's mania of Aryanization (or whitening) but supportive of Hitler's program of patriotism and racial solidarity, even excusing the Third Reich's persecution of Jewish people (Andrews 1991, 153; Butler 1998, 120–21; Davis 1999, 182–86). By aligning itself more closely with fascism and Integralism over the course of the 1930s, the Front increasingly alienated moderate and left-wing sectors within the African Brazilian community. Eventually, this prompted disaffected individuals in São Paulo to form rival organizations such as the Clube Negro de Cultura Social (Black Club of Social Culture) and Frente Negra Socialistas (Black Socialists Front) (Andrews 1991, 154).

By 1932, the *Clarim* began criticizing Viega's authoritarianism, leading to the first major fissure between the Black Front and the leading African Brazilian newspaper. Viega countered by condemning the newspaper for not being actively engaged in the African Brazilian struggle. The *Clarim* continued its attacks until the Black Front militia—which was involved in often violent confrontations with the Black Front's opponents—vandalized the newspaper's offices. This activity intensified criticism by both whites and African Brazilians and led to a decline in the Front's membership. Eventually, this dispute led to a split between the *Clarim* and the Black Front. In 1933, the Front organized its own bimonthly newspaper, *A Voz da Raça* (Butler 1998, 118, 123–26; Taylor 1978, 32, 36–37).

Brasilidade *and Vargas's New Racial State*

The decline of the Front came rapidly when Vargas outlawed all political parties in 1937—a year after the Black Front became an official party. On November 10, 1937, Vargas masterminded a coup that made him dictator until 1945. In December 1937, he installed the fascist-inspired corporatist Estado Novo. This decision was largely in response to the escalating social tension and conflict engendered by the plethora of competing political and economic interests. Since 1930, these opposing forces had sought to define the new political order, resorting to armed violence on several occasions. Vargas's justification (or pretext) was that the government had uncovered the "Cohen Plan," a document that described the unfolding of a vast communist conspiracy (Andrews 1991, 146–47, 154–55; Taylor 1978, 32, 33–37).

The period between 1937 and 1945 was a high point of authoritarian rule in Brazil. Political and intellectual freedoms were severely restricted, especially political dissent and opposition. Mass-based organizations that could potentially threaten the state were either repressed (such as the Integralist movement) or brought under state control (such as the labor unions) (Andrews 1991, 155). Organizations like the Black Front, which were too small or fragmented to pose a threat, were allowed to dissolve. Although the Estado Novo did not view the Black Front as a cause for immediate concern, Vargas viewed it as potentially dangerous. He considered leftists a threat, and some white leftists backed the Front. Indeed, one such organization, the Alliança Nacional Libertadora (National Liberation Alliance), promoted African Brazilian equality and supported an unsuccessful attempt to organize a Black Front chapter in the university district of Rio de Janeiro (Andrews 1991, 154–55; Davis 1999, 189–91; Taylor 1978, 34).

Vargas not only decreed that discussing racial conflict or calling attention to racial discrimination adversely affected national pride but also believed that organizations like the Front, which were strictly political in nature and explicitly racial in composition, impeded progress toward national cultural (and racial) unification. Yet the whitening ideal bequeathed to Vargas by his predecessors also presented him with a serious dilemma. In other words, explicit support of racial hierarchy and whitening contradicted Vargas's populist, developmentalist, and nationalist agenda. The resolution of this contradiction necessitated a new, inclusive, and uniquely "Brazilian" narrative of national identity that would legitimate the nation's ambition as an emerging nation-state and promise as a world power (Taylor 1978, 34; Winant 2001, 226).

Always the strategist, Vargas fully embraced and institutionalized racial democracy as the official national ideology and understood that Brazil's greatest liability—the black peril—could also become its greatest asset. This led to a critical reevaluation of the ongoing attempt to stamp out African Brazilian cultural expression, which could now serve to advance his larger agenda for national integration under the rubric of *brasilidade* or "Brazilianism." *Samba, candomblé, capoeira* (which had now been transformed into a stylized martial art / dance form), and other forms of African Brazilian cultural expression once viewed as "primitive" could now be considered emblematic of Brazil's racial democracy in action.[4] Consequently, Vargas made racial democracy ideology a cornerstone of

---

4. Some have argued that slaves blended dance steps and acrobatics with the attack and defense moves of *capoeira* to disguise it as a recreational or ritual dance and prevent it from being prohibited by slave masters. Eventually, African musical instruments such as the *berimbau* and the *atabaque*

administrative policy for preserving African Brazilian cultural expression, while simultaneously maintaining a belief in the principle of whitening through miscegenation (Davis 1999, 83–177, 188).

Vargas's stance dovetailed with Freyre's reinterpretation of Brazilian national identity as *lusotropicalismo* (or "Portuguese tropicality"), which extolled Brazil as the outpost that reflected par excellence Portugal's unique history of creating egalitarian racially and culturally blended societies in the tropics. Through his historical and ethnographic writings, Freyre rearticulated Brazilian understandings of both "nation" and "race" by framing Brazil as an open and fluid racial order that was a synthesis of its three parent racial and cultural components. Freyre's revisionist work significantly influenced Brazilian national culture, and also reshaped Brazil's image abroad. Beginning with his 1933 work *Casa Grande e Senzala* (The Masters and the Slaves), Freyre alleged, among other things, that the egalitarian nature of the Portuguese colonizers had given rise to pervasive miscegenation in Brazil. This dynamic had an invigorating, rather than enervating, effect on the Brazilian racial makeup and gave rise to "kinder, gentler" race relations than those of the United States (Winant 2001, 226–29). Not only was slavery more benign in Brazil than elsewhere in the Americas (most notably the United States), but the racial order that emerged out of slavery also displayed a noticeable absence of racial conflict and a more unified society, in contrast to the U.S. segregationist policies buttressed by the one-drop rule.

In addition, Freyre recognized and legitimated the permanence and depth of the African Brazilian and Native American contributions to Brazilian national culture and society and celebrated the racial and cultural blending that many earlier authorities had considered abhorrent.[5] Thus, Freyre's work was a significant departure from previous analyses in that it called into question and undermined the scientific racism and whitening ideology of the abolitionist era and the early First Republic (Winant 2001, 226). Yet his celebration of Brazil's racial inclusiveness, its hybridity (and sexuality), ultimately served to justify, rather than critique, both the racial order and Vargas's national integration agenda based on *brasilidade* (D. Silva 1989, 166–67; Winant 2001, 226–28). As a result of Freyre's work race

---

were added. In Rio *capoeira* developed almost exclusively as a form of fighting, whereas in Bahia it also continued to develop as a type of ritual martial art/dance (Almeida 1986, 1–30; Butler 1998, 186–89; Moulthrop 2001).

5. Freyre's First Afro-Brazilian Congress of Recife, a conference held in 1934, furthered his goal of examining and celebrating the African-Brazilian contribution to Brazilian culture and society. The Congress involved the collaboration of academics from various disciplines, as well as grassroots and popular musicians, artists, religious practitioners, culinary specialists, and so on. That said, more radical African-Brazilian critics concerned about addressing racial inequality have often described the conference as "culturalist" and "folkloristic" (Brookshaw 1986, 118–19; Butler 1998, 42–45).

consciousness was viewed as deleterious to a truly inclusive Brazilian national culture and identity, which Freyre captured with the notion of a Brazilian meta-race, or "beyond race" *(alem raça)* (Nobles 2000, 87, 97–98, 117). Accordingly, Brazil was depicted as capable of a racial integration unimaginable elsewhere—particularly in the 1930s era of Jim Crow, not to mention the Third Reich—an image that defused racial conflict far more effectively than whitening ideology could ever do (Winant 2001, 226–28).

Ultimately, the preservation and perpetuation of African Brazilian culture (e.g., *samba, capoeira, candomblé,* and so on) under the rubric of *brasilidade* would have the dual benefit of providing empirical evidence of racial democracy and marketing Brazil's racial democracy abroad, attracting tourist dollars during Carnival. These annual festivities would become the great national celebration of racial democracy as personified in the *mulata,* the utmost symbol of the sanctified sexual objectification of African Brazilian women and the commodification of *brasilidade* wrapped into one marketable package. Samba schools, an institution that had originated as part of a culture of resistance among African Brazilians, were required to incorporate events and individuals in the national history that would further project Brazil's racially democratic image.

In the decades that followed, samba schools would increasingly rely on corporate and state funding to mount ever more lavish and expensive floats and parade displays during Carnival. Furthermore, candidates seeking public office would be able to use samba schools during election campaigns by offering increased subsidies in exchange for votes, rather than promising real social structural change. Carnival euphoria and the celebration of heavily African Brazilian influenced popular culture—particularly music and dance—as national culture, along with the gradual, yet token, integration of mulattoes into the national soccer team, helped foster the illusion of an inclusive racial democracy. Simultaneously, these phenomena served as a form of social control by diverting attention away from larger socioeconomic inequities (Davis 1999, 83–177; Parker 1991, 136–64; Raphael 1990, 73–78; Rodrigues 1984, 3–14, 137–40; Sheriff 1999, 3–28; Vianna and Chasteen 1999, 32–76).[6]

After having reached its nadir during the Vargas regime, the Black Front was reorganized as the União Negra Brasileira (African Brazilian Union) with Raul Amaral as the general president. However, May 13, 1938, just days after the unsuccessful Integralist uprising in Rio de Janeiro and, symbolically, the fiftieth anniversary of abolition, marked the last public gathering of individuals involved with the Black Front (Andrews 1991, 155). African Brazilian cultural organizations such as the São Paulo–based Black Club for Social Culture participated in the anniversary celebration with a nationally created "Black Commission for the

---

6. Lecture given by Guerreiro Ramos at the University of California, Los Angeles, in 1974.

Fiftieth Anniversary of the Abolition of Slavery." Yet this public spectacle seemed to be another official attempt to rouse popular support without offering broader political or social structural change. According to some sources, the club was allowed to continue functioning only as a cultural entity and had to eliminate the word *negro* from its name. This was, in effect, a return to the 1920s, when *clubes de baile* (or dance clubs) provided African Brazilians with the only sites for social engagement (Davis 1999, 190–92).

Until the end of Vargas's dictatorship in 1945, explicit political discourse by African Brazilians was forced underground. Meanwhile, the *Clarim da Alvorada* continued publication after the Black Front ceased operations. In 1946, after the end of the Vargas regime, the newspaper pressed for the formation of the Associação dos Negros Brasileiros (Association of African Brazilians), which was to be a rejuvenated Black Front. The idea was not greeted with enthusiasm and died when the *Clarim* ceased publication in 1948. Although the Black Front had numerous successors in the 1940s and 1950s (O Teatro Experimental do Negro, União dos Homens de Côr, Associação Cultural do Negro), none of these organizations achieved its prominence (Davis 1999, 190–92; Taylor 1978, 37).

The Racial Politics of Black Art

World War II made Brazilians more responsive to the dangers of ideologies premised on racial superiority. Also, in 1943, President Vargas and U.S. president Franklin Delano Roosevelt met to discuss collaborating against fascism in Europe. The following year Brazilian troops were deployed in Italy to battle the Axis powers. This made Brazilians even more conscious of and vocal about the contradictions of living under a dictatorship while their young men, including African Brazilians, fought and died in Europe for the cause of democracy. By the end of the war, the Estado Novo had already given way to a new period of democratization. On February 20, 1945, the *Correio da Manhã* (*The Morning Courier*), disregarding the censorship of the press, published an article by former presidential candidate José Américo de Almeida that criticized the regime. Almost two months later, the Vargas administration announced a general amnesty of all political prisoners, which paved the way for presidential elections at the end of the year. In that election, General Eurico Gaspar Dutra, a Vargas ally, won a resounding victory as president. Though Vargas left his mark on the new generation, his dictatorship ended as a wave of antifascism swept over Brazil (Davis 1999, 192–95).

The end of Vargas's dictatorship in 1945 coincided with the end of World War II and the assertion of new emancipatory and egalitarian demands by the disenfranchised. The aspirations of previously colonized populations in Asia, and particularly in Africa, were key elements of these new initiatives. In Brazil, a group of activists led by Abdias do Nascimento, the leading pan-Africanist and black nationalist in modern Brazilian history, explicitly sought to position Brazil within pan-Africanist discourse. The focus was primarily on African Brazilian cultural initiatives and organized under the banner of *quilombismo,* which took its name from the *quilombos,* or runaway slave settlements of the seventeenth century (Davis 1999, 196; Winant 2001, 228). Thus in the period after 1945, black arts, cultural groups, and urban organizations reasserted themselves. African Brazilian newspapers flourished; social and political clubs, as well as trade union organizations, appeared in urban centers, most notably in São Paulo and Rio de Janeiro. More explicitly political initiatives were articulated in a national black constitutional convention organized by São Paulo activists. They were seeking to formulate a platform of demands to be presented at the upcoming Constituent Assembly, which was charged with the task of writing the new constitution for the Second Republic (Andrews 1991, 182).

As more Brazilians increasingly spoke out for democratic reforms in the late 1940s, African Brazilians once again envisioned the possibility of being incorporated as equals into Brazilian society. Consequently, they embarked on the second major mobilization in the post-abolition era: the Black Experimental Theater (O Teatro Experimental do Negro). Abdias do Nascimento, along with other African Brazilian intellectuals and cultural workers, spearheaded the Black Experimental Theater, which was founded in October 1944 and lasted until 1968. Benefiting from the lessons learned from organizations such as the Black Front, the theater endeavored to balance political and social denunciation with promoting positive African Brazilian values and racial equality. It sought to achieve these goals through three distinct trajectories: theater and culture, national African Brazilian forums, and publications (Davis 1999, 192–203; Nascimento 1967, 37–53).

One of the goals of the Black Experimental Theater was to help African Brazilians cast aside their feelings of inferiority. Moreover, it believed that European Brazilians would change their conventionally negative images of African Brazilians if they saw them engaging in nonstereotypical activities. Through a host of nontheatrical projects, including its journal *Quilombo,* national African Brazilian conferences, and African Brazilian Studies seminars (to name a few), the Black Experimental Theater sought to further the cultural and psychological education of whites and African Brazilians. From the beginning, it was open to individuals of all racial identities, and welcomed whites as long as they supported the premises of the theater. Moreover, it and its founders were no less patriotic than the modernists a decade earlier. The theater promoted its own sense of a *brasilidade* that opposed racial discrimination as an undemocratic practice that undermined the integrity of the nation. Thus, it called for the implementation of antidiscrimination statutes within the parameters of Brazil's legal and constitutional structure, which the organization hoped would legitimize its struggle. Remarkably, several of the Black Experimental Theater's recommendations seemed to prefigure U.S. affirmative action initiatives that emerged in the late 1960s (Davis 1999, 194–96, 199; Hanchard 1994, 106–8; Paixão 2004, 791).

Although the Black Experimental Theater never gained as much popular support as the Black Front, its influence extended throughout Brazil. It became the major African Brazilian venue for the discussion and dissemination of ideas surrounding race in Brazil. In particular, *Quilombo,* published between 1948 and 1951, provided such a forum for Brazilian thinkers, both black and white. The publication included a column titled "Racial Democracy," which promised to highlight events and issues that would undermine the racial democracy ideology—particularly its assimilationist underpinning—in order to forge a new conception of racial democracy based on genuine egalitarian integration. Not surprisingly, almost two decades after the publication of his *Casa Grande e Senzala,* Freyre reaffirmed his belief in Brazil's racial democracy in *Quilombo.* Although Freyre acknowledged the existence of color prejudice, he pointed out that Brazil had never been racially polarized. At the same time, Freyre cautioned that Brazilians should be vigilant against separatists who sought to perpetuate racial divisions. Freyre's appearance in *Quilombo* at the time of the publication's inauguration legitimized the Black Experimental Theater's existence in the public perception. Yet it also indicated the extent to which it was either willing, or felt compelled, to avoid projecting itself as a separatist organization (Davis 1999, 196–97; Nascimento 2004, 223).

The modernists were anti-foreign (particularly with regard to the United States), in the sense that they perpetuated the notion that Brazilian race relations were more harmonious than those in the United States. The Black Experimental Theater identified the problematic implications of this perspective, which initially gained it a reputation for being influenced by U.S. racial thinking. Many Brazilian writers and newspapers accused it of receiving U.S. financial backing, although it unequivocally reaffirmed its loyalty to Brazilian national development. Indeed, it acknowledged that the absence of legal segregation distinguished Brazil from the United States but argued that informal barriers to racial equality made African Brazilians feel segregated de facto. Moreover, the standard of living of African Brazilians in the 1940s was far below that of African Americans. In addition, legalized segregation in the United States actually encouraged the formation of black consciousness by orienting mulattoes toward blacks. By contrast, Brazil's racial democracy ideology, coupled with whitening through miscegenation, thwarted the formation of black consciousness. The Black Experimental Theater considered miscegenation and the mulatto escape hatch to be tantamount to sanctioned ethnocide of African Brazilians (Davis 1999, 199–202).

The Black Experimental Theater did point out that African Brazilians had maintained their African cultural identity in ways that African Americans had not been able to do. But they attributed this to the large number of slaves that were *boçal* or African born, rather than to any innate egalitarianism of the Portuguese colonizers, the Catholic Church, or the Brazilian national character. The number of slaves, plus the longer duration of the Brazilian slave trade, helped African culture survive in myriad forms. This was a testament to African Brazilian resistance, despite attempts to destroy it (Davis 1999, 201–2; Walker 1989, 17–21).

Both the Black Experimental Theater and the Black Front sought to link their cause with pan-African concerns throughout the Americas and globally, although the theater's efforts were more vigorous and wide-ranging in this area. The Black Experimental Theater also called attention to Brazil's exclusion of African Brazilians in national life and provided an opportunity for African Brazilians to learn about the achievements of African-descent individuals abroad (Davis 1999, 196). For example, *Quilombo* published articles on world-renowned African American entertainers such as Josephine Baker, Marian Anderson, and Katherine Dunham. Dunham, an internationally recognized dancer, was herself a victim of discrimination while visiting São Paulo on tour in 1950. Despite holding advance reservations, which had been previously confirmed in person by her white secretary, Dunham was denied entrance to a hotel. As a result of the Dunham incident, Congressman Afonso Arinos de Mello Franco introduced antidiscrimination legislation that prohibited racial discrimination in public accommodations. The bill passed as Law No. 1390 and became known as the 1951 Afonso Arinos Law. Yet the Arinos law contained a very limited and restricted definition of racial discrimination and treated infractions as misdemeanors rather than felonies (Davis 1999, 200; Nascimento and Nascimento 1992, 33–36).

Following the Dunham incident, the Black Experimental Theater moved to a more aggressive level of political engagement. In the late 1950s, it sent a letter to all political parties in the Federal District asking them to develop programs that would stimulate interest in African Brazilian concerns. The letter requested explicitly that these organizations list all their African Brazilian candidates. These efforts were unsuccessful, largely because the national political culture did not consider African Brazilians to be a legitimate interest group.

In addition, the Black Experimental Theater promoted African Brazilian beauty contests, which took place between 1947 and 1950, in order to undermine the long-standing perception that African Brazilians are physically unattractive. There were two annual pageants celebrating the most beautiful African Brazilian women in the nation's capital: the *Rainha das Mulatas* (Queen of the Mulattas) and the *Boneca de Pixe* (Tar Baby or Black Doll), whose contestants were respectively young mulatto and black women.[7] Yet press coverage of the two pageants differed significantly. One newspaper revealed its own and Brazil's qualified acceptance of mulattoes and their implicit rejection of blacks when it stated that the *mulata* is "the only peaceful solution" to the racial problem in Brazil. "Only through her can the race cleanse itself." This media portrayal of the mulatto woman as Brazil's racial salvation was, however, undermined when the same newspaper referred to her as the proverbial sex object: "She is, above all, the glorification of the flesh and of the sins of the flesh" (Turner 1992, 79). For the black pageant, the newspapers provided photographs of the contestants and the most basic factual information (i.e., their names, their opinions about the contest, when the coronation would be held). There do not appear to have been any interviews with the general public concerning the national importance of the black beauty contests. Moreover, the black contestants were never portrayed in the media as being representative of Brazil's racial democracy, in contrast to their mulatto counterparts. Rather, the media gave modest praise, reaffirming stereotypic views of black women as "self-sacrificing and hard working" (80).

The Culture of Racial Resistance: White Domination and a "War of Maneuver"

Subverting the Escape Hatch

Even during the most oppressive periods of Brazilian race relations, black and multiracial individuals have countered with forms of resistance. This racially defined opposition has been occasionally expressed through armed revolt. More typically, this resistance has moved both outward, to the margins of society, and

7. In one source "Boneca de Pixe" is listed as "Peixe," which translates as "Fish Doll" (Davis 1999, 197, 212). In other sources, including Nascimento's own account of the TEN, the term is listed as "Boneca de Pixe," which translates as "Tar Doll" (or "Tar Baby"), although a more common spelling for the word "tar" is *piche* (Nascimento 1967; Turner 1992, 76–81). Given the racial underpinnings of the term "Boneca de Pixe," it would seem that "Boneca de Peixe," which has no explicit racial reference, would be a less likely term. However, use of "Boneca de Pixe," given its pejorative meaning, would seem to contradict the goal of increasing racial self-esteem and public acceptance of the beauty of the black woman. On the one hand, the term may have reflected internalized racism. In other words, as a normative part of vernacular culture, the term's racist implications were largely invisible and remained unquestioned. Alternatively, appropriation of "Boneca de Pixe" may have been a form of subversion to imbue this derogatory term with positive value and respectability by simply using it in public discourse, thereby helping to increase racial self-esteem.

inward, to the relative safety of their own exclusive (and excluded) communities. Although this isolation has provided African Brazilians with relative comfort and security, it has also deprived them of a power base from which to mount opposition or make inroads into the mainstream political process (Omi and Winant 1994, 80–81).

Following Gramsci, Omi and Winant describe this process as a *war of maneuver:* a conflict between disenfranchised and subordinated groups and a dictatorial and dominant power. In a racial *war of maneuver,* black and multiracial individuals necessarily have devoted themselves principally to projects aimed at self-preservation (Omi and Winant 1994, 80–81). This has included everyday, small-scale forms of opposition in which individuals (such as Gama and Lima Barreto) have spoken out against racial oppression, or have fought for African Brazilian rights. This opposition has also included larger-scale collective challenges, such as those mounted by the Black Guard, Black Front, and the Black Experimental Theater, which have allowed black and multiracial individuals to develop social alternatives to the repressive racial order.

Each of these racial projects has been a discursive or cultural initiative that has interpreted, represented, or explained racial dynamics by means of identity politics. The goal has been to rescue racial identities from the dominant society's distortion and erasure. Simultaneously, each racial project has also been a political initiative, with the goal of organizing and redistributing resources. At times, the state has been called upon to play a significant role, as in the struggle to abolish slavery and the demands for equal rights for African Brazilians. Both types of initiatives have variously contested the ternary racial project and the divisiveness perpetuated by the mulatto escape hatch. None of these strategies succeeded in dismantling the mulatto escape hatch; at best they only subverted or partially closed it.

Besides a few voices in the mulatto press during the 1830s (which tended to frame protest in terms of partisan politics, rather than race), multiracial individuals rarely discussed racism as a force keeping free people of color in a position of second-class citizenship during slavery. Exceptions to this occurred during periods of crisis or "political opportunity" within the white political establishment, when discussion of racial issues coincided with anticolonial, antimonarchy, and antislavery movements. At such junctures, the issue of race was often coupled with, overshadowed by, or subsumed under more general political and economic agendas. This was particularly evident when the abolition campaign gained full momentum after 1870, or when Free Coloreds became involved in the mass-based movement that instigated the flight of slaves from the plantations in the 1880s. At both moments, the political and socioeconomic advantages and disadvantages of slavery superseded humanitarian concerns and issues of racial solidarity. Blacks, whites, and mulattoes fought together on both sides of the abolitionist struggle (Flory 1977, 205, 208, 210, 220).

Prior to that time—when Gama began to wage his war against slavery and racial inequality—any abolitionist was considered a seditious radical. However, a European Brazilian might have been dismissed as a misguided, yet benevolent and self-sacrificing liberal, but a mulatto would have been condemned as an ungrateful upstart or treated as a belligerent rebel to be silenced. Even after the abolition of slavery, the Brazilian racial order remained rabidly anti-black. African Brazilians still required white patronage in order to achieve vertical social mobility. Thus, Lima Barreto, whose discursive and political initiatives criticized Brazil's ruling elite for pursuing material wealth and whiteness at the expense of the black and mulatto masses, had difficulty getting his works published. Individuals such as Gama and Lima Barreto, who broke the code of silence on questions of racial oppression, faced significant opposition and paid a high price for their subversive activities. They not only risked losing what support they had from patrons in the white elite but also generally operated without the collective support of other African Brazilians, which limited the scope of their efforts.

Collective forms of resistance had a more immediate and broader, if limited, impact on the racial order than relatively isolated expressions of individual agency. The Black Guard was one such form of collective agency and was squarely situated within the traditional framework of African Brazilian organizations. This was reflected in its genesis from a social club, its secret organizational structure, and its adoption of Princess Isabel as somewhat of a patron saint, as well as the religious-like tenor of its fraternal oath (Trochim 1988, 287). Yet the Black Guard's cultural initiative sought to breach the racial comportment line by overcoming the invidious distinctions that had historically divided blacks and mulattoes and prevented other traditional African Brazilian organizations from promoting African Brazilian racial solidarity in the war against racial inequality.

The Black Guard was also an attempt by African Brazilians to address the issues of social and economic reform and political participation. Yet its use of violence, although understandable in the context of labor relations in the post-abolition period, was a serious tactical mistake in the political sense. In addition, the organization's support of the monarchy (and its concomitant focus on attacking Republican opposition), while perhaps functional in rallying the majority of politically unsophisticated ex-slaves, was equally problematic. In effect, the Guard's leaders involved their organization in political battles of secondary importance to the African Brazilian masses. Opponents of social and economic reform were thus able to exploit these weaknesses in order to discredit not only the Black Guard but also the entire reformist movement (Trochim 1988, 287). Whites were able to thwart the Black Guard's attempts to gain recognition as an independent African Brazilian political movement by arguing that African Brazilians were ignorant tools of the Princess and her abolitionist entourage. Ultimately, the whole campaign for social and economic reform collapsed when the monarchy was overthrown on November 15, 1889. Thus, African Brazilians lost a key opportunity to force the European Brazilian power structure to deal with racial discrimination and economic exploitation (299).

The failure of the Black Guard to promote racial solidarity, socially acceptable forms of political participation for African Brazilians, and solutions to the problems of race and class discrimination was only part of the more general failure to supplement abolition with further social and economic reforms. Still, the experience of the Black Guard highlights the fact that serious, if largely unsuccessful efforts were made to bring African Brazilians into the economic and political mainstream. Yet the backlash against the Black Guard's collective militancy, particularly its use of violence, may have prompted many African Brazilians to abandon direct assaults on the racial comportment line and follow more traditional and assimilationist paths of individual socioeconomic advancement (Trochim 1988, 299–300).

Closing the Escape Hatch

Although blacks and mulattoes in São Paulo did not originally consider themselves primarily as "black," blackness became the basis of a shared experience of subordination and exclusion. Awareness of this shared experience paved the way for initiatives such as the Black Front. Like the Black Guard, the Black Front also sought to bridge the color divide and mobilize blacks and mulattoes into a cohesive force in the war against racial inequality. Yet the Front had a more immediate and broader, if still comparatively limited, impact on the racial order than the Black Guard. At the turn of the twentieth century, a small cadre of African Brazilian activists in São Paulo began to articulate a racial ideology that rejected the traditional distinction between blacks and multiracial individuals based on color, instead assuming a racial identity as *negros*. This rearticulation of blackness through a cultural initiative that included mulattoes as well as blacks was similar to the formation of African American identity in the United States and would become a central organizing principle of African Brazilian political discourse throughout the twentieth century. This radical usage of *negro* sought to imbue the term with not only positive but also political significance. This was considered a prerequisite to gaining support for the Black Front and forging a power base among its potentially large constituency (Butler 1998, 57–58, 88–112; Fernandes 1969, 187–233; Taylor 1978, 25, 28–39).

Nevertheless, the Front was unable to gain broad national support. This was especially true in the Northeast, particularly Bahia, which had the largest African Brazilian population. Many African Brazilians in the region considered a racial identity grounded in the concept of blackness to be in conflict with their self-identities and day-to-day social reality. The economic structure in the region also hampered racial mobilization. The Northeast was still dominated by agrarian interests; urbanization and industrialization (except in Recife) lagged far behind that of the Southeast. Thus, there was no restructuring of the Northeastern economy that might have given rise to new social sectors capable of challenging the agricultural and commercial interests that had dominated the political structure in places like Bahia since the colonial era. In Bahia's capital of Salvador, the pre-abolition pattern of African Brazilian economic exploitation persisted in the rural areas. The political culture was shaped by fiefdoms unable or unwilling to forge broader interest-based coalitions. Mass constituencies of any type, particularly race-based ones, were not viable as power bases. Consequently, the Black Front was unable to mobilize an African Brazilian population that was largely composed of nonliterate rural peasants still bound economically and psychologically to the plantation, or an urban population that tended to view sociopolitical injustice in economic and cultural rather than racial terms (Butler 1998, 130–13; Taylor 1978, 34–36).

In São Paulo, the dismantling of local power bases and Vargas's encouragement of corporatist politics created a greater potential for popular empowerment than in Salvador. However, neither situation was conducive to the formation of a strong African Brazilian interest group. Many middle-class black and multiracial individuals in the Southeast had the same antipathy toward race-specific organizations that urban African Brazilians in the Northeast did. Despite the Front's call for racial unity, there were various aspects of the Brazilian racial order, even in the urban Southeast, which discouraged the formation of a broad-ranging collective identity and a common sociopolitical agenda. For example, after slavery was abolished, no formal legislation was implemented restricting the economic or social activities and advancement of African Brazilians, or mandating residential segregation. Furthermore, the franchise and incorporation into the body politic were based on literacy, not race (Taylor 1978, 34–36).

More important, the Black Front was unsuccessful in shattering the illusion of inclusion perpetuated by the escape hatch, which had been effectively manipulated for generations by Brazil's political and economic elite. Theoretically, individual mulattoes and blacks could achieve vertical social mobility as far as their skill, intelligence, and competence would take them. Most African Brazilians accepted the egalitarian tenets of racial democracy ideology, which provided hope for an improvement in their status, even as their personal experiences with discrimination may have contradicted those tenets (Taylor 1978, 34–36). A call for racial unity by the Front, especially within the context of national unity, thus seemed redundant to many blacks and mulattoes—particularly the African Brazilian bourgeoisie. They criticized the Front's emphasis on "racial" issues and asserted that individual achievement would gain European Brazilian respect and acceptance. Yet support from the African Brazilian bourgeoisie was essential if the Front was to win political campaigns, raise funds for its activities, or secure new members and leaders. The Black Front's failure to reach the larger African Brazilian middle class, along with its failure to mobilize in the Northeast, were probably two of the most important factors in its demise (Marx 1998, 256–57; Taylor 1978, 35–37).

Another problem for the Front was the lack of political experience among Viega dos Santos and other Front leaders. Despite the focus on electing Front members or sympathizers to the Chamber of Deputies, the organization was unsuccessful in gaining support among African Brazilians who exercised the franchise. The Front elected none of its members to any office. Moreover, it never devised any legislative agenda to assure African Brazilian equality or economic opportunity that African Brazilians and liberal whites might have supported. Nor did the Front create alliances or cultivate support among important European Brazilian organizations, though this was partially because most European Brazilian organizations refused to acknowledge "race" as a central organizing principle (Marx 1998, 256–57; Taylor 1978, 36). In addition, class differences among the membership of the Front stifled communication between the leadership that often consisted of educated mulattoes and blacks, and the rank-and-file members who were African Brazilians with little or no formal education. Also, the former were variously supportive of the organization's authoritarian (and pro-fascist) structure, whereas the latter tended to view the Black Front's structure and philosophy as too similar to those of ultra-conservative groups such as the Integralists.

Although the Front continually reiterated its goal of integrating African Brazilians into all aspects of national life, it never devised any long-range strategies for doing so. And though it spoke in vague terms about "reeducating" whites, the only education program it sought to implement was for African Brazilians. And because it had neither the financial nor organizational resources to build schools or create scholarships for African Brazilian students, it solicited funds to support the organization's educational activities from the most impoverished Brazilians. Few African Brazilians with teaching experience or technical expertise assisted the organization, and the Black Front repeatedly proposed more activities than the African Brazilian population could reasonably support (Taylor 1978, 36–37).

Moreover, the Front in a sense had embraced the racial democracy ideology it professed to be fighting. It perhaps naïvely assumed that simply exposing egregious cases of racial discrimination would prompt Brazilians to demand an end to the injustice. To some extent, this faith in the nation's ability to implement rapid reform was reinforced by the Front's relatively easy successes in its direct action campaigns against discrimination in some public venues. However, with the establishment of the Estado Novo, numerous facilities returned to their exclusionary policies (Fernandes 1969, 187–233; Marx 1998, 255–56; Taylor 1978, 36–37).

The Front's ability to promote African Brazilian culture on a national level was likewise limited. The organization never received support from the Ministry of Education and Public Health. Conferences held by the Front received little national attention. Many in the press and government criticized the Front as an extremist movement that was adapting certain concepts—in particular a "social politics of races" (Davis 1999, 190)—that were contrary to the civil and constitutional order and the nationalist agenda. More important, however, were the labor codes that conveyed to many workers (of all racial backgrounds) the message that Vargas was the "father of the poor." Despite escalating inflation, government pay increases tended to discourage opposition to the regime. The state and political elite also lured the masses by promoting traditional values and perpetuating the illusion of their own self-identification with the masses through the rhetoric of *brasilidade.* Yet the Estado Novo sought to maintain the supremacy of upper-class whites and instituted a policy grounded in deep-seated prejudices against African Brazilians (190–91).

Although the Black Front lasted only six years, it was a bold attempt to create an effective national organization that fought for the political and economic interests of African Brazilians and sought to prepare them for competition in an increasingly urban industrial society. Embittered and disillusioned by the Front's failures, members of the African Brazilian middle class rejected proposals for a new African Brazilian political organization after the demise of the Black Front. When the dictatorship fell in 1945 and Brazil embarked on a new experiment in democracy—the Second Republic—many African Brazilians devoted themselves to the individualistic pursuit of opportunities (Andrews 1991, 156; Taylor 1978, 38).

The Black Experimental Theater's cultural initiative sought not only to elevate blacks and mulattoes in the national consciousness but also to provide a critique of and antidote to the ideology of *branqueamento* (whitening) by furthering negritude and black self-esteem. Yet at times it presented a new "positive" stereotype of the happy-go-lucky African Brazilian, which originated in the negative stereotype of the "savage black." This dynamic was part of a larger international countercultural trend in which blackness (or negritude) served as a conduit for a return to a primordial (and thus fundamentally prerational) state prior to the domination of intellect and reason in the modern West as well as Europe's rise to global dominion. This primitivist rearticulation of blackness, however strategic and subversive, was nevertheless underpinned by essentialism. It not only confirmed that African Brazilians were intrinsically different from whites but also could have the unsavory consequence of justifying the former's social and economic dependence on the latter (hooks 1995, 23–31; Rosenau 1992, 5–7; Wilber 1996, 131, 159).

The Black Experimental Theater attempted to represent the African Brazilian voice on a national level and to implement political initiatives that would mobilize an African Brazilian electorate. Yet these efforts were largely unsuccessful, as the national political culture discouraged mobilization around racial identities and did not view African Brazilians as a legitimate interest group. Also, individual supporters, both black and white, had different ideas about how to promote African Brazilian interests. Many individuals who first joined the Black Experimental Theater were artists primarily interested in advancing theater. They viewed political activities as secondary to art. Others were intent on educating the masses about their own contribution to Brazilian culture or encouraging mobilization and dialogue through newspapers and discussions (Davis 1999, 205).

On the one hand, the mass migration to the cities of rural and impoverished African Brazilians with limited or no formal education presented communication barriers between the leadership of the Black Experimental Theater and these masses, as had been the case with the Black Front. This in turn presented obstacles to political, economic, and cultural mobilization. Moreover, political uncertainty and repression discouraged mass protest. On the other hand, *brasilidade* provided a framework that promoted the integration of African Brazilians as essential members of the national family, thus making race-based mobilization seem unnecessary. Furthermore, education, money, and social prominence could enhance individual (albeit assimilationist) integration into dominant European Brazilian culture, especially for select mulattoes.[8] Many opponents thus viewed the Black Experimental Theater's tactics as segregationist, racist, and influenced by the United States, rather than an attempt to forge an African Brazilian identity premised on egalitarian pluralism in the struggle for egalitarian integration into the national community. However, *brasilidade* had become such a powerful force that African Brazilian antiracism went hand in hand with unequivocal affirmation of Brazilian patriotism. In short, African Brazilian militancy remained a subset of Brazilian nationalism rather than a competing ideology (Davis 1999, 188, 196, 199).

8. Conversation with Abdias do Nascimento after performance of Black Experimental Theater playwright Rosario Fusco's *Auto da Noiva* at Indiana University in 1969.

Although the Black Experimental Theater staged several plays by African American dramatists, whites wrote most of the theater's Brazilian plays. Moreover, individuals from the bourgeoisie largely commandeered it. The theater was designed to forge a positive sense of blackness as the basis for a self-esteem and collective racial consciousness within an African Brazilian population that was economically and educationally unprepared for it. As a result, it found itself performing before largely European Brazilian audiences (which was a de facto implementation of its program to educate whites). Eventually, the theater had to cease its activities because of a lack of financial resources and adequate professional organization, though the military coup of 1964 dealt the final blow (Brookshaw 1986, 284–85; Davis 1999, 203).

Finally, the Black Experimental Theater also attempted to challenge the white aesthetic that viewed African Brazilians as physically unattractive. Cultural initiatives such as the two annual beauty contests ("Miss Tar Baby" and "Miss Mulatto"), however, were riddled with contradictions. Together, they epitomized what many African Brazilian activists had been trying to eradicate since the early 1900s: the notion that lighter-skinned African Brazilians, whose features were less characteristically African, composed an echelon separate from and superior to darker individuals with a more African phenotype. The most beautiful *mulata* was typically referred to as *rainha* (the queen), whereas the most beautiful black woman was called *Boneca de Pixe* (Miss Tar Baby). This differentiation of African Brazilian contestants by phenotype, and the accompanying hierarchical valuation of whiteness over blackness, indicated how the Black Experimental Theater unwittingly sanctioned one of Brazil's racial stereotypes and was complicit in its own political and psychological manipulation. Moreover, this phenomenon underscored the extent to which its own program of increased African Brazilian racial self-esteem was undermined by the very ideology it sought to overturn, which left wide open the mulatto escape hatch it had sought to close (Davis 1999, 197; Turner 1992, 79–80).

The Black Guard and Black Front focused on the political sphere, whereas the Black Experimental Theater focused largely (though not exclusively) on cultural concerns refracted through a political lens. Each sought to articulate an African Brazilian identity premised on egalitarian pluralism. Each sought to challenge the dominant assimilationist ideology by promoting a social order in which both African Brazilians and European Brazilians would have equal access to all aspects of the public sphere, with the choice of inclusion in the private sphere in the manner of egalitarian integration. Accordingly, the black and mulatto populations would be linked by virtue of their shared dissimilarities to the white population; yet, the uniqueness of the mulatto population would not be diminished and the white population would not be excluded. Rather, the goal was to establish a horizontal (as opposed to hierarchical) and thus egalitarian relationship that valorized the two previously subordinated and excluded groups.

The Black Experimental Theater was perhaps the most rigorous in exposing the racial democracy doctrine as a sinister myth that had resulted not in an egalitarian blending of African Brazilian and European Brazilian racial/cultural differences into a more inclusive transracial/transcultural commonality (column a in Figure 1). Rather, it had resulted in an inegalitarian integration of African Brazilian racial and cultural distinctiveness into the normative European Brazilian culture (column b in Figure 1). These dynamics, along with the mulatto escape hatch, allowed token socioeconomic mobility for a privileged few multiracial individuals (and some rare blacks), who were then co-opted into an alliance as insiders. In turn, this obscured gross inequities between whites and the African Brazilian masses in education, jobs, income, and health typified by pervasive inegalitarian pluralism: a de facto apartheid. These two inegalitarian dynamics are shown in columns b and f. The vertical relationship depicted in column b allows for a limited amount of linkage between the three populations contingent upon their approximation to the norm image of the dominant white population. However, this trend is juxtaposed with the more pervasive one based not only on separation but also on the eventual exclusion of the black and multiracial populations, depicted in column f.

Despite their critique of the Brazilian racial order, the Black Guard, Black Front, and Black Experimental Theater were committed to fulfilling Brazil's racial democracy ideology. They strove to integrate African Brazilians into the racial order as equals rather than maintaining them as a separate group. Yet all three ultimately succumbed to pressure to assimilate to the dominant European Brazilian cultural and political order. Accordingly, the Black Guard, Black Front, and Black Experimental Theater were forced to operate within the limitations of the racial order rather than against it. This was manifest, among other things, in the need for white patronage, which constrained a more radical critique. Nevertheless, all three movements variously sought to overcome the divisiveness of the mulatto escape hatch and the ternary racial project in order to unify blacks and mulattoes into a racial plurality as African Brazilians. Accordingly, they contested the hierarchical relationship of whiteness over blackness by rearticulating the dichotomization of whiteness and blackness as distinct categories of experience. To accomplish this aim, these strategies deployed binary racial projects that breached the secondary color divide between mulattoes and blacks and reinforced the primary racial divide between *negros* and *brancos* in a manner similar to that between blacks and whites in the United States.

four THE U.S. PATH

The Binary Racial Project

Either Black or White: The Origin of the Binary Racial Project

The differences between racial formation in "Anglo" North America, that is, the U.S. North and Upper South, and racial formation in Brazil and other areas of South America, Central America, and the Caribbean, can be attributed to different trajectories of colonization. North Carolina and further northward—particularly New England and the Mid-Atlantic colonies of New York, New Jersey, Pennsylvania, and Delaware—were settled by large numbers of Europeans with families. Parity between the sexes was established quickly and continued throughout the colonial period (Bender 1978, 36; Fowler 1963, 30; Harris 1963, 79–94; Nash 1982, 162, 279). European patterns of domestic life were thus reestablished. The white family formed by legal marriage remained the standard social unit in Anglo North America, impeding permissive attitudes toward miscegenation. In Latin America, the interracial family based on extended concubinage or common-law marriages was a social necessity, and thus more acceptable.

English settlers in Anglo North America, like Portuguese settlers in Brazil and Spanish colonizers in the Caribbean, were unsuccessful at exploiting Native Americans as a captive labor force, unlike Spanish colonizers in Mexico and Peru. The less densely populated Native American communities in Anglo North America were rapidly decimated by Old World diseases. Also, many Native Americans resisted enslavement and encroachment on their lands by escaping into the interior. Moreover, Britain had a surplus of individuals who were eager to settle in the New World, whereas France, Spain, and Portugal were plagued by a chronic labor shortage when they began colonization in the seventeenth century (Harris 1964, 79–94).

The passage from Britain to Anglo North America, however, was expensive, which made emigration difficult. Therefore, Britain developed the system of European indentured servitude to meet its developing agricultural labor needs in the colonies during the seventeenth century. Large numbers of indentured servants were forced into servitude involuntarily, sometimes as punishment for rather minor crimes or simply kidnapped off the streets of Europe. All lived and worked in circumstances that differed little from that of slaves (Breen 1987, 110; Fredrickson 1981, 59–62). Nevertheless, indentured servitude was typically a contractual arrangement of temporary duration between two parties, in which the price of passage from Europe was advanced in exchange for usually five to eight years of voluntary labor. Furthermore, laws provided indentured servants with some protection during their servitude. Although the laws were inconsistently enforced, indentured servants could use the courts if they thought their rights were being violated. Despite the high mortality rate of early European indentured servants, they were accorded full membership in the colonist community upon completing their servitude, and granted "freedom dues" to facilitate their transition. Some former indentured servants became landowners, and a few even rose to positions of influence in colonial society. Most, however, remained propertyless and poor (Fredrickson 1981, 62; Harris 1963, 79–94; Ringer 1983, 63–64).

Throughout the early colonial period, the Anglo North American colonies of the North and Upper South were overwhelmingly comprised of white yeomanry, former indentured servants, and wage earners. Although African slavery gradually became established in the 1650s and 1660s, the sheer size of the European American population partially explained the limited introduction of slavery in the region. Compared to a total white population of approximately 369,200, there were only about 50,000 slaves in all Anglo North American colonies in 1715. At no time during the colonial period did African Americans outnumber European Americans in any colonies of the North or Upper South. This was the case even as their numbers expanded more rapidly than European Americans, or when they became a sizable portion of the population, as was the case for example in Virginia over the course of the eighteenth century (Foner 1975, 188–89).

During the early seventeenth century in the Upper South, when the African American population was comparatively small, the distinction between the white indentured servant and the black slave was less precise than that between bonded and free. Indentured men and women from the British Isles were bought and sold in the same markets with indentured and enslaved Africans, and were bequeathed in the same wills. They shared similar working conditions, and many jointly resisted bondage by running away together (Williamson 1980, 7, 38). Both groups were represented among the "giddy multitude" of slaves, indentured servants, and the landless poor among the free classes. In 1676 this sector of society took part in Bacon's Rebellion, one of the larger in a series of uprisings that occurred between 1660 and 1683 in Virginia, to the consternation of the planter elite. Indeed, many former indentured servants had become disillusioned with the New World's promise of opportunity, particularly the lack of available land. This discontent became not only a source of social unrest but also a cause for concern on the part of the planter elite (Breen 1987, 109; Fredrickson 1981, 62).

In addition, indentured servants and slaves shared the same living quarters such that in the private sphere, phenotypical differences were somewhat accommodated in the form of egalitarian pluralism. Miscegenation in the manner of egalitarian integration was not legally prohibited, despite strong social prejudice against it (Dyer 1976, 311–12; Nash 1982, 173). This is indicated by the small, but significant, number of blacks and whites of both sexes who married or formed common-law unions and had legitimate offspring, alongside more widespread clandestine and fleeting liaisons that resulted in births out of wedlock. However, the latter largely involved the rape and extended concubinage of indentured and slave women of African descent by European American masters or overseers.

Over the course of the eighteenth century, African Americans and European Americans achieved a balance between the sexes in their respective communities, except on the newly opening frontier. Yet the initial shortage of women in both populations contributed to widespread early miscegenation. Among Africans, there were at least three men for every two women; among whites, men outnumbered women by as many as three or four to one, especially in the South (Tenzer 1990, 58). Given this gender imbalance, as well as the harsh realities of frontier life, marriage proposals in the early colonial period were often made on the basis of the opportunity to protect and procreate. Free white men married African slaves, sometimes the only women they knew, and white female servants accepted offers of marriage from black men, both slave and free. However, this latter pattern, whether in the form of casual sexual relations, common-law relationships, or legalized marriage, was more stigmatized and less common because the few available white women were at a premium among European American males (Hodes 1997, 44–46; Russell, Wilson, and Hall 1992, 11–12).

Similar processes in the cultural domain accompanied these racial dynamics. There was not only an accommodation of differences in beliefs, values, customs, and artifacts in the manner of egalitarian pluralism but also mutual exchange between African and European culture that became the basis for a significant blending in the manner of egalitarian integration. This was fostered in part by the existence of African and European centers of reference, which were often equal in demographic significance, if not population size. Transplanted components from a variety of African cultures helped shape an evolving African American culture, which was also influenced by (and influenced in turn) the Anglo North American core culture. For example, a significant amount of black vernacular expression (e.g., music, dance, language, and the culinary arts) has been incorporated into Southern culture, not to mention U.S. popular culture. Even the distinctive linguistic features of the Southern dialect are a creolization of West African and English speech patterns originating largely in the south and west of England. Although whites were generally unaware of their own transformation in this process, by the end of the colonial period, blacks and whites had forged a new Southern culture that in varying degrees was a blend of both. Demographics in Anglo North America made this phenomenon more common in the Upper South than the North and, indeed, less extensive than in Brazil and other parts of Latin America, including "Latin" North America (the lower Mississippi Valley, the Gulf Coast, and South Carolina). However, nowhere in the Americas did egalitarian cultural integration through social intercourse transfer to equitable treatment in the educational, political, and socioeconomic arenas (Alger 2003, 9–13; Berlin 1974, 10–11; Nash 1982, 141, 170–78, 185–97; Piersen 1993, 99–100; Sobel 1987, 3–20).

By the eve of the American Revolution, Africans and Europeans were becoming a new people: African Americans and European Americans. The memories of British life were losing their meaning, and individuals of European descent were increasingly viewing themselves less as European and more as Americans of English, Scottish, Welsh, or Irish descent. After more than a century of enslavement in the English colonies, second-hand accounts of Africa were also losing their significance for new generations of American-born blacks. Indeed, by the third decade of the eighteenth century, and long before the official abolition of the slave trade in 1808, American-born blacks with no first-hand knowledge of Africa far outnumbered African-born blacks (Nash 1982, 141, 170–97).

With the shift from indentured servitude to slavery in the late seventeenth century, the importation of African slaves expanded to meet labor needs.[1] Yet whereas European indentured servants worked on small yeoman farms, African slaves were engaged primarily on large plantations that cultivated cash crops such as tobacco, rice, indigo, and eventually sugar cane and cotton. Thus it became increasingly necessary to ensure white dominance over the growing number of African Americans. During the next several decades, cumulative court decisions and enactments of the colonial legislatures gradually institutionalized servitude in perpetuity for African Americans and relegated their legal status to that of property. As slavery became entrenched over the course of the late seventeenth

---

1. Africans proved to be a cheaper source of labor than European indentures. In the North, however, African slave labor was primarily an urban phenomenon involving a minority of farm hands, artisans, and personal servants. In contrast, Africans in the South formed a significant portion of the population, replacing Native American slaves and eventually European indentures in urban domestic and artisanal sectors, and comprising the agricultural labor force (Harris 1963, 79–94).

and early eighteenth centuries, it became inextricably intertwined with African ancestry in the Anglo North American mind.[2]

By the mid-eighteenth century, the dramatic increase in the number of slaves was matched by an equally dramatic reduction in the number of white indentured servants. The influx of African slaves squeezed white servants out of the harsher and less skilled tasks, which enhanced their vertical mobility. Even free African Americans found themselves increasingly competing with free white labor in occupations that had been open to them as slaves. The enhanced social mobility of white laborers not only eroded the previously shared experience between European American indentured and formerly indentured servants and African Americans but also diverted the attention of the former away from the class oppression they continued to share with the latter. In addition, by the 1660s colonists had defeated Native Americans in the coastal region and pushed them beyond the perimeter of English settlement. Consequently, many former indentured servants and their descendents had increased opportunities to purchase land (Ringer 1983, 63–64). The resulting racial segmentation spawned a concomitant distancing, if not outright hostility, among white workers toward African Americans, whom they perceived as economic competitors. Consequently, the ruling elite had the foundation for building a wall of white racial solidarity and privilege without undermining their own class interests (Breen 1987, 109–19; Foner 1975, 227; Williamson 1980, 28–29).

Yet slavery hardly could have been preserved unless barriers to sexual relations between African Americans and European Americans—particularly indentured or formerly indentured white servants—were also maintained and strengthened. Accordingly, Southern colonies, and some Northern colonies, simultaneously began criminalizing sexual relations and intermarriages between whites and blacks. It is highly significant, however, that the first antimiscegenation laws passed by Virginia and Maryland in the 1660s and 1680s primarily centered on

---

2. In the South, slavery remained intact into the last half of the nineteenth century. However, Massachusetts (1641) and Connecticut (1650) were the first colonies to legally recognize slavery. Though slavery was not deeply entrenched in the North, its role in industry and commerce was significant, if not a mainstay of the economy. Slaves were utilized as urban domestic servants, porters, coachmen, dockworkers, workers in the distilleries and manufactories, artisans, and farm hands in lumbering, dairying, and other enterprises requiring heavy labor. Northerners also built substantial fortunes in the Atlantic slave trade by supplying the South with loans and ships. The capital for the plantation economy was from Northern banks, and slave trafficking became a primary source of income for many Northern merchants and traders. Indeed, New England traders brought more Africans into slavery than any other Americans. Virginia (1661) and Maryland (1663) followed Massachusetts and Connecticut in giving legal sanction to African slavery, which in turn, led the way in passing laws that subjected African Americans, rather than whites, to servitude in perpetuity (Berlin 1974, 5; Foner 1975, 188–89; Spickard 1989, 239–38).

regulating sexual relations and marriages between European women—particularly
indentured servants—and African-descent slave men. Later statutes stipulated that
free white men who married or became sexually involved with African American
women, slave or free, would incur the same fines and penalties imposed on free
white women (Dyer 1976, 309–33; Fredrickson 1981, 102–4; Jordan 1962, 183–200;
Tenzer 1990, 56–68).[3]

The earliest laws did not forbid interracial unions. Rather, they sought to discourage miscegenation by imposing stiff fines or severe penalties ranging from
banishment to whippings, or imposing additional terms of servitude upon white
indentured women. They also stipulated that children born of these relationships would be held in bondage for extended periods of time. With the passage
of these and similar statutes, slave owners had an economic incentive to coerce
black slave men and white indentured women into marriage to increase the
number of bound servants, despite the antipathy toward such unions. This abuse
was so widespread that in 1681 an act was passed in Maryland that placed stiff
fines on the masters and ministers performing such marriages (Dyer 1976, 309–33;
Jordan 1962, 190; Tenzer 1990, 56–68; Williamson 1980, 8–11).

By the middle of the eighteenth century, however, laws were passed to prohibit
all interracial unions (particularly between black males and white females), in or
out of wedlock.[4] These relationships threatened the sanctity of white womanhood
and the integrity of the white family, both of which were pivotal to preserving
the racial purity and numerical self-perpetuation of the European American
community, as well as maintaining the intergenerational transmission of white
wealth, power, privilege, and prestige. Even in those colonies—and eventually

3. Between 1705 and 1725, authorities in many of the other colonies from New Hampshire to
North Carolina were coming to conclusions not unlike those of Virginia and Maryland. Legislation
that passed in colonial North Carolina (1715) and various other colonies differed from Virginia and
Maryland more in detail than in principle (Fowler 1963, 48). Restrictions against interracial sexual
relations and marriages were enacted in some of the Northern and Mid-Atlantic colonies as well,
particularly Massachusetts (1705), Pennsylvania (1725), and Delaware (1721), despite the relatively
small number of blacks in the former two and the smaller proportion of slaves in the latter as
compared to the South. In Pennsylvania, especially in the vicinity of Philadelphia, where European
American indentures and African American slaves fraternized in great numbers, interracial unions
between white indentures (both men and women) with black slaves were common and the number
of mulattoes was high. One community known as "Mulatto Hall" became entirely multiracial and
was ostracized and isolated by whites. Finally, in 1725–26 Pennsylvania enacted a law prohibiting all
interracial unions and remanded the multiracial children of white women to servitude for thirty-one
years (Williamson 1980, 11).

4. Six of the Southern colonies penalized sexual relations between blacks and whites. Except for
South Carolina and Delaware, four prohibited intermarriage between blacks and whites. Among the
seven Northern colonies, only Massachusetts and Pennsylvania implemented restrictions. Yet both
colonies prohibited interracial sexual relations as well as racial intermarriage (Fowler 1963, 62–81).

states—where unions between blacks and whites were allowed, these relationships— whether informal or legal marriages—carried painful social consequences (Fowler 1963, 62–81; Fredrickson 1981, 102–4).

These legal and informal restrictions did not result in a marked decrease in miscegenation. The key change was a shift in public attitudes. Rape and extended concubinage involving white slave masters (or overseers) and women of African descent, whether slave or free, continued to be tolerated. These relationships had no legal standing, posed little threat to the slave system, and would become the source of most subsequent miscegenation. Legal prohibitions against racial inter-marriage provided the ideal solution to the Anglo North American patriarchy's labor needs, its extramarital sexual behavior, inadmissible sexual desires, and its obsession with maintaining white cultural and racial "purity" (Nash 1982, 282, 285). Accordingly, this patriarchy established an economic and political system, as well as a cultural ideology, grounded in racial, gender, and class oppression. These social forces granted them the power to control the productive (and to some extent reproductive) labor of not only African American men but also African American and European American women. As long as miscegenation was restricted largely to white male exploitation of African American women, it did not threaten the racial order, especially since these men typically disavowed their mulatto offspring (Fredrickson 1981, 106; Ginsberg 1996, 5; Higginbotham 1978, 40–46; Tenzer 1990, 62, 63). This practice had the dual advantage of divesting the mulatto offspring of white slave masters of the privileges associated with paternity and increasing the number of individuals held in bondage.

The One-Drop Rule: White Domination and the Illusion of Racial Purity

Although these laws were specifically enacted to deter miscegenation, African and European cultural, phenotypical, and ancestral blending were perhaps less feared than the challenge multiracial individuals implicitly presented to white domination and the subordination of blacks. Yet the legal status of free mulattoes (and free people of color generally) was ambiguous at best up to the time of the American Revolution. Colonial Black codes were riddled with inconsistencies, which allowed free African-descent Americans to enjoy some areas of legal equality with whites. Some earned substantial amounts of money and became independent landowners and employers of servants. They enjoyed the rights of citizenship (including the right to vote, despite heated opposition) and occasionally held minor offices.

The North and Upper South

Moreover, during the early colonial period, whites in the North and Upper South did not seem averse to racially assimilating into the white population those Free Coloreds who were the most phenotypically and culturally European American, and economically successful. However, multiracial individuals were not granted this privilege to the same extent as in Brazil and various other areas in Latin America. For example, in 1785, Virginia allowed mulattoes to be legally white if their African ancestry was less than one-fourth, although most whites found this policy too liberal. In 1832, Virginia lawmakers exempted light-skinned free people of color from new restrictions on Free Colored rights if they applied to the county courts "with satisfactory evidence" that they were white (Berlin 1974, 162). However, only those who were indistinguishable from European Americans could be assimilated as whites; others remained socially identified with the Free Colored population, although legally distinct from it.

When slaves began pouring into the Anglo North American colonies in the early eighteenth century, whites began restricting the legal rights of Free Coloreds, although they had begun to chip away at those rights sporadically in the 1660s. As the numbers of Free Coloreds began to expand in the late eighteenth and nineteenth centuries, their status deteriorated even further. Some Southern legislatures began to make private emancipation by slave owners more difficult by imposing taxes on free mulatto women and denying equal rights to free mulattoes in a variety of categories—including the right to vote and carry a firearm. Others barred Free Coloreds from holding office, serving in the militia, and testifying against whites. In addition, legislatures restricted their interstate travel and migration, requiring them to carry passes giving proof of their free status or risk being fined, expelled from the state, or even kidnapped into slavery (Berlin 1974, 7–9, 49, 90–97; Higginbotham 1978, 42, 48, 62, 175; Williamson 1980, 10, 11, 25–31, 49, 98, 236).

The deterioration of Free Colored status after the American Revolution resulted in part from their significant increase due to the abolition of slavery in the North by the end of the colonial era and the emancipation of many black and mulatto slaves in exchange for military service in the Upper South.[5] Their worsening plight during the post-Revolutionary decade was also attributable to the darkening of the population, which stemmed from the successful escape and large-scale indiscriminate manumission of many black slaves, particularly in the Upper South. This manumission had been partially inspired by the short-lived

5. Vermont abolished slavery in 1777, followed by Massachusetts and Pennsylvania in 1780, Connecticut and Rhode Island in 1784, New York in 1799, and New Jersey in 1804.

libertarian fervor generated by the American Revolution. Yet some owners merely sought to relieve themselves of the responsibility and expense of maintaining slaves that were considered unproductive and provided little financial return (Berlin 1974, 3–5, 7–9, 16, 30–35, 49, 60, 90–99, 162).

These changes in the post-Revolutionary era were accompanied by an even greater concern with precise legal definitions of racial categories. In the colonial era, only Virginia and North Carolina specified legal definitions of blackness. Both colonies designated as black anyone with African American ancestry three generations removed; at times, North Carolina legislators investigated the fourth generation removed. In other words, any free person with an African American parent, grandparent, great-grandparent, and sometimes a great-great-grandparent—up to one-eighth or one-sixteenth African American ancestry—could be deemed black and subject to laws regulating Free Coloreds. Other colonies appear to have implemented similar policies without writing them explicitly into law (Berlin 1974, 97–98).

Yet as the status of Free Coloreds declined in the late eighteenth century, distinctions between them and whites had more serious social implications than previously. If strict legal fractions of blackness prevented the infiltration of light-skinned African Americans into the ranks of whites, this also presented the possibility of relegating some "swarthy" whites to the subordinate status of Free Coloreds. To prevent such mishaps, Virginia lowered the racial divide in 1785 and defined as black anyone having one African American forebear in the previous two generations, that is to say, anyone with a black parent or grandparent. States in the Upper South, such as Kentucky and Missouri, generally adopted the Virginia rule. North Carolina implemented a similar statute, except when marriage to a white person was concerned, in which case legal blackness was pushed back into the third generation (Berlin 1974, 97–99, 163; Mencke 1979, 8–11).

Eventually two states in the Lower South, Florida and Mississippi, implemented the Virginia standard. However, much of the lower South, including Georgia, Tennessee, Alabama, and Texas, eventually adopted a stricter law, extending the line back three generations. Georgia lawmakers, in particular, mandated that individuals enjoying the rights and privileges of free whites could be taken to court if their ancestry was in doubt. Those found to have more than one-eighth African American ancestry were pushed into the community of Free Coloreds. No other state enacted a similar measure, but many legislatures in the lower South and some Northern states would follow Georgia's lead and eventually raise the racial divide. It was a fine legal distinction—though informally, whites generally considered as black everyone with African American ancestry (the one-drop rule), no matter how remote (Berlin 1974, 97–99, 163; Mencke 1979, 8–11).

The Lower South

The racial order in the U.S. Lower South ("Latin" North America) initially differed from that in the North and Upper South ("Anglo" North America). This originated in the early patterns of Spanish and French settlement in the lower Mississippi Valley and the Gulf Coast, and English settlement in South Carolina (and to a lesser extent, Georgia), which followed the Latin American model. White settlers were few in number and primarily single males, who first formed liaisons with Native American women and, after the introduction of slavery, with African-descent women. As in the rest of the Americas, there were formidable barriers to intermarriage. Informal unions, however, were tolerated, if not encouraged, by the prevailing moral code (Berlin 1974, 109; Williamson 1980, 14–15).

In fact, despite legal restrictions, interracial unions became such an accepted social practice in Louisiana that they developed into an institution called *plaçage*. This involved relationships, sometimes lasting for life, contracted between white men and women of color. The white male provided financial support for his multiracial offspring according to an agreement negotiated with the young woman's parents (usually her mother). However, he could maintain his interracial family on one side of town while simultaneously maintaining his life in white society, including marriage to a white woman if he desired. This arrangement of institutional, if not legal, concubinage, along with the Quadroon Balls that emerged at the turn of the nineteenth century, enabled wealthy white men to maintain romantic and sexual liaisons with African-descent women, specifically multiracial women. Because most women of African descent were brutalized, auctioned, and enslaved, the *plaçage* system gave these mistresses the illusion of relative equality with free white women, despite its classism, sexism, and racism (Foner 1970, 406–30; Rankin 1977–78, 379–416).

Compared to Anglo North America, the more socially sanctioned miscegenation in "Latin" North America—and Latin America generally speaking—coupled with the preferential liberation of slave mistresses and their multiracial offspring, made it easier for multiracial individuals early in colonial French Louisiana to enter the free classes. A similar pattern evolved in Spanish Alabama and Florida, particularly in and around Mobile, Pensacola, and St. Augustine. Free Coloreds filled interstitial economic roles—particularly in the artisanal, manual, and skilled trades—and became integral to the economy because of an insufficient numbers of whites. Because whites and most Free Coloreds shared bonds of ancestry and culture, whites viewed them as natural and valuable allies against the black slave majority, which often entailed suppressing slave uprisings, as well as capturing and returning fugitive slaves (Berlin 1974, 130–32; Garvin 1967, 1–17; Landers 1999, 1–28, 229–53; Lempel 1979, 54–56; Mencke 1979, 4–5; Thomas 1911, 335–37; Williamson 1980, 43–35).[6]

Moreover, the region's comparatively favorable situation for multiracial individuals was enhanced by the fact that the European monarchs in France and Spain during the colonial period saw Free Coloreds as a potential military counterforce against independence-minded whites and necessarily provided some protection of their rights (Berlin 1974, 5, 110–12, 130–32; Garvin 1967, 1–17; Landers 1999, 1–28, 229–53; Lempel 1979, 54–56; Thomas 1911, 335–37). By granting multiracial individuals privileges superior to those of blacks but inferior to those of whites, both the Crown and the colonists in "Latin" North America won their loyalty while maintaining white domination and control. In fact, many of Louisiana's multiracial citizens were slaveholding planters in parishes such as St. Landry, Iberville, and Plaquemines (Williamson 1984, 22–23). Some of them had the means to live in luxury, receive an education in Europe, and, most important, "to maintain themselves with poise and dignity in a white-dominated world" (Mills 1977, 78).

Under Spanish rule (1769–1803) the population of free people of color expanded rapidly, both by natural increase and because of comparatively lenient manumission policies. In particular, Spanish law codified a customary practice known as *coartación,* which gave slaves the right to self-purchase based on a price stipulated by the master or arbitrated by the court. Simultaneously, Spanish authorities attempted to curb the public and private activities of free women of color, in part responding to the growing number of white women who saw them as rivals. In 1785, they passed legislation forbidding free women of color from wearing jewels and feathers and forcing them to wear their hair bound in a kerchief. Officials eventually sought to outlaw the Quadroon Balls. Nevertheless, the *plaçage* system continued unabated. Furthermore, some legalized unions were contracted between European American men and African-descent women when Spanish authorities granted dispensation in individual cases. Both types of relationships were important sources for the continued numeric growth and wealth of Free Coloreds, particularly because mistresses of color and their mulatto offspring often received sizable inheritances from wealthy white progenitors. These relationships also furthered the "mulattoization" and Europeanization of Louisiana's Free Colored population (Domínguez 1986, 24; Hanger 1997, 7; Hazzard-Gordon 1989, 14–25; Rankin 1977–78, 381).

6. Both the larger numbers and higher proportion of blacks in the total population in the Lower South, as compared to the Upper South, is striking. For example, blacks were an estimated 51.1 percent of the population of South Carolina in 1708, 64.0 percent in 1721, and 70.6 percent on the eve of the American Revolution (Foner 1975, 203–5; Williamson 1980, 34–35). By 1731, blacks in lower Louisiana outnumbered whites by a ratio of more than 2 to 1. Slaves remained about 55 percent of the total population of lower Louisiana during the late eighteenth century and into the first half of the nineteenth century (Hall 1992a, 174, 176, 278).

On November 30, 1803, France regained control of the colony through negotiations with Spain (which had secretly transferred the colony to France on October 1, 1800). Twenty days later, France transferred Louisiana to the United States (Bell 1997, 29; G. Hall 1992a, 276; Hanger 1997, 7–8). By the time of Louisiana's annexation by the United States, Free Coloreds had increased fourfold to almost eight thousand, largely resulting from the influx of émigrés fleeing the revolution in Saint-Domingue. Whites in Louisiana attempted to prevent their entry through legislation, but lax administration or humane attitudes on the part of government officials limited enforcement. Though whites feared the growth of Free Coloreds through immigration, they were more concerned about the black slave majority. Therefore, they tended to see the prosperity of multiracial individuals as hindering any potential alliance between Free Coloreds and black slaves. Acutely aware of their rights and interests, as well as of their fragile position, Free Coloreds correspondingly acted with considerable cohesiveness. Consequently, Louisiana became home to the most numerically significant and economically integrated population of Free Coloreds in the South. These same factors also heightened the distinction between multiracial and black, which further bolstered the dominant position of whites (Berlin 1974, 98–99, 104–17, 163; Domínguez 1986, 23–24; Haskins 1975, 32–33; Hazzard-Gordon 1989, 15; J. Johnson 1992, 52–53; Mencke 1979, 1–19; Rankin 1977–78, 380–82; Sterkx 1972, 94).

Anglo and Latin North America Compared

The fact that whites were a majority in the North and Upper South diminished any need to utilize multiracial individuals as interstitial labor in the economy, or to differentiate individuals of varying degrees of African ancestry in order to gain the collaboration of multiracial individuals, whether slave or free, against a black slave majority. Throughout the antebellum period in Anglo North America, most individuals of African descent, multiracial as well as black, were slaves. There is little evidence to support the notion that house servants or concubines were invariably multiracial; most worked in the field along with blacks. Yet mulattoes were, when compared to blacks, disproportionately represented among the free in all regions of the North and South.

There is little data on the exact size and status of the multiracial segment of the Free Colored population prior to the 1850 census. This is partially because black and multiracial individuals had not been counted separately on previous censuses. However, in 1850, federal enumerators were instructed for the first time to designate whether African Americans (Negroes) were black or mulatto by recording a "B" or "M" respectively on the census schedule. According to the 1850 data, mulattoes composed a larger percentage (24.8 percent) of the African-descent population in the North than in the nation as a whole (11.2 percent) (Census 1918, 210).[7] The numbers of Free Coloreds in the Upper South (203,702) exceeded those in the Lower South (34,485) and composed a larger percentage of the total African-descent population (12.5 percent versus 3.5 percent, respectively) (Berlin 1974, 137; Cohen and Greene 1972, 10, 14).

Yet only a small number of mulattoes lived in the North, and the multiracial segment of the Free Colored population in the Upper South was predominantly rural, of humble European American origins, and of modest means. Furthermore, there were larger numbers of blacks in the ranks of Free Coloreds in the Upper South (78,556 mulattoes and 125,146 blacks) than in the Lower South (23,683 mulattoes and 10,802 blacks), because of the large-scale manumissions that took place around the time of the American Revolution. Although the Upper South was home to greater numbers of Free Coloreds and mulattoes, as well as greater numbers of mulattoes among Free Coloreds, the percentage of mulattoes in the ranks of Free Coloreds in the Upper South (38.6 percent) was only little more than half of the percentage in the Lower South (68.7 percent). Moreover, Free Coloreds in the Lower South were typically urban and from comparatively well-to-do European American origins (Berlin 1974, 216; Mencke 1979, 15, 19).

The Free Coloreds gained their freedom through various means. Some enlisted in either the British or American forces during the American Revolution. Others had been emancipated by legislation or court decisions, while some gained freedom through self-purchase or through relatives and friends who purchased their freedom for them. Still others were born of free parents or of mothers who were free, while some escaped from slavery (Foner 1975, 498). However, the population originated through preferential emancipation from servitude (both indenture and slavery) often granted to the offspring of interracial unions, who were generally freed after a specified term of servitude if the mother was white, or perhaps manumitted by a conscience-stricken white father. Nevertheless, whites in Anglo North America successfully prevented Free Coloreds from integrating into mainstream society as their equals, with the result that most of them remained nonliterate, propertyless, and poor (Berlin 1974, 3, 110, 218, 245; 1998, 44–46, 332–38, 354–57).

Although Free Coloreds in the North and the Upper South ultimately performed an important role in the artisanal and skilled trades, there were always a sufficient number of whites—particularly impoverished European immigrants—who could fill interstitial roles in the economy. Indeed, European immigrants to some extent functioned as "situational mulattoes" in the North and Upper South, often engaging in racial conflict with Free Coloreds because of labor competition.

7. By 1850, of course, the entire African-descent population in the North was free.

Long before the abolition of slavery, however, the heavily mulatto Free Coloreds had established lifestyles that differentiated them from the slave masses (and by extension, the masses of blacks). Some achieved a certain amount of education and economic security; a few developed lifestyles that paralleled, and even mirrored, the social and cultural life of whites. Consequently, a more European phenotype and sociocultural orientation among African Americans became visible markers of elite status (Allen 1994, 14; Mencke 1979, 3, 5, 9).

The majority of Free Coloreds lived in precarious economic circumstances, if not in grinding poverty, and all existed in an ill-defined penumbra between servitude and freedom. However, the status of antebellum Free Coloreds in the Lower South differed from that of Free Coloreds in the North and Upper South. Free Coloreds, particularly mulattoes, experienced a status similar to that of multi-racial individuals in South America, Central America, and the Caribbean, though it was not as elevated as in those regions. For example, Free Colored mulattoes in the Lower South were not extended a white racial identity, in proportion to their social prominence as well as behavioral and physical approximation to European norms, to the same extent as light-skinned mulattoes in some other parts of Latin America. Moreover, Free Coloreds in the Lower South numbered fewer than in places like Brazil (Bender 1978, 37; Forbes 1971, 30–33; Fredrickson 1981, 119–20; C. Hall 1992, 238–42; Hanger 1997, 93, 107; Landers 1999, 129; Williamson 1980, 19, 29).

Yet the Latin North American ternary racial project provided circumstances that allowed Free Colored mulattoes (and free people of color generally) just enough room to carve out a sense of dignity in a world that barely tolerated them. The populations in Charleston, Savannah, and Gulf ports such as Natchez, Mobile, Pensacola, and New Orleans included many individuals who achieved some education, accumulated some property, and experienced markedly elevated lives. Consequently, Free Coloreds in the Lower South not only achieved a relatively favorable status but also enjoyed the most secure position of free people of color anywhere in North America, despite the generally oppressive conditions (Berlin 1974, 110, 114–17, 178–79, 216; Forbes 1971, 30–33; Haskins 1975, 32–33; J. Johnson 1992, 53; Lempel 1979, 43, 54–56; Mencke 1979, 14–19; Rankin 1977–78, 380–82).

From White Domination to White Supremacy: Maintaining Racial Privilege

After several unsuccessful attempts to settle in North America, the English finally established a colony in Jamestown, Virginia, in 1607 under a royal charter granted to the Virginia Company of London. Initially, the settlers relied on their own labor and in the process constructed a "colonist" society (Ringer 1983,

37–40, 51). This took place within the organizational framework of the Virginia Company, which eventually was formed as a distinctive territorial and political community under the Crown. The General Assembly of the colony was composed of elected representatives and generally modeled itself after Parliament. The assembly gave the colonists a voice in the company's decision-making process and provided them with a "politically generated consensual framework" (53) that unified them as a people with a sense of community (37–64).

During the first half-century of colonization, individuals who paid for their own passage from Europe were granted fifty acres of land and fifty additional acres for each individual whose passage they covered. Others contracted themselves out as indentured laborers who worked on company land for a designated period, for which the company paid the cost of transportation and other expenditures. This led to the development of a political economy dominated by yeoman planters who owned and worked small farms of a few hundred acres. It is unclear whether or not and to what extent these indentured servants were voting constituents of the early colonial political structure. In the early colonial period, all males were granted the right to vote once they completed their indenture, although only property owners were allowed to hold elective office. Throughout the later colonial period, however, property ownership became a prerequisite for the franchise (Ringer 1983, 49, 53–54, 61–64).

Sociologist Benjamin Ringer argues that while the colonist society was being constructed, a "colonialist" society was also being assembled. The building of this society had already begun with the conquest of Native Americans, and was further established through the involuntary servitude of Africans, which began in 1619. The legal status of African Americans in this colonialist society was gradually defined under the regime of the small yeoman planters, who at the time were the colonist elite and still relied primarily on the labor of European indentured servants. Yet by the end of the seventeenth century, their fortunes sharply declined. By the first half of the eighteenth century, large plantation owners not only replaced the yeoman planters as the new elite of the colonist society but also consolidated the colonialist society that relied primarily on African American slaves as a source of labor (Ringer 1983, 64–69). The other twelve colonies were also beginning to solidify their dual structures, although each reflected a distinctive configuration of the colonist-colonialist dynamic based on its unique heritage and demographics.

Like Virginia, the colonialist society that eventually emerged in Massachusetts toward the end of the eighteenth century was built on the conquest (and removal) of Native Americans and the enslavement of African Americans. Although slaves were never an important source of labor in Massachusetts or a significant portion of the total population, profits from the slave trade were an important source of capital accumulation for much of the merchant class in the region. Furthermore, slavery in Massachusetts was comparatively less brutal, manumissions more frequent, and antislavery sentiments more prevalent. Nevertheless, in the early colonial period, white colonists in Massachusetts imposed various restrictions on Free Coloreds as part of an evolving inegalitarian pluralist racial structure that persisted long after abolition. Meanwhile, most European Americans were extended the rights of membership in a more broadly based "civic culture" (Fuchs 1990, 7–12, 16) that was the foundation of the "people's domain" (Ringer 1983, 78–79).

According to Ringer, the various versions of this colonist-colonialist duality survived the American Revolution and were incorporated in the transformation of the former English colonies into a federated nation-state (Ringer 1983, 71). The colonist heritage manifested itself in the Declaration of Independence, the Constitution, and the Bill of Rights. The Constitution, for example, formulated a new structure of governance for what its preamble identifies as "We the People." The Bill of Rights was added to the Constitution to provide a legal-normative protection of the people's sovereignty. It carves out a sphere of rights and immunities that is the preserve of the people as individuals and protects them from the arbitrary use of authority and power by the state or federal governments (92). Likewise, the colonialist heritage originating in African American slavery emerged intact with the writing and final ratification of the Constitution in 1791, though slavery is neither mentioned nor endorsed anywhere in the document (91–103). In effect, white colonists were transformed into citizens of what historian Alexander Saxton calls the "White republic," which was anchored in the rights and sovereignty of the people (Saxton 1990, 1–18). This society integrated each individual European American into the body politic as an equal. Meanwhile, African Americans were retained in a racially inegalitarian pluralist society (or colony) located within the United States, yet outside the people's domain (Miller 1996, 16–24).

This dynamic is evident in three sections of the Constitution. The first is section 2 of Article 1, which apportioned representatives for each state based on population, according to a formula which counted each African American slave as three-fifths of a person. This provision reflected a compromise between the South's desire to count individual slaves as whole persons, despite their legal status as property, and the North's concerns with the potential political advantage this would give the South. The reference is not, however, to African American slaves but rather to "all other persons" (Ringer 1983, 99).

In section 9 of Article 1, slave states were granted the right to import slaves until 1808 without interference from the federal government. Yet the slave trade was highly contested by many delegates. This provision was a compromise between the North's desire to place a limitation on slavery's survival by essentially attacking it at the source—the Atlantic slave trade—and the South's economic investment in maintaining the institution. Once again, slaves are referred to not directly but rather through a reference to the "migration and importation of such Persons as any of the States now existing shall think proper to admit" (Ringer 1983, 99).

The third paragraph of section 2 of Article 4 was written expressly to address the Southern states' concerns about the extradition of fugitive slaves. Like the other provisions, it refers, however, not to "slaves" but rather to "person[s] held to service or labor" (Ringer 1983, 99). The clause required the state in which escapees were found to return the slaves to the state or party from which they had escaped (99–103).

Both Northern and Southern delegates participated in intense debate over the first two provisions. Ultimately, little sacrifice was required on the part of the North except a willingness to agree to a sectional compromise that respected the South's investment in the political economy of slavery. Neither provision, for example, required their home states to actively support slavery. The provisions merely gave constitutional legitimacy to slavery as practiced within the borders of the various Southern states (Ringer 1983, 100–103).

The third provision, however, did require the Northern states to comply with certain mandates and essentially sanctioned property in slaves throughout the nation. The delegates from the Northern states were curiously silent on this third provision (Ringer 1983, 101–2). According to some historians, this silence indicates that the Massachusetts model of colonist-colonialist duality had already become imprinted in the North by the end of the colonial era. Accordingly, the Northern delegates, more through "deliberate design than casual indifference" (103), were sending African Americans a message that they did not have rights in the people's domain and should not consider the North a safe haven (Finkelman 1987, 188–225). This argument is plausible, given that Northern supporters of abolition often upheld notions of African American racial inferiority and were sympathetic to the idea of removing free African Americans from the United States to the Caribbean or West Africa. The First Congress made even more explicit the sole inclusion of whites in the people's domain (and the concomitant exclusion of African Americans). While the Founding Fathers in Philadelphia had already implied that a racial restriction was applicable to those already living within the boundaries of the United States, the First Congress extended this restriction to immigrants seeking naturalization (Ringer 1983, 99–103). The bill, which granted citizenship to "any alien, being a free White person" who fulfilled stipulated residency requirements, passed both houses and was signed into law on March 26, 1790 (109–10).[8]

8. The phrase "White person" remained on the books for 162 years, until the McCarran Act of 1952, although an attempt was made to remove it from the naturalization laws during Reconstruction. As a concession, individuals of African birth and descent were made eligible for citizenship, though immigrants from Asia were not. Thus, the 1790 law that guaranteed the inclusion of white

Approximately seventy years after the passage of the First Naturalization Law, Supreme Court Chief Justice Taney spelled out the underlying premise of this racial restriction in the *Dred Scott* case of 1857. Scott was a Missouri slave who had been taken by his master to live in free Illinois and eventually Wisconsin Territory. After returning to Missouri, Scott sued his master for his freedom on the grounds that he had become a citizen by virtue of having resided in states that prohibited slavery. Yet a fundamental question facing the Court was whether Scott, as an African American, could ever become part of the people of the United States (Fuchs 1990, 91; Ringer 1983, 103–7). The Chief Justice decided that even emancipated African Americans could not "compose a portion of the people" and were not "constituent members of this sovereignty" (Ringer 1983, 104). In other words, the word "citizens" in the Constitution did not include, and was never intended to include, African Americans. Consequently, they "could claim none of the rights and privileges" afforded citizens (104, 105).

Ringer points out that European Americans were thus the superordinate group in the racially inegalitarian pluralist ("colonialist") social system, and the only group in the egalitarian integrative ("colonist") social system comprising the people's domain. They could move without restraint between the two social orders and did so to protect their wealth, property, power, privilege, and prestige in both. White domination was not only the linchpin between the two systems but also the mortar that held them together into a seemingly unified and logical social order. Indeed, since the colonial period, the plantation elite had presided over both these societies and saw no contradiction between them. The colonist society was composed of subjects; the colonialist society was composed of objects (Ringer 1983, 69, 108, 157–58).

According to Gunnar Myrdal (*An American Dilemma,* 1944), these attitudes and practices underpinned a "racial creed" that breached what he defined as the "American creed." The American creed was based on the egalitarian principles enshrined in the Declaration of Independence, the U.S. Constitution, and Bill of Rights. It proclaimed that all individuals were born equal with inalienable rights to "freedom, justice, and fair opportunity" without regard to racial or ethnic group membership (Ringer 1983, 3).[9] Yet Myrdal's analysis operated on the erroneous premise that the racial creed, rather than having been built into the social and legal-normative fabric of the United States, was an aberrant and irrational phenomenon. However, when the Founding Fathers wrote the legal-

---

immigrants in the people's domain was used almost a century later to deny citizenship to Chinese and Japanese immigrants.

9. For a more lengthy discussion, see Myrdal 1944, 1:4–5.

normative foundation for the racial creed into the Constitution, they were only consolidating a process that had been under way since the early colonial period.

Nevertheless, African Americans, ever mindful of the universalistic language of the Constitution, would take advantage of the unstable racial equilibrium created by the tension between the two creeds and their respective social systems. They continually challenged the legitimacy of the inegalitarian pluralist society supported by the racial creed that excluded them from the people's domain and prevented them from enjoying the rights of the American creed as guaranteed by the Constitution (Nash 1990, 79–83; Ringer 1983, 180). This struggle between the American and racial creeds for control of the destiny of African Americans would not only become the prototype for the experience of all racialized "others" but also tear at the fabric and soul of the nation for generations to come.

The contradiction between the American and racial creeds was exacerbated over the course of the eighteenth and nineteenth centuries by the increasing demand for cheap labor and the ensuing expansion of African slavery. To resolve this contradiction, a number of prominent European and European American thinkers attempted to replace the doctrine of monogenesis (one origin for a single human species) with a theory of polygenesis that declared Africans and their descendants a species separate from and inferior to whites. According to this theory the "races" were different species of humans, rather than superficial variations within a single human species; thus, the American creed and its promise of constitutional equality simply did not apply to people of African descent.

Part of the debate centered on whether an African civilization had ever existed, in order to substantiate claims of inherent white cultural superiority over blacks (Young 1994, 60–165). A major emphasis, if not obsession, in writing on the topic was the history of Egypt and the question of hybridity in human reproduction. In fact, it was in the United States where the most concerted "scientific" effort took place to prove that the Egyptians were, and had always been, white or "Caucasian" (Drake 1987, 1:132–37; Elbashir 1983, 19–26; Haller 1971, 72). Skeletal material from Egypt was selectively measured and classified in order to achieve this goal (Sertima 1976, 110–11). There were a few Egyptologists who claimed that the average degree of racial blending within the general population varied from period to period but was, in a general sense, "multiracial" (Drake 1987, 1:31, 62–75, 134). They also agreed that blacks were numerous in Egypt. Yet they argued that their social position in ancient times was that of servants and slaves, whereas the kings, priests, and military—the elite—were white (Sertima 1976, 108–10). Accordingly, Egypt served as an ancient historical precedent for a white society with black slaves, justifying the "natural" place of blacks in the U.S. South.

Although useful for the Southern defense of slavery, this argument still remained vulnerable to the question of hybridity. Consequently, scientific racists made a double argument: the difference between the species of humans was permanent, and this permanence was preserved thorough the laws of hybridity by the degeneration and eventual infertility of any hybrid crossing between them. The supposed infertility of the hybrid offspring was held up as proof that blacks and whites were biologically different species. This argument buttressed claims that any breakdown of the social divisions between blacks and whites in the United States would lead to pervasive racial hybridization (or "mongrelization"), which in turn would cause the white race to decline and eventually die out altogether (Young 1994, 160–65). The term "miscegenation," in fact, originated in the United States in 1864 during the Democratic Party's campaign for the presidency; it was coined in a pamphlet titled "Miscegenation: The Theory of the Blending of the Races." Inflaming racial fears was necessary to gain support for the continued enslavement of African Americans and the segregation (or repatriation to Africa) of those who were free.[10]

Antimiscegenation sentiments were thus not only central to the ideology of white racism and supremacy but also rationalized slavery in the years leading up to the Civil War and the continued exclusion of African Americans from the American creed's promise of constitutional equality. At the end of the nineteenth century, draconian measures were taken to ensure this exclusion through the institutionalization of Jim Crow segregation. In particular, the one-drop rule would sustain the generalized system of both legalized and informal segregation that prevented blacks from having avenues of contact as equals with whites. Moreover, this rule assured that most subsequent miscegenation in the United States would be from European Americans (largely males) into the African-descent population (largely females) and from multiracial individuals to blacks. Accordingly, the one-drop rule became Anglo North America's solution to preserving white cultural and racial "purity," and maintaining, at least theoretically, absolute white dominance, privilege, superiority, and social control (Ginsberg 1996, 5).

The Post-Abolition Racial Order: From Racial Dictatorship to Herrenvolk Democracy

In the wake of the American Revolution, differences between North and South were overshadowed by their common interest in uniting the former colonies

---

10. Some individuals assume the term "miscegenation" is derived from adding the prefix *mis-* (Anglo-Germanic for ill, wrong, or unfavorable) to "cegenation." The word is actually derived from the

into one nation. This was achieved through a variety of compromises between the North and South at the expense of African Americans. Yet regional tensions increased over the course of the nineteenth century as new territories were acquired after the Louisiana Purchase (1803) and the Mexican American War (1846–48). This resulted in intense debate and a series of other compromises over the propagation of slavery in the newly acquired territory. The South felt that it needed new slave states to maintain its political influence. Before the Civil War the Southern economy and social order were largely founded on plantation slavery. These mutually dependent institutions produced the staples, especially cotton, from which the South derived its wealth. The North had its own great agricultural resources, was always more advanced commercially, and was also expanding industrially. Consequently, it was economically and politically interested, if not always morally interested, in limiting the spread of slavery into the new territories. A series of legislative actions, beginning most notably with the Missouri Compromise of 1820, were passed by Congress to limit the spread of slavery, but compromise with Northern and Southern interests was always kept in mind (Fogel 1989, 281–386).

Yet sectionalism grew stronger with each new state that was incorporated into the Union. The election of Abraham Lincoln in 1861 was the death knell to further expansion of slavery. He vowed to keep the nation united and the new Western territories free of slavery. Many Southerners feared he was not sympathetic to their way of life and would not treat them equitably. In addition, differences between the Northern states (which included the Midwestern and Western states) and the Southern states had become so great that compromise was no longer possible. It became apparent to the South that the North was bent on undermining and ultimately destroying the institution of slavery and its way of life. The gradual breakdown of the compromise between the increasingly divergent interests of the agrarian South and the urban North was pivotal in the secession of the Southern states and the subsequent Civil War (Fogel 1989, 281–386).

A first major confrontation between the American and racial creeds occurred during "Black Reconstruction" (1865–77) following the Civil War. With the enactment of the Thirteenth, Fourteenth, and Fifteenth Amendments and other Reconstruction legislation, the United States seemed to be reshaping its duality into a single society in which African Americans would gain full membership in the people's domain.[11] Yet this effort collapsed with the Hayes-Tilden Compromise

---

Latin words *miscere* (to mix) and *genus* (race). In addition, miscegenation between blacks and whites has been falsely characterized as the crossing of different species, not geno-phenotypical variations of the same species (Lay 1993, 165; Miller 1996, 12).

11. Lincoln's Emancipation Proclamation was a military measure to end slavery only in the states in rebellion that were under Federal control. Congress passed the Thirteenth Amendment (1865) to

of 1877, which ushered in a period generally called White Redemption. In this compromise, the southern Democratic supporters of Samuel Tilden gave the Northern Republican supporters of Rutherford B. Hayes the disputed votes in the presidential election of 1876 in exchange for removal of federal troops that had occupied the South to ensure compliance with Reconstruction legislation. This withdrawal allowed the South to handle the "Negro Problem" as it saw fit without interference from the federal government (Fuchs 1990, 96–98; Russell 1994, 139–41).

In no region of the United States were the effects of this change felt more acutely and dramatically than in Louisiana, where Southern whites mobilized against racial democracy in the 1896 Supreme Court decision *Plessy v. Ferguson* (Davis 1991, 8–9, 52–53; Olsen 1967, 112). The *Plessy* decision enforced legal segregation in the public sphere, so long as separate facilities were equally maintained. This affirmation of de jure equality was meaningless, given the de facto inequality endorsed by the decision. *Plessy* also required a series of dialectical jugglings by the Supreme Court to reconcile these grounds with the Reconstruction amendments (Ringer 1983, 215–16; Davis 1991, 61).

To achieve this, the Court divided the people's domain into two institutional realms. One was a large institutional area of behavior and practice—the "social" realm—in which the guarantees of the Constitution and the American creed no longer automatically applied. The other was a smaller institutional area—the "legal-political" realm—in which these mandates did apply. The Court, however, did more than create a legal vacuum for the social realm. It gave constitutional sanction to the doctrine of egalitarian pluralism—"separate but equal"—while giving local and state governments the authority to ratify statutes that legalized discriminatory practices in the manner of inegalitarian pluralism. Thus, the Supreme Court virtually rendered null and void the effects of the Fourteenth and Fifteenth Amendments. It included into the supreme law of the people's domain the principle of racial difference, separation, and "social inequality" as a justifiable basis to enact state legislation and perpetuate customary practices in the private and social realms of the community (Ringer 1983, 246).

The Supreme Court essentially imbued the racial creed and the racist beliefs of European Americans with a "status and sanctity" (Ringer 1983, 246) they had previously lacked. Prior to Reconstruction, the American creed was the sole foundation for the legal-normative code of the people; the racial beliefs and values

---

ensure that slavery was permanently abolished throughout the United States. The Fourteenth Amendment (1868) grants all persons born or naturalized in the United States citizenship and equal protection under the laws. The Fifteenth Amendment (1870) gives all male citizens the right to vote. The Civil Rights Acts of 1866 and 1875 declared respectively that all persons born in the United States were citizens, and provided everyone the right to equal treatment in public places and transportation.

articulated in law referred to a class of beings who were not included in the domain of the people. The rearticulation and new legitimization of the racial creed during the post-Reconstruction period, however, was subsequent to African Americans gaining legal membership in the people's domain, implying they were ostensibly governed, as were European Americans, by the tenets of the American creed (246–47). Thus, the new racial creed—a "thinly disguised version" of the former doctrine (246)—became a part of the legal-normative framework of the people. Consequently, it carried relatively equal weight as the American creed in terms of its applicability to African Americans. Thus, Reconstruction's promise of freedom, opportunity, and equal citizenship was broken, in favor of the reconstruction of African American servitude and the redemption of white supremacy (Steinberg 1989, 153–200).

In Louisiana, as elsewhere in the South, state-mandated segregation was established in public transportation and, shortly thereafter, in public facilities and schools. Jim Crow laws were extended to nearly every facet of life. From 1896 to 1904, the U.S. Supreme Court upheld Southern strategies to deprive African Americans of the right to vote, which the Fifteenth Amendment had granted them. The Court also upheld the segregation of all public facilities, including schools and housing (although it insisted that they be equally maintained, in keeping with the equal protection clause of the Fourteenth Amendment). In the North, theaters, restaurants, hotels, housing, and schools were also segregated in practice, even where the law forbade it (Zack 1994, 98–99).

The climate of the military branches also reflected these trends. During World War I, segregated African American military units did not receive the same support that European American units did. After returning from the "war to save democracy," many patriotic African American soldiers were lynched in their uniforms during the urban race riots of the early 1920s (Fuchs 1990, 99; Wintz 1988, 13). These riots erupted in Southern cities, as well as in New York, Tulsa, Oklahoma, and Springfield, Illinois. White mobs murdered African Americans and wantonly destroyed their property. Many African Americans had armed themselves and fired back at white mobs (Wintz 1988, 13).

White racism was not limited to the judicial and legislative branches and the military but was also reflected in the attitudes and policies of the executive branch. In 1906, President Roosevelt dealt harshly with black troops involved in the Brownsville race riots, falsely stating to Congress that lynchings were precipitated by the sexual assault of white women by black men. President Taft endorsed restrictions on African American suffrage and began segregating federal offices in Washington, D.C., a policy that was expanded during Woodrow Wilson's administration. President Harding denounced racial amalgamation (Fuchs 1990, 99; Wintz 1988, 7–8; Zack 1994, 98–99).

The impact of this reconfigured racial creed was felt in the North and South. Enslavement and exclusion in the North and South were the chief means through which U.S. society had been racialized. Slavery, in particular, was central to U.S. notions of freedom and democracy. However, the racial creed in the North never attained the closure of that in the South, as slavery had been abolished by the early nineteenth century. African Americans were, in fact, afforded a greater measure of political and legal privileges in the people's domain, including at various times the right to vote. Yet the North's legacy of African American subordination and imposed inferiority stamped an inegalitarian pluralist edifice of racial segmentation, discrimination, and exclusion on the region (Ringer 1983, 247).

After the Civil War, the natural choice for labor in the expanding industrial North would have been the recently freed African Americans. Desperate to retain African Americans as the cheap labor force in the South after the Civil War, Southern agricultural interests locked them into debt peonage and sharecropping. Northern industrialists were not, however, averse to hiring African Americans when it suited their interests (e.g., to replace white workers who went on strike for higher wages). They particularly welcomed African Americans during the First and Second World Wars when the conscription of many white males and reduced European immigration created a labor shortage. Indeed, the promise of economic opportunity lured many African Americans to Northern cities. Furthermore, an economic depression, massive flooding, extensive crop failures caused by the cotton boll weevil, and the mechanization of agriculture production in the South contributed to a loss of jobs in cotton production and other misfortunes. Jim Crow laws in the South also prompted African American migration northward (Fuchs 1990, 100; Steinberg 1989, 201–7; Wintz 1988, 13–14; Zack 1994, 98).

That said, seemingly pliant European immigrants had been brought in to work in the urban industrial North dating back to the antebellum era, and in the process displaced African Americans in the few jobs they had secured. This process was repeated with each successive wave of European immigration. Despite being the targets of discrimination themselves, European immigrants rapidly adopted anti-black sentiments in the competitive social and economic struggle with African Americans. Accordingly, as part of their rite of passage to legitimating their rights to the privileges of whiteness, they came to share the same beliefs of other European Americans: African Americans were not entitled to the rights and protections of the people's domain (Ringer 1983, 266).[12]

---

12. Although some native white workers supported abolition and the cause of the North in the Civil War, they generally held on tenaciously to the separate and elevated status bestowed by a white racial designation. Race, apart from economic interests, was already present in the way native

The political consequences of this racialization, therefore, resulted in the formation of a white racial dictatorship based on *herrenvolk* (or "master race") democracy. Accordingly, racialization eclipsed the economic interests of the white working class by bonding European Americans of all socioeconomic backgrounds into a racially unified force directed against all people of color, particularly African Americans. It tended to homogenize distinctions among those deemed racially different from whites, while simultaneously leveling ethnocultural differences among European Americans. Race was thus constructed as a universal and permanent social difference, which denied commonalities between European Americans and Americans of color across a host of categories (e.g., economics, citizenship, and at its most extreme, a shared humanity) (Winant 1994, 39–43).

These attitudes and policies had unique implications in "Latin" North America after France and Spain ceded their territory in Louisiana and the Gulf ports of Mobile and Pensacola to the United States through the Louisiana Purchase Treaty of 1803 and the Adams-Onís Treaty of 1819. Overwhelmed by an English-speaking majority, individuals of French and Spanish cultural orientation (or Creoles) of all racial backgrounds remained aloof from the new arrivals, which they correctly perceived as threatening their cultural and political survival. They fought to maintain French (or Spanish) civil law, their unique cultural traditions, the teaching of French (or Spanish) in public schools, and Creole dominance over local and regional governments. However, the Latin American ternary racial project was gradually replaced with a binary racial project, which by the early twentieth century designated as black all individuals of African descent. Ultimately, multiracial individuals were reduced to the subordinate status of blacks, deprived of citizenship, politically disenfranchised, and eventually segregated from European Americans (Domínguez 1986, 28–50, 113–15, 134–40; Gould 1996, 28–50; Haskins 1975, 118–20; Logsdon and Bell 1992, 189–261).

As part of their strategy for achieving this goal, Anglo North Americans concentrated on securing economic, political, and social dominance by minimizing ethnocultural differences between themselves and their European Creole counterparts in order to build a united ethnoracial white front against all individuals of African descent. Though many Free Coloreds (or Creoles of color) felt that the Louisiana Purchase Treaty assured them equal citizenship in the United States,

---

white workers recognized themselves in the nineteenth century and was intrinsic to the manner in which they viewed other concerns. Accordingly, their class identity was itself racialized, and class formation drew upon fears of economic competition, wage cutting, and even replacement by nonwhite labor. This explained why the white working class felt more threatened by emancipated African American labor (or conquered Mexican or immigrant Asian labor) than by the flood of European immigrants in the late nineteenth century. It also explained why the native white working class formed—with a few short-lived exceptions—racially exclusive organizations (Winant 1994, 39–43).

the new Anglo-American rulers not only denied their petitions for equal citizenship and civil rights but also systematically began to erode their existing rights. Moreover, Anglo North Americans showed no desire to extend to even the wealthiest and lightest of the multiracial elite a legal white racial identity, or any of the privileges associated with that status (Domínguez 1986, 113–15; Logsdon and Bell 1992, 205–7). Meanwhile, Creoles of color in Mobile and Pensacola, who became U.S. citizens through the Adams-Onís Treaty, were initially exempted from restrictions later enacted against Free Coloreds. However, by the 1840s and 1850s, the legislatures of Alabama and Florida began enacting restrictive laws aimed at Free Coloreds that did not specifically exclude Creoles of color (Gould 1996, 40–44).

Multiracial individuals in Louisiana and the Gulf ports thus came to be viewed less in terms of their national ethnocultural origins as Franco-Hispanics, and more in terms of their ethnoracial origins as individuals of African descent. Consequently, they were not only redefined as black but also denied citizenship and suffrage until the passage of the Reconstruction amendments. Even these legal rights were circumvented by Jim Crow segregation, as well as through the implementation of "understanding clauses" and "grandfather clauses," poll taxes, and literacy tests.[13] By the first decades of the twentieth century, the one-drop rule became the legal definition for blackness in some Southern states, and the "commonsense" definition throughout the United States (Davis 1991, 55–58). State after state enacted legislation to void interracial marriages (Tenzer 1990, 65–66).

The Anglo North American occupation of Northern Mexico, particularly the territory of California, and the subsequent racialization of the Mexican population, provides an interesting contrast to the experience of Creoles of color in the Lower South. After the conquest, annexation, and subsequent colonization of what would become the U.S. Southwest through the Mexican American War (1846–48), Mexicans—who are largely multiracial individuals of Native American and European American descent (*mestizos*)—were legally guaranteed citizenship and suffrage. These rights were protected by the 1848 Treaty of Guadalupe Hidalgo with Mexico, and by the U.S. Constitution.

Yet the social structural position the Mexican population would occupy in California was largely unscripted. Although most Mexicans were dark-complexioned

---

13. Southern states adopted an "understanding clause," or a "grandfather clause." This allowed individuals who could not pass the literacy test to register to vote, if they could demonstrate that they understood the meaning of a specific text in the state constitution to the satisfaction of the registrar, or were descended from someone eligible to vote in 1867, the year before African Americans attained the franchise. Poll taxes were enacted in Southern states between 1889 and 1910, which disenfranchised many poor whites as well as blacks.

mestizos who were phenotypically more Native American than Spanish, many were of partial African descent. In fact, African ancestry was widely dispersed among all social classes, including the elite. This was largely due to extensive miscegenation in Mexican society, which fostered not only a ternary racial project but also notably fluid racial markers and a tendency to "lighten" the racial categorization of individuals with increased vertical social mobility. For example, social practice allowed multiracial individuals to purchase certificates of "whiteness" called *cédulas de gracias al sacar* (literally "thanks for getting out of it"), which erased their Native American and/or African origins. This certification not only gave them legal status as *Españoles,* and even greater opportunity for vertical social mobility but also enhanced the comparatively more fluid racial demarcations between "pure" Spaniards (or whites), light *mestizos,* and mulattoes. Consequently, the memory of African forebears was forgotten, if not ignored or successfully concealed by the many light-skinned Spanish-identified descendants of the Southwest's first families.

Thus, it is difficult to determine whether and to what extent Anglo North American colonizers were aware of the African ancestry in the Mexican population, or what impact knowledge of that ancestry had on their attitudes toward Mexicans, especially if African ancestry was not phenotypically discernible or distinguishable from Native American ancestry. Furthermore, the largest subordinate population in the region was Native American, rather than an enslaved African population. At the time the United States acquired California from Mexico, slavery had been abolished for nearly twenty years; few African slaves remained. Consequently, this inhibited the establishment of a racialized social order based on the one-drop rule as in Louisiana. What seems evident is that Mexicans were perceived to be largely *mestizos* of predominantly European and Native American descent, irrespective of any African ancestry or phenotypical traits they might have had. Multiracial individuals in California and the Southwest thus came to be designated more in terms of their national ethnocultural origins than their ethnoracial origins. Correspondingly, Mexican Americans were extended an official white racial identity, despite the fact that they were not "white" in the Northern European sense.

Though Mexican Americans were extended a white legal status, in practice it was frequently disregarded, much as their rights to U.S. citizenship. Moreover, the extension of white racial privilege was not necessarily intended to include the entire Mexican American population. Rather, the prime beneficiaries of these privileges, and those deemed most worthy of integration into the new racial order, were the light-skinned ranchero (and merchant) elite in Texas, New Mexico, Arizona, and California. They identified themselves as *Españoles* (Spaniards) and were considered white under the racial policies that had prevailed during Mexican rule. As the one-drop rule was not applied to indigenous ancestry, this segment of the Mexican population was not automatically designated as Native American (Almaguer 1994, 1–74; Forbes 1971, 30–33).

The Civil War and Reconstruction ended the previous distinction between slave and free. Moreover, the loss of those few privileges that had been associated with color during the antebellum period, in conjunction with the hostility of whites that accompanied the rise of Jim Crow segregation, led to a shift in the political consciousness of the multiracial elite toward an alliance with blacks. In this coalition, they provided a number of leaders in the early fight for civil rights because of the relatively better opportunities for social, cultural, and intellectual advancement their color had given them in comparison to the black masses (Mencke 1979, 3, 23–24; Williamson 1980, 81, 87–88).

Nowhere was this shift more clearly demonstrated than in the 1920s among the vanguard of the Harlem Renaissance. Although the Harlem Renaissance attracted both black and multiracial individuals, the descendants of the mulatto elite led the way. Largely a product of the "talented tenth,"[14] which itself was disproportionately made up of the multiracial elite, this vanguard assumed a leadership role in defining and describing African Americans to themselves and the larger U.S. society. The emergence of this "New Negro" in Harlem was closely tied to New York becoming the new land of opportunity for African Americans in the first two

14. Henry L. Morehouse, a patron of liberal arts study for African Americans, coined the term "talented tenth" in 1896 to refer to a class of highly educated and morally upright African Americans who he hoped would constitute a vanguard for the black masses. In 1905, W.E.B. Du Bois, cofounder of the National Association for the Advancement of Colored People (NAACP) and founder of *The Crisis*, the monthly publication of the NAACP, appropriated Morehouse's term when he called upon a cadre of exceptional African Americans to become "leaders of thought and missionaries of culture among their people" (Gates and West 1996, 156–57; Banks 1996, 47). Du Bois would have vehemently rejected any notion that membership in the talented tenth was based on color. If, however, color was not explicit in Du Bois's concept of the talented tenth, it was certainly implicit, given the confluence of color, culture, and class in the socioeconomic structure of the African American community. That said, the concept of the talented tenth must be viewed in the limitations of the historical context and was one of the various tactics in the war of maneuver African Americans deployed in the struggle for equality.

Notably, Du Bois became critical of the class egoism and failure of the African American elite to provide strong leadership, particularly as he shifted more toward Marxist thought. Consequently, he reassessed his notion of the talented tenth out of concerns that educated African Americans would use their intellectual and social capital for personal gain rather than collective uplift. Du Bois rearticulated the concept of the talented tenth as a leadership that would seek "the just distribution of wealth" (Gates and West 1996, 163) and be imbued with a transformative as well as global vision of mass development (Gates and West 1996, 161, 162; James 1997, 18–27). In addition, Du Bois gave greater attention to the moral and political agency of the working class in the struggle for racial justice. He referred to this reassessment of the talented tenth as the "Doctrine of the Guiding Hundredth" (Gates and West 1996, 177).

decades of the twentieth century, just as Washington, D.C., had been during and after Reconstruction. Between 1914 and 1930, there was a significant migration of African Americans of all colors and classes from the South to the North.

African Americans became part of the growing metropolitan areas that formed the twentieth century's urban ghettos—most famously Chicago's South Side and New York's Harlem. The same job opportunities that attracted African Americans to the North also attracted African-descent populations from Latin America and the Caribbean. Because of this deluge of black migrants and immigrants, the African American population in New York City increased by 250 percent between 1914 and 1930, when it reached 327,706; virtually all African American New Yorkers lived in Harlem. But this African American mecca was a segregated ghetto and slum. Thirty percent of all dwellings lacked bathing facilities; the death rate from tuberculosis was five times greater than for whites in Manhattan, and schools were segregated. Limited employment for blacks resulted in their predominant employment in domestic service and unskilled labor and their exclusion from skilled blue-collar, clerical, and professional work. As Naomi Zack points out, it is impressive, if not miraculous, that the leaders of the Harlem Renaissance forged a positive sense of cultural identity and awareness in such circumstances, not to mention the hostilities of the larger racial ecology of the United States (Wintz 1988, 13–14, 20, 27–29; Zack 1994, 98–99).

Although it began in New York, the Harlem Renaissance extended to Chicago, Washington, Atlanta, and other cities with large African American populations. Though part of the "New Negro Movement," it also attracted the attention of European Americans and reflected a mutually beneficial, egalitarian integration of many whites and blacks. Some individuals were genuine patrons of the arts who sought to expose the white world to this tremendous outpouring of talent, despite the complicated and often contradictory motivations and consequences of this patronage (Gubar 1997, 95–133, 153–56; Hutchinson 1995, 1–28; Lemke 1998, 17–20; Washington 2003, 54–57; Woodson 1999, 7–9). The Harlem Renaissance also influenced the thinking of many white intellectuals (European and American) espousing different forms of pragmatism and cultural nationalism, who in turn helped shape the Harlem movement. For example, anthropologist Franz Boas challenged the scientific racism on which the eugenics movement and other racist projects were premised, whereas Robert Park, originator of the famous Chicago School of Sociology, supported the endeavors of African Americans to build their own institutions and culture (Hutchinson 1995, 61–77, 42–61). Other European Americans were racial voyeurs who looked to Harlem as a place for "releasing themselves" from the constraints of Protestant American values through the "carefree" and "uninhibited" lifestyle of African Americans (Riggs

1986). Their appropriation of blackness, which they saw as chic, exotic, or risqué, often bordered on cultural grand larceny, and did not imply a willingness to exchange white privilege for the hipness or "cool" they associated with black life. Neither did it translate into racial equality for African Americans in the nation's civic culture and body politic (duCille 1996, 27).

By denying African-descent Americans equality with European Americans, the changing circumstances in the first quarter of the twentieth century, including enforcement of the one-drop rule, furthered the process of "intraracial democratization" between black and multiracial individuals. These circumstances would serve as the basis for mass mobilization and collective action in the twentieth-century struggle for civil rights—a struggle in which the multiracial elite would continue to provide leadership. Even given the heightened racial consciousness, the racial attitudes of the Harlem Renaissance vanguard were different from the eugenics movement, at one extreme, and Black Nationalism, at the other. Many of the Harlem Renaissance artists and thinkers had close personal and professional relationships with European Americans. Some married interracially, and a few even explored the multiracial experience in their writing. Yet the clear message conveyed in Harlem Renaissance writings was that the only meaningful future for multiracial individuals involved the full embrace of black identity. If, therefore, the Harlem Renaissance was a "rebirth" of African American identity, and at the same time an important "interracial moment" (Nash 1999, 141–45), it was also a "still birth." The protagonists of the Harlem Renaissance sacrificed the concept of multiracial identity as an "intellectual weapon" and "theoretical wedge" (Zack 1994, 99) against the essentialized conceptualization of biological race and racial categories, as well as white racism and the dichotomization and hierarchical valuation of blackness and whiteness.

The "pan-African Americanism" forged by Harlem Renaissance leaders such as W.E.B. Du Bois, Jean Toomer, Countee Cullen, Langston Hughes, Zora Neale Hurston, and James Weldon Johnson was therefore somewhat paradoxical. This vanguard turned for inspiration to the black experience—to African American culture and the vitality of African American art, music, and social relations—and engaged with the question of what it meant to be an African American. They sought to achieve this identity through a new appreciation of southern rural African American life, the human dignity of African American slaves, and early twentieth-century African American urban poverty. Yet they simultaneously fused this vision with their own European American sociocultural tradition.

This "double consciousness" was best captured by W.E.B. Du Bois, the most prominent African American during those years. He was co-founder of the National Association for the Advancement of Colored People (NAACP) and founder (in 1910) of The Crisis (its monthly publication), which he edited until

1934. This duality was not, however, seen as an actual racial "twoness." Rather, Du Bois meant that blacks were products of two warring cultural identities and nations—one American and the other African American. By forging a hybridized "Afro-Saxon" tradition within an African American cultural framework, the Harlem Renaissance vanguard were perhaps able to act out their own multiple backgrounds without daring to confront them fully. Multiple racial ancestries, therefore, were overridden by a single racial identity and a bicultural experience forged in the U.S. context. The Harlem Renaissance leaders could not, or would not, even conceptualize a multiracial identity intermediate to black and white constructed on egalitarian premises (Gaines 1996, 9–10; Zack 1994, 99–101).

Naomi Zack argues that any critique of the Harlem Renaissance's rejection of multiracial identity must consider the limitations of the contemporary racial order and can be meaningful only in light of the alternative choices that were available later (Zack 1994, 99–101). The one-drop rule was not a neutral theoretical demarcation but an expression of the virulent racist sentiment that pervaded white society in the early twentieth century (99). It reinforced the low regard in which European Americans held African Americans and the stigma they attached to African ancestry.

Although the Harlem Renaissance elite embraced the one-drop rule and set themselves up as spokespeople for the black masses, this role would ultimately fall to Marcus Garvey, the more militant pan-Africanist from Jamaica, who declared that he spoke for the "untalented ninetieth" (Kellner 1987, xiii). The leaders of the Harlem Renaissance were representatives of the "talented tenth" and maintained an elite class position in the African American community, no matter how they may have denied or sought to transcend that fact. They were also numerically few and touched relatively few people. Yet they challenged the racial elitism of the past, and as harbingers of the future, embodied the prospect for social change.

By the end of the second decade of the twentieth century, individuals of varying degrees of African ancestry were more evenly distributed throughout the upper, middle, and lower sectors of the African American social structure; wealth and cultural attributes had become more important than color alone in determining social prestige. Nevertheless, a disproportionate number of the elite remained considerably more European in appearance and culture than the black masses (Mencke 1979, 24; Williamson 1980, 129). This was partially because these individuals had continued to benefit from the advantages vested in them over generations. Also, despite changing political alliances, many resisted their loss of status by withdrawing more self-consciously unto themselves (Russell, Wilson, and Hall 1992, 25). Yet the cumulative effects of forced endogamy and "internal miscegenation" (Myrdal 1944, 135; Williamson 1980, 120–21) between multiracial individuals and blacks reached such a point by the 1920s that the majority of African Americans were becoming multiracial. Indeed, after the 1920s the census ceased to differentiate between blacks and mulattoes.

Officially and informally, individuals of a more European phenotype gradually came to regard themselves, and were regarded, less as multiracial and more as light-skinned blacks (Mencke 1979, 28; Williamson 1980, 112–14, 125). Seven of the Southern states—including Louisiana—adopted the one-drop rule as the official definition of blackness. Virginia abandoned its one-fourth rule in 1910 and settled for one-sixteenth on the assumption that lesser amounts could not be detected, though it explicitly adopted the one-drop rule in 1930. Seven states resorted to the one-eighth rule early in the century. This allowed some persons to be classified as white who appeared to be partly black, or who had at least some African forebears and had been known as black (Davis 1991, 55).

Regional variations notwithstanding, European Americans had little inclination to recognize either legal or informal social distinctions among individuals of African descent. Blacks and mulattoes were counted in each census from 1850 to 1920 (except 1880 and 1900). In 1890, census enumerators were instructed to be careful to distinguish between blacks, mulattoes, quadroons, and octoroons. "Black" was to be used to describe individuals who had three-fourths or more African ancestry, "mulatto" for persons who had three-eighths to five-eighths African ancestry, "quadroon" for individuals of one-fourth African ancestry, and "octoroon" for persons who had one-eighth or less African ancestry. In practice, however, the differences between words describing varying degrees of African ancestry had little significance beyond their usage in the creation of hierarchy among African Americans (Davis 1991, 11–12, 57; Lee 1993, 75–94; Williamson 1980, 114).

That said, the preoccupation with degrees of African ancestry on the 1890 census reflected paranoia about invisible blackness or "cryptomelanism," and the possibility of multiracial individuals crossing the racial divide and "contaminating" the European American population. The resulting "mongrelization" would ultimately lead to the decline of Anglo-American civilization. This concern reached new heights in the eugenics movement of the early twentieth century, which held that mental and other qualities, including "frailties" and "debilitating propensities," were mostly inherited. Eugenicists advocated preserving (and "improving") Anglo North American "racial stock" as a "master" or "super" race by encouraging the reproduction of people only of exceptional intelligence. They also advocated eradicating inferior elements through sterilization and other means. The eugenics movement succeeded in getting Congress to pass national-origins quota legislation, notably the Immigration Act of 1924. This legislation restricted the immigration of Southern and Eastern Europeans—who had begun arriving in large numbers beginning in the 1890s—as well as East Asians and

Asian Indians, who were completely prohibited from immigrating. However, no limits were placed on immigration from Latin America (Davis 1991, 13; Smedley 1993, 270, 276, 285–87).

This obsession with degrees of blackness also reflected an attempt to police the boundaries of whiteness and prevent multiracial individuals from taking advantage of white privilege. If, however, European ancestry, and a white racial designation and identity—along with the advantages of white racial privilege—have been intertwined, they have not always been synonymous. For example, Irish, Italian, and Jewish immigrants from Eastern Europe were not initially allowed membership carte blanche in the white republic or the full benefits of the *herrenvolk* democracy. They were European in origin and thus racially white, which meant they were not denied the right to naturalization and citizenship, notwithstanding various attempts to restrict or limit their immigration. Yet these immigrants and their descendants acquired white identities only after protracted struggle. This was aided in no small part by varying degrees of cultural assimilation and socioeconomic mobility—which distanced them from their original pariah status—and more important, their comparatively greater approximation to the dominant Anglo-Protestant ideal.

Thus, the phenotypical criteria for integration into the Anglo-Protestant dominated mainstream—indeed, white racial identity itself and legitimate membership within the white republic—gradually expanded from the original Northern European American ideal to include all European Americans. The possibility of racial assimilation is the last standing requirement for assimilation and the most visible one. It is, therefore, simultaneously a prerequisite and a corollary, along with cultural assimilation, to full entry into the mainstream society dominated by white Anglo-Protestants. In the process of assimilating, each of these waves of European immigrants and their descendants eventually has been granted the status as "insiders." Despite persistent gender and class inequality among European Americans, they have nevertheless been rewarded with white racial privilege, particularly greater egalitarian structural integration in the educational, political, and economic domains of social order. They have necessarily internalized in varying degrees the ideology of white racism and white supremacy, especially discriminatory attitudes and behavior toward blacks, in exchange for significantly, if not completely, discarding their ties to their ethnocultural backgrounds (Cunningham 1965, 22–36; Decaro 1992, 17–19; Ignatiev 1995, 1–6, 178–88; López 1996, 111–53; Roediger 1991, 6–40; Rogin 1996, 3–18; Sacks 1994, 78–102; Saxton 1990, 1–20; Williams 1990, 15–48, 77–87, 131–47).[15] Consequently, assimilation is

15. This does not deny that these groups have influenced to some degree the dominant Anglo-Protestant core culture in the form of transcultural integration. For example, typically "American" phenomena such as the Christmas tree, Easter, hamburgers, hot dogs, the covered wagon, the Kentucky rifle, and a significant number of American beers are German American in origin (Sowell 1981, 43–68).

at best a patronizing integration that creates the illusion of power sharing without dominant Anglo-Protestants actually giving up control.

The structural disadvantages that formally and informally held (and continue to hold) African-descent Americans disproportionately at the bottom of society in terms of occupation, education, and political participation precluded their integration into the U.S. social order. Other groups of color have been excluded in varying degrees by pervasive de jure and de facto inegalitarian pluralism and faced significant continuing racial discrimination, despite the impressive socio-economic and educational gains they have made. Yet the experience of African-descent Americans has differed significantly from that of European Americans, as well as from that of other groups of color generally, because of the strict enforcement of the one-drop rule. The U.S. racial order would thus have to make a significant leap in order to incorporate African Americans in the pattern of European immigrants and their descendants, as well as various other groups of color. As long as the one-drop rule remained intact, it would reproduce an African American group identity and experience distinct from that of European Americans in the larger society. Furthermore, it would preclude the differentiation of multiracial individuals in the racial order, as well as the formation of a multiracial identity as a part of U.S. racial common sense and a socially acceptable means of personal identification.

five THE U.S. PATH LESS TRAVELED

Contesting the Binary Racial Project

The Path of Least Resistance: "Passing"

In the United States, multiracial individuals of African American and European American ancestry for the most part have internalized the one-drop rule and identified themselves as black. Resistance to rules of hypodescent, however, has challenged both legal and commonsense constructions of blackness. European American control over the boundaries between black and white has always been relative rather than absolute. One historical form of individual resistance has been "passing," a radical form of integration in which individuals of a more European American phenotype and cultural orientation make a clandestine break with the African American community, temporarily or permanently, in order to enjoy the privileges of the dominant white community. Compared to frontline battles against racial inequality, passing may seem merely opportunistic—a way of accepting the racial status quo. If viewed as part of a spectrum of tactics, however, passing may be seen as an underground "conspiracy of silence" that seeks to beat oppression at its own game (Stonequist 1937, 184). As a form of racial alchemy, passing exposes the political motivations behind racial categories and seeks to turn oppression on its head by subverting the arbitrary line between white and black (Daniel 2002, 49–55).

Going Underground

Passing has meant deliberately shifting one's racial reference group from black to white and should not be confused with situations where racially blended individuals are mistaken for white. Though sociocultural factors are important, passing is necessarily employed by individuals who are already genotypically (and thus phenotypically) more European American than African American (Day 1932, 7–12; Stonequist 1937, 184; Williamson 1980, 101, 125–26). Those unable to pass as European Americans have often adopted "Latin" or other non-English names; some have passed as members of other groups of color (e.g., Asians or Native Americans) perceived as having a more privileged status in the racial hierarchy (Williamson 1980, 125–26).

From the 1920s to the 1940s, no book on African Americans or race relations was complete without a section on passing. The phenomenon was the topic of several films and was dealt with extensively by both African American and European American novelists (Berzon 1978, 140–61; Spickard 1989, 333–35). It is difficult to say whether passing has actually decreased since the civil rights gains of the late twentieth century. However, these legislative and judicial victories have given African-descent Americans greater access to sectors of society from which they were previously barred, thus removing the most immediate impetus behind passing (Daniel 1992b, 91–107; Spickard 1989; 1992; George 1999, 18–21, 34, 36).

It is noteworthy that during the era of segregation, the most common form of passing was the discontinuous type. Whether for reasons of practicality, revenge, or amusement, discontinuous passing was a brief trip across the racial divide for an evening in a white restaurant or theater or a more comfortable seat on the train (Daniel 2002, 50; Spickard 1989, 335; George 1999, 18–21, 34, 36). Sometimes people of African American descent have migrated to other parts of the country, where they have passed as white, but have continued identifying as black when returning to visit friends and family back home. Many held day jobs as whites, returning to the African American community at night. In the 1920s, Walter White (1893–1955) became an undercover operative for the NAACP and temporarily crossed the racial divide in order to accomplish the dangerous task of investigating lynchings in the South (Daniel 2002, 49–55; Davis 1991, 56; Spickard 1989, 335). All have experienced the anxiety of operating in two different and antagonistic worlds, while simultaneously struggling to keep each world separate. Precautions had to be taken against the possibility of being exposed, deliberately or unwittingly, by an acquaintance, although African Americans typically honored an unwritten code of silence on this score. Individuals sometimes displayed an evasiveness or aloofness in public that might have indicated their efforts to conceal their "real" racial identity (Daniel 2002, 49–50; Piper 1992, 13–15).

Continuous passing, which involves a complete break with the African American community, has been the most sensational form of crossing over, although it has been studied disproportionately to the number of individuals who probably practiced it prior to the civil rights era of the 1950s and 1960s. Because passing is a clandestine affair, it is not possible to pinpoint its origins or to know how many people engaged in it, whether sporadically or permanently (Daniel 1992b, 93). It is possible that a few offspring of the first contact between African Americans and European Americans in the early colonial period passed as white. Most of these first-generation individuals, however, would have had enough discernible African ancestry to prevent their passing as white, even if they had so desired. Passing plausibly became easier for successive generations of multiracial individuals, as procreation with each other and with whites decreased the number of genes inherited from West African antecedents and increased phenotypical approximation to European Americans. Indeed, most individuals who have passed as white have inherited few, if any, genes from West African ancestors. Only about 1–5 percent of the genes of European Americans are derived from African American antecedents, although the total of European Americans with West African forebears numbers in the millions (Davis 1991, 21–22).

Passing in general, and continuous passing in particular, became more appealing as legally sanctioned discrimination increased, first with the codification of slavery in the late seventeenth century and then with the restrictions on both manumission and free people of color in the late eighteenth century. Throughout the antebellum period, the near-white appearance of many runaway multiracial slaves facilitated their escape into the population of Free Coloreds—in part because whites associated freedom with mulattoes and slavery with blacks—and in many cases eventually into the population of European Americans (Berlin 1974, 160). For example, Thomas Jefferson's son Beverly and daughter Harriet, conceived with his multiracial slave Sally Hemings, supposedly ran away from the Monticello estate where they had been slaves and passed as white in Maryland and Washington, D.C. Jefferson freed Eston, another one of his sons with Hemings, and his brother Madison in his will; Eston subsequently vanished into white society in Wisconsin. John Wayles Jefferson, Eston's son, served as a white lieutenant colonel of the Eighth Wisconsin during the Civil War. Madison established himself in the African American community in Ross County, Ohio, and remained there until his death. Yet his son, William Beverly Hemings, crossed the racial divide and served in a white regiment—the 73rd Ohio (Nash 1999, 106; Rothman 1999, 165–70; Stanton and Swann-Right 1999, 107).

The "great age of passing," particularly continuous passing, occurred between 1880 and 1925, undoubtedly in response to Jim Crow legislation (Davis 1991, 21–22; Williamson 1980, 102). Because of the need for spatial mobility and anonymity, continuous passing was more common among men than among women, and occurred more frequently in the urban North (particularly during the first great migration of 1900–1925) than in the rural South (Spickard 1989, 336). However, it is impossible to produce hard numbers, and estimates are largely conjectural (Williamson 1980, 100–103). Some sociologists have placed the number of passers during this period at ten to twenty-five thousand per year; others have estimated the numbers above a hundred thousand annually (Williamson 1980, 103).

European American alarmists of the era, fearing "racial mongrelization" and the decline of Anglo North American civilization by "cryptomelanism" (or invisible blackness), tended to exaggerate these figures. Certain African American leaders used these numbers as an indictment of racial oppression in the United States. Other African Americans saw the inflated figures as fitting revenge on European Americans. Many social scientists also welcomed high numbers as proof that the assimilationist model was as applicable to African Americans as it was to European Americans and would thus provide a solution to "the race problem." The most recent (and careful) calculations, made in 1946, estimated that 2,500–2,700 individuals crossed over annually. These estimates were calculated by tracking for several decades demographic discrepancies in census data that showed an increase in the European American population and a decline in the African American population that could not be accounted for by increased immigration and births, or emigration and deaths, respectively. These modest figures are probably more accurate (Burma 1946, 18–20).

Like discontinuous passing, the continuous sort has most often been a means of gaining access to positions of wealth, power, privilege, and prestige. Some may also find it a way of escaping the disdain of African Americans who have viewed them as less than black (Stonequist 1937, 186–88; Piper 1992, 4–32). Continuous passing is a gradual process in which emotional ties to African Americans are severed as ties to European Americans are achieved, as opposed to a sudden break with the African American community (Drake and Cayton 1962, 166–67). The final break comes when the benefits of becoming white are felt to outweigh the costs of being black. Nevertheless, continuous passing often exacts a considerable price; it is usually extremely difficult for a person to say farewell to family and friends, or to leave without saying anything at all (Spickard 1989, 335–36). If some passers became "white liberals," opening doors that otherwise would be closed to individuals of African descent, others, out of the constant fear of being exposed as impostors, adjusted to their new identities by overcompensating, or even surpassing, the most rabid white racist to prove their credentials as European Americans (Daniel 2002, 49–55; Davis 1991, 56).

The Straight and Narrow Path: Blue-vein Societies, Triracial Isolates, and Louisiana Creoles of Color

Passing is necessarily an individual strategy available to a small percentage of multiracial individuals, and probably only a minority of individuals who could pass have done so. Those who have been unwilling or unable to pass often have sought to counter subordination through the formation of elite societies within the African American community. The multiracial elite were convinced that they suffered from stereotypes stemming from the behavior of the "untutored" and "submerged" black masses, who possessed little knowledge of or appreciation for "the laws governing society." Consequently, they remained aloof from the black masses and vigorously opposed any form of segregation that would restrict them to social spaces marked distinctly for African Americans (Gatewood 1990, 37, 46, 53). Restrained by their pride, however, from attempting to mingle in European American society, where they would be rebuffed, these multiracial elites tended to withdraw into their own exclusive social worlds through the formation of "blue-vein societies." The degree of one's acceptance into this social network depended on approximation to the dominant European American psychosomatic norm, particularly skin color that was light enough to show one's veins. The multiracial elite also valued straight hair, sharp features, and European culture and thought, thus distancing themselves from the image typically held of blacks. Their escape from blackness was illusory, however, for they never achieved social equality with whites.

The Light Brigade

Despite their elitism and attempts to distance themselves from the black masses, the multiracial elite was sympathetic to less fortunate African Americans. They were aware that they constituted a privileged class of a stigmatized minority and considered themselves an aristocracy with a legitimate "right to govern socially and a responsibility to serve by example and take action in the cause of racial uplift" (Gatewood 1990, 45–46, 68). Although their interest in the moral and intellectual uplift of the black masses was patronizing, the multiracial elite genuinely saw itself as the solution to the race problem. The elite argued that if they were "given rights as rapidly as they merited them," they would be inspired, and in turn inspire "the fellows of the lower grade" (46). But the multiracial elite often found its efforts thwarted by the condescension of European Americans on the one hand and criticism from blacks on the other. Few possessed the wealth and leisure to contribute on the scale their critics expected of them. Plus, their ambivalence toward the larger African American community was heightened by the numerous problems of the ever-increasing population of unskilled and low-income blacks in the cities. Not even the most civic-minded among the elite could easily avoid feeling a sense of futility (50).

The formation of multiracial elites was primarily an urban phenomenon; rural African American communities generally lacked the socioeconomic resources for color stratification to develop. In urban areas, color combined with sociocultural and socioeconomic factors to heighten differences among individuals of African descent. Virtually every major urban center has had a section where predominantly multiracial individuals have resided (Russell, Wilson, and Hall 1992, 25). Cities such as Charleston, Philadelphia, Nashville, Louisville, New Orleans, Boston, New York, Atlanta, and particularly Washington, D.C., to mention only a few, have been well known for their "blue-vein" societies (Berzon 1978, 164–87; Mencke 1979, 25; Wright 1985, 134–37).

Despite their social stature, the multiracial elite could hardly be described as wealthy when one considers the enormous fortunes of late nineteenth- and early twentieth-century European American families such as the Carnegies, Asters, Guggenheims, Vanderbilts, and Rockefellers. Nearly all of the multiracial elite was part of a "working aristocracy" (Gatewood 1990, 27, 63), despite pretensions, leisurely aspirations, an elevated standard of living, or the educational opportunities they provided their children. Yet the majority enjoyed a degree of financial security unknown to most African Americans (and many European Americans as well) that dramatized the economic gulf between themselves and the black masses. For the day laborer or even the skilled worker, the economic resources of physicians, public school teachers, administrators, and attorneys—primarily servicing the African American community—government employees, certain businessmen and businesswomen, faculty members of the prestigious African American universities, and others constituted a degree of wealth almost beyond comprehension. The multiracial elite also included families identified with such service trades as catering, barbering, and tailoring, which brought them into regular contact with elite whites. Some of the multiracial elite inherited wealth; others accumulated substantial property, especially in real estate (52).

Great financial wealth was not a prerequisite for membership in the multiracial elite. They surrounded themselves with books, paintings, fine furniture, and musical instruments, but these things did not require great fortunes (Gatewood 1990, 44). More important than money were European ancestry (preferably aristocratic) and a more European phenotype; personal qualities such as education, industry, thrift, sobriety, and fastidiousness in speech, manner, and dress; and matters of circumstance such as wealth, professional standing, and sometimes, close social contact with European Americans. All these characteristics combined to qualify one for membership in or marriage into a numerically small and select elite (Berzon 1978, 168; Mencke 1979, 24–26). It is uncertain whether there were actually churches with front doors painted a shade of light brown to discourage entrance by persons of a darker hue, but religious affiliation did frequently follow color, cultural, and class lines. In each city, the elite attended two or three high-status churches. Multiracial individuals often gravitated toward Episcopal, Congregational, Presbyterian, and Catholic churches and away from Baptist or Methodist churches (except Methodist Episcopal), though there were numerous exceptions to the rule, such as the Fifth Street Baptist Church in Louisville, Kentucky (Daniel 1992b, 95–96; Gatewood 1990, 272–73, 298–99; Wright 1985, 134–37).

Disdainful of gaudiness and ostentation, the multiracial elite dressed "tastefully" at social gatherings, spoke "flawless" English, and exhibited all the earmarks of education, sophistication, and wealth. Graduates from Yale, Harvard, Cornell, Oberlin, and other prominent European American institutions of learning were counted at social gatherings among Washington's elite. African American preparatory schools such as the Palmer Institute in North Carolina, M Street High School (later renamed Dunbar) in Washington, D.C., and historically African American colleges such as Howard University, Atlanta University (later renamed Clark Atlanta) in Georgia, Hampton Institute in Virginia, Morgan University in Baltimore, Spelman Women's College in Atlanta, and Fisk University in Nashville became bastions of the multiracial elite.

Certain Greek fraternities and sororities on these campuses have been accused of partiality to individuals of a comparatively more European phenotype. The famous Cotton Club, particularly at its inception, was notorious for excluding all but the most phenotypically European women of African descent from its chorus line; African Americans, regardless of phenotype, were prohibited from patronizing the establishment (Gatewood 1990, 44, 61; Russell, Wilson, and Hall 1992, 28, 30). There were also the infamous paper bag and comb tests that prohibited entry to social dances and the like of all persons darker than a brown paper bag and whose hair was too curly to allow a comb to pass through smoothly (Berzon 1978, 168; Gatewood 1990, 62). To this day, elite African American social clubs such as the Links and Jack and Jill—founded in 1938 and 1946, respectively—have a disproportionate number of individuals of more "visible" European ancestry, although social and cultural orientation associated with economic affluence now serve as equally, if not more, important criteria for membership (Graham 1999, 42–43; Russell, Wilson, and Hall 1992, 25).

As European Americans became more obsessed with the delusions of their own racial purity, exclusivity, and superiority over individuals they designated as "Negroes," African Americans embraced the identifier "Negro"—as well as the one-drop rule—which they considered mutually beneficial to black and multiracial individuals. Publicly, the multiracial elite assumed positions of cultural and political leadership within the larger African American community, which now increasingly combined both blacks and mulattoes. Socially, they removed the formal barriers against marriage with darker-skinned African Americans, retaining them only as matters of personal preference, snobbery, and what was later defined as "colorism" (Zack 1994, 96).

Runaways and Refusniks

Scattered throughout the eastern United States, particularly in the Southeast, there have been some two hundred or more communities of varying combinations and degrees of mainly European American, Native American, and African American descent, commonly called triracial isolates. They are pluralistic in nature, like the blue-vein societies. Yet the latter formed an urban elite within the African American community, whereas triracial isolate communities have historically lived apart from both blacks and whites on the fringes of villages and towns, or in isolated rural enclaves. Some have been small communities located in hilly, swampy, or densely wooded areas somewhat inaccessible to the general public, with as few as fifty persons, whereas the Lumbees, for example, have had as many as forty thousand members (Brooks 1998a, 1998b).

In the early twenty-first century, large numbers of individuals remain in these rural communities as unskilled laborers or agricultural workers. However, some triracial communities boast of prosperous farmers, college graduates, and professionals. Since the mid-twentieth century, many individuals from these communities have migrated to the cities. This trend, along with increased intermarriage (generally with European Americans), has led to the extinction of many communities and the loss of collective identity (Berry 1963, 31–33). Prominent individuals partially descended from some of these communities include actress Heather Locklear. In a recent interview she mentioned that her mother's lineage is predominantly Scottish, and her father's includes Lumbees, from Robeson County, North Carolina.[1] Although they have much in common, and have been collectively designated by social scientists as triracial isolates, many of these communities vehemently reject any such labeling (Kennedy and Kennedy 1997, 91, 92, 99–102, 164). In fact, it would be erroneous to think of them as one identifiable group. Commonalties have less to do with actual cultural bonds

---

1. A reader wrote in to Walter Scott's "Personality Parade" *Parade Magazine:* "'I belong to a Native American tribe called the Lumbee, and Locklear is a common last name. That makes me wonder: Is Heather Locklear part Native American?' . . . Locklear, who was contacted by the magazine about the question responded, 'Yes, I *am* part Lumbee—way, way back on my father's side.'. . . Her maternal ancestors were predominantly Scottish" (Scott 1998, 2). Ms. Locklear was a recipient of the 1999 First Americans in the Arts Awards for her continuing role on Fox TV's *Melrose Place*. First Americans in the Arts is a nonprofit organization dedicated to improving the image and visibility of Native Americans in the entertainment industry. Proceeds from the annual First Americans awards ceremony go to a scholarship fund for Native American students pursuing careers in entertainment (Finn 1999).

than with similarities in experience and in living conditions that unite them in their refusal to accept the U.S. binary racial project and the one-drop rule (Wilkins 1989, 1–2).

Since evidence is scanty, the exact origins of these groups and their names are unknown. This is compounded by the fact that at different times in the antebellum period, depending on the determination of the enumerator, the same families in some communities were listed variously as white, mulatto, or free people of color (Blu 1980, 3, 39–51). To complicate matters further, the last term did not become interchangeable with the categories of free mulatto and free black until the mid-nineteenth century. Up to that time, it had been a rather elusive term that included Native American reservations; Native American rural communities; multiracial populations of Native American, European American, and African American descent; multiracial populations of European American and African American descent; and free blacks. The communities probably evolved from frontier settlements that became magnets for runaway slaves, trappers, homesteaders, adventurers, deserters, outlaws, outcasts, and nonconformists of all racial backgrounds, but "internal miscegenation" fostered by self-imposed isolation led to a generalized blending over time (Berry 1963, 31–41).

The triracial isolates have been known by a wide variety of names. New York has been the home of the Van Guilders, the Clappers, the Shinnecock, the Poospatuck, the Montauk, the Mantinecock, and the Jackson Whites. In Pennsylvania, they have been called Pools; in Delaware, Nanticokes; in Rhode Island, Narragansetts; in Massachusetts, Gay Heads and Mashpees; in Ohio, Carmelites. Maryland has its Wesorts; West Virginia, its Guineas; and Tennessee, its Melungeons.[2] There are the Ramps, Issues, and Chickahominy in Virginia; the Lumbees, Haliwas, Waccamaws, and Smilings in North Carolina; Chavises, Creels, Brass Ankles, Redbones, Redlegs, Buckheads, and Yellowhammers in South Carolina. Louisiana has also been home to many triracial communities (Berry 1963, 1–30).

Some of the labels, such as Chavis and Creel, are family names, although many others, such as Brass Ankle and Redbone, are externally imposed, and are clearly meant to be epithets. As such, they are anathema to those who bear them. Names such as Chickahominy and Nanticoke, which suggest Native American derivation, are borne proudly. Some individuals in these communities would readily be taken as Native American. Others are indistinguishable from whites; however, many clearly show varying degrees of African ancestry. Enclaves in St.

2. Recent DNA tests indicate that the Melungeons are of Native American (approximately 5 percent), African (approximately 5 percent), and European (approximately 83 percent) descent. The study also showed approximately 7 percent of the samples matching populations in Turkey, Syria, and northern India (Kennedy 2002).

Landry Parish, Louisiana, in Gouldtown, New Jersey, and in Darke County, Ohio, have always acknowledged their African ancestry, though they have somewhat isolated themselves from the mainstream of society and have differentiated themselves from other locals of African descent (Berry 1963, 1–30).

In the U.S. South, any term describing a racially blended background generally has included African ancestry, been equated with mulatto, and been translated into black. Thus, most of these communities have affirmed only two components— Native American and European American—if they acknowledged their multiracial ancestry at all (Blu 1980, 1–8). Consequently, triracial isolate communities have tended to deny African ancestry and prize indigenous origins, despite having retained little to no knowledge of either Native American culture or tribal affiliations and being culturally indistinguishable from local whites (Berry 1963, 11–12, 33, 166–71; Wilkins 1989, 11–12). In this sense, the triracial isolate quest for identity appears to be more reactionary than revolutionary. Yet these communities have manipulated the U.S. binary racial project to their advantage and have forged a ternary racial project, which has destabilized binary racial thinking (Wilkins 1989, 1–2).

This positive bias toward indigenous ancestry is partly explainable by the fact that it has never carried the stigma that has been consistently attached to African ancestry (Crowe 1975, 158–61). Furthermore, the smallest amount of Native American ancestry could qualify individuals for federal assistance, voting rights, and land claims—meager privileges that have not always been available to blacks. By the twentieth century, the Native American threat to continued U.S. territorial expansion had been sufficiently neutralized through extermination to facilitate the romanticization of Native Americans and afford many whites the luxury of viewing indigenous ancestry as a source of pride (Borowich 1996, 17–18; Crowe 1975, 158–61; Snipp 1986, 247–51). This romanticization has changed, depending on U.S. attitudes and policies. Nevertheless, it appears all the more ironic and tragic, given that contemporary Native Americans are far more excluded than African Americans (generally speaking) from achieving political, economic, and educational equity in the mainstream of society (Feagin and Feagin 1996, 224–28, 280–83).

Moreover, if racial composition and ancestry have always determined who is African American, there is by contrast no universally accepted definition of Native American (Berry 1963, 1–9). The definitions employed by the U.S. Census Bureau and the Bureau of Indian Affairs have often contradicted each other, and both agencies have shifted policies overtime. The Bureau of Indian Affairs includes on its rolls only those individuals entitled to bureau services. Acceptance by a tribe, however it may be defined, in conjunction with proof of at least one-quarter degree of indigenous ancestry, is generally required. For census purposes, self-definition has been the prevailing policy for all racial and ethnic groups since 1970. In the past, however, enumerators were instructed to record as Native American only those individuals enrolled on reservations or listed in agency rolls, persons of one-fourth or more indigenous ancestry, or individuals regarded as Native Americans by their communities (Berry 1963, 7–9).

Although these regulations were applied primarily to multiracial individuals of Native American and European descent, or to individuals who were perceived to be completely indigenous, some state codes, and the census in 1930 and 1940, applied the same criteria to individuals of Native American and African descent, as well as to those of Native American, African, and European descent. However, such individuals typically have been classified as black. Although some African Americans have accused the triracial isolate communities of donning feathers in order to escape the stigma of being black, various triracial groups have cast their lot with African Americans. Some individuals have even committed the "unforgivable sin" of marrying blacks. Most, however, have historically maintained a strong anti-black prejudice that has helped bolster support for their own identity by whites. The clearest example of this came during the era of segregation. Denied entry into white schools, numerous triracial communities not only refused to attend schools and use public facilities for African Americans but gained support for establishing their own public restrooms and education facilities, as well as separate sections in churches and theaters (Berry 1963, 106–7, 115–18, 188).

Prevented by society from affirming all of who they were without also being classified as African American, yet unable to claim residence on a reservation or prove that they met the ancestry requirements, various triracial communities have used the flexibility in the definition of Native American to their advantage (Forbes 1988, 203; Wilkins 1989, 1). By 1980, the Lumbees of North Carolina, the Nanticokes of Delaware, the Houma in western Louisiana, and the Poospatuck of Long Island, New York, after a prolonged struggle, succeeded in officially changing their classi-fication from mulatto to nontreaty Native American. Although this status excludes them from government benefits, it places them on the indigenous side of the racial divide. Many have become active in Native American affairs; however, their claims to indigenous status have been met with reluctance, if not resistance, from treaty or reservation groups (e.g., the Cherokee, the Comanche, and the Choctaw) that qualify for federal subsidies (Berry 1963, 137–38; Blu 1980, 77–90; Borowich 1996, 60–65, 74–83; Thornton 1987, 210–12; Census 1980).

Groups such as the Jackson Whites and the Issues have succeeded in negotiating alternative identities as "other non-whites" (Berry 1963, 157, 163; Census 1980). Although some individuals have always passed for white, groups such as the Brass Ankles and the Melungeons, who fought for white legal status, succeeded in their local communities, if not with the government (Berry 1963, 185–86, 190; Blu 1980, 43, 182).[3] Other communities have enjoyed a status just below that of whites; elsewhere their status has been hardly distinguishable from that of blacks. Overall, they seem to have occupied a status intermediate to both. The costs incurred have included the denial of African ancestry, sometimes the casting-off of darker relatives, and the avoidance of any suspicion of association with blacks (Berry 1963, 173, 188).

The French Resistance

The history of multiracial individuals in Louisiana and the Gulf ports after annexation by the United States is in many ways a synthesis of other strategies of resistance to the one-drop rule. Nevertheless, the region displays unique features of its own, stemming largely from the fact that the early patterns of settlement in the U.S. Lower South followed the Latin American model (Berlin 1974, 108–32; Mencke 1979, 10–11; Hall 1992b, 58–90; Williamson 1980, 14–15). The comparatively more favorable circumstances in this region began to change following U.S. annexation during the early part of the nineteenth century. With the concomitant extension of the one-drop rule, Creoles of color began the long quest to preserve their intermediate status, as they watched Louisiana's ternary racial order polarize into black and white (Domínguez 1986, 28–50, 134–40; Gould 1996, 28–50; Logsdon and Bell 1992, 201–61).

By the time of the Civil War, the ethnocultural tension between Anglo Americans and Creoles of European descent abated as both groups united in support of white racial purity and devised criteria in which Creole was redefined as having only Spanish and French ancestry (Domínguez 1986, 141–48, 150–53). Abandoned by their white brethren, many Creoles of color nevertheless had a vested interest in the Southern way of life (close to one in three families owned slaves) and thus supported the Confederacy in a desperate attempt to arrest further erosion of their status (Haskins 1975, 50; Rankin 1977–78, 387). With the Union capture of New Orleans, most switched their loyalties, hoping that with emancipation, racial prejudice also would fall. However, Union victory not only brought a loss of wealth and property but also furthered the deterioration of their status, because all individuals of African descent were now free. Many Creoles of color resisted this decline by denying any similarity or community of interests with ex-slaves and English-speaking African Americans. Others, benefiting from the generational inheritance of social, cultural, and intellectual advantages, provided a majority

---

3. Since the late 1990s there has been a change in these attitudes. This "new" Melungeon identity seeks to deconstruct the hierarchical premises upon which the "old" Melungeon identity rested by acknowledging and embracing African ancestry (see http://www.melungeons.org/).

of the political leadership of the black masses, serving as state senators, representatives, and even state officials in the Reconstruction government (Domínguez 1986, 134–37; Haskins 1975, 50–57).

This struggle reached a crescendo with the implementation of Jim Crow segregation and other discriminatory practices. A number of prominent Creoles of color retained the hope that something could be done to rescind these unjust laws, retain the hard-won franchise, and arrest the segregationist tide (Logsdon and Bell 1992, 204). In 1891, they formed the Comité des Citoyens (Citizens' Committee), with the goal of mobilizing Creole resistance to state-imposed segregation (Bell 1997, 280–81). One of the Committee's first acts was to test the constitutionality of a railroad segregation statute—the 1890 Louisiana Separate Car Law—that required individuals of African descent to ride in special streetcars and railway carriages (Haskins 1975, 61). The Committee chose Hommeré A. Plessy, a young Creole artisan and community activist—who was of one-eighth African descent and thus indistinguishable from European Americans—as the perfect candidate to challenge the absurdity of this type of segregation.

The Citizens' Committee, in cooperation with the *Crusader* newspaper, was the vehicle for negotiation on behalf of New Orleans's Creoles of color. On June 7, 1892, the Committee set its plan in motion when Plessy boarded the East Louisiana Railway in New Orleans and took a seat in the segregated white coach of the train. When approached by the conductor for his fare, Plessy declared himself to be an individual of African descent. He was asked to move to the car reserved for coloreds but refused. He was arrested, removed from the train, and fined (Bell 1997, 280; Davis 1991, 8–9, 52–53; Olsen 1967, 112).

Plessy was bound over to the criminal court of the parish of New Orleans. His plea, presented by his attorney, James C. Walker, but probably written by another attorney, Albion W. Tourgée, contained fourteen specific objections to the segregation statute. Among these was the argument that "the Statute impairs the right of passengers of the class to which Relator [Plessy] belongs, to wit: Octoroons, to be classed among white persons, although color be not discernible in the complexion, and makes penal their refusal to abide by the decision of a Railroad conductor in this respect" (Olsen 1967, 74).

With Plessy's arrest, the Committee asserted the separate-car law abridged "the privileges and immunities of the Citizens of the United States and the rights secured by the 13th and 14th Amendments to the Federal Constitution" (Olsen 1967, 280–81). Plessy and his supporters took his case to the local court. They won their first suit against the separate-car law for trains that crossed the state borders, but the law was upheld on appeal (Olsen 1967, 81–85).

Part of Plessy's case rested on the question of racial definition. In the "Brief for Hommeré Plessy" prepared by Tourgée, the issue was raised to point out the arbitrary nature of the racial classification and to challenge the state's (or anyone's) authority to define blackness:

> Is not the question of race, scientifically considered, very often impossible of determination?
>
> Is not the question of race, legally considered, one impossible to be determined, in the absence of statutory definition? . . .
>
> The Court will take notice of the fact that, in all parts of the country, race-mixture has proceeded to such an extent that there are great numbers of citizens in whom the preponderance of blood of one race or another, is impossible of ascertainment, except by careful scrutiny of the pedigree. . . .
>
> But even if it were possible to determine preponderance of blood and so determine racial character in certain cases, what should be said of those cases in which the race admixture is equal. Are they white or colored?
>
> There is no law of the United States, or of the State of Louisiana defining the limits of race—who are white and who are "colored." By what rule then shall any tribunal be guided in determining racial character? It may be said that all those should be classified as colored in whom appears a visible admixture of colored blood. By what law? With what justice? Why not count every one as white in whom is visible any trace of white blood? There is but one reason, to wit, the domination of the white race. (Olsen 1967, 81–85)

The argument was not that someone such as Plessy was entitled to the rights and privileges accorded to European Americans because he was predominantly white and his African ancestry was indiscernible. Rather, Plessy and his counsel were indicting the legality of enforced segregation. The brief identified the fact that racial segregation was based on the patently absurd notion that a trace of African ancestry could disqualify a person from the rights of equal citizenship.

When state courts denied Plessy's arguments against the 1890 law, the Committee proceeded to the nation's highest court (Olsen 1967, 81–85). On May 19, 1896, the Supreme Court not only upheld the lower court's decision but also gave constitutional sanction to the "separate but equal" doctrine. It denied that segregation was oppressive as long as facilities were equally maintained. However, the Court made no formal judgment on the legal definition of blackness. Considering that definitions varied from state to state, such a ruling would have been beyond its jurisdiction. Instead, the Court took what might be called informal judicial notice of what it assumed to be racial commonsense: an African American was anyone with any traceable amount of African American descent (Davis 1991, 8–9, 52–53; Davis 2001, 193–94; Olsen 1967, 112). Thus, the Plessy decision set a judicial precedent for future court rulings on legal definitions of blackness. In accordance with the decision, Plessy appeared before the New Orleans's Criminal District Court in January 1897, pled guilty, paid a fine of $25, and was discharged (Olsen 1967, 81–85).

Creoles of color, who prior to the 1890s had enjoyed a status separate from blacks, were dealt the final blow by the full installation of segregation and suddenly found themselves pushed into the larger African American community. Those who did not welcome the changes left for Mexico and the Caribbean, where racial lines were more fluid, and where color, rather than ancestry, was the primary criterion used to define race. Others moved to Florida, Kansas, and particularly California, where they crossed the racial divide or formed Creole residential enclaves. Many went north, where they passed for white. A smaller number passed for white in Louisiana by destroying the birth records in St. Louis Cathedral (the only legal proof of their ancestry). It has been estimated that in Louisiana, probably one hundered to five hundred African-descent Americans crossed the racial divide every year from 1875 to the 1890s. In a desperate search for solace and seclusion, still others refused to learn English, remained staunchly Catholic, and sought refuge within the narrow confines of their own world in New Orleans north of Canal Street, particularly in the Seventh Ward (Domínguez 1986, 223–24; Haskins 1975, 64). Over time, the multiracial clan of Metoyers on Cane River emerged as a pluralistic enclave (Mills 1977, xvii–xxx, 247–50; Williamson 1980, 21–22). In both cases, this racial seclusion was often accompanied by a rejection of association with both whites and blacks, as well as a denial of African ancestry, similar to many of the triracial isolate communities.

The Culture of Racial Resistance: White Domination and a "War of Maneuver"

Even during the most oppressive periods of U.S. race relations, multiracial individuals have countered with their own forms of organization and identity. Some have moved inward to the relative safety of their own exclusive (and excluded) communities. Others have chosen to move outward to the margins of society. However, in both cases, isolation deprived them of a power base from which to oppose or participate in the mainstream political process.

Like their black and multiracial counterparts in Brazil, multiracial individuals in the United States prior to the civil rights movement engaged in a *war of maneuver*. Confronting a dictatorial and comprehensively dominant power, multiracial individuals, like all subordinated "Others," devoted themselves primarily to racial projects aimed at self-preservation (Omi and Winant 1994, 80–81). These *war of maneuver* tactics included everyday, small-scale, or individual forms of opposition, such as passing. They also entailed larger-scale collective challenges, such as those mounted by multiracial elites societies, which allowed multiracial individuals to develop an internal society as an alternative to the repressive racial order. Generated by racist pressure that has rewarded whiteness and punished blackness, the tactics of resistance devised by multiracial individuals were prompted less by the forced denial of their European American ancestry than by the subordination they experienced and the denial of privileges that such ancestry is supposed to guarantee.

Subverting the One-Drop Rule

The goal of passing, as reflected in its political initiative, has been primarily utilitarian—that is, to gain access to social and economic opportunities of the dominant European American culture. The cultural initiative of passing is perhaps its most subversive aspect (Stonequist 1937, 193). Passing has been associated primarily with the adoption of a "fraudulent" white racial identity by an individual who is defined as African American according to the customary social and legal definitions of blackness based on rules of hypodescent. Thus, passing has necessarily involved moving away from one's previous life as African American, both in terms of space (geographically) and time (one's experiential past). If European Americans have historically maintained a "possessive investment" (Lipsitz 1998, vii) in "whiteness as property" (Harris 1995, 276–91), then passers have crossed the racial divide—and indeed "trespassed" (Ginsberg, 1996:3)—to become "racial thieves" (Daniel 2002, 83). They have pirated an identity that allows them to escape racial subordination and gain privileges and status that are not "rightfully" theirs (Ginsberg 1996, 3–5).

Passing also questions several problematical assumptions, including the notion that identity categories such as race are inherent and unalterable essences. Indeed, the cultural logic of passing is posited on a supposedly more "authentic" and "true" African American identity that existed prior to the assumption of a "false" white identity. However, passing not only exposes racial difference as a continually emerging distinction devoid of any essential content but also reduces whiteness to the realm of histrionics. It attests to the fact that whiteness can be enacted, donned, or even discredited, if not convincingly performed. This shows the anxieties about racial status and hierarchy created by the potential of boundary violation by someone who has mastered the art of racial cross-dressing and disguise (Ginsberg 1996, 3–5).

Moreover, the discursive dimension of passing challenges the "race-as-objective-reality position," which presupposes that race is fixed in biological fact. Race is supposedly visible in phenotypical features such as skin and hair color—epidermal schema of racial difference. Indeed, difference (or "otherness"), in this case "race," must be seen to be guarded against, for if it cannot be seen, then one's own identity can be called into question. Passing therefore forces reconsideration of the cultural association of the physical body with race, and of the assumed visibility of this identity category, while calling into question the whole notion of a true (or authentic) and false identity (Ginsberg 1996, 16).

Collective racial projects such as the formation of blue-vein societies composed of multiracial elites were a cultural initiative that sought to rescue multiracial identities from distortion and erasure by the dominant society. They also entailed a political initiative that sought to counter systematic subordination and the arbitrary line between white and black through the formation of pluralistic elites within the African American community. By emphasizing light skin, straight hair, and narrow features, as well as European culture and thought—including gentility and social discretion—multiracial individuals formed elite societies that made it possible to distance themselves from the image typically associated with blacks. Moreover, this "genteel performance" allowed them to achieve vicarious, if not actual, parity with whites (Gatewood 1990, 182).

The political initiative of the multiracial elites was aimed at economic gain, enfranchisement, and so on. Even as they championed the struggle for the rights of the black masses, the multiracial elites maintained at least an implicit bias toward the dominant psychosomatic norm image to support their own self-interest. They argued that their sociocultural and physical whiteness entitled them to special privileges and made them more deserving than blacks of full integration into the U.S. mainstream. Having internalized Eurocentrism and the oppression embedded in the U.S. racial order, this elite became perpetrators of a divisive and pernicious "colorism" among individuals of African descent, which had significant socioeconomic implications. Yet by recreating the dominant norm image through the formation of blue-vein societies within the subordinate African American community, the multiracial elite also brought into sharp focus the illogic of hypodescent, which deemed as inferior, and as "black," individuals who were white in every visible respect (Gatewood 1990, 67–68, 347–48).

The multiracial elite, small and lacking vast wealth or power, lived largely in a state of racial denial. They convinced themselves that they were achieving acceptance among European Americans and could make similar gains for the black masses (Gatewood 1990, 67–68, 347–48). This elite never abandoned its mission of service to and racial uplift of less privileged African Americans. This legacy, despite its value, is diminished by the negative consequences of the colorism that they also bequeathed to subsequent generations of African Americans.

Passing, along with the formation of blue-vein societies by multiracial elites, challenged the binary racial project and subverted the one-drop rule, but neither actually broke the rule. In fact, both tactics confirmed the enduring power of this rule and the racial order it supported. These projects also tended to be Eurocentric and maintained the hierarchical relationship between whiteness and blackness characteristic of the racial order. Nevertheless, passing and the formation of blue-vein societies should be seen as legitimate tactics in the struggle against racial oppression.

Breaking the One-Drop Rule

Other collective racial projects, such as the triracial isolates and the Louisiana Creoles of color, implemented more extreme tactics than the blue-vein societies. The formation of blue-vein societies made it possible for multiracial elites to use their racial and cultural whiteness to challenge the legal liabilities attached to the social designation of blackness. Regarding themselves, however tenuously, as part of the larger African American community, the multiracial elite sought to maximize their legal rights, and the rights of the black masses by extension, without necessarily seeking to overturn official racial classifications that buttressed social inequities.

The triracial isolates and the Louisiana Creoles of color, by contrast, challenged these social inequities through the formation of alternative communities "outside" the social and cultural parameters of the African American community. Triracial isolate appeals for changes in official racial classification have been supported by a political initiative aimed at securing separate schools, enfranchisement, government benefits, and so on. Taking into account the historical importance of the state in the politics of racial exclusion, particularly in enforcing racial definitions, these communities have often called upon it to play a significant role in the pursuit of these goals. Though some groups eventually succeeded in officially changing their earlier classification as mulattoes to nontreaty Native Americans, they were still excluded from most government benefits. Nevertheless, they staked a claim on the indigenous side of the racial divide. However, entries on the census indicating identification with most of these rural multiracial enclaves have remained in the "other" category since the 1970 census (Thornton 1987, 210–12; Census 1970, 1980, 1992).

Unlike the triracial isolates, the Louisiana Creoles of color have not pursued changes in official racial classification that would place them outside the parameters of legally defined blackness. At their most extreme, the Louisiana Creoles sought to counter systematic subordination and to compensate for the arbitrary racial divide perpetuated by the rule of hypodescent through the formation of communities that operated on the periphery of both the black and white communities. Accordingly, they have viewed themselves, and sometimes been viewed in turn, as a racially intermediate group separate from blacks and whites in a manner similar to the triracial isolates.

In 1910, the Louisiana Supreme Court distinguished between the terms "negro" and "person of color" to designate black and multiracial individuals (Gatewood 1990, 84), although these official distinctions had few legal implications. Moreover, they did not appear to have made a significant difference in the everyday treatment of Creoles of color. Indeed, for the better part of the twentieth century, they have been considered legally black. They have accordingly been subjected to the indignities of blackness even when they have considered themselves, and been considered by others, as an elite stratum or a French cultural variant within a larger "pan–African American" community.

This trend has been mirrored in the census, where in 1970, "Creole" write-in entries in the race question were reassigned to the "black" category if the respondent resided in Louisiana. Outside this region, the entry remained in the "other" category. In 1980, this write-in entry was recoded as black, regardless of location (Census 1970, 1980). Yet by emphasizing their light skin, straight hair, and narrow features, as well as Catholicism and French culture and thought, Louisiana Creoles of color have been able to cushion the impact of their legal blackness, and (like blue-vein societies) achieve at least vicarious, if not actual parity, with whites (Berzon 1978, 162–87). However, radical Creoles of color (e.g., the Citizens' Committee) argued neither for white status nor for an intermediate status that carried with it some of the legal rights and privileges of whiteness. Despite the elitism that has characterized the self-identity of Louisiana Creoles of color, these radicals focused on issues of racial composition to show the arbitrary nature of racial classification and to challenge anyone's authority to define blackness (Mencke 1979, 3, 23–24; Williamson 1980, 81, 87–88).

The formation of the Louisiana Creoles of color and triracial isolates, like passing and the formation of blue-vein societies, was motivated by the legal system of segregation or inegalitarian pluralism that sought to control the potential threat to white dominance posed by individuals of African descent. Although the triracial isolates and Louisiana Creoles of color did not dismantle the one-drop rule, they were successful in varying degrees at breaking the rule. They thus created alternative third identities (or ternary racial projects) in a manner similar to Brazil that challenged the U.S. binary racial project, as well as the comportment line between blacks and whites. Yet all these tactics of resistance had an inegalitarian dynamic that has generally involved contesting the dichotomization of blackness and whiteness but maintaining the hierarchical valuation of whiteness over blackness.

part two CONVERGING PATHS

six A NEW U.S. RACIAL ORDER

The Demise of Jim Crow Segregation

The Civil Rights Movement: Integrating the Public Sphere

From the end of Reconstruction through the first half of the twentieth century, the U.S. social order was rife with tension generated by conflict between the American and racial creeds. Supporters of the former envisioned the full integration of all individuals as equals into the mainstream of society. Adherents of the latter enforced a racial contract premised on inegalitarian pluralist exclusionary policies. Neither side was successful in eclipsing the power of the other. In the South, most states immediately grasped the import of the Supreme Court decisions supporting the racial creed's "separate but equal" doctrine. They expanded the institutional area of practice and behavior that came under the jurisdiction of this doctrine—the social realm. However, they sought to do this without trespassing into the institutional area still protected by the American creed—the legal-political realm (Fuchs 1990, 152–54; Ringer 1983, 246–47).

The efforts by some Southern states to breach this limit head-on were met with punitive court rulings. Still, devices as "literacy," "understanding," and "grandfather" clauses circumvented the application of the American creed's tenets (e.g., voting rights). These tactics excluded African Americans from the people's domain, placing them beyond the reaches of the American creed. Ultimately, these machinations proved vulnerable because the Court never completely abandoned the Fourteenth and Fifteenth Amendments, although the Court's commitment during this period to protecting the political and legal rights of African Americans appeared to be more fiction than fact (Fuchs 1990, 152–54; Ringer 1983, 247).

In the North, the conflict between the two creeds was more intricate. The American creed seemed to be dominant, since the Northern states did not have Jim Crow statutes. Yet European Americans in the North practiced a de facto inegalitarian pluralism, which reaffirmed the racial creed, albeit in a more informal or "segmented" manner (Ringer 1983, 251). Despite laws requiring equal access in public accommodations, European Americans were unwilling either to extend to African Americans full membership in the social realm or allow them to compete as equals in the pursuit of wealth, power, privilege, and prestige. Northern whites effectively eliminated African Americans as competitors by only hiring them for low-paying jobs and only selling or renting homes to them in residential areas with the least desirable housing (247–51).

The legal framework created by the Supreme Court delineated a private sector within the people's domain, which gave European Americans in the North license to exclude African Americans from European American places of employment and residential communities. In addition, the local courts were placed at the disposal of European Americans to enforce various private exclusionary agreements, such as restrictive covenants in housing. This racial segmentation was solidified with the Great Migration of African Americans northward during and after World War I. These dynamics, along with the hardening of racial segregation in the South, generated a national climate of racial fear. African Americans not only expressed public indignation at the implementation of the "separate but equal" doctrine but also balked at compliance with its mandates. European Americans in the South responded with repressive legal and extralegal tactics to keep African Americans "in their place." In the North, racial tensions exploded in a series of violent urban riots. Yet increasing racial segmentation in employment and housing limited direct contact, which in turn prevented overt racial conflict from exceeding certain limits (Ringer 1983, 215–16, 251–52, 276–85).

Even as the Supreme Court gave legal sanction to the "separate but equal" doctrine in the Southern states, it limited how much European Americans could constitutionally deprive African Americans of the legal-political rights gained through the Reconstruction amendments. Nevertheless, for years, states were considered to have exceeded these limits only if they approved statutes that explicitly violated these legal-political rights or in which the racially discriminatory purpose was obvious, despite claims of universal applicability (e.g., the grandfather clauses) (Ringer 1983, 286–87, 296).

In addition to challenging state legislation, the Court maintained that discriminatory actions of state officials should not be treated as those of private individuals exempted from compliance with constitutional mandates. Rather, they were to be considered behaviors of state agents and therefore under the jurisdiction of the Constitution. Furthermore, the Court expanded the meaning of agent or agency of the state to encompass political parties and voluntary associations the state had charged with electoral responsibilities. Accordingly, it shifted some of the state's functions to organizations in the private realm that were exempt from such constitutional mandates. The Court thus rejected any attempts by the states to sidestep their constitutional responsibilities to African Americans in the legal-political realm. Only beginning in the 1930s and 1940s did the Court decisively challenge state actions that had discriminatory consequences but in fact had no explicit legislative purpose to discriminate. For example, any continuous pattern of exclusion or significant underrepresentation of African Americans on jury service was increasingly considered "prima facie" evidence of discriminatory action by the state (Ringer 1983, 286–88, 296). Moreover, the Court expressed a greater inclination to limit the power of the state in areas formerly considered under its jurisdiction. It declared unconstitutional the racially exclusionary practices of the "White primary," which were designed to prevent blacks from choosing candidates for office. The Court also extended its rulings to all elections and primaries, not just those relating to federal office (Bloom 1987, 89–90; Ringer 1983, 291–97).

Despite the Supreme Court's heightened determination during the 1940s to apply nondiscriminatory standards in the legal-political domain, it still accepted inegalitarian pluralism in the form of de facto racial segmentation and de jure segregation in the social realm. As long as the Court failed to address the unequal treatment of African Americans in the social realm, it could not prevent racial inequities from seeping into the legal-political domain (Fuchs 1990, 152–54; Ringer 1983, 297). Though the Court had originally maintained that separation in the social realm must be founded on equal availability and quality of public resources and facilities, Southern whites over the next five decades focused exclusively on the principle of separation. Meanwhile, the Court itself appeared more focused on reaffirming and strengthening this principle than on addressing the question of equality (298).

Since the founding of civil rights organizations in the early part of the century, such as the NAACP, African Americans focused on the "equal" part of the Plessy doctrine. Aware that European Americans would be unwilling to devote the resources necessary to maintain two separate and equal societies, activists and civil rights attorneys waged a legal battle to set a judicial precedent that would test, and ultimately overturn, the constitutionality of the separate but equal doctrine. After several decades of agitation and litigation against Jim Crow segregation, the results were coming to fruition by the middle of the twentieth century. By the late 1930s and early 1940s, the Court began to investigate the "equal" part of "separate but equal" and found that failure of the state to meet standards of equity undermined the legitimacy of maintaining racial separation (Fuchs 1990, 153; Ringer 1983, 298, 301–12).

By midcentury, the United States began to move toward official repudiation of legal inegalitarian pluralism. In 1948, President Truman issued a presidential decree ending segregation in the Armed Forces and the federal civil service. After the end of World War II the NAACP's Legal Defense and Education Fund, under the leadership of Charles Hamilton Houston and his protégé Thurgood Marshall, set its sights on winning a case that would overturn Plessy. In 1952, a brief was filed with the Supreme Court leading to the Court's 1954 decision ending segregation in public schools—*Brown v. Board of Education*. Chief Justice Warren, speaking for a unanimous Court, declared that separate was inherently unequal and therefore unconstitutional. With this decision, the Court undermined the legal foundations of inegalitarian pluralism and stripped the racial creed of its constitutional scaffolding (Fuchs 1990, 157–58; Ringer 1983, 308–10, 346–54). The *Brown* ruling thus became the benchmark for other court decisions that delegitimized racial inegalitarian pluralism—whether in the form of segmentation or legalized segregation—in all the major institutional domains of the social realm, from public transportation to public recreation. In addition, the Court withdrew the apparatus of the state from supporting those practicing discrimination in the private sphere, depriving them of access to mechanisms of legal coercion and political control (Bloom 1987, 89–91; Ringer 1983, 311, 318–20).

White officials in some border states immediately endeavored to comply, in part, with *Brown*. However, whites in the Deep South—including elected state and local government officials and private citizens—denounced the federal government, which they alleged had usurped its power through the Supreme Court. They defied the Court's edicts and revived the doctrines of "interposition and nullification" (Ringer 1983, 426), which harked back to the period leading up to the Civil War (Bloom 1987, 96–101). Over the next decade, tensions grew as the Court pushed to delegitimize the racial creed into the farthest reaches institutionally, in the social realm, and geographically, in the South (Ringer 1983, 425).

In 1955, African Americans boycotted segregated buses in Montgomery, Alabama, the first in a series of events that over the coming decade brought Dr. Martin Luther King Jr. to the forefront of the civil rights struggle. King was aware that African American pressure would need the backing of the Supreme Court (Ringer 1983, 442–48). As the civil rights movement launched its campaign of "civil disobedience" in the South, it became apparent that even the backing of the Court was not enough to overcome white resistance. African Americans would need the full measure of federal authority, including the executive and legislative branches, while simultaneously forging a national coalition with European American liberals in the North (442–48, 461–62). This strategy culminated in the 1963 March on Washington, which forced President Kennedy to become an active participant in the question of civil rights. Kennedy introduced legislative proposals for the landmark Civil Rights Act of 1964, which ironically was passed as a direct consequence of his assassination. Subsequent brutality during the voter registration drive in Selma, Alabama, not only elicited cries of indignation across the nation but also prompted President Johnson to submit a voting rights bill to Congress with the force absent from all previous voting rights legislation (445–62).

The 1964 Civil Rights Act, the 1965 Voting Rights Act, and the Fair Housing Act of 1968 were part of a legislative package mandating that all institutional aspects of the people's domain were to be governed under a common legal-normative framework based on the American creed. The task that had begun during the "First Reconstruction" had been completed almost one hundred years later in the "Second Reconstruction." This shift was directly linked to the combined pressures of the civil rights movement and its interracial coalition, as well as the nationwide revulsion against the racial brutality of the Deep South, which was engendered by television news coverage of the civil rights struggle (Fuchs 1990, 159–68; Ringer 1983, 327–39).

Equal But Separate: The Racial Creed and the New Pluralism

The early civil rights movement had integration as its goal. The NAACP, National Urban League, and Southern Christian Leadership Conference (SCLC) sought the integration of all individuals as equals under the tenets of the American creed. The movement initially focused its energies on the Southeast, where whites opposed integration most viciously (Omi and Winant 1994, 96–97). At the time, racial injustice was generally understood to be a matter of prejudiced attitudes or bigotry. In the liberal tradition of Myrdal (1944), the solution to the "American Dilemma" was believed to reside in the abolition of discriminatory practices, which would involve overcoming such attitudes, and the achievement of tolerance, specifically among European Americans. Thus, the early civil rights movement reflected these views and sought to overcome racial prejudice by appealing to the moral conscience of the nation (Omi and Winant 1994, 69).

The limitations of the integrationist vision were revealed when a wave of uprisings swept across the urban central cities outside the Southeast, in places like Los Angeles, Detroit, Newark, and Washington, D.C., from 1964 to 1968. These uprisings not only exposed de facto inegalitarian pluralism but also led to a tactical shift in the African American struggle for equality. Radical organizations, such as the Student Nonviolent Coordinating Committee (SNCC) and the Black Panthers, rejected the integrationism of Martin Luther King and advocated Black Nationalism, Black separatism, and Black power (inspiring similar rhetoric among other communities of color—such as "brown power" among Latinas/os, "red power" among Native Americans, and "yellow power" among Asian Americans). These groups argued that racism excluded people of color from the protections guaranteed by the American creed and the nation's founding documents. Communities of color, they maintained, were doomed to perpetual dehumanization and exploitation as subordinated and excluded racial groups (Omi and Winant 1994, 101–4).

This ideology drew parallels between African Americans (and other communities of color in the United States) and colonized people of the Third World. This "colonial analogy" emerged in the 1960s as the rallying cry for Malcolm X, Kwame Touré (formerly Stokely Carmichael), and the Black Panther Party. It also caught the attention of scholars such as Robert Blauner, Robert L. Allen, William K. Tabb, and others, who reframed the experiences of people of color in the United States as a form of "internal colonialism" (Ringer 1983, 531). In this way, the colonial analogy gained a "respectability" and scholarly pedigree (Bloom 1987, 186–213; Fuchs 1990, 184–89; Ringer 1983, 466–559).

According to the colonial analogy racial inequality and injustice are not simply products of individual prejudice and discriminatory behavior. Prejudice and discrimination have deeper roots and are embedded in the very structure of society; they are the products of centuries of systematic exclusion and exploitation of racially defined "minorities." Thus, the combination of prejudice and discrimination, along with the institutionalized power to enforce them, defined the concept of "racism" at the end of the 1960s. In turn, the term "racism" (which had surfaced occasionally in the past) increasingly became part of the lexicon of racial "common sense" (Omi and Winant 1994, 101–4).

By the late 1960s, the ambiguous success of the civil rights movement had led to a redefinition of the meaning of racial inequality and to a break with the integrationist vision of leaders like Dr. King. Integration had become identified with the problematic concept of "the melting pot" and was too approximate, in the view of more radical thinkers, to assimilation, or inegalitarian integration. The melting-pot ideology, by which immigrants were expected to assimilate themselves into the dominant Anglo-Protestant culture, worked well enough for most European immigrants and their descendants but effectively excluded individuals of color. In practice, the melting pot meant assimilation for European-descent individuals and apartheid for groups perceived as racially different. Consequently, these pluralists were suspicious of any notion of integration without a critique of hierarchy. Many felt that the best way for any oppressed group to achieve equality was to recover their collective sense of self through a process of dissimilation that would create intergroup accommodation of mutually respectful and separate racial and ethnic groups with equal status in both law and fact (Omi and Winant 1994, 101–4). In this new scenario, group pluralism was envisioned as voluntary, rather than mandated and enforced by European Americans under state-sanctioned apartheid. More important, if people of color chose to integrate, they would do so with the bargaining power of equals.

Compensatory programs such as affirmative action are needed to redress the injustices of the past. Like the racial creed, affirmative action requires that one take racial differences into account; both are pluralistic. Unlike the racial creed, which is inegalitarian, the purpose of affirmative action is not to exclude individuals on the basis of racial group membership, or to submerge their group identity, but to permit them for the first time to enjoy the rights promised to all under the American creed. Affirmative action, therefore, was a response to these previous and continuing race-conscious attitudes and policies, in order to achieve equality without denying difference. And although affirmative action and other programs represented the culmination of African American protest, it was not until the late 1960s and the advent of black militancy that African Americans were able to exert the political pressure necessary for their implementation.

Generally speaking, those individuals who supported integration, in contrast to those who supported pluralism, sought to redefine (or reaffirm) universal humanism and support democratic principles of individual free association. They acknowledged the legacy of racism without perpetuating the Manichaean distinction between "white guilt" and people of color as "innocent victims." Nevertheless, integrationists often predicated their vision on a myopic understanding of egalitarian pluralism. Many believed that focusing on epidermal differences reinforced a divisive us/them dynamic that undermined basic democratic principles. Consequently, they frequently misunderstood the admittedly abrasive and often chauvinistic rhetoric of many radical pluralists. They interpreted what was actually a defensive stance against racial oppression premised on egalitarian pluralism as an offensive maneuver to overthrow European American domination and replace it with a new domination by people of color (column e in Figure 1).

Some integrationists also erroneously believed that the repudiation of white supremacy and the elimination of legal discrimination had caused race to decline in significance. Many were coming to view government enforcement of anti-discrimination regulations as detrimental rather than helpful. Some even argued that government programs were contrary to the American creed and had gone too far in "balancing" the scales of racial justice, leading to "reverse discrimination" against whites.

By the 1970s, the racial movements of the previous two decades had lost their vitality and coherence as the result of repression, co-optation, and fragmentation. Meanwhile, the economic, political, and cultural crises of the 1970s eroded the clarity in the terms "racism" and "racial discrimination" and led to a backlash by conservative forces that attempted to dismantle the moderate gains that had been achieved. Despite such setbacks, the race-based movements of the 1950s and 1960s set the stage for the general reorganization of U.S. politics and created "the great transformation" of racial awareness (Omi and Winant 1994, 96). Race was henceforth considered a preeminently social phenomenon, something that not only penetrated state institutions and market relationships but also shaped individual identities, families, and communities. The racial movements of the period, therefore, were the first "new social movements" to extend the concerns of politics to the terrain of everyday life. The goals, particularly those formed around identity politics, did not seek merely to resist the oppressive racial order or to bring about greater material rewards but rather to transform racial identities by dismantling the oppression and marginality embedded in them (Darnovsky, Epstein, and Flacks 1995, xii–xv; Hunter 1995, 320–46; Johnston, Laraña, and Gusfield 1994, 7).

Taken together, these two interrelated dimensions—the critique of the integrationist paradigm as assimilationist and the emergence of new social movement politics premised on egalitarian pluralism—constitute an oppositional framework by which to assess the racial politics of the 1960s. However, the subsequent waning of the movements articulating oppositional paradigms left a vacuum in racial theory and politics. This opened the political space for the resurgence of the assimilation paradigm in the 1980s. Nevertheless, the persistence of the racial meanings and new racial identities that developed during the 1960s continue to shape politics. They remain the most formidable obstacles to the consolidation of a new oppressive racial order based on the overwhelmingly dictatorial racism of the past. The movements themselves could disintegrate, the policies for which they fought could be reversed, and their leaders could be co-opted or destroyed. Yet the new racial collective subjectivities they forged during the 1960s and 1970s have endured (Omi and Winant 1994, 90).

The *Loving* Decision: Integrating the Private Sphere

The dismantling of Jim Crow segregation and the implementation of civil rights legislation during the 1950s and 1960s dissolved the formal apparatus barring individuals of African descent from interacting with whites as equals within both the public and private spheres. The greater frequency of whites and blacks living in the same neighborhoods, working in the same offices, and attending the same educational institutions led to increased friendships, dating, and intermarriage across traditional racial/cultural boundaries (Davis 1991, 68–73; Roberts 1994, 57–74; Spickard 1989, 278–79; Tucker and Mitchell-Kernan 1990, 209–19). By 1967, the number of marriages between African Americans and European Americans were increasing in the North and the West. Meanwhile, legal prohibitions against such marriages remained on the books of only the seventeen Southern and Border states.

In March 1967, Maryland (which, along with Virginia, had been among the first to ban miscegenation) repealed its law. On June 12, 1967, the U.S. Supreme Court, in the case of *Loving v. Commonwealth of Virginia*, which involved interracial couple Mildred Jeter (an African-descent American) and Richard Perry Loving (a European American), ruled unanimously that the Virginia statute violated the equal protection clause of the Fourteenth Amendment (Roberts 1994, 57–74). The *Loving* decision overturned several centuries of legalized barriers to interracial marriage. Along with the Fair Housing Act of 1968, it was part of the dismantling of apartheid in the private structural sphere and followed the elimination of all other forms of legalized racial discrimination and segregation in the public sphere.

The *Loving* decision was not accompanied in the South by massive resistance or violence, as had been the case in the aftermath of the *Brown* decision and the passage of the Voting Rights Act. Several states, nevertheless, were slow in nullifying their statutes, and federal and state courts found it necessary to direct defiant clerks and registrars to issue licenses to interracial couples. If this decision was not received with massive backlash in the South, data collected by Robert E.T. Roberts indicate there was neither an immediate upsurge in black-white interracial marriages (Roberts 1994, 57–74). In the 1960 census, there were 51,000 black-white couples in the United States; in the 1970 census, there were about 65,000 black-white unions among the nation's 321,000 interracial couples. By the 1980s, the number of interracial couples was approaching 1 million, including 599,000 white-"other race" unions and some 167,000 black-white unions. According to census data the number of interracial couples steadily increased such that by the 1990s there were approximately 1.5 million interracial unions, of which 883,000 were white-"other race" unions (most of whom identified as Latina/o) and 246,000 were between blacks and whites (Funderburg 1994, 26; Lee and Bean 2004, 228–29; Monroe 1990, 14; Taylor-Gibbs 1989, 323; Tucker and Mitchell-Kernan 1990, 209–19). Data from the 2000 census reveal that the number of married couples with partners of different races had risen to approximately 3.1 million, of which 335,308 were black-white unions (Frey 2003, 7; Census 2000).[1]

---

1. The 2000 census data are not directly comparable with 1990 (or earlier) census data, because the Census Bureau did not previously differentiate between unmarried and married couples in reporting data on interracial unions. For the 2000 census, the Census Bureau reported separate figures for married and unmarried interracial couples, including figures for same-sex couples (Simmons and O'Connell 2003; Tavia Simmons, U.S. Census Bureau, Fertility and Family Statistics Branch, pers. comm., April 28, 2005).

Despite this substantial increase nationally over the decades since the *Loving* decision, states with the lowest percentages of African Americans have the highest percentages of African American men and women who outmarry, whereas nationwide very low percentages of white women and men marry African Americans. As a result, in the South, where there is a high concentration of African Americans, the percentage of African Americans and European Americans who are interracially married is far lower than other geographic regions.

According to 1970, 1980, and 1990 census data, the percentage of European American husbands with African American wives increased slightly, while the percentage of black husbands with white wives more than doubled.[2] Although marriages of black grooms to white brides are far more numerous than those of white grooms to black brides, there are regional differences as well as changes over the years. For example, in New England during the late nineteenth century the first combination exceeded the second by a large margin. During and after Reconstruction, when intermarriage was permitted in the South for a brief period during the 1870s and 1880s, most interracial marriages were between European American males and African American females. This pattern prevailed in the District of Columbia before 1940 but has since reversed. In 1990, the groom was black and the bride white in 65 to 75 percent of marriages between blacks and whites in states where more than 8 percent of all marriages included black partners. This combination ranged from about 80 to well above 90 percent of marriages between blacks and whites in states where not more than 1.2 percent of marriages included a black partner (Roberts 1994, 59–74).

Since 1967, black male–white female marriage has predominated in the South, but to a lesser extent than elsewhere. A much higher percentage of intermarried African American husbands and European American wives reside in the West than in other regions. Moreover, higher proportions of European American husbands with African American wives reside in the Northeast and West than in the South and North Central regions. These trends are particularly true in urban centers on the West Coast, such as Seattle, San Francisco, and Los Angeles,

---

2. The number of black women who outmarry has increased and stems in large part from the ravages of poverty, drugs, high mortality, and incarcerations, which have removed a disproportionate number of African American males from the pool of potential marriage partners. Furthermore, declining university enrollments and graduation of black men as compared to black women has also taken its toll. Considering that most individuals marry within the same socioeconomic class even when they outmarry racially, many African American women, particularly college-educated women, must seek partners outside the African American community if they desire to marry someone of equal class standing. These partners are disproportionately European American by virtue of their sheer size in the national population, especially in the white-collar environments where one is mostly likely to find college-educated African American women (Muwakkil 2005; Randolph 1989, 154, 156–62; Root 2001, 71; Staples 1988, 187–90).

which appear to have the highest rates of interracial marriage in the continental United States (Roberts 1994, 57–74).[3]

According to 1980 and 1990 census data outmarriage rates for blacks and whites, as well as for other racial and ethnic groups, are positively associated with educational attainment and are highest among the middle and upper classes (Lieberson and Waters 1988, 211–13; Qian 1997, 263–76).[4] A sample of marriage data from seventeen states in 1980 revealed that European American and African American partners in interracial marriages have more years of education than those in endogamous marriages. While only 9 percent of black grooms who married black brides had completed college, 13 percent of black grooms who married white brides held college degrees. Twenty-four percent of white grooms who married black brides had college degrees, whereas only 18 percent of white grooms who inmarried had completed college (Roberts 1994, 57–74).

Although outmarriage rates tend to increase with educational attainment, and intermarriages specifically between European Americans and African Americans are increasing, individuals from comparatively smaller racial and ethnic groups (Native American, Asian and Pacific Islander) have higher rates than either European Americans or African Americans (Lieberson and Waters 1988, 171; McDaniel 1996, 282; Sanjek 1994, 105, 113–14). Nevertheless, the majority of intact marriages or consensual unions in the United States (about 92 percent) involve one spouse (or unmarried partner) who is white, because European Americans compose such a large proportion of the total national population.[5] This is especially

3. The 2000 census data indicate that California, Florida, Oklahoma, Texas, and Washington have the largest number of intermarriages and Hawaii, the highest proportion of intermarriages (35 percent) (Root 2001, 6–8; Simmons and O'Connell 2003, 11).

4. Increased education and income seem to decrease racial bias and increase openness to inter-marriage, except at the very top of the Anglo-Protestant elite, whose very existence has historically has been predicated on endogamous marriage patterns (Spickard 1989, 307–11).

5. Some have argued that the lower intermarriage rates between European Americans and African Americans, as compared to rates of intermarriage between European Americans and various other Americans of color, is indicative of the continuing greater social distance between these groups and less mutual receptivity toward interracial marriage. Furthermore, African Americans generally diverge more from the dominant European American somatic norm than do the members of other groups of color.

The comparatively higher intermarriages rates between European Americans and Americans of color—including African Americans—compared to the lower rates of intermarriage among the various communities of color, can be attributed in part to the fact that all communities of color have European Americans as the most significant "racial other" reference group, more so than each other. Consequently, they are necessarily somewhat "bicultural" (or at least bi-referential) with regard to European Americans, as well as to their own communities of color. This interracial pluralism among various communities of color is in part derivative of the long history of spatial distance and social separation from each other perpetuated by dominant European Americans. This differentiation also originates in egalitarian pluralism wherein they have sought to retain their own communal cultural

true among Native Americans and Japanese Americans, for whom intermarriages with European Americans have become normative (OMB 1997a, 36901). According to 1990 census data, the nonwhite partner in 22 percent of all interracial couples was Native American / Alaska Native; in 31 percent, Asian / Pacific Islander; in 14 percent, African American; and in 25 percent, "other race" (most of whom were of Latina/o origin). Tabulations based on 2000 census data reveal that nearly 75 percent of marriages involving Native Americans / Alaska Natives and 29 percent of marriages involving Asians are interracial, compared to just 13 percent of marriages involving African Americans (Frey 2003, 7, 10).

Trends among Latinas/os are somewhat difficult to gauge because their official classification ("Hispanic") is constructed as an "ethnic" rather than a "racial" category. Consequently, "Hispanics" may claim any one of the various populations the Census Bureau classifies as racial groups (e.g., white, black, Native American, Asian American, Pacific Islander) (Otten 1991; Sanjek 1994, 110–14). However, reports based on 1990 census data revealed that approximately 26 percent of Latinas/os were married to partners who were not of Latina/o origins, although rates varied among the particular national origin groups (i.e., Cuban Americans, Puerto Ricans, Mexican Americans, and so on) (OMB 1997a, 36901; Sanjek 1994, 110–14). According to demographer William Frey, based on 2000 census data, nearly 30 percent of marriages involving a Latina/o partner were intermarriages, similar to the rate among Asian Americans (Frey 2003, 7, 10).[6] Nationwide, in 2000, 3.1 percent of all marriages (1.7 million) involved one Latina/o and one non-Latina/o spouse, while 5.7 percent of all marriages (3.1 million) involved individuals of different racial groups, according to Census Bureau tabulations (Census 2001; Simmons and O'Connell 2003, 11–12).

Although statistical surveys historically have failed to provide reliable figures on the population of offspring from interracial unions, census data indicate that the number of children born of interracial parentage grew from less than one-half million in 1970 to about 2 million in 1990. In 2000, just over 4 percent of all children (approximately 2.9 million) were identified as having two or more races (Lugaila and Overturf 2004, 15).[7] Considering that most interracial marriages

---

patterns, thus minimizing their mutual "biculturation" with each other. Increased contact over the last few decades has engendered new forms of conflict but has also facilitated the increased formation of primary relationships (friendships, dating, and intermarriage) among these communities of color. This will likely result in increased intermarriage (McDaniel 1996, 282; Sanjek 1994, 105, 113–14; Spickard 1989, 6–19, 343–72).

6. It should be noted that Frey treats the "Hispanic" identifier as a racial instead of an ethnic category in his tabulations (Frey 2003, 7).

7. An additional 7.6 percent of children were identified as "some other race" alone (Lugaila and Overturf 2004, 15). The race question for the 2000 census provided the option of checking more than

involve a white partner, the majority of children born to these unions have one European American parent. For children in interracial families with one white parent, the other parent was Native American in approximately 34 percent of the cases, Asian American in 45 percent of the cases, and African American in only 20 percent of such cases, based on 1990 census data (OMB 1997a, 36901). Data on birth certificates indicate that this trend has grown significantly over the last three decades. In 1968, only 28 percent of all births with at least one Native American or Alaska Native parent listed the second parent as European American (6,900); in 1994, it had increased to 45 percent (23,000) such that for every 100 children born to two Native American parents, 140 have one parent who is European American and one who is Native American (OMB 1997a; Usdansky 1992).

Among births to Asian American / Pacific Islander parents, the percentage of births in which the second parent was listed as European American was 28 percent in 1968, approximately 32 percent between 1971 and 1979, and 26 percent in 1994. The most significant increase has been among Japanese Americans. According to the most recent data, 139 children are born to one Japanese American parent and one European American parent for every 100 children born to two Japanese American parents (OMB 1997a, 36901; Usdansky 1992; Williams-León and Nakashima 2001, 6). However, at least in California and the Southwest, the largest number of multiracial offspring born during the 1990s had one European American and one Latina/o parent (24.4 percent white mother / Latino father; 22.9 percent Latina mother / white father) (Boxall and Herndon 2000; Gold 2000; OMB 1997a, 36901). In California alone, couples with one Latina/o partner and one European American partner accounted for 53 percent of all "multiracial/ethnic births" in 1997, based on a study of California Vital Statistics Birth Records (Tafoya 2000, 6). It is still unclear, however, what percentage of these offspring actually identify as "multiracial/multiethnic," rather than either Latina/o or European American.[8]

There was a marked increase in births of children of black/white parentage, from 2 percent (8,800) in 1968 to 9 percent (63,000) in 1994 (OMB 1997a, 36901; Funderburg 1994, 11–12; Taylor-Gibbs and Hines 1992, 223). Despite statistical limitations, the total population of children of black/white parentage, ranging in age from infants to young adults, is believed to number from 600,000 to several million (OMB 1997a, 36901; Funderburg 1994, 11–12; Taylor-Gibbs and Hines 1992, 223).

---

one box. However, some parents may have chosen to use the "some other race" option to signify a multiracial identity for their children.

8. Trends among multiracial/multiethnic individuals of partial Latina/o descent are difficult to measure when analyzing census data. These individuals are neither permitted to check both Hispanic and non-Hispanic origins on the ethnicity question, nor provided with the Hispanic identifier on the race question (OMB 1997a, 36901).

Among black and white couples, there is a considerable range of opinions as to how children's identity should be developed and supported. Some say that their children are human above all else and that race is irrelevant. Many raise their children as black and teach them African American survival skills. A significant number of couples, however, incorporate both black and white backgrounds in socializing their offspring and use a variety of terms to describe them, such as, "rainbow," "brown," "mélange," "blended," "mixed," "mixed-race," "biracial," "interracial," and "multiracial" (Wardle 1987, 55). The common denominator among these terms, however, is that they challenge formal policies and informal social attitudes that maintain a system of racial categorization premised on the one-drop rule.

The Multiracial Movement: Dismantling The Binary Racial Project

Although past individual experiences mostly remain unknown and unreported, there have been cases of notoriety, such as Jean Toomer and Philippa Duke Schuyler, who sought to follow the road less traveled by embracing both their African American and European American backgrounds. Several groups for interracial families (the Manasseh Societies, Penguin Clubs, Club Miscegenation) that emerged between the 1890s and 1940s also helped multiracial individuals affirm their black and white backgrounds (Daniel 2002, 96).

Nathan Eugene "Jean" Toomer (1894–1967) was a prominent writer of the Harlem Renaissance. Toomer's masterpiece *Cane* (1923) weaves together contrasting portraits of the love lives and sensibilities of African Americans in the rural South and urban North. The middle section of the book explores the psychological conflict of the multiracial elite. Although *Cane* is generally considered a novel, at times the work is more poetry than prose, slipping from one form into the other almost imperceptibly (Bone 1965, 80–89; Bontemps 1969, vii–viii; Gayle 1976, 117–23; Whitlaw 1974, 81–83; Woodson 1999, 28–46). *Cane* reflects Toomer's "deepening appreciation" of his African American background and his immersion in the African American community in a way that he could never feel for his European American background or the white community (Bontemps 1969, viii). Ironically, Toomer does not appear to have embraced a singular African American identity. That *Cane* is a structural and stylistic hybrid reflects the author's more general challenge to the arbitrary nature of the categories and boundaries that influenced his personal identity (Woodson 1999, 29, 31–33, 45).

In the summer of 1922, Toomer sent a collection of his writings to Max Eastman and his assistant Claude McKay, the editors of the *Liberator*. They accepted some of the pieces enthusiastically and requested biographical material from the author. Toomer responded with the following:

> Racially, I seem to have (who knows for sure) seven blood mixtures: French, Dutch, Welsh, Negro, German, Jewish, and Indian. Because of these, my position in America has been a curious one. I have lived equally amid the two race groups. Now white, now colored. From my own point of view I am naturally and inevitably an American. I have strived for a spiritual fusion analogous to the fact of racial intermingling. Without denying a single element in me, with no desire to subsume one to the other, I have tried to let them function as complements. I have tried to let them live in harmony. (Bontemps 1969, viii)

and

> Human blood is human blood. Human beings are human beings. . . . No racial or social factors can adequately account for the uniqueness of each—or for the individual differences which people display concurrently with basic commonality. (Kerman 1987, 341–46)

Toomer's problematization of blackness cannot be framed as "passing," at least not in the sense in which this concept has traditionally been defined (although he allegedly did pass as white at various times in his life). Rather, the underlying premise of Toomer's identity and his immersion in the mysticism of George Gurdjieff's metaphysics reflects a desire to transcend racial categories altogether. Toomer's goal was to embrace an identity that sought a spiritual synthesis analogous to multiraciality without the particularlism of race. He embraced this identity privately and did not publicly engage the social forces arrayed against a multiracial identification (Hutchinson 1993, 226–50; Woodson 1999, 31–45; Zack 1994, 110–11).

Philippa Duke Schuyler (1931–67) was the daughter of George Schuyler, the renowned and controversial African American journalist of the Harlem Renaissance, and Josephine Cogdell, a European American dancer, artist, heiress of a Texas rancher, and granddaughter of slave owners. The Schuylers were prominent in African American intellectual, political, and cultural circles and entertained dignitaries from all over the African diasporic world. Their daughter Philippa, who was reading and writing at the age of two-and-a-half, playing the piano at four, and composing music at five, was often compared to Mozart. Philippa was exposed to African culture and history, and to the classical music tradition of

Western Europe. She also became acquainted with many prominent intellectual, cultural, and political figures of African descent from the United States and abroad (Talalay 1995, 60, 93, 191).

Suffering the double oppression of racism and sexism, Philippa was largely rejected by the European American elite classical music milieu. She found audiences abroad, however, where she flourished as a performer and composer. She traveled throughout seventy countries in South America, Africa, Asia, and Europe, performing before royalty and heads of state. Eventually Philippa also became an author and foreign correspondent reporting on events around the globe, from Albert Schweitzer's leper colony in Lamberéné, Gabon, to the upheavals in the Belgian Congo. She spent her final days reporting on the turbulent conflict in Vietnam. While in Vietnam, Philippa co-founded the Amerasian Foundation, an organization that provided relief to the offspring of U.S. servicemen and Vietnamese women. On May 9, 1967, Philippa's life was cut short tragically in a helicopter crash while she was on a mission of mercy to evacuate children to Da Nang from a Catholic orphanage in Hue (Talalay 1995, 60, 93, 191).

Philippa experienced many of the ambiguities and conflicts that naturally surround multiracial identity in a society that views black and white as mutually exclusive and hierarchical categories of experience. During her lifetime, social forces were significantly more hostile than they are today to a multiracial identity that values both these backgrounds. In retrospect, the Schuylers seem hopelessly naive, and perhaps somewhat narcissistic, in hoping that Philippa would replace popular images of "hybrid degeneracy" with notions of "hybrid vigor." Nevertheless, their struggle to integrate African American and European American backgrounds in their daughter's identity, along with Philippa's own struggle to be both black and white, were significant departures from the norm.

Several groups—the Society for the Amalgamation of the Races in San Francisco in the 1920s; the Manasseh Societies (named after the biblical Joseph's half-Egyptian son) in Milwaukee, Chicago, and Des Moines, between 1892 and 1932; Club Miscegenation in Los Angeles; and groups in Washington, D.C., and Detroit during the 1940s—provided interracial couples with support and sought to help multiracial individuals affirm both their black and white backgrounds (Spickard 1989, 302, 333).

The best documented of these groups is the Chicago chapter of the Manasseh Society, which was already in operation by 1892. Though it disintegrated in the late 1920s, the surviving members retained a measure of informal solidarity well into the 1950s (Drake and Cayton 1962, 145–46). The Society was formed as a mutual benefit organization and had as many as seven hundred members in its heyday. It owned a cemetery plot, had elaborate burial rituals, and hosted social activities, including an annual picnic and dance. Its annual ball was one of the high points of the social season (Cozart 1909, 27–33). The club's motto was "Equal Rights for All," and it elevated intermarriage to a social good. Society members, who generally were stable working-class couples, performed elaborate initiation ceremonies for the induction of new members. They carefully scrutinized all new candidates for membership, barring common-law unions and individuals of "questionable" moral character. The Chicago chapter was especially sensitive about its reputation during the period of the Great Migration, during which a wave of "illicit" interracial relationships swept the city and made all interracial couples suspect (Drake and Cayton 1962, 145–46). Reverdy Ransom, a well-known A.M.E. clergyman in Chicago who performed services for many couples of the Manasseh Society, claimed that contrary to popular opinion, European Americans involved in such marriages were not of the "lowest stratum" of white society. Many of their children often became attorneys, physicians, and teachers (Gatewood 1990, 177–78).

The mere existence of such organizations as the Manasseh Society demonstrates that interracial couples felt themselves to be sufficiently anomalous to need psychological and social support from other intermarried couples. Although the Manasseh Society had become an established part of the associational complex of the African American community in Chicago by 1910, European Americans largely rejected the organization. African Americans, if they did not ostracize these couples outright, did not necessarily receive them with warmth. For the most part, interracially married couples were outcasts who had to make substantial provision for their personal security and comfort (Drake and Cayton 1962, 145–46; Gatewood 1990, 177–78).

The identity configuration exemplified by Jean Toomer and Philippa Schuyler, and supported by the membership of these early organizations, prefigured the contemporary "new" multiracial identity. This identity is embraced by growing numbers of individuals and is supported by similar contemporary organizations that emerged in the decades following the removal of the last antimiscegenation laws in 1967 (Brown and Douglass 1996, 323–40). In 1979, interracial couples in Berkeley founded I-Pride (Interracial/Intercultural Pride) to provide general support for interracial families. Their more specific purpose was to petition the Berkeley public schools to reflect the identity of their offspring by including a multiracial designator on school forms.[9] Their efforts resulted in the Berkeley public schools adopting "interracial" as a new identifier on school forms for the

9. I-Pride is the oldest support organization still operating. Yet the first such organization was Citizens for Classification of Interracial Children (CCIC), which was formed on October 19, 1978, in Seattle, Washington. Along with the support it provided interracial families and multiracial individuals, CCIC also sought to get the federal government to include an "interracial" category on all official forms,

1979–80 school year, making it the first such designator in U.S. history. In 1980–81, however, California state education officials restricted the category to internal district uses only, citing federal reporting requirements that did not permit such a classification (Fernández 1995, 4).

By the 1990s, what had began as a somewhat marginalized racial project expanded to include a growing number of similar support groups and educational organizations. This led to a full-scale social movement whose constituents, along with other supporters, began pressuring states to change procedures for collecting official data on race, particularly on the decennial census, so that multiracial individuals could be statistically enumerated. The organizations behind the multiracial movement have included thirty to forty support groups, with names such as Multiracial Americans of Southern California in Los Angeles (MASC), the Biracial Family Network in Chicago (BFN), the Interracial Family Alliance in Atlanta (IFA), the Interracial Family Circle in Washington, D.C. (IFC), and a national umbrella organization called the Association of MultiEthnic Americans (AMEA) (Brown and Douglass 1996, 323–40). Other organizations have included A Place for Us/National (APUN), which is a national nondenominational religious support network for interracial families; Project RACE (Reclassify All Children Equally), an advocacy, informational, and educational organization; and the Center for the Study of Biracial Children, an informational and educational organization. There have also been several national periodicals, including *Interrace, New People,* and *Mavin*—which address the concerns of the interracial/multiracial community—as well as *Interracial Voice* (*IV*) and *The Multiracial Activist* (*TMA*), which are advocacy journals on the internet. Although reflecting sometimes radically different, if not mutually hostile political perspectives, these publications provide a public forum for the discussion of issues related to multiracial-identified and transracially adopted individuals, as well as individuals in interracial relationships (Bhattacharyya, Gabriel, and Small 2002, 60–87; Brown and Douglass 1996, 323–40; Grosz 1989, 24–29).[10]

---

including the upcoming 1980 census. The CCIC was successful in getting the Washington State Human Rights Commission to submit a policy recommendation to the Seattle Board of Education to permit public schools to include a category for multiracial children on school forms. However, it does not appear to have succeeded in getting compliance with this recommendation. In addition, the organization had ceased operations by the time activists in I-Pride and other organizations began mobilizing for changes on the 1990 census (Cheers 1978, 14–16).

10. Other organizations have included My Shoes, which is a support group for multiracial-identified individuals who appear phenotypically European American, Honor Our New Ethnic Youth (HONEY), Getting Interracial Families Together (GIFT), and Multiethnics of Southern Arizona In Celebration (MOSAIC).

The complexities of multiracial identity are not limited to the experiences of individuals of partial African descent but encompass a wide variety of backgrounds. However, the movement has been disproportionately composed of black-white couples—particularly those involving European American women and African American men—and their offspring. Though only a small percentage of the larger national population of interracial families, their overrepresentation is due to the unique legacy of attitudes and policies that have crystallized around blackness in race relations—and more specifically, racial jurisprudence—in the United States. Yet the key leadership of the movement has been disproportionately composed of multiracial adults.

The number of active participants in the multiracial movement, particularly those involved with the census debate in the 1980s and 1990s, is indeed only a small percentage of the total population of multiracial-identified individuals—itself only 2.4 percent of the national population according to 2000 census data (Jones and Smith 2001, 2–4; Williams 2005, 53–54). That said, the multiracial movement has encompassed a wide variety of organizations and concerns quite apart from the census. Beyond its leadership and membership, there is a wider circle of participants throughout the United States who have played a greater or lesser part in the movement. There is also a general constituency of potential supporters who are vaguely sympathetic to the movement's objectives.

Though this larger constituency includes individuals from various class backgrounds, the movement originated as the result of political projects and interventions led largely by professionals and white-collar workers. Indeed, the leadership and advisory boards of two organizations, MASC and I-Pride, have consisted disproportionately of individuals with postgraduate degrees and included a cadre of academics—the largest among all of the support groups. Most of these scholars have been in the vanguard of new research and teaching on interracial relationships and multiracial identity. They have not only helped formulate strategy but also enhanced the credibility of the movement through public speaking, appearances in the media, and testimony at congressional subcommittee hearings (held between 1993 and 1997) to discuss changes in the collection and tabulation of official racial/ethnic data (Bhattacharyya, Gabriel, and Small 2002, 60–87; Daniel 2002, 123–24).

The West Coast, particularly California and Hawaii, has the highest concentration of interracial couples and the largest number and highest proportion of multiracial-identified individuals. This helps to explain why the multiracial phenomenon as a racial project has had a more immediate impact on patterns of race relations on the West Coast (Bhattacharyya, Gabriel, and Small 2002, 66–87; Jones and Smith 2001, 2–4; Simmons and O'Connell 2003, 11–12). California, in particular, has been a major center of multiracial activism, as well as academic research and university courses on multiracial identity.[11] The University of California, specifically the Berkeley and Santa Barbara campuses, has the longest-standing university courses on this topic in the United States. Despite this unique regional concentration, the multiracial movement has led to noticeable changes in racial discourse in the national public sphere. Consequently, the multiracial phenomenon has become a more normative part of everyday understandings and presentations of racial identity in the national media and national consciousness. That said, the gap between California's seemingly anomalous pattern of race relations and that of the rest of the United States undoubtedly will narrow if racial intermarriages continue to increase, and if there is a continued growth in the number of individuals who identify as multiracial, an option that only has been available officially since 2000.

Although these support, educational, and advocacy groups have been comprised primarily of black and white couples, as well as children who, like Philippa Schuyler, are the "first-generation" offspring of these unions, many organizations also have included a smaller number of "multigenerational" individuals whose experience is similar to that of Jean Toomer. This latter identity encompasses individuals who have parents and/or generations of ancestors that have been socially designated as black (although they have multiple racial/cultural backgrounds) but have resisted identifying solely with the African American community (Daniel 2002, 93–96).

The first-generation experience is based on identifying with *parents from more than one racial/cultural reference group* and generally involves the concrete and immediate experience of those backgrounds in the home and/or extended family. Meanwhile, in the multigenerational experience these specific backgrounds typically are not concretely delineated in the home and/or extended family. This experience is primarily based on identifying with *more than one parent racial/cultural reference group* in the more abstract genealogical past. Consequently, multigenerational individuals more commonly refer to themselves as "multiracial" because this designator more specifically captures their identification with many backgrounds and ancestors, whereas first-generation individuals more frequently refer to themselves as "biracial." However, first-generation and multigenerational individuals use "mixed" as the most common alternative way of describing themselves (Daniel 2002, 103; 1996, 128–29). The lack of a formally recognized multiracial-designated and identified community in the United States, and the accompanying sense of "peoplehood," continues to affect

---

11. Seattle has become an increasingly important center of multiracial activism since the founding of the Mavin Foundation.

both contemporary first-generation and multigenerational individuals, despite the recent emergence of a new multiracial identity. However, first-generation individuals, particularly teenagers and young adults, have begun to form a significant cohort of peers in both public and private interaction with each other (e.g., at school, recreational activities, and so on).

Multigenerational individuals on the other hand, particularly adults, have often experienced a long-standing sense of personal racial isolation. A variety of organizations and forums have formed independently of the support groups for interracial couples and their offspring specifically to address multigenerational concerns (e.g., the Melungeon Society, Tan American Community Forum, the Amerigroid Society of America, the Tirah Society, Famlee, and Mis-ce-ge-NATION) (Daniel 2002, 124). In addition, many multigenerational individuals have vicariously identified with multiracial populations in South Africa or Latin America, which have been acknowledged in their respective societies for centuries. Others have identified vicariously with multiracial communities in the United States (such as the Louisiana Creoles of color), although they have had no known genealogical ties, personal experience, or contact with these communities. Generally, this sense of isolation has been reduced significantly when these individuals have met other multiracial-identified individuals (either first-generation or multigenerational). This has been the case with interactions in various support groups such as MASC.

Multigenerational individuals whose backgrounds include antecedents from various triracial isolate communities and Louisiana Creoles of color are to some extent exceptions to this experience of isolation. Yet many of these individuals tend to identify and designate themselves primarily as "Creole," or members of their respective triracial communities and only secondarily as "multiracial." This new identity is neither based on the desire to gain special privileges, nor is it synonymous with the psychosocial pathology of colorism traditionally associated with triracial isolate and Louisiana Creole identity. Accordingly, it differs from past identities in that it resists both the dichotomization *and* hierarchical valuation of cultural and racial differences (Anthony 1995, 1–3; Domínguez 1986, 172–76; Dorman 1992, 620–21; 1996, 166–79; George 1992, 222, 240–43; Haskins 1975, 127–28; Hirsch 1992, 262–319; Kennedy and Kennedy 1997, 91, 92, 99–102, 164).

This change in attitudes toward African American ancestry reflects the heightened pride and black consciousness that has affected all individuals of African descent since the 1960s. Many Creoles of color experienced an intense sense of personal conflict during the height of the civil rights and black movements in the late 1960s and early 1970s, when a black identity was widely adopted by African-descent Americans, including the majority of multiracial adults—first-generation or multigenerational (Daniel 2002, 86–88). Yet they also began to realize, like others before them, the advantages of joining forces, at least politically, with blacks in the fight for civil rights (Daniel 2002, 10; Domínguez 1986, 172–76; Dorman 1992, 620–21; 1996, 166–79; Haskins 1975, 127–28; Hirsch 1992, 262–319).

Thus, growing numbers of Creoles have begun to rearticulate an identity that displays a greater openness to inclusion under a larger "Pan African American" identity. This new Creole identity relinquishes the legacy of racial and cultural isolation, which was an attempt to escape the stigma attached to blackness, but without discarding other beliefs, values, customs, and artifacts originating in their French and Spanish heritage. Others seek to affirm a Creole identity that remains distinct from African Americans, similar to that of Puerto Ricans and Cuban Americans. For the most part, Puerto Ricans and Cuban Americans have multiple ethnoracial/ethnocultural backgrounds, and also acknowledge, as do many blacks, their African ancestry, in conjunction with their other ancestries. However, these groups generally display singular ethnoracial/ethnocultural identities as Latinas/os (or Hispanics) and therefore do not necessarily consider themselves African American, although many do variously identify as African Latinas/os or African Hispanics (Comas-Dias 1996, 167–90). Another variant of this new Creole identity might be described as "multiracial." This identity is not, however, indicative of individuals who simply acknowledge the presence of African ancestry—in conjunction with other ancestries—in their background. Rather, it replaces this configuration with one that references their sense of "we-ness" in and kinship with the multiple racial/cultural backgrounds in their genealogy.

The contrast between the multigenerational and the contemporary first-generation experience is further underscored because the latter is frequently viewed as being a more justifiable basis for a multiracial identity. This is related in part to the removal of antimiscegenation laws in 1967 and the subsequent liberalization of the social ecology. More specifically, the first-generation experience generally originates in the context of marriage, which includes an element of choice. Marriage confers equal legal status on both partners and, by extension, equal legitimacy to both parents' identities (Davis 1991, 128–29). The one-drop rule, therefore, has been less consistently enforced, both de jure and de facto, in the experience of contemporary first-generation offspring.

The classification policies at the National Center for Health Statistics, and to some extent, the Census Bureau, have reflected this more relaxed application of the one-drop rule to contemporary first-generation offspring. The former previously classified multiracial children in terms of the "minority" parent; the latter classified them in terms of the father's racial/cultural identity. Since the 1980s, both agencies have shifted to a formula relying on the identity of the mother (Fernández 1995, 5; Lee 1993, 83). Many multiracial children who have European American mothers thus have been designated as "white," though in neither case have they have been designated as "biracial." Since the mid-1960s, however, some adoption agencies have described multiracial children as "racially mixed" or "biracial." This policy has not been devised to challenge the one-drop rule per se. Rather, it sought to attract white adoptive parents by appealing to Eurocentric bias in the larger society, in order to hasten the removal of these children from public institutions (Davis 1991, 128–29).

By contrast, this flexibility is not readily extended to the identity of multi-generational individuals. Not only does their experience carry the explicit or implicit stigma of concubinage, rape, and illegitimacy, but also the parents and families of these individuals have been considered African American by the larger society, and to some extent have identified themselves with the African American community. Multigenerational individuals of European American and African American descent, therefore, find themselves at odds not only with the larger society and the African American community but also with first-generation individuals. African Americans often accuse them of choosing to identify as multi-racial to escape the societal stigma attached to "blackness," given that most African-descent Americans have some European American ancestry in their genealogy. Meanwhile, some first-generation individuals contend that their own biracial experience is the legitimate starting point for a blended identity (Daniel 1996, 129).

Many multigenerational individuals have expressed disappointment to find that after all the years of struggle to express a multiracial identity some first-generation individuals do not view them as "authentic." This is all the more unsettling because of the sense of kinship they feel with first-generation individuals. Yet all multiracial-identified individuals must develop constructive strategies for resisting the one-drop rule, regardless of whether they are first-generation or multigenerational. This device challenges their comfort with their backgrounds and continually assigns them a socially defined identity that contradicts their personal identity (Root 1990, 185–205). Thus, it is myopic to restrict the parameters of the new multiracial identity—as some individuals have argued—to the experience of first-generation individuals born since the removal of the last antimiscegenation laws in 1967. This perspective ignores and invalidates the experience of earlier generations of first-generation individuals, as well as generations of their offspring, who have struggled, and continue to struggle, to liberate themselves from the shackles of hypodescent.

Race, Research, and Revisionism: From Marginality to "Liminality"

Prior to 1980, the growing multiracial population had received limited attention from educators, researchers, sociologists, and mental health professionals. Furthermore, the extant research was outdated, contradictory, or based on small-scale case studies of children who were experiencing "problems" with identity and were referred for psychological counseling (C. Hall 1992, 250–64). In the case of children of African American and European American parentage, most professionals stressed the importance of learning to cope as African Americans, because society would view them as such. Consequently, their mental health was assessed in terms of how successfully or unsuccessfully they achieved an African American identity. These counselors (whose approaches were often based on misinterpretations of sociologist Robert E. Park's theories) argued that marginality itself was necessarily pathological and the source of life-long personal conflict. It was characterized by divided loyalties, ambivalence, and hypersensitivity, caused by the mutually exclusive nature of black and white racial identities (Park 1928, 881–93; Stonequist 1937, 10–11, 24–27).

Admittedly, these theories emerged at a time when the United States was significantly more hostile to the affirmation of a multiracial identity. Accordingly, the prevailing ideology focused on the "psychological dysfunctioning" of multiracial offspring as a justification for discouraging miscegenation, rather than on the social forces that made psychological functioning problematic (Lempel 1979, 247–99). Thus, certain theorists (e.g., Stonequist) distorted, or at least misinterpreted, Park's actual theory of marginality. They also overshadowed other contemporary theorists who argued that marginality could potentially imbue individuals with a broader vision and wider range of sympathies because they were able to identify with more than one racial/cultural reference group (Antonovsky 1956, 57–67; Goldberg 1941, 52–58; Green 1947, 167–71; Kerchkhoff and McCormick 1955, 48–55).

The theories on "negative" marginality have been further refuted by theories formulated since the 1970s and by data collected since the 1980s (Gist 1967, 361–65; Miller 1992, 24–36; Poston 1990, 152–55; Root 1992, 3–11; Williams-León and Nakashima 2001, 3–10; Wright and Wright 1972, 361–68). In turn, the concept of "positive" marginality has gained greater acceptance among health professionals and in the larger society. There is a growing consensus that multiracial-identified individuals may variously experience some of the ambiguities, strains, and conflicts that accompany marginality in a society that views black and white identities as mutually exclusive categories. However, these feelings can be counterbalanced by increased sensitivity to commonalities and an appreciation of the differences in interpersonal and intergroup situations, as an extension of their feelings of kinship with both blacks and whites (Daniel 1996, 135).

The new multiracial identity differs from that of African Americans—who for the most part have multiple racial/cultural backgrounds but a single-racial/cultural identity as black (Forbes 1988, 271). Indeed, as Los Angeles psychologist Patricia Johnson has argued, the intrapsychic development of multiracial-identified individuals is different from that of single-racial identified individuals ("Biracial

Children of Interracial Divorce," *Oprah Winfrey Show*, Harpo Productions, October 7, 1994). Nor is the new multiracial identity analogous to Manuel Ramirez's multicultural identity model (Ramirez 1983, 100–117). Ramirez's model is applicable to any individual, irrespective of genealogy or ancestry, who displays a general openness and sensitivity to racial and cultural differences, has an affinity with the values, beliefs, and customs of more than one racial/cultural context, or blends aspects of these contexts into a new personal synthesis, because of exposure to multiple racial/cultural groups. Though there are similarities between the behavior of individuals who display Ramirez's multicultural identity and those who exhibit the new multiracial identity, there are considerable differences in the subjective motivations behind these respective identities.

The new multiracial identity is indicative of individuals who, in direct response to the multiple racial/cultural backgrounds in their genealogy, reference their sense of "we-ness" in and feel kinship with both black and white communities. This identity is based, however, not on biological notions of race but on ancestry.[12] Exposure to these backgrounds enhances feelings of kinship. Simple awareness of those backgrounds, however, can catalyze this sentiment, while lack of contact does not preclude its presence (Daniel 1996, 134).

Individuals who identify with the new multiracial identity experience differences in affinity toward their black and white backgrounds. Myriad variables determine this process. Data reveal that the outcome is influenced less by the extent to which individuals display phenotypical traits commonly associated with their parent reference groups and more by the impact that society, peers, and family have had on their personal history (Bradshaw 1992, 77–90; Field 1996, 211–26; C. Hall 1992, 250–64; D. Johnson 1992, 37–49; Root 1990, 185–205; Wallace 2001, 40–94).

Information obtained from the extensive research on multiracial-identified individuals since the late 1980s indicate that many affirm an "integrative" multiracial identity that references both black and white communities. Individuals displaying such an identity are aware of being both similar to and different from their black and white reference groups but may, under certain circumstances,

---

12. Biological and ancestral notions of race overlap but are not synonymous. The former is based on one's genetic inheritance irrespective of ancestral background. The latter is grounded in the ancestors in one's lineage or genealogy, irrespective of genetic concerns, and is the basis of the new multiracial identity. That said, the new "ethnic DNA test" offered by a growing number of companies has complicated this relationship between biology, ancestry, and identity. The test involves swabbing the mouth and mailing a sample for DNA analysis, which can pinpoint the geographical origins of the various portions of an individual's genetic makeup. This technology may have the unintended consequence of reifying the link between ancestry, biology, and identity. Yet increased awareness of the myriad ancestors in one's genealogy and DNA inherited from them would also call into question any lingering notions of racial purity and most likely prompt larger numbers of individuals to display more fluid monoracial, if not actual multiracial, identities (see Kaplan 2003).

lean toward either a European American or African American orientation. These individuals tend to be first-generation offspring, because of the likelihood of exposure to both backgrounds in the home and/or extended family (Daniel 1996, 136; Field 1996, 211–26; Rockquemore and Brunsma 2002, 41–48; Renn 2004, 67–93; Root 1990, 185–201; Tizard and Phoenix 1993, 46–66).

Other individuals express a "pluralistic" multiracial identity that blends aspects of both parent reference groups and moves fluidly between the two. Generally, however, they consider themselves to be neither black nor white but rather part of a new primary reference group composed of individuals sharing a multiracial identity, though they may variously have a European American or an African American orientation (Daniel 1996, 137; Renn 2004, 67–93; Rockquemore and Brunsma 2002, 41–48; Root 1990, 185–205; Wallace 2001, 121–25, 147–52). Multi-generational individuals more consistently embrace a pluralistic identity, because they frequently have not experienced both parental backgrounds in either the home or extended family. Meanwhile, first-generation offspring express an identity that operates variously out of both the pluralistic and integrative models. Most individuals exhibit an identity that manifests itself in varying shades of gray on the integrative-pluralistic continuum (Daniel 1996, 135–36; Renn 2004, 67–93; Rockquemore and Brunsma 2002, 41–48; Wallace 2001, 121–25, 147–52).

Given the multidimensional nature of the new multiracial identity, those individuals who display it are neither totally dependent nor completely free from the cultural predispositions and sociocultural conditioning of any given racial group in their backgrounds (Adler 1974, 23–40; Brown 1990, 319–37). The psycho-social configuration of their identity is based on a style of self-consciousness that involves a continuous process of "incorporating here, discarding there, responding situationally" (Adler 1974, 25). Individuals maintain no rigid boundaries between themselves and the various communities in which they operate. Not having fixed or predictable parameters, their identity has multiple points of reference but no circumference, because it manifests itself *on* the boundary (Anzaldúa 1987, 77–91; Daniel 1996, 134; Renn 2004, 67–93; Wallace 2001, 121–25, 147–52). Individuals do not, however, experience this liminality (Turner 1969, 94–130; Trubshaw 1995), or sense of being "betwixt and between," in a way that either precludes an affinity with both blacks and whites or translates into the marginality and its attendant pathologies of social dislocation and personal alienation traditionally ascribed to multiracial individuals (Daniel 1996, 121–39; Kich 1996, 263–76; Root 1990, 185–205; Williams-León 2001, 146–61; Williams-León and Nakashima 2001, 3–10).[13]

---

13. Liminality can also be observed among individuals who are simultaneously members of two or more culturally distinct groups, such as second-generation immigrants, recent migrants from

The multiracial movement has sought to make it possible for individuals to embrace the new multiracial identity by dismantling the one-drop rule and the binary racial project, as well as their implicit and explicit hierarchical valuations. As a racial project, the movement involves both a cultural initiative that interprets racial dynamics by means of identity politics and a political initiative that seeks to bring about changes in official racial classification. Any such changes would have consequences in the distribution of resources, such as the enforcement of civil rights legislation and claims, tracking historical and contemporary patterns of discrimination, and achieving social and economic equity. However, interracial couples and multiracial-identified individuals have not mobilized specifically to achieve gains in these areas. Rather, the immediate goal has been to rescue multiracial identities from distortion and erasure by the continued enforcement of the one-drop rule. The new multiracial identity politics demands that both dominant and subordinate groups make major and complex changes in definitions of self and community, difference and hierarchy, which go well beyond gaining increased advantages in the political economy.

Traditional explanations of social movements relying on relative deprivation, resource mobilization, and responses to political opportunities, while useful, have limited applicability to collective action by interracial couples and multiracial-identified individuals, because they do not adequately analyze the related process of identity formation. Identities have little power to shape group members' actions until they involve more than simple awareness among members that they constitute a group, although this self-conscious collective subjectivity (defining the "who" or "object" of social mobilization) is a prerequisite for collective action. Once established, however, a racial or ethnic identity becomes not only a lens through which individuals interpret and make sense of the world but also a starting point for action. Correspondingly, identity shapes how other issues and interests are perceived and can be acted upon in the formation of a social movement (Cornell and Hartmann 1998, 86; Marx 1995, 159–60).

Stephen Cornell and Douglas Hartmann argue that ethnoracial (and ethnocultural) groups and identities are formed by the ongoing interaction between "assignment" (what others say individuals are) and "assertion" (who or what individuals claim to be). Groups as collective subjectivities do not simply respond to circumstantial factors or build identities within the constraints imposed by external forces. The interaction between identity and external circumstances is intrinsic to the logic and process of group formation (Cornell and Hartmann

country to city, and women in nontraditional roles. These phenomena share a similar process of proceeding from "either/or" to "both/neither."

1998, 73–80, 85). According to Candace West and Sarah Fenstermaker, race and racial identity are more than individual characteristics or some vaguely defined set of role expectations, but rather are accomplished in daily interactions with others. The accomplishment of race renders the social dynamics based on race as "normal" and "natural," and legitimizes ways of organizing social life. This in turn reaffirms institutional practice, the racial order, and the respective power relations associated with them (West and Fenstermaker 1995, 21–22, 23–24).

Accountability of individuals to race categories is the key to understanding the maintenance of the racial order in the United States. Situated social action contributes to the reproduction of racialized social structure and systems of domination, whose entrenched ideas, practices, decisions, and procedures construct dichotomous racial hierarchies that exclude, control, and constrain human agency. Nevertheless, individuals are active agents in constructing, maintaining, reproducing, transforming, deconstructing, and reconstructing their identities. Moreover, those identities are capable of reconstructing circumstances via the actions they set in motion. Identities, and the groups that display them, change over time as the forces that impinge on them change, and as the claims made by both group members and others change (Cornell and Hartman 1998, 73–80, 85, 101; West and Fenstermaker 1995, 19).

Considering that the U.S. racial order is continually constructed in everyday life, it follows that under certain conditions, individuals acting as singular or collective agents resist pressures to conform to those social forces. The new multiracial identity represents a form of resistance displayed by individuals who attach equal value to their European American backgrounds and identify with European Americans without diminishing the value attached to their African American backgrounds and affinity with the experience of African Americans. This resistance to the U.S. binary racial project and the shared racial liminality originating in identification with more than one racial group are what bind multiracial-identified individuals together. This racial liminality constructs identities and becomes an integral, fundamental part of the self-conception of multiracial individuals.

This is not to suggest that interracial couples or families involved in transracial adoption do not experience liminality. Indeed, they experience liminality as members of different racial reference groups that are combined in their interracial and transracial relationships. This in turn may provide the experience of liminality by virtue of their difference from normative single-racial marriage and family patterns in the United States (Kelley 1999, 12, 15–19; McKay and Hall 1996, 63–78; Rosenblatt, Karis, and Powell 1995, 32–33; Simon and Alstein 1987, 33–39). However, these experiences differ from the "multiracial" experience, which is based on identification with two (or more) different backgrounds in one's genealogy.

Considering the many types of liminality, there has been some debate over whether multiracial-identified individuals actually form a group. Some have questioned whether the experience of liminality in and of itself can be a valid defining characteristic for group formation. Furthermore, it has been argued that within the greater multiracial experience, individuals with the same or similar backgrounds (e.g., black-white, white-Asian) have more in common with each other than with other multiracial-identified individuals. Accordingly, this precludes a "pan-multiracial" experience and identity, which some argue is a prerequisite to the contention that multiracial individuals form a group (Thornton 1992, 321–25).

Despite the myriad differences in backgrounds, experiences, and identities, and the fact that the experience of multiraciality is refracted through the lenses of sex/gender, class, and a host of other social categories, the common denominator among multiracial-identified individuals is the direct experience of liminality originating in identification with multiple backgrounds. It is this shared experience that has been instrumental in the formation of a multiracial collective subjectivity, irrespective of the specific backgrounds that give rise to and define various multiracial experiences and identities. Most multiracial-identified individuals will never know, meet, or even hear of each other. Yet in their minds lives the image of their communion (or "imagined community") (Anderson 1983, 57), which provides connections across social and geographical space, as well as across time (Cornell and Hartmann 1998, 98).[14]

The Culture of Racial Resistance: From "War of Maneuver" to "War of Position"

In the past, interracial couples and multiracial individuals have counterpoised their own forms of organization and identity in a *war of maneuver* against the dehumanization and enforced invisibility imposed by the white power structure. They lacked a power base from which to wage a *war of position* that would achieve strategic incursions into the mainstream political process. The multiracial movement has a natural affinity with these previous projects. There is a parallel between the appeals of the triracial isolates and those of the new multiracial movement for changes in official racial classification. The historical circumstances that gave rise to the Manasseh Societies in the late nineteenth and early twentieth centuries

14. Observation of students at the University of California, at Los Angeles, Santa Barbara, and Santa Cruz, and public behavior at local support group meetings and regional and national conferences on the topic of multiracial identity and interracial marriage.

seem to parallel those which gave rise to similar contemporary support groups since the 1967 *Loving* decision. Both periods were characterized by social isolation caused by the unsupportive racial climate in the larger society, yet also provided opportunities for increased interracial marriage. Many other similar organizations that formed during the 1940s and 1950s in Los Angeles, Washington, D.C., and Detroit were not in response to any national trend of increasing interracial marriages per se. Nevertheless, interracial military families returning after World War II to the United States from abroad—particularly Europe—where many had experienced comparatively greater acceptance, formed these organizations to provide mutual support, as previous groups had done and contemporary ones are doing now (Spickard 1989, 276–77).

For the most part, the founders of contemporary support groups have not, however, drawn inspiration from previous groups when inaugurating their organizations. In fact, they have generally been unaware that such groups existed.[15] In addition, the motivation for the triracial isolates' appeals for changes in racial classification differs significantly from those of the multiracial movement. The former originated in the desire to escape the social stigma of blackness, whereas the latter originates in the desire to embrace an identity that reflects the various backgrounds in one's genealogy.[16] Consequently, the multiracial movement cannot be viewed as part of a continuous collective tradition of racial resistance, as has been the case with the struggle of African Americans (Spickard 1989, 276–77). The multiracial movement is more directly related to the African American civil rights movement that dismantled Jim Crow segregation. After World War II, African Americans and other subordinated racial groups made sustained strategic incursions into the mainstream political process. Indeed, the 1950s and 1960s were among the most racially turbulent periods in postwar U.S. history (Omi and Winant 1994, 95–98). The racial minority movements of that period achieved comparatively limited but real reforms in their struggle for racial justice and equality.

Prepared in large measure by tactics deployed under conditions of the *war of maneuver,* the struggles for voting rights, the sit-ins, and boycotts to desegregate public facilities, the urban rebellions of the mid-1960s, and the political mobilizations of Latinas/os, Native Americans, Asian Americans, and Pacific Islanders dramatically transformed the U.S. political and cultural landscape. These gains provided the diverse institutional and cultural terrain upon which the racial state could be confronted in a *war of position* (Omi and Winant 1994, 95–98). New conceptions of racial identity and the meaning of race, new modes of political

---

15. Observation of public behavior at local support group meetings and regional and national conferences on the topic of multiracial identity and interracial marriage.

16. Observation of attendees at the founding meeting of the AMEA, November 1989.

organization and confrontation, and new definitions of the state's role in promoting and achieving "equality" were explored, debated, and contested on the battleground of politics. These new social movement politics would later prove "contagious," leading to the mobilization of other groups—students, feminists, gays, and eventually, interracial couples and multiracial-identified individuals— who have drawn upon the African American struggle "as a central organizational fact or as a defining political metaphor and inspiration" (97). Indeed, many of the interracial couples as well as multiracial-identified adults in the vanguard of the multiracial movement came of age in the 1960s and were actively involved in the civil rights movement.[17]

Although the civil rights movement ended legalized segregation in the public sphere and led to the removal of restrictions against interracial marriages, the one-drop rule continued to operate throughout the 1960s and 1970s. It is part of what sociologist Pierre Bourdieu defines as the doxa, that is to say, the sphere of sacred, sacrosanct, or unquestioned social concepts or dogmas that have acquired the force of nature (Bourdieu 1977, 159). Despite the increase in black-white intermarriages in the decade immediately following the *Loving* decision, the 1970 and 1980 censuses, the first to allow self-identification, indicated that most parents identified their multiracial children as black (Waters 2000, 30–31). Because the only alternative was the "other" box, it is possible that many couples selected "black" in the tradition of the one-drop rule but were actually raising their children as biracial. These data also reveal more about the parents than the children. Nevertheless, most black-white interracial couples continued to identify their offspring as black as late as 1980. The 1980 census shows that roughly 70 percent of such offspring were identified as African American by their parents, regardless of whether the mother or father in the marriage was black (Lieberson and Waters 1988, 16).

That said, the one-drop rule paradoxically sowed the seeds of its own demise. By drawing boundaries that solidified blackness, this mechanism had the unintended consequence of forging a black group identity that provided the basis for mass mobilization and collective action. This in turn led to the dismantling of Jim Crow segregation and ultimately paved the way for the removal of the last laws against intermarriage in the 1967 *Loving* decision. The *Loving* decision led to a growth not only in the number of interracial marriages but also in the births of "first generation" (or biracial) offspring. Many interracial couples began challenging and seeking to dismantle the one-drop rule by imbuing their children with pride in both their black and white backgrounds.

17. Observation of public behavior between 1989 and 1998 at local support group meetings and regional and national conferences on the topic of multiracial identity and interracial marriage.

At the dawn of the 1980s, there was no organized collective mobilization against enforcement of the one-drop rule, with the exception of I-Pride. By the 1990s, however, what had begun as a racial project organized by and largely limited to I-Pride had expanded to include a critical mass of similar grassroots support groups and educational organizations and forums. The network began pressuring the racial state to change procedures for collecting official data on race—particularly on the decennial census—so that multiracial-identified individuals could be statistically enumerated. This provided not only the cultural terrain upon which other oppositional political projects could be mounted but also an inroad to the institutional process through which the racial state could be confronted in a *war of position*. Informal resistance to the one-drop rule escalated and expanded to include a formal dismantling of that device at the municipal, state, and federal levels.

The multiracial movement's primary political focus in terms of action campaigns has been aimed at changing bureaucratic procedures in the collection of racial and ethnic data. There has been some lobbying—particularly at the state level—for legislative change, but greater emphasis has been put on letter writing, phone calls, public appearances in the media, and testimony at hearings. The relatively "quiet" nature of the multiracial movement differentiates it significantly from the public displays of mass mobilization in boycotts, demonstrations, sit-ins, and uprisings of the civil rights era. Yet the carriers of the new multiracial identity have benefited, as have other individuals of African descent, from the comparatively more fluid intergroup relations and from socioeconomic gains of the civil rights era. This identity represents a logical step in the progression of civil rights, the expansion of strategies, and the achievement of both socioeconomic equity and a "holocentric" racial self.

The new multiracial identity challenges the American binary racial project, and the dichotomization of whiteness and blackness, as have other manifestations of multiracial identity. Yet it differs from previous multiracial identity projects (e.g., passing, blue-vein societies, Louisiana Creoles of color, triracial isolates), which were motivated by the legal system of segregation that sought to control the potential threat to white domination posed by individuals of African descent. Consequently, those tactics were less a response to the forced denial of one's European ancestry and/or cultural orientation and more a reaction to being subordinated and being denied the privileges that these criteria implied. Accordingly, they operated out of inegalitarian integrationist and pluralist dynamics by maintaining the hierarchical valuation attached to African American and European American racial and cultural differences.

The new multiracial identity resists the one-drop rule and the binary racial project as well as their hierarchical and dichotomous valuations. It thus recognizes the commonalities among blacks and whites and at the same time appreciates the differences. Here, categories of experience are viewed as relative, rather than absolute extremes. Accordingly, this identity builds on the egalitarian pluralist tenets of the racial movements of the 1960s, which sought to achieve the equality of difference. Simultaneously, the new multiracial identity resuscitates the integrationist goals of the 1950s by seeking to replace assimilationist integration with a more egalitarian dynamic.

seven A NEW BRAZILIAN RACIAL ORDER

A Decline in the Racial Democracy Ideology

Prelude to the Decline: Brazilian Race Relations in Global Perspective

The Brazilian elite appropriated racist theory from Europe and the United States to formulate their solution to the "Negro problem." However, they abandoned two of its principal tenets: the belief in absolute racial differences and the degeneracy of multiracial individuals. By rejecting the existence of intrinsic racial differences, whitening through miscegenation provided Brazil an escape from the determinism of "scientific" racism. This whitening ideology was also reconciled with the existence of a sizable population of individuals designated as multiracial (or mulatto) in Brazil. Of course, it was quite arbitrary to conceptualize a single category of Brazilians as mulatto, considering that African phenotypical traits (not to mention African ancestry) were widespread throughout the entire population, including large numbers of self-identified and socially designated whites. Yet belief in this intermediate category of individuals was central to Brazilian racial thinking, as well as to eliminating the "black peril" (Skidmore 1974, 76–77).

During the first two decades of the Republic, the Brazilian elite maintained an abiding faith in the ideal of whitening, which rationalized a process that supposedly was already transpiring. The whitening ideology and the alleged lack of discrimination granted Brazil a feeling of moral superiority over technologically more developed nations like the United States, where bitter racial divisions and systematic domination and exclusion of African Americans and other communities of color prevailed. With its supposedly more tolerant attitudes, Brazil was eliminating the "Negro problem" through black attrition (Skidmore 1974, 76–77, 209).

European American visitors acknowledged Brazil's progress in solving the race problem. These opinions reached as high as the Oval Office, where President Theodore Roosevelt had a very favorable reaction (Skidmore 1974, 68, 76–77).

For much of the twentieth century, many African Americans, including sociologist E. Franklin Frazier, became ardent supporters of Brazil's "solution" to the race problem through miscegenation and social integration (Hellwig 1990, 4–59; 1992, xi–xiii, 47–50, 123, 125, 133). They used the image of Brazil as a racially democratic, color-blind paradise to instill hope among African Americans, who, long after the legal abolition of slavery, lived in social, economic, and political servitude.

Some African American leaders were so inspired by Brazilian race relations—or so discouraged by those in the United States—that they considered Brazil a potential refuge, akin to a black homeland. By the middle of the twentieth century, however, some African Americans who visited Brazil observed the subtleties of race and class discrimination and began to question its prevailing image. Still, some of the most prominent African American scholars endorsed Brazil's racially democratic image, even when their observations and personal experiences contradicted that image (Hellwig 1990, 4–59; 1992, xi–xiii, 47–50, 123, 125, 133).

As the mystique of Brazil's racial democracy proliferated across the globe, the United States continued to practice legalized apartheid. Brazil joined the Allied forces in World War I, and again during World War II to defeat Nazi Germany (and its racist doctrines). However, this did not prompt the Brazilian elite to question their own racial thinking. Even after racist theories were being repudiated by the scientific establishment and in the larger global public sphere in the years prior to and following World War II, Brazilians continued to support the whitening ideal and the belief that Brazil was in fact becoming progressively whiter. However, as this ideal rested on increasingly disreputable notions of racial superiority and inferiority, it would be rearticulated as racial amalgamation or integration. This framed the whitening ideal as a more egalitarian solution to the race problem (Skidmore 1974, 207–10).

The censuses conducted between 1900 and 1930 did not collect data on color supposedly because such data were unreliable and ambiguous. Yet the 1940 census not only returned to the use of color designations but also seemingly supported claims of an increasingly amalgamated (and whiter) Brazil. In addition, one purpose of the census was to "reeducate" children of immigrants to assume the appropriate ethnoracial identity of white and the appropriate national identity as Brazilian, instead of maintaining ethnocultural identification with their various national origins. Otherwise, they might "harbor political sympathies with the fascist regimes [in Europe], and organize themselves accordingly" (Nobles 2000, 93, 98).

The 1940 census employed the color categories of *branco*, *preto*, and *pardo*, as well as *amarelo* (yellow) for the recent Asian immigrants (primarily Japanese). The *pardo* category, which in the census of 1890 had been applied strictly to multiracial individuals of *preto* and *branco* descent, became an overarching term for individuals who did not fit the categories *preto, branco,* or *amarelo.* According to the census data, the multiracial population had declined from 41.4 to 21.2 percent between 1890 and 1940. The white population had grown from 44 to 63.5 percent during the same period. This was due more to the massive immigration of Europeans than an actual increase in miscegenation or racial self-recoding of multiracial individuals as whites (Nobles 2000, 98, 99, 101; Skidmore 1974, 44–46).

Brazil's external racial points of reference remained unchanged until the end of World War II but altered radically afterward. The defeat of the Third Reich also brought an end to Nazi racist doctrines of Aryan superiority. In addition, the independence movements that swept across Asia and Africa threw off the yoke of European colonialism and further called into question the notion of European supremacy. Also, the United States had moved toward official repudiation of legal inegalitarian pluralism, beginning with President Truman's 1948 mandate ending segregation in the armed forces and the federal civil service (Skidmore 1974, 210–14).

Previously Brazilians had been on the defensive when discussing their nation's racial past and future. By midcentury, they found themselves taking the offensive. This reached a climax in 1951 when the Ministry of Foreign Relations released a pamphlet contrasting Brazilian race relations favorably to those in the United States. The pamphlet was published in English and included a foreword by Gilberto Freyre, which clearly indicated the goal of promoting a flattering image of Brazil abroad. Ironically, in that same year, the Brazilian Congress found itself in the awkward (and rather unprecedented) situation of finding it necessary to pass legislation, the Afonso Arinos law, making racial discrimination in public and private accommodations and employment a criminal offense. This legislation was more symbolic than reflective of a genuine commitment to racial equity, considering there was no government apparatus or attempt to investigate possible discrimination in public facilities. What is important, however, is that the Arinos law was passed in response to an incident involving an African American dancer, Katherine Dunham, who filed a discrimination suit after being refused accommodations in a São Paulo hotel while touring in Brazil (Dzidzienyo 1987, 33–34; Skidmore 1974, 209–12).

Comparisons with the United States became even more awkward as African Americans launched their civil rights movement. By the end of the decade, Jim Crow segregation had lost the sanction once given by white supremacist ideology, despite bitter resistance from many European Americans. Furthermore, the removal of the last formal vestiges of apartheid profoundly shifted the legal reality of the U.S. racial order. Later statutes authorized the federal government to penalize citizens found guilty of discrimination on the basis of race, color, or creed

(Bloom 1987, 96–101; Fuchs 1990, 405–8, 453–57; Ringer 1983, 386–423, 426–42; Skidmore 1974, 210–11).[1]

By the late 1960s and early 1970s, Brazilians could no longer claim moral superiority over the United States, which had politically (as well as scientifically) repudiated racism. In addition, being of African descent had become a source of cultural pride and political power in both Africa and the United States. Brazilians were still digesting the implications of these changes well into the 1970s. Though the United States maintained a binary racial project, supported by the one-drop rule, it had removed all legal barriers to racial equality. Indeed, race had become a legal means for gaining government assistance in securing equality in employment, education, and housing (Fuchs 1990, 174–89, 406–8, 453–57; Ringer 1983, 386–423; Skidmore 1974, 210–13). The United States was pursuing public policy that actively promoted equal opportunity and affirmative action in the name of redress and social justice, which mandated integration of African Americans (and other "minorities") into the larger social structure, "even if only in token numbers" (Skidmore 1974, 212).

The majority of the Brazilian elite, however, continued to believe that all Brazilians had equal access to the channels of vertical mobility. The lack of improvement in the social status of African Brazilians was attributed to questions of class and culture, not race. Since millions of whites experienced similar disadvantages at the lowest levels of society, policymakers could easily dismiss the idea of implementing race-specific programs, which they most likely would have considered racist and against the universalist and color-blind tenets of the Brazilian constitution. The question of racial equality was thus subsumed under broader concerns relating to social class. By addressing the larger class issue, so the argument went, the racial question would also be addressed, albeit indirectly (although the issue of class inequality itself has rarely received sufficient attention) (Skidmore 1974, 212–13).

The Decline Begins: A Crack in the Racial Democracy Ideology

In the context of the scientific racism of the 1930s and 1940s, anthropologist Gilberto Freyre's works formalized Brazil's image as a racial democracy and gave it the legitimacy of a social scientist's stamp. In the wake of Hitler's Third Reich, the idea of Brazil's racial democracy was so persuasive that a group of scholars

1. In the United States, the state, however begrudgingly, supported the civil rights movement. Legalized racial discrimination could not have been dismantled without state backing. In Brazil, the state has historically been apathetic, if not explicitly hostile, to questions of racial inequality and partially responsible for the fact that a civil rights movement has been slow to develop.

was commissioned to discover the formula for a harmonious social order typified by Brazil. In 1950, Columbia University and the state of Bahia sponsored a joint research project on social change in Bahia. The research was expanded later that year when the United Nations Educational, Scientific, and Cultural Organization (UNESCO) granted funds for a large-scale analysis of race relations.[2] Charles Wagley (Columbia University) and Roger Bastide (École Pratique des Hautes Études, Paris) were among the foreign scholars who carried out field research in Brazil. René Ribeiro (Joaquin Nabuco Institute) and Luís Costa Pinto (University of Brazil) conducted other UNESCO-funded research in Recife and Rio de Janeiro, respectively. Wagley and his students collaborated in Bahia with Thales de Azevedo (University of Bahia), while Bastide worked with Florestan Fernandes in São Paulo. Fernandes eventually established a prominent school of social science research at the University of São Paulo, along with his students and fellow researchers Fernando Henrique Cardoso and Octávio Ianni (Reichmann 1999, 9, 23–28; Skidmore 1974, 215–17; Wood and Carvalho 1988, 135–53, 215–16).

Inspired by Freyre's formulation of racial democracy, these projects were initially designed to explore and document the absence of racial prejudice and discrimination in Brazil. Empirical data about Brazilian race relations did not, however, correspond to these expectations. These scholars used the most up-to-date research techniques to reveal an intricate web of correlations between phenotype, culture, and class in determining social stratification, despite the conspicuous absence of institutionalized barriers to equality. Though opinions differed on how physical appearance might influence future social mobility, researchers generally agreed that Brazilians who were phenotypically more African were disproportionately located at the bottom of society in terms of education, occupation, and income (Skidmore 1974, 216; Wood and Carvalho 1988, 135–53).

That said, the UNESCO studies operated largely from a Marxist perspective, which tended to reduce racial dynamics to class analyses. Indeed, the leading voice among the UNESCO researchers, Florestan Fernandes, argued that racial thinking was a remnant of slavery and thus a relic of the colonial and precapitalist past. The studies also suggested that a class struggle would largely eliminate the race problem and open the path for socialism, which would finally signal Brazil's sociopolitical maturity. Yet Fernandes, unlike other UNESCO researchers, recognized the centrality of race. Indeed, Thales de Azevedo, Marvin Harris, and others studying the Brazilian Northeast during the 1940s and 1950s hypothesized that

2. UNESCO was founded November 16, 1945, as an educational and cultural organization that would embody a genuine culture of peace. The goal was to develop the intellectual and moral solidarity of humanity, and by so doing, prevent the outbreak of another world war. "About UNESCO" (http://portal.unesco.org/en/ev.php-URL_ID=6207&URL_DO=DO_TOPIC&URL_SECTION=201.html).

class inequalities and cultural attributes had more impact on everyday social relations than race or physical appearance. In addition, Harris and Wagley followed Freyre's line of reasoning and argued that the absence of the one-drop rule in Brazil led to a situation in which racial identity was more flexible and fluid than in the United States (Winant 2001, 219–29).

The scholars of this Bahian School did agree that the overwhelming majority of the affluent were white and that most African Brazilians were impoverished. They also recognized the existence of racial stereotypes and prejudices but did not view these as the source of discrimination. Rather, individual integration into the white-dominated mainstream was contingent on the African Brazilian's cultural orientation and class position. The conclusion was that discriminatory behavior emerged from Brazil's rigidly stratified class structure, which coincidentally corresponded to racial stratification. However, once African Brazilians achieved sufficient income or education, they would be fully accepted by whites (Pierson 1967, 349; Skidmore 1974, 215–17; Wood and Carvalho 1988, 135–53).

During this same period, several UNESCO researchers and other scholars also began disputing the long-held belief among Brazilian and some U.S. commentators and investigators that Brazil's allegedly more equitable post-slavery race relations could be traced back to a slave system more humane than that of the United States. They did not, however, provide any primary data to support these claims. Empirical analyses of Brazilian slavery revealed that the physical treatment of slaves equaled and may have exceeded the level of dehumanization recorded anywhere, although there was general agreement that slave societies throughout the Americas were brutal. This documentation not only challenged the Brazilian elite's belief in the more humane nature of Brazilian slavery, along with the image of the kind and paternal Brazilian slave master but also demonstrated there was no correlation between slavery and post-slavery race relations (Degler 1971, 67–75; Skidmore 1974, 217).

In the early 1960s, scholars of the São Paulo School were among the first to confirm the significance of race (or phenotype) apart from culture and class in social stratification. These scholars accused the Brazilian elite of clinging to the false belief that racism had disappeared with abolition, and that phenotype was no longer a barrier to socioeconomic mobility. Fernandes, the leader of the São Paulo School, captured this best in his famous phrase describing Brazil as having "the prejudice of having no prejudice" (Fernandes 1969, xv). The São Paulo social scientists argued that the racial democracy ideology had been maintained in order to perpetuate the notion that Brazil's "relative underdevelopment or the lack of individual initiative," rather than race, was the source of the abject social and economic status of African Brazilians (Skidmore 1974, 217).

While acknowledging the existence of racial barriers to socioeconomic mobility, the São Paulo scholars reasoned that racial stratification endured primarily because African Brazilians had been "handicapped" by slavery. Consequently, they were unable to "adapt" to labor market competition in the post-abolition period (Reichmann 1999, 25). As Marxist scholars, they argued that opportunities for socioeconomic advancement would increase with national economic growth made possible by industrialization and capitalist development. This would incorporate African Brazilian workers into the industrializing economy as well as distance them from the handicapping legacy of slavery. Furthermore, development would minimize social inequalities among all groups, thereby strengthening class identities and weakening those based on race. The São Paulo scholars, therefore, agreed with their Bahian counterparts in arguing that the correlation between color and social status was a transitory phenomenon and that class-based cleavages would eventually integrate African Brazilians (Reichmann 1999, 25; Wood and Carvalho 1988, 135–53).

By the time of João Goulart's presidency (1961–64), the weight of data compiled by both Brazilian and foreign social scientists had begun to erode Brazil's image as a racial democracy, at least in academic circles. Support of this ideology in sectors of officialdom and among the public remained largely unchanged. Nevertheless, journalists provided anecdotal evidence of a pattern of subtle yet unmistakable racial discrimination. The question was no longer whether but how physical appearance, particularly skin color, influenced life chances. Nevertheless, Brazilians could still boast that they had escaped the United States's distorted white supremacist ideology and avoided its long history of violent urban disturbances (Skidmore 1992–93, 49–57).

Yet the Goulart presidency was a time of great political and economic unrest. Some of this could be attributed to a growing negative sentiment toward U.S. and other foreign business interests in Brazil. The environment was conducive to a social revolution, with political groups on the left and right competing for influence and power. Ultimately, Goulart's regime leaned toward socialist politics and politically influential peasant and labor groups. The regime also dealt with forces that were hostile to these concerns, including external ones (e.g., the United States) and internal ones (e.g., socioeconomic elites) (Burns 1993, 430–44). This orientation was supported and encouraged by Goulart's brother-in-law, Leonel Brizola of the Brazilian Workers' Party (PTB), then governor of Rio Grande do Sul, whose political agenda was counter to the interests of both the United States and many in Brazil's socioeconomic elite. For example, Brizola insisted on the expropriation or nationalization of foreign-owned public utilities in his jurisdiction such as a U.S.-owned subsidiary of the International Telephone and Telegraph Company. This policy of nationalization fully consolidated Goulart's agenda in socialist ideology and politics (Andrews 1991, 188–89; Burns 1993, 437; Freeland 1992, 11–15; Mitchell 1985, 97–98).

According to political scientist Gregory Freeland, all the ingredients were in place during the Goulart regime for the growth of a mass-based African Brazilian social movement: an avowed democratic administration, various established African Brazilian groups to commandeer the struggle for equality, and encouragement from the well-publicized accomplishments of the African American civil rights movement (Freeland 1992, 11–15). Yet African Brazilian groups were unable to forge a strong power base grounded in racial issues and an African Brazilian constituency. The political parties and labor organizations considered demands specific to African Brazilians to be incompatible with, if not inimical to, class-based initiatives aimed at eradicating social inequality. Any significant African Brazilian political activity functioned under the sponsorship of labor parties that claimed to represent the concerns of African Brazilians as part of the larger transracial working class. Nevertheless, some African Brazilian groups worked with labor organizations, despite the difficulties of nurturing and establishing an independent posture based on race (Freeland 1992, 11–15; Mitchell 1985, 97–98).

Still, Freeland argues that this situation worked to the advantage of African Brazilians. First, it afforded them political opportunities that had not previously existed. African Brazilians were members of several parties, and some of their concerns were incorporated in party platforms. Second, the experience they gained in working with unions and political parties—particularly in terms of strategic and organizational skills—proved valuable during subsequent military regimes when African Brazilians were forced to cease all political organizing. Those African Brazilians—particularly the professional and intellectual elite—who chose not to participate in unions or avoided direct participation in politics during the Goulart presidency focused their attention on social, cultural, and educational activities. Ironically, this strategy would also prove advantageous following the 1964 military coup that led to a crackdown on Goulart supporters and leftist groups (Freeland 1992, 11–15).

The Crackdown: The Racial Democracy Ideology Under Military Rule

Goulart's already unstable regime began to disintegrate because of increasing polarization among Brazil's various factions. Mass demonstrations calling for Goulart's impeachment and resignation were accompanied by increased anti-communist sentiment. The Goulart administration might have survived this turmoil had leftist factions not splintered into opposing groups that were unable, or unwilling, to cooperate on any level. Therefore, the regime was vulnerable to forces of opposition—particularly the powerful military. On March 31, 1964, the military overthrew Goulart and seized power. It called for and installed a "new order" (Freeland 1992, 15) based on modernization, "ostensibly to rid the nation of corruption, communism, and economic chaos" (Kennedy 1986, 201).

The 1964 revolution was a response to the sudden upsurge in leftist sympathies and activities, a severe slump in the economy, and spiraling inflation (Foran 1997a, 1997b; Kennedy 1986, 201). The primary goal of the military government was "popular demobilization and the strengthening of elite political control." (Kennedy 1986, 202). To further these goals, as well as promote rapid economic growth while curbing inflation, the military promulgated a series of constitutional amendments, institutional acts, and executive orders aimed at strengthening governmental authority.

The installation of the military regime was devastating for peasants and urban workers. Individual and collective bargaining, for example, was effectively eliminated, which weakened and systematically destroyed organizing among African Brazilian workers. Also, the military government's policy of pitting government-backed industries against small industries led to the ruin of the latter, increasing African Brazilian unemployment. Furthermore, the government pursued a policy of distributing land arbitrarily to corporations and government projects, forcing African Brazilian peasants off their farms. When they protested their dispossession, the military regime responded with repressive and violent measures (Freeland 1992, 11–15).

During military rule (1964–85), political organizing was violently suppressed. Efforts to mobilize along racial lines were deemed "racist," "subversive," and a threat to national security, and were punishable by detention, imprisonment, and even torture. Individuals who organized to address a problem that the state declared did not exist were themselves viewed as creating a problem and accused of having been infected with a contagion imported from the United States. Many individuals were imprisoned; others emigrated or were exiled. Among the vocal critics of Brazilian race relations leaving "voluntarily" for the United Sates were Abdias do Nascimento, a founder of the Black Experimental Theater (which ceased activities after the military coup of 1964), and African Brazilian social scientist Guerreiro Ramos. Others remained in Brazil but met in cultural enclaves that were largely ignored by the authoritarian regime (Davis 1999, 203; Skidmore 1974, 49–57).

The military dictatorship was formalized with the Institutional Act No. 5, which was implemented to counter opposition from students and workers protesting the effects of economic constraints on wages and suppress an armed revolutionary struggle waged by urban guerrilla organizations. The constitution and civil rights were suspended, and Congress was dissolved for an indefinite period. This gave the security apparatus of the military freedom to repress. Institutional Act No. 5 also resulted in the stringent enforcement of Executive Order 314 (enacted in 1967), which imposed heavy censorship of the media. Its goal was to prohibit the "spreading of false information that could imperil the republic" or provoke "conflict between the social classes . . . racial hatred or discrimination" (Kennedy 1986, 202). What followed was perhaps the most far-reaching censorship campaign in the Western hemisphere. This involved full-scale police repression—including the kidnapping and persecution of students—combined with direct and indirect censorship of all forms of media and cultural activities.

Authorities banned, seized, or burned books considered subversive. Periodicals were subject to prepublication review, and newspaper articles were partially or totally censored if deemed "part of a subversive plan that puts national security at risk." Writers, publishers, television newscasters, and intellectuals were subject to brutal police interrogation and often were immediately imprisoned. Under such conditions, authors resorted to self-censorship by seeking "safe" themes and eschewing topics that accurately portrayed the social condition of the masses. Correspondingly, the racial democracy ideology became even more crucial and was systematically and staunchly defended by Brazil's ruling elite. Studies and reports on racial discrimination were among the National Security Council's 1969 list of subversive topics (Kennedy 1986, 203). The national security laws could be interpreted in such a way that even the discussion of racial discrimination could be considered subversive. By 1969, university faculty such as Fernandes, Cardoso, and Ianni, who were conducting research on race relations in Brazil, were branded as subversives and given "involuntary" retirement. When a 1970 BBC news documentary *Panorama* suggested that racial discrimination existed in Brazil, military leaders quickly denounced the documentary as a fabrication (Dzidzienyo 1979, 6; Freeland 1992, 16; Lovell-Webster 1987, 1).

The censorship of public discussion on racial issues was paralleled by the fact that no racial data were collected in the 1970 census. The rationale was that racial data were notoriously unreliable, given that definitions of racial categories lacked uniformity. In actuality, government officials were seeking to promote the notion that there was no correlation between race and differences in education, jobs, income, and health. This also deprived researchers (and therefore the public and politicians) of data that would verify how poorly African Brazilians fared in terms of these and other social indicators (Lovell-Webster 1987, 1–6; Skidmore 1985, 24–41). The enactment of the national security laws, combined with the implementation of massive censorship, nurtured a political climate that was hardly conducive to expressions of black consciousness, particularly those associated with political protest. Thus, African Brazilian political and literary expression came virtually to a standstill.

The Black Movement: Dismantling the Ternary Racial Project

The veil of silence cast over the discussion of racial inequality was not lifted until the "abertura democrática" (or democratic opening), beginning in the early 1970s, which required the military to loosen its grip on the reigns of power. This set the stage for a revitalized black consciousness movement, which was also fueled by other factors. These included the growing racial tension in Brazil, the civil rights movement in the United States, the decolonization of African countries—particularly the Portuguese colonies of Angola, Guinea-Bissau, and Mozambique—and the subsequent shift in foreign policy when Brazil launched its drive for new markets in Africa.

During the democratic opening, black consciousness first emerged in "cultural" phenomena, which were less threatening to military authorities. These included the urban "Black Soul" movement composed of large numbers of underemployed working class African Brazilian youth—mainly in Rio de Janeiro and Salvador—who were inspired by African American cultural developments. These youth crowded into all-night clubs to dance to the "soul music" of African American singers such as James Brown, Isaac Hayes, and Aretha Franklin, and filled movie theaters to see "Black" American films such as *Wattstax, Claudine, Superfly,* and *Shaft.* They adopted English-language phrases such as "soul" and "Black-power kids," colorful clothes, elaborate handshakes, and "Afro" hairstyles as part of an evolving culture of opposition that rejected traditional African Brazilian culture (e.g., samba).[3] The latter had been co-opted by European Brazilian society and had become central to maintaining racial democracy ideology (Burdick 1992a, 27; Fontaine 1981, 141–62; Hanchard 1994, 111–19).

Displays of black consciousness in the early 1970s were also evident in the formation of "study" groups and cultural associations, such as the Centro de Cultura e Arte Negra, the Grupo Evolução, the Grupo Negro, and the Sociedade de Intercambio Brasil-Africa. Some groups, such as the Instituto de Pesquisa das Culturas Negras and the Centro de Estudos Afro-Asiáticos have been traditionally composed primarily of middle-class professionals and intellectuals.

3. Observations of public behavior in Rio de Janeiro, 1977–78. The most recent expressions of this phenomenon include the adoption of reggae music and Rastafarianism in two of the most metropolitan Brazilian cities—Salvador and Rio de Janeiro—along with the adoption of U.S. funk and hip hop music (Sansone 2003, 111–40).

Others, like the Centro de Articulação de Populações Marginalizadas, have claimed the grassroots working class as their base. Many of these entities initially styled themselves as "research centers" to avoid repression by the military. They organized lectures, debates, and exhibits to enlighten African Brazilians and the public-at-large on Brazil's African heritage. More important, they provided forums for meetings among activists and intellectuals to discuss racial issues.[4] Some cultural groups, such as the Instituto de Pesquisa Afro-Brasileiras, have emphasized an African Brazilian identity rooted in an African cultural/racial lineage. Others, such as Rio de Janeiro's Grupo Cultural Afro-Reggae, which emerged in the 1980s, have focused on an African Brazilian identity rooted in the New World experience (Barcelos 1999, 155–77; Burdick 1998a, 3–4).

The same period that gave rise to "Black Soul" also witnessed a rebirth of traditional African Brazilian cultural expression such as samba and related phenomena through the formation of carnival groups such as *blocos afros* (Olodúm and Ihê Aiyê). Beginning in the 1970s, samba schools began dealing explicitly with racial inequality and were no longer willing to use racial democracy as a theme. The music, dance, and lyrics of samba, along with *capoeira*, became important conduits of black consciousness and affirmed a culture of opposition, particularly among African Brazilian workers.[5] In addition, African Brazilian religious practices that had also been co-opted, such as *candomblé* and *umbanda*, became vehicles for black consciousness. *Umbanda* became one of the fastest-growing religions in Brazil during the 1980s and 1990s. Blacks, mulattoes, and whites came together to become possessed by and seek guidance from a variety of Brazilian spirits, including deceased slaves and Native Americans. In addition, blacks worshiped spirits such as Zumbi, the African Brazilian leader of the Palmares quilombo (or runaway slave settlement) that held off a Portuguese assault for decades in the seventeenth century. Zumbi has also been an important symbol for secular organizations in the black movement (Burdick 1992a, 27; 1998a, 60).

Despite the significance of African-derived religious expression, most Brazilians have practiced some form of Christianity. Religious groups, such as the Agentes de Pastoral Negro, and leaders have issued official statements on racial inequality and encouraged grassroots activism. Catholicism and Pentecostalism, in particular, have provided support for black consciousness in the form of African Brazilian martyrs and saints. One of the most popular symbols is Anastácia, an eighteenth-century African Brazilian slave, with a following among older African Brazilian women. According to the legend, the jealous wife of a slave owner unjustly accused

---

4. Observations of public behavior at the Instituto de Pesquisas das Culturas Negras and Centro de Estudos Afro-Asiáticos, Rio de Janeiro, 1977–78.

5. Observations of public behavior at Carnival in Rio de Janeiro, 1977–78.

the virgin slave Anastácia of seducing her husband. As punishment, the wife forced Anastácia to wear an iron mask for the rest of her life. Anastácia's legend represents a harsh critique of the master class and refutes the image of the kind and paternal Brazilian slave master (Burdick 1992a, 27).

More explicitly political expressions of black consciousness emerged in the late 1970s with the formation of organizations such as the Unified Black Movement (O Movimento Negro Unificado, MNU). The first national African Brazilian political organization to form since the 1937 banning of the Black Front, the MNU emerged out of protests in May 1978 on the steps of São Paulo's Municipal Theater. Coinciding with the anniversary of the abolition of slavery, African Brazilians organized in several major cities. Specifically, they protested in response to the murder by police of an African Brazilian taxi driver named Robson Luiz and the expulsion of three African Brazilian youths from a yacht club where they were playing as part of a volleyball team. Although these events were not particularly unusual, they were catalytic in the formation of the MNU. In addition, exiled African Brazilian activist Guerreiro Ramos, as well as Abdias do Nascimento, who co-founded the MNU, returned to Brazil (Andrews 1991, 146–56; González 1985, 120–33; Hanchard 1994, 104–29; Mitchell 1985, 95–119).

The MNU comes the closest to being a national civil rights organization. The organization's platform has supported the position that African Brazilians constitute an underclass whose labor maintains the wealth and power of the European Brazilian elite. Its methods have ranged from demanding recognition of important historical events involving African Brazilians to calling for economic, social, and political reforms. The MNU has demonstrated against police brutality, fought in courts for the enforcement of existing antidiscrimination laws in the workplace, and provided logistical support for improved health care, the rights of prostitutes, battered women, and street children (Burdick 1992a, 24).

The MNU was originally antagonistic toward African Brazilian cultural organizations, which activists accused of being not only apolitical but also reactionary and co-opted. Yet the MNU has itself been the target of criticism. Some have focused on the organization's ideologically narrow and leftist orientation. In addition, the MNU has been criticized for being too aggressive in pushing black consciousness. For many African Brazilians, black identity is simply a fact of life, as questions of socioeconomic survival take precedent over identity politics. Indeed, many have not seen the connection between identity politics and the larger issue of eradicating structural racism (Barcelos 1999, 161–63; Burdick 1998b, 150–52; Covin 1996, 39–55).

Beginning in 1988, the MNU initiated a task of self-criticism, prompted by several factors. One factor was the glaring rift between the "cultural" and "political" trajectories of the black movement. Another was the increasing popularity of carnival groups at a time when the MNU's presence in and effect on the African Brazilian masses was minimal. Accordingly, MNU members wanted to tap into the political potential of this constituency by collaborating with cultural groups. For example, in 1988, the MNU displayed a large canvas of Anastácia at one of its rallies, which some observers interpreted as an attempt by the organization to connect with the masses through popular Christianity and recoup its losses to the rapidly growing Pentecostal movement. By the 1990s, the MNU had not only gained a fuller appreciation of cultural work but also recognized that cultural organizations were doing important political work in forging black consciousness. The MNU decided that its members should join and work with cultural organizations rather than perpetuate a further rift in the black movement. Its current position is that a combination of "cultural politics" and "political culture" will provide a strong platform upon which African Brazilians can articulate their demands (Barcelos 1999, 155–77; Covin 1996, 39–55).

Other more politically engaged organizations have included the União de Negros pela Igualdade (Burdick 1992a, 24–25; 1998a, 3–4). Since the late 1980s, a growing number of organizations like Criola in Rio and Geledés in São Paulo have focused on the concerns of African Brazilian women (Burdick 1998a, 3–4; Hanchard 1994, 119–29). Indeed, African Brazilian women face challenges in mobilizing alongside both the larger black and feminist movements. They have encountered obstacles in gaining greater recognition of sexual/gender inequality in black movement political organizations such as the MNU, which have traditionally been male dominated. At the same time, many African Brazilian men objectify African Brazilian women as the least desirable and least powerful of all social actors. Similarly, the women's movement in Brazil (much as in the United States) has focused more on the concerns of middle-class white women and less on questions of racism. Some activists argue that African Brazilian women must constitute an independent political force capable of dialogue on an equal basis with the women's and black movement as well as with other progressive sectors. The goal is to sensitize white feminists and African Brazilian male activists to the contradictions inherent in sexual and racial discrimination and the link between them (Carneiro 1999, 217–28).

Race, Research, and Revisionism: Cracking the Racial Democracy Ideology

Sufficiently large and reliable sets of socioeconomic data based on color did not become widely available to researchers until the 1980s, after the long-awaited release of the 1976 National Household Surveys (PNAD). In fact, it was only in 1976 that census officials settled on consistent definitions of color categories. A new generation of social scientists (mostly white) not only helped reinstate the race question on the 1980 census but also—with the support of the Ford Foundation—rigorously analyzed the data in the 1976 PNAD, as well as the 1980 census and previous censuses (Htun 2004, 77; Reichmann 1999, 25–26; Skidmore 1992–93, 53; Telles 2003, 31–48).

Sociologist Carlos Hasenbalg and demographer Nelson do Valle Silva were among the first in the late 1970s and early 1980s to disaggregate persuasively class variables from the effects of racial discrimination, and their findings bolstered activists' claims about the significance of race in social inequality (Reichmann 1999, 29). Further research conducted by Silva, Hasenbalg, and other social scientists beginning in the 1990s confirmed and expanded on these analyses. This groundbreaking research uncovered glaring disparities in the areas of health, income, and education between whites, who constitute approximately 54 percent of the population, and African Brazilians, who constitute approximately 46 percent. Most African Brazilians earn substantially less than whites performing the same type of labor and generally fare worse in terms of employment (Reichmann 1995, 35–36; Toni 2004). For example, 90 percent of Brazil's six million housekeepers (or domestics) are African Brazilians (Kane 2004). Racial inequalities in employment and earnings indicate that African Brazilians achieved lower financial returns than whites on their investments in education, particularly at higher educational levels (Silva 1985, 42–55; 1999, 67–82; Silva and Hasenbalg 1999, 53–66). In addition, African Brazilians have higher rates of infant mortality, a greater risk of going to prison, and a lesser chance of entering and staying in a university (Adorno 1999, 124, 128; Hasenbalg 1999, 61–84; Lovell-Webster 1987, 2–6; Lovell and Wood 1998, 90–109; Margolis 1992, 7; Wood and Carvalho 1988, 139, 135–53).

Data indicate that African Brazilians are two and a half times more likely than whites to be nonliterate. Only 12.1 percent of whites are nonliterate, as compared to 29.3 percent for *pardos* and 30.1 percent of *pretos* (Roland 1999, 197). Black and multiracial children are also disadvantaged when they enter school. All else being equal, African Brazilian children enter school later, leave school earlier, and at all ages display a lower probability of being in school than white children (Beato 2004, 774; Lovell and Wood 1998, 90–109). Furthermore, the proportion of African Brazilian children who have no access at all to school is three times greater than that of whites. Educational opportunities for children across racial groups improve with higher socioeconomic status. Yet marked differences in access to education remain, even at higher family income levels. In addition, data indicate that white children display significantly greater rates of progression through school than African Brazilian children: 71.6 percent of *pretos* and 68.7 percent of *pardos*, but only 31.6 percent of whites, fail to complete eight years of schooling. Furthermore, whites are five times more likely than multiracial individuals and nine times more likely than blacks to obtain university degrees: 13.6 percent of whites enter college as compared to 1.6 percent of *pretos* and 2.8 percent of *pardos*. Meanwhile, 4.2 percent of whites, but only 0.6 percent of African Brazilians, have graduated from college (Burdick 1998a, 1–2; Silva and Hasenbalg 1999, 55–57).

Although 32 percent of whites are poor, more than 62 percent of African Brazilians are impoverished; in fact, African Brazilians are half as likely as whites to have running water or a working toilet in their homes. The median income of an African Brazilian family averages 43 percent of that of a white family, and an African Brazilian worker receives on average 57 percent of the salary of a white worker similarly employed (Jeter 2003; Toni 2004). Whites are not only more likely than African Brazilians to be college graduates, but African Brazilian professionals, such as physicians, teachers, and engineers, also earn 20 to 25 percent less than their white counterparts. Indeed, the highest-paid 10 percent of African Brazilians earn just 24 percent of what the highest-paid European Brazilians earn (Rocha 1988, 25). Overall, whites hold the highest-paying jobs, earning as much as 75 percent more than blacks, and 50 percent more than multiracial individuals (Burdick 1998a, 1–2). Furthermore, white high school graduates have higher incomes on average than African Brazilian college graduates (Toni 2004). Color discrimination shapes occupational outcomes, as employment agencies have historically stressed "good appearance," implying a preference for whites in certain positions. Even the national job service (SINE) is reported to have previously used a secret code number to designate certain types of employment for whites (Rocha 1988, 25). African Brazilian women, particularly blacks, are uniquely disadvantaged by virtue of the interlocking systems of class, cultural, racial, and gendered oppression. They earn less, occupy lower-status jobs, receive fewer years of education, and have a higher rate of mortality from debilitating diseases than white women (Burdick 1998a, 1–2; Castro and Guimarães 1999, 105–8).

As part of their statistical research Hasenbalg and Silva also reexamined the concept of the mulatto escape hatch. They pinpointed how the racial divide, in terms of overall socioeconomic stratification, is primarily located between whites and the African Brazilian masses and only secondarily between mulattoes and blacks. Accordingly, the intermediate positioning of the majority of those 40 percent of Brazilians who are considered multiracial is much closer to blacks than was previously thought. Like blacks, multiracial individuals have been largely excluded from the most prestigious professions, such as medicine, law, academia, upper-level government, and the officer and diplomatic corps. Even entry-level jobs in the primary labor force that require a "good appearance," such as receptionists, secretaries, and bank tellers, or even minimal authority, such as entry-level federal employees, are effectively closed to the majority of mulattoes (Burdick 1992b, 41). The multiracial population, along with the 5 to 6 percent of African Brazilians identified as black, remains disproportionately at the bottom of society in the secondary labor force (Dzidzienyo 1987, 23–42). Once in the labor market, wage differentials persist, even after controlling for education and job experience, which suggests the continuing significance of color-based wage discrimination in urban labor markets (Beato 2004, 775–76; Nobles 2000, 161; Reichmann 1995, 36).

Class and culture can compensate for skin color, hair texture, and other somatic features of obvious African origin for select multiracial individuals. Though the popular saying that "money whitens" is utilized as proof of Brazil's alleged racial democracy, it paradoxically evinces the central and yet tacitly ignored fact of white privilege. The assumption is, however, that once individuals break out of the working class and gain the symbols of a more prestigious social status, they are no longer treated as second-class citizens and are magically transformed into ersatz, if not actual, whites by the cleansing properties of the mulatto escape hatch. The mulatto escape hatch notwithstanding, Hasenbalg and Silva found that *pretos* and *pardos* not only have a more difficult time breaking out of the working class than whites do but also suffer increasing disadvantages with vertical class mobility.

Whites and African Brazilians experience similar disadvantages at the lowest levels of society, which gives credence to the argument that social inequality is based primarily on class. Yet whites overcome these disadvantages once they have made educational gains, which themselves have become increasingly important in influencing labor market outcomes. Moreover, whites are more successful at the intergenerational transferal of their achieved status, given the same starting point. Both *pretos* and *pardos* are handicapped by the cumulative disadvantages of previous and persistent racial discrimination that hamper, if not preclude, their ability to pass on wealth, power, privilege, and prestige from generation to generation (Hasenbalg 1985, 25–41; Silva 1985, 42–55).

However, Hasenbalg and Silva's research had some problematical conclusions. They did not find the differences between the socioeconomic status of *pardos* and *pretos* to be statistically significant, which led them to reject Degler's mulatto escape hatch. By contrast, research conducted in the 1990s by sociologist Ana Maria Goldoni found differences between the two populations to be statistically significant, justifying a consideration of *pardo* as a distinct category from *preto* (Goldoni 1999, 181–93). The multiracial and black populations, collectively speaking, are very similar in terms of socioeconomic status and share more with each other than with whites, yet the social location of the two populations is not exactly the same. Multiracial individuals, unlike their black counterparts, have been able to enter the primary occupational tier in greater numbers as public school teachers, journalists, artists, clerks, and low-level officials in municipal government and tax offices. Moreover, they get promoted more easily and earn more than blacks. In addition, rates of intermarriage and residential integration between multiracial individuals and whites are higher than between whites and blacks (Burdick 1992b, 41; Hasenbalg, Silva, and Barcelos 1989, 189–97; Silva 1985, 42–55; Telles 1993, 141–62; 1992, 186–98).[6]

Hasenbalg and Silva's rejection of Degler's mulatto escape hatch may have been partly influenced by their professional training in the United States (Telles 2004, 54–55). Accordingly, they tended to conflate the primary racial divide between European Brazilians and African Brazilians with the U.S. binary racial project. Ultimately, Hasenbalg and Silva may have been using this analysis in support of the black movement's efforts to downplay and counter the divisive color distinctions reflective of Brazil's ternary racial project, which historically thwarted political mobilization of black and multiracial individuals. Accordingly, they viewed the application of the binary racial project—which has been instrumental in mobilizing all individuals of African descent in the United States against racial inequality—as a tactical strategy that would further mobilize black and multiracial individuals in Brazil.[7]

Yet, in this process, these researchers misinterpreted Degler's underlying thesis. Degler does not imply that multiracial individuals, collectively speaking, are significantly better off than blacks or gain access to the prestigious ranks of whites by virtue of their multiraciality. Rather, the mulatto escape hatch has informally awarded a few "visibly" or socially designated and exceptional multiracial individuals the rank of situational whiteness in accordance to their approximation to the dominant psychosomatic norm image. Moreover, this mechanism has over time allowed millions of other individuals who have African forebears but who are phenotypically white to be socially designated as white. Even the presence of some phenotypically African traits has not precluded a self-identification or social designation as white, highlighting the ambiguity of credentials distinguishing white and multiracial Brazilians.

The mulatto escape hatch has historically brought with it a rejection of any association with being African Brazilian to avoid the stigma attached to blackness. This has tended to neutralize multiracial individuals' concern for the plight of

6. Much as in the United States, the majority of marriages in Brazil (approximately 80 percent) are racially endogamous. Although multiracial individuals appear to outmarry to blacks and whites in about equal proportions, black-white intermarriage is comparatively rare (Hasenbalg, Silva, and Barcelos 1989, 189–97; Telles 1992, 141–26).

7. Public statements made by Carlos Hasenbalg and Nelson do Valle Silva at the Center for Afro-American Studies 1980 symposium "Race and Class in Brazil: New Issues and New Approaches," University of California, Los Angeles, February 13–14, 1980.

the African Brazilian masses. Since the 1970s, however, many multiracial individuals have realized that the promise of integration (albeit assimilationist) the escape hatch holds out is, generally speaking, a hollow one. Consequently, many previously multiracial-identified (and a few white-identified individuals) have begun to identity as *negros* or African Brazilian. Activists point to this shift in identification as proof of the success of MNU (and other organizations) in forging a black consciousness (Burdick 1992a, 23–27). Yet this change is also related to the fact that by the early 1970s, many black and mulatto students, who were admitted to college in unprecedented numbers as a result of the dictatorship's policy of subsidizing private universities in the late 1960s, were becoming aware that a college degree did not automatically counterbalance the liabilities of a darker skin color in seeking employment. Many began venting their frustration by challenging the racial democracy ideology and becoming activists in the black movement (Burdick 1992a, 25; Turner 1985, 73–94).

However, some of these multiracial individuals have been accused of seeking to compensate for their shift in identification by parlaying their socioeconomic and cultural advantages into leadership status in the black movement. Anthropologist John Burdick has observed that the leadership—and a significant part of the support base—of organizations such as the MNU has been composed primarily of professionals, intellectuals, and upwardly mobile students from the bourgeoisie, many of whom have been African Brazilians of comparatively lighter complexion. Florestan Fernandes previously made similar observations, finding that multiracial individuals have historically been at the helm of black movements in Brazil as they were in the United States of the early 1900s (Burdick 1992a, 25–26; Fernandes 1969, 208–9).[8] According to several of Burdick's informants, this apparent "mulatto monopoly" on leadership positions in some organizations explains the aversion of some darker African Brazilians to participate in consciousness-raising programs. As one of Burdick's informants explained, "Look and see who is there at the top. It is people whose skin doesn't look like mine. These

8. In Brazilian racial consciousness the term "mulatto" has historically encompassed the *mulato claro* (light mulatto), the *mulato medio* (intermediate mulatto), and the *mulato escuro* (dark mulatto). The term *mulato claro* is more or less synonymous with "light-skinned African American," such as former Miss America Vanessa Williams (although some Brazilians would consider her "white"). However, Brazilians typically refer to intermediate and dark mulatto types when they think of mulatto. For example, African American singers Donna Summer and Diana Ross were often described as "mulatto" in Brazilian advertisements in the late 1970s. Many of the "mulatto" leaders in the black movement fall into the intermediate and dark mulatto categories, although there are some "light mulattoes" among them. Observations of video documentaries on the black movement such as *Orí* (1989) and *We Don't Begin—We Continue* (1989), as well as billboard signs, television advertisements, magazines, and public behavior in Rio de Janeiro and Salvador, 1977–78, and *Raça Brasil* magazine, 1998–2004.

movements are a way for them to say they are black, to figure out a new way to stay on top of us" (Burdick 1998b, 152). In addition, African Brazilians from the bourgeoisie, who view racial politics as their primary concern, often find themselves talking past working-class African Brazilians, who consider these concerns to be of secondary significance.

Turning Black Pride into Black Power: The Battle for the Black Electorate

The lack of unity among African Brazilians is not the only obstacle confronting the black movement. Brazil's national political culture has historically discouraged, if not thwarted, mobilization around raced identities (Barcelos 1999, 164). In union and party politics in the 1940s and 1950s, racial issues were never part of official platforms, although African Brazilians held important leadership positions. During this period, Vargas's Brazilian Workers' Party (PTB), the Brazilian Communist Party (PCB), and the Social Progressive Party (PSP) actively recruited African Brazilians. Many African Brazilians supported the PTB, especially in the state of Rio de Janeiro, because of its social security policies and strong anti-immigrant stance, which enhanced their employment prospects. They also supported the party because its populist ideology espoused integrating African Brazilians as equals (Reichmann 1999, 14–19). Union leaders affiliated with Vargas's National Labor Department, many of whom were African Brazilian, were offered leadership roles in the new PTB. Even during the Goulart administration, a majority of the European Brazilian groups supporting African Brazilians did so under transracial or class-based ideologies. During the São Paulo elections in 1982 and 1986, the few African Brazilian candidates who ventured into the political fray did not run on race-based platforms but rather emphasized working-class issues (Valente 1986, 25–33, 107–16).

The military government that came to power in 1964 sought to fragment the opposition and prolong authoritarian rule by permitting multiple parties to organize. The opposition did fragment, but the military failed to anticipate that some elite opposition leaders would address the question of racial inequality, as well as mobilize and incorporate African Brazilians. Leonel Brizola, a veteran leftist politician who spent fifteen years in exile and one of the founders of the Democratic Workers Party (PDT)—the PTB's factious offshoot—was the first major white politician to prioritize racial inequality as a national problem. Indeed, the PDT boasts more African Brazilian party officials than any other party. Brizola sought to capture the hybrid character of Brazil's socialist agenda by giving the name *socialismo moreno* (brown socialism) to the PDT's populist ideology (Johnson 1998, 101–2; Reichmann 1999, 15). African Brazilian activist, educator, and playwright Abdias do Nascimento served as a PDT federal senator, substituting for Darcy Ribeiro in the late 1980s and in the mid-1990s, and was Rio's first Extraordinary Secretary for the Defense and Promotion of the African Brazilian Population of Rio de Janeiro (Burdick 1992a, 25; Dillion and Silva 1987, 155–76; Reichmann 1999, 15).

The socialist Workers' Party (PT), which was established in 1979, has given racial concerns less consideration. Yet a significant African Brazilian leadership emerged within it as well. In addition, the PT has elected by far the largest number of African Brazilian representatives to Congress (Johnson 1998, 107). Luisa Erundina, PT mayor of São Paulo (1989–92), established the Municipal Department of Black Coordination (A Coordenadoria do Negro) to fight racial discrimination. However, the program was poorly funded and plagued with leadership struggles, which significantly diminished its impact on the São Paulo social order. Meanwhile, African Brazilians in Salvador, Bahia, attempted to translate their numerical dominance into greater political power in the 1988 and 1992 city council elections. The 1992 municipal elections displayed a remarkable diversity in terms of the candidates' backgrounds, and African Brazilians fared better than in previous elections. Nevertheless, white male politicians clearly controlled greater political capital, indicating that politics remains preeminently a white and male domain (Oliveira 1999, 167–77).

Although black elected officials and political representation in Brazil has increased over the last two decades, in the 1980s and 1990s, whites continued to be overrepresented, and African Brazilians, much as African Americans, significantly underrepresented in national politics. Indeed, the number of African Brazilians holding office is still minuscule in comparison with the United States. African Brazilians have held but a handful of the 559 seats in the National Congress (Feagin and Feagin 1996, 265–66; Johnson 1998, 102–17; Robinson 1994, 40); nevertheless, they have become visible in elective office as never before. Before the 1980s, very few African Brazilians were leaders in national parties or had been elected to the Congress (González 1985, 120–34; Johnson 1998, 101; Mitchell 1985, 95–119; Reichmann 1999, 15–16). According to political scientist Ollie A. Johnson III, since 1983, at least twenty-nine African Brazilian representatives have served in the Congress. Seventeen have been elected for two or more terms. In the Chamber of Deputies, African Brazilians were 4 of 479 members (0.84 percent) between 1983 and 1987, 10 of 487 members (2.05 percent) between 1987 and 1991, 16 of 503 members (3.18 percent) between 1991 and 1995, and 15 of 513 members (2.92 percent) between 1995 and 1999. In the Senate, the number of

African Brazilians has remained small, but their overall percentage is greater than that of African Brazilian deputies.[9] This increased presence has had a noticeable impact on Brazilian politics and society.

During this period, Nascimento became the first African Brazilian federal deputy, and later senator, to speak openly in defense of African Brazilians from within the National Congress. As a federal deputy in the 47th Legislature, Nascimento spoke out vehemently against racism, the racial democracy ideology, and pervasive poverty among African Brazilians. In addition, he requested that the Chamber of Deputies publish his speeches and proposals as an eventual six-volume series, *Combate ao racismo* (Fight Against Racism) (Johnson 1998, 109). As a senator, Nascimento articulated key policy positions of black movement organizations. He documented the subordinate position of African Brazilians and presented legislation that would penalize racial discrimination, promote affirmative action, and establish an African Brazilian national holiday. Although his legislative proposals rarely passed, Nascimento used the Congress as a forum to educate his congressional colleagues, African Brazilians, and all Brazilians on the issue of racial inequality. Benedita da Silva, a former domestic, was elected June 1987 as the PT representative to the National Congress from the *favelas* of Rio de Janeiro. She was the first woman and African Brazilian woman to serve as a federal deputy, a senator, and eventually vice governor of Rio de Janeiro (1996–2002). In 2002 Silva became the first African Brazilian female state governor (Rohter 2002).[10] Silva has played a major role in articulating the demands of African Brazilians (Johnson 1998, 97–117).

During the writing of Brazil's current constitution in 1986–88, MNU activists were instrumental in calling for a National Convention of African Brazilians for the Constitution, which promoted debates on the constitutional process in hundreds of towns and cities. The intense lobbying by African Brazilian members of Congress, Carlos Alberto Oliveira and Benedita da Silva, combined with these grassroots debates helped bring about the inclusion of a constitutional amendment that made racial discrimination a crime without bail. In addition, the 1988 constitution guaranteed practically all Brazilian adults (including the nonliterate) the right to vote. Yet there remain substantial challenges in mobilizing blacks and mulattoes as an electorate that would support African Brazilian candidates or a black-based political agenda (Burdick 1992a, 24; Johnson 1998, 97–117).

9. Other African Brazilians have been elected as governors: Albuíno Azeredo in Espírito Santo and João Alves in Sergipe (Freeland 1992, 6).

10. Silva took over the reigns of power as vice governor (April–December 2002) after then governor Anthony Garotinho stepped down nine months early to run in the 2002 presidential election.

The Culture of Racial Resistance: From "War of Maneuver" to "War of Position"

In the past, African Brazilians counterpoised their own forms of organization and identity in a *war of maneuver* (e.g., the Black Guard, Black Front, Black Experimental Theater) against the dehumanization and enforced invisibility imposed by the white power structure. They lacked a significant power base from which to mount a *war of position* that would achieve strategic incursions into the mainstream political process. Groups involved in racial mobilization in the early half of the twentieth century, such as the Black Front, sought to increase African Brazilian education and skill levels to help integrate them into the developing national economy. The racial mobilization in the mid-1940s and 1950s, typified by the Black Experimental Theater, maintained these goals but was more critical of Brazilian race relations.

Prepared in large measure by new tactics deployed under conditions of the *war of maneuver,* racial mobilization in the 1970s generated an even more radical critique of the Brazilian racial order. This was facilitated in part by the "democratic opening" beginning in the early 1970s, which gradually transformed Brazil's political and cultural ecology. These gains provided the institutional and cultural terrain upon which other oppositional political projects could be mounted in order to confront the racial state in a *war of position.* New conceptions of racial identity and the politics of culture, new modes of political organization and confrontation, and new definitions of the state's role in achieving equality were debated and contested on the political battleground.

By the 1980s, African Brazilian groups had begun to focus greater attention on political culture. This can be explained in part by the liberalization in government policies, which enhanced their ability to carry out and maximize political initiatives and interests during the process of democratization. The black movement has sought to move beyond traditional centers of action (e.g., cultural centers, union halls, and university seminar rooms) into the legislature, where they have pressed for civil rights statutes requiring increased racial equity in the media, multinational corporate managerial positions, and "high-tech" employment, among other demands (Freeland 1992, 30).

Politicians who were successful in consolidating political democracy were also receptive to the demands of civil society, which created channels of communication between the state apparatus and social movements. Consequently, movement organizations, like the MNU, inevitably engaged in party politics. They persuaded a number of political parties to include antiracist concerns in their platforms, create commissions on racial issues, and nominate African Brazilian candidates to run for office. Through their electoral victories, political activities, and support of race-specific public policies, African Brazilian politicians have pressed white political actors and the general public to address racial inequality (Burdick 1992a, 24; Freeland 1992, 30).

The black movement has achieved many political victories, yet is confronted with a national political culture that has consistently discouraged mobilization around specific racial identities (Barcelos 1999, 164). Increasingly, however, African Brazilian groups have sought the support of traditional parties in advancing an explicit black agenda and black candidates, although not necessarily supporting a particular party. Thus, African Brazilians have become increasingly visible in elective office as never before, and African Brazilian politicians have used their positions to explicitly advocate for the African Brazilian masses (Freeland 1992, 17–32).

While black movement organizations, including the MNU, have not garnered enough momentum to be considered a mass movement, they have supported successful political campaigns, as well as drawn public attention to issues of racism. Indeed, like earlier oppositional groups, one of the MNU's prime goals has been to awaken people to the fact that Brazil's racial democracy ideology is a myth. That is to say, the culture of Brazil is no inclusive transracial/transcultural commonality resulting from an egalitarian blending of African Brazilian and European Brazilian traditions but the product of the inegalitarian integration of African Brazilians into the European Brazilian world through the elimination of African Brazilian racial and cultural distinctiveness. More important, these dynamics have allowed socio-economic mobility for only a privileged few multiracial individuals (and some rare blacks), who are then co-opted into an alliance with whites as "insiders."

By focusing on how race, apart from class, determines social inequality, the MNU and other African Brazilian organizations and activists have sought to highlight the de facto apartheid that racial democracy ideology has masked. This de facto apartheid is a form of inegalitarian pluralism whose end result can only be the exclusion of black and multiracial Brazilians from the mainstream of Brazilian life.

Accordingly, activists have rearticulated the dichotomization of blackness and whiteness in order to challenge their hierarchical ranking. To achieve this goal they sought to sensitize individuals to the notion of African ancestry by replacing the commonsense notions of color reflected in the terms *preto* and *pardo* with the racial term *negro* (African Brazilian). The goal of forging a united African Brazilian community premised on egalitarian pluralism to challenge the dominant assimilationist ideology and achieve a more equitable society has frequently encountered blatant hostility from sectors of the political and cultural establishment. Some critics, for example, have termed the MNU as "un-Brazilian" and have accused it of mindlessly imitating the United States's civil rights movement and racial thinking. Others have viewed the organization's pluralist goals as a type of reverse apartheid. Instead, what activists have sought is to maintain mutually respectful and differentiated African Brazilian and European Brazilian racial/cultural groups—egalitarian pluralism. Both African Brazilians and European Brazilians would have equal access to all aspects of the public sphere, with the option of integrating in the private sphere—egalitarian integration. In other words, African Brazilians could choose to integrate on their own terms, as opposed to assimilating into the European Brazilian culture.

Traditional explanations of social movements relying on relative deprivation, resource mobilization, and responses to political opportunities, while useful, provide insufficient analyses of the related process of identity formation. Identities have little power to shape group members' actions until they involve more than simple awareness among members that they constitute a group. Individuals must be aware of themselves as part of, or integrated into, a group. Defining the "object" of social mobilization must logically precede collective action. A racial or ethnic identity becomes not only a lens through which individuals interpret and make sense of the world around them but also a starting point for social action. Correspondingly, definitional issues shape how other issues and interests are perceived and can be acted upon in the formation of a social movement (Cornell and Hartmann 1998, 86; Marx 1995, 159–60).

In addition, accountability of individuals to race categories and identities is key to understanding the maintenance of the Brazilian racial order. It is a means by which situated social action contributes to the reproduction of racialized social structure and systems of domination, whose ingrained ideas, practices, and procedures erect racial hierarchies that exclude, control, and constrain human agency. Nevertheless, individuals are active agents in constructing, maintaining, reproducing, transforming, and reconstructing their identities (West and Fenstermaker 1995, 19). Considering that the Brazilian racial order—as well as the ternary racial project and the escape hatch—is continually constructed in everyday life, it follows that under certain conditions, individuals acting as singular or collective agents resist pressures to conform to those social forces.

Cultural initiatives involving identification as *negro* represent just such a form of resistance by individuals and groups who seek to mobilize black and multiracial individuals into an African Brazilian constituency based on the notion of ethnoracial origins (e.g., African ancestry). However, movement activists, particularly those associated with political organizations such as the MNU, commonly state that the African Brazilian masses are not receptive to their message of positive black identity and denunciations of racism. They attribute this to the fluidity and ambiguity of racial identities, which has not only led to a vague awareness of color prejudice and discrimination but also diluted voices against the brutalities of racial discrimination. Indeed, the little systematic evidence available in the 1980s and 1990s suggests that the African Brazilian masses were largely unaware of the MNU and its activities (Burdick 1992a, 25–26; 1998b, 150–52; Sheriff 2001, 192–94).

Yet Burdick and anthropologist Robin Sheriff insist that this argument calls for careful assessment (Sheriff 2001, 46, 114–17). Lack of popular support of and as well as limited direct involvement in black movement political organizations does not necessarily mean ignorance of and indifference toward those organizations, or ignorance of color prejudice and discrimination. Indeed, most of Burdick's "lifelong black" informants could identify color prejudice and discrimination in their lives. They also displayed a wide range of awareness of the black movement and a variety of reasons for their lack of involvement. More neutral reasons given included a "lack of time." Those who gave more negative reasons often felt that many black movement political organizations are more interested in self-promotion and with resolving the identity ambiguities of elite African Brazilians than with addressing the everyday problems of racism faced by people who have no such identity ambiguities (Burdick 1998b, 139–52).

Of course, these and other similar conundrums are prevalent among popular social movements, which tend to be commandeered by individuals of higher socioeconomic status than the majority of their targeted constituency. The latter may see little benefit in "assuming blackness," which they consider to be a predicament of individuals who are "confused" about their racial identity. Statements such as "we are all *negros*," which inform the social practice of the black movement, require that individuals identify themselves as *negros* to be active participants in movement organizations. Naturally, this practice excludes people of African descent who are averse to acknowledging and identifying with it. It may also exclude self-identified *negros* who express general sympathy for the objectives of fighting discrimination and valorizing an African Brazilian identity, but who view the objective of building a unified African Brazilian identity as less appealing personally. Consequently, Burdick suggests there may be a large black movement constituency that remains relatively untapped. Arguably, to tap it may require overcoming ideological barriers *within* the black movement itself (Burdick 1998b, 139–52).

eight THE U.S. CONVERGENCE
Toward the Brazilian Path

From Racial Dictatorship to Racial Democracy: Metaracism and the Color-Blind Society

African Americans have been vocal in their opposition to a multiracial identity. Many fear this identity will undermine their integrity and solidarity, as have "passing" and the formation of blue-vein societies. Those multiracial identity projects were not only products of the Eurocentrism in the larger society but also responsible for a divisive and pernicious "colorism" among African-descent Americans. Colorism has historically perpetuated the divide between the less privileged black masses and the privileged few by granting preferential treatment to individuals who more closely approximate European American cultural norms and appearance.

A Decline in the Significance of Race?

Intraracial stratification among African-descent Americans based on skin color has varied in intensity regionally and historically. Some argue this phenomenon was reduced significantly by the emergence of the black movement in the late 1960s and early 1970s. Yet recent research by Michael Hughes and Bradley R. Hertel, as well as Verna Keith and Cedric Herring, found that educational attainment, occupational opportunities, and family income increased considerably with lighter skin (Johnson and Farrell 1995). Significantly, this research, based on the National Survey of Black Americans (1979–80), found no appreciable difference between data complied in 1950 and in 1980 (Hughes and Hertel 1990, 1105–20; Keith and Herring 1991, 760–78).

While all of the 2,107 African Americans in the national survey had approximately the same minimum level of education—twelve years—darker-skinned African Americans earned only 70 cents for every dollar that lighter-skinned African Americans earned. Between all African Americans and all European Americans with approximately twelve years of education, lighter-skinned African Americans earned about 58 cents for every dollar European Americans earned. Most revealing, however, were the employment percentages for both groups in high-status and high-paying professional and managerial occupations. Approximately 29 percent of all European Americans were employed in such jobs but only 15 percent of all African Americans, which is nearly a two-to-one ratio. Moreover, this was roughly the same ratio between lighter-skinned and darker-skinned African American employment percentages (27 percent versus 15 percent, respectively). In fact, very light-skinned respondents were substantially more likely to be employed as professional and technical workers than those with a darker complexion, who were more likely to be manual laborers and service workers.

A 1996 Los Angeles study of 2,000 male subjects confirms the importance of skin color in determining differences not only in employment but also in unemployment. Being African American and darker-skinned reduced the odds of working by 52 percent. Only 8.6 percent of European Americans were unemployed, as compared to 23.1 percent of African Americans. Lighter-skinned African American men were more likely than their darker-skinned counterparts to be employed, although their rate of unemployment (20 percent) was still higher than that of European American males. Controlling for educational attainment, darker-skinned African American men were still more likely to be unemployed than their lighter-skinned counterparts; indeed, the unemployment rate for lighter-skinned African American men was only slightly higher than the rate for European American men with comparable schooling (Johnson and Farrell 1995). None of the researchers strongly support the argument that the correlation between skin color and stratification outcomes among African Americans is merely the result of accumulated benefits passed on to lighter-skinned individuals because of their families' higher educational and socioeconomic status. On the contrary, skin color is a form of "racial capital" that continues to operate as an important stratifier in the larger society independent of family background.

Explanations of how and why this is the case differ. Hughes and Hertel conclude that skin color operates as a "diffuse status characteristic" in the larger society, although other phenotypical characteristics, such as hair texture, eye color, and nose and lip shape are also important (Hughes and Hertel 1990, 1105–20). This suggests that European Americans—particularly males—who are generally responsible for making upper-level management and administrative decisions, are more likely to employ, even if only unconsciously, individuals who more closely approximate European Americans in physical appearance, believing they are making impartial decisions based on competence or other criteria. Keith and Herring, by contrast, hold that this selection process may not be so unconscious and unintentional. Similar research in social psychology and organizational demography consistently finds an expressed preference for coworkers of the same race. European Americans may express a preference for lighter-skinned over darker-skinned blacks because the former are perceived to be closer to whites in terms of racial and assumed behavioral and attitudinal characteristics (Russell, Wilson, and Hall 1992, 127–28; Shellenbarger 1993; Tsui, Egan, and O' Reilly 1992, 549–79).

Whether the preference is based on conscious aesthetic preferences and feelings of comfort that minimize social distance, or simply on unconscious decisions, one is immediately struck by the fact that a significant number of African American "firsts" in the post–civil rights era were all light-skinned. Consider, for example, Thurgood Marshall, the first African American Supreme Court Justice (1966); Edward W. Brooke, the first African American senator to be elected since Reconstruction; Patricia Harris, the first African American woman cabinet member (1976); David Dinkins, the first African American mayor of New York; L. Douglas Wilder, the first African American ever elected governor; General Colin Powell, the first African American chairman of the Joint Chiefs of Staff and former secretary of state (and possibly the only black candidate that could pull in large numbers of votes from the largely white neoconservative right as a Republican presidential candidate), to mention only a few.

In the media, entertainment industry, and world of high fashion—to name only a few obvious areas—there are advantages that accrue to those who more closely approximate the dominant European American aesthetic pervading those cultural spheres (Njeri 1988a; Russell, Wilson, and Hall 1992, 134–62). African American anchors for the nationally syndicated news media, both male and female, are disproportionately light-skinned individuals. However, the trend with African American men is more complicated and varies according to the industry, that is, film, modeling, and news media. Lighter-skinned males have an advantage over darker-skinned males in terms of overall aesthetic appeal in the mainstream modeling industry and news media, but darker-skinned males may have an edge in the film industry. Yet white advertisers and fashion designers are said to express an almost routine and unabashed preference for white female models, and secondarily for lighter-skinned African-descent American models, if they select African American female models at all ("Light and Dark" 1997). The most prestigious modeling work—magazine cover spreads—is almost the exclusive domain of white or very light skinned models of African descent. And African American models in general get significantly fewer calls from modeling agencies than white models do ("Light and Dark" 1997; Russell, Wilson, and Hall 1992, 35–37, 134–62).

The Miss America Pageant is perhaps one of the best case studies of this aesthetic bias. Until 1950, rule 7 of the regulations governing the pageant reportedly stated that contestants had to be in good health and "members of the white race." By the 1970s, African Americans and other groups of color (although in small numbers) were accepted as contestants in the pageant, and by the early 1980s five African American women and one woman of partial African American descent had been crowned Miss America (Vanessa Williams in 1984; Suzette Charles, who completed Williams's disrupted reign; Debbye Turner in 1990; Marjorie Judith Vincent in 1991; Kimberly Aiken in 1994; and Erika Harold in 2003) (Banet-Weiser 1999, 123–52; duCille 1996, 27–28).[1]

However, the body types, attire, and hairstyles of these women of African American descent hardly differ, if at all, from those of the European American contestants. Indeed, it is significant that Vanessa Williams, the first black Miss America, is very light skinned, with gray-green eyes and light hair. Whatever moments of popularity and acceptance "black looks" may have enjoyed in the pageant, the svelte white female represents the dominant somatic norm image in most circles, both public and private. No African American woman has won, or is likely to win in the near future, the title of Miss America wearing an Afro, braids, dreadlocks, or displaying "strong" West African facial features (Banet-Weiser 1999, 123–52; duCille 1996, 27–28). The fact that a few women of African American descent have been crowned Miss America is an important shift from previous policies of complete exclusion. Yet this far from proves that the commercial beauty culture has acknowledged African Americans as "beautiful" per se. Rather, it suggests that the commercial beauty culture has absorbed, validated, and commodified only that "blackness" which is a suitable reproduction of whiteness (duCille 1996, 27–28).

Given the continuing devaluation of blackness and normalization of skin color bias in the larger society (Russell, Wilson, and Hall 1992, 127–28), many African Americans have internalized the same color bias as European Americans. This is not surprising, considering the power the latter have to impose their ideals through control of U.S. institutions, not the least of which is the mass media. Consequently, skin color has an impact not just on African American job placement, earnings, and other indicators of social status but more important, on African American self-worth (Bond and Cash 1992, 874–88; Hall

1. The 2003 winner of the Miss America pageant, Erika Harold, is a "first-generation" offspring of an interracial marriage. Her mother is of black, Native American, and Russian descent; her father is of Greek, German, Welsh, and English ancestry. Although embracing all parts of her background, Harold stated in an interview that she identifies most with her African American background (Fosten 2003).

1995, 101). Studies have found that lighter skin color is related to feelings of increased attractiveness, self-control, general personal satisfaction, and happiness in love, popularity, physical and emotional health, as well as feelings of intelligence, success, and career development (Russell, Wilson, and Hall 1992, 67–68; Thompson and Keith 2001). Darker-skinned African American men may develop a sense of being powerless to effect change in their lives and achieve wealth, power, privilege, and prestige through channels available to lighter-skinned males. In fact, studies have found that among darker-skinned men, only those scoring low on subjective powerlessness were able to overcome the impediments of their skin color (Keith and Herring 1991, 765; Russell, Wilson, and Hall 1992, 38–39; Thompson and Keith 2001).

For African American women, skin color is even more central to personal identity and self-worth. U.S. culture values physical beauty in women as much as it values intelligence, political influence, and physical strength in men. Indeed, women's self-worth in the process of socialization typically develops in part from observing and internalizing what others think about them, much more than is the case for men. Consequently, the attributes that society assigns to "attractive" and "unattractive" African American females in terms of skin color have profound implications for their psychosocial development. Intelligence and financial success may compensate for darker skin among males, which in turn mediates the negative impact that darker skin may have on their sense of self-worth. However, darker-skinned women—particularly those with more "West African features"—may be viewed as unattractive no matter how intelligent and successful (Russell, Wilson, and Hall 1992, 38–42, 68; Thompson and Keith 2001, 15).

Notwithstanding the negative influence of darker skin on feelings of self-worth and socioeconomic mobility, one could argue that socioeconomic mobility for dark-skinned individuals has increased and continues to rise. Larger numbers of African Americans have gained admission to top academic institutions and received professional, high-paying jobs, regardless of the shade of their skin. But changes in the relationship between race and opportunity over the last few decades, combined with the persistent Eurocentric bias in the larger society, have afforded lighter-skinned individuals even greater access to wealth, power, privilege, and prestige. Thus, a positive correlation between lighter skin color and socioeconomic status remains. Stratification based on phenotype is one of several different but related and interconnecting systems of stratification that feed on and reinforce one another (Graham 1999, 393; Marriott 1991; Okazawa-Rey, Robinson, and Ward 1987, 91–92). This "matrix of oppression" allots unearned social advantages and rewards to individuals in terms of sex/gender privilege, racial privilege, light-skin privilege, and class privilege (Feagin and Feagin 1996, 53–54; McIntosh 1992, 70–73; West and Fenstermaker 1995, 13–16, 19, 31–33).

The confluence of these systems of privilege ensures that African Americans, regardless of gender, color, and class, are subject to collective racial oppression. African American women are subject to a "double oppression" in relation to both European Americans and African American men. Darker-skinned African American men also are subject to a "double oppression" originating in the convergence of social inequities based on both race and color; darker-skinned African American women experience a "triple oppression" based on gender, race, and color (Collins 1990, 40–48; Russell, Wilson, and Hall 1992, 39, 131; Segura 1986, 48). Darker-skinned African American women from the less privileged socioeconomic classes may actually experience a "quadruple oppression" involving gender, race, color, and class. However, both gendered racism and gendered colorism in social stratification may be mediated by socioeconomic factors. That is, a more privileged socioeconomic status may mitigate the negative impact of a darker skin color, and a lower socioeconomic status may be offset by a lighter skin color for both men and particularly women (Russell, Wilson, and Hall 1992, 39, 131).

Nevertheless, the official repudiation and discrediting of white supremacist ideology and the dissolution of legalized inegalitarian pluralism have led to the increased integration and affluence of the African American bourgeoisie, particularly in business and politics.[2] These developments opened some doors to the black working class by expanding opportunities for educational achievement. Consequently, the number of individuals who have achieved upper- and middle-class status as large and small capitalists, entrepreneurs, professionals, and white-collar workers now make up between 16 and 30 percent of African Americans—depending on whether the percentage is measured in relation to the means of production, occupation, or household income of $35,000 or more (Boston 1988, 1–53; Lacayo 1989, 58–68; Small 1994, 50–51, 117–27; Wilkerson 1992, 113–20).

Many have argued that the growth of the African American bourgeoisie proves that the United States increasingly rewards education and technological expertise largely independent of race, so that race has declined as a factor in social stratification.[3] Racism, through this lens, is viewed only as a secondary

2. In 1970, there were 1,469 African American elected officials nationwide. By 2001, the number had reached a high of 9,101. Center for Political and Economic Studies (http://www.jointcenter.org/).

3. African American economist Thomas Sowell contends that a free market can eliminate racial discrimination if the market is truly free or uncontrolled and educational opportunities are reasonably equal for all groups (see Sowell 1975, 1983, and 1984). African American sociologist William Julius Wilson makes a similar argument (see Wilson 1980 and 1987). However, when Wilson speaks of the declining significance of race, he is neither ignoring the legacy of previous racial discrimination nor suggesting that racial discrimination no longer exists. Rather, his central argument is that there has been a change in the

cause of poverty among African Americans. Although African Americans may have been subjected to racial discrimination in the past, the situation has been ameliorated, making the correlation between race and socioeconomic status insignificant. Disadvantage is more a matter of class than of race, and of cultural impediments like family instability, unemployment, juvenile delinquency, low aspirations, and so on. In other words, it is argued that a historical "culture of poverty" among African Americans undermines their chances of upward socio-economic mobility (Feagin and Sikes 1994, 26, 26–29; Sowell 1984, 76–77, 139; Wilson 1980, 19–23, 122–54, 167–79; 1987, 3–19).

This belief—that the United States has transcended racism—commonly referred to as "metaracism" (Kovel 1970, xi, xxix, xxx–xxxiii, liv–lv, 211–30, 234, 247)—became the cornerstone of U.S. racial etiquette during the last two decades of the twentieth century. It is false. Racism has simply gone underground (Omi and Winant 1994, 113–36). Only a select few African-descent Americans have moved from the margin to gain increased access to socioeconomic resources, and many of those structural gains are circumscribed and easily eroded. Further-more, the black masses, which make up 70 to 84 percent of the African American population (Boston 1988, 8, 41–53; Lacayo 1989, 58–68), have been retained dis-proportionately in service and blue-collar jobs in the secondary labor force. Some are locked into the ranks of the underemployed and unemployed on the periphery of society, and in the informal economy, because of the continuing legacy of de facto—yet no less deleterious—inegalitarian pluralism (Conley 1999, 11; Hacker 1992, 93–133; Landry 1987, 78–93; Wilson 1980, 122–54; 1987, 3–19).

This is not to suggest that the status of African Americans has not improved significantly. Certainly, African Americans made important gains relative to European Americans during the 1940s and the 1960s. But whether they are signif-icantly better off depends on what is being measured, and how. The current aver-age occupational status of African Americans has improved no matter how it is measured. African Americans are included in the economic mainstream in ways that were unheard of half a century ago. Absolute gains in years of formal education are significant. And formal political involvement at both the local and national levels has increased dramatically.

Despite these gains, the condition of African Americans has not improved unambiguously (Carnoy 1994, 13–21; Hochschild 1995, 39–43). Although the income gap between African Americans and European Americans has been

---

"relative role" race plays in determining African American life chances in the modern industrial period. This is as reflected in the changing impact of race in the economic sector—and, in particular, the changing importance of race versus class for social mobility—that has led to the increasing significance of class.

slowly closing, the gap in socioeconomic status remains enormous. Black adults are still two and a half times as likely as whites to be unemployed. This gap exists at virtually every level of education. If one includes "underemployment"—that is, "falling completely outside the labor force, being unable to find full-time work, or working full-time at below poverty-level wages"—then the black-white ratio in major urban centers over the past few decades has risen from the customary two-to-one disparity, to almost five to one (Bobo, Kluegel, and Smith 1997, 18; Lichter 1988, 771–92). Conservative estimates are that young, well-educated African Americans with work experience and other characteristics comparable to those of European Americans still earn 11 percent less annually (Bobo, Kluegel, and Smith 1997, 18). Furthermore, studies have documented continued direct labor-market discrimination against African Americans at both low-skill entry-level and more highly skilled positions. Some studies indicate that even highly skilled and accomplished black managers encounter "glass ceilings" in the corporate sphere, prompting some analysts to suggest that African Americans will never be fully admitted into the power elite (Bobo, Kluegel, and Smith 1997, 18–19; Waldinger and Bailey 1991, 291–323).

The black-white gap in employment and earnings almost seems insignificant compared to differences in wealth, which is in many ways a more reliable indicator of one's quality of life than income (Bobo, Kluegel, and Smith 1997, 18; Conley 1999, 1–13; Feagin and Feagin 1996, 256–57; Oliver and Shapiro 1995, ix–52). The median net worth (including assets other than earnings, such as property, savings, investments, and so on) of the African American household is $4,604, while the median net worth of the European American household is $44,408, or ten times greater (Bobo, Kluegel, and Smith 1997, 18–19). Furthermore, white households with incomes between $7,500 and $15,000 have "higher mean net worth and net financial assets than black households making $45,000 to $60,000" (Starr 1992, 7–16). In other words, even European Americans near the lower end of the white income distribution have more wealth than African Americans near the upper end of the black income distribution. Furthermore, the types of assets held by European American households are quite different from those held by African American households. Almost three-quarters of African American households' assets (but less than half of European American households' assets) are held in durable goods such as housing and vehicles. European American households hold more than three times as much of their wealth in interest-bearing bank accounts or stock shares than do African American households (Feagin and Feagin 1996, 256–57).

African Americans, including the upper and middle classes, occupy a uniquely disadvantaged position in terms of housing, which demographers Douglas Massey and Nancy Denton describe as "hypersegregation" (Massey and Denton 1993, 1–10, 74–78, 81, 83, 144, 148). Hypersegregated groups are "extremely racially isolated from whites on four of five standard measures of residential segregation" (Bobo, Kluegel, and Smith 1997, 18; Massey and Denton 1993, 1–10, 74–78, 81, 83, 144, 148). According to 1980, 1990, and 2000 census data for large metropolitan areas, African Americans and Latinas/os rank as hypersegregated from whites, in contrast to Asian Americans (although Asian American and Latina/o groups vary individually in terms of these conditions). African Americans are the only group in which this trend does not decrease with increased socioeconomic status (Denton 1994, 49–81; Massey and Denton 1993, 9, 73, 85–87, 144; Wilkes and Iceland 2004, 23–36).

In the past, African Americans of all socioeconomic classes lived largely in the same racially segregated residential enclaves, particularly in cities. As the African American bourgeoisie has gained in residential mobility over the last few decades, they are no longer confined to those urban areas to the same extent as previously. Yet they are still largely shut out of affluent European American residential areas, especially in the suburbs. If and when middle-class African Americans succeed in breaking through residential barriers in numbers that exceed the racial comfort level of European Americans (generally between 10 and 20 percent), whites begin moving out and the neighborhoods eventually become all black (Hacker 1992, 35–38; Steinhorn and Diggs-Brown 1999, 36–37).

Tired of this "white flight," and the many obstacles to gaining entry to white residential communities, many affluent African Americans who want to live in areas with a "high quality of life" are increasingly settling in predominantly middle-class black communities outside the central cities. This pattern reinforces the growing trend toward "resegregation" that stabilizes identifiably African American enclaves (Darden 1994, 85–90; Feagin and Sikes 1994, 243–48, 264–71; Steinhorn and Diggs-Brown 1999, 36–37). In addition, there is growing evidence that mortgage lenders (not to mention realtors and landlords) discriminate against African Americans (Bobo, Kluegel, and Smith 1997, 19). Studies indicate that racial bias is a significant determinant even after controlling for financial resources and credit history.

The United States is integrated only to the extent that European Americans and African Americans come into contact with each other more frequently in public places and, significantly less often, in the private sphere. If their lives intersect more than previously, most European Americans and African Americans still tend to live in separate, mistrustful, unequal, and sometimes mutually downright hostile worlds. Indeed, except perhaps for attendance at Sunday church services, housing is the single most inegalitarian pluralist aspect of life in the United States (Hacker 1992, ix; Steinhorn and Diggs-Brown 1999, 3–28). Moreover, racial patterns in housing and education have made real egalitarianism all but unattainable, despite the grand illusion perpetuated by the United States, that egalitarian racial integration is imminent.

From Racial Apartheid to Racial Amnesia

During the Johnson and Nixon administrations of the late 1960s and early 1970s, civil rights mandates as well as affirmative action and other compensatory programs were perceived as a way to rectify the inequalities fostered by the racial creed.[4] By the time of the Reagan-Bush administration in the 1980s, many whites and some privileged blacks and other individuals of color began to assert that civil rights legislation, and the ostensibly more tolerant attitudes that followed from it, had removed the most egregious racial barriers preventing equality and advancement of communities of color, particularly African Americans. Neoconservatives and the new right (and Republican party-based politics) that emerged during this period co-opted the terms "individualism" and "fairness" embodied in the American creed to dismantle the very civil rights and affirmative action apparatus that was implemented to fulfill those principles (Laham 1998, 1–132, 195–216; Myers 1997, viii–xiii; Omi and Winant 1994, 109–36; Pinkney 1984, 32–45).

The neoconservative and new right corporate and political elite gained support for this agenda by preying on the fears of those working-class European Americans who occupied an already tenuous position in the U.S. economy. This group increasingly felt themselves somewhat disenfranchised, a situation that was now supposedly exacerbated by "unfair preferences" given to racial minorities. White working-class individuals were framed as victims of a liberal and left-wing agenda that has supposedly been waging war against "traditional American values"—values they purportedly share with the neoconservative and the new right power elite (e.g., Christianity, pro-life, prayer in school, and so forth). All the while, that neoconservative and the new right power elite has pushed for and implemented an agenda of privatization and market privilege that has favored wealthy European Americans and has actually harmed the white working class. Consequently, the white working class has unwittingly become complicit in supporting policies that have worsened its own economic plight and that of the working class in general (Frank 2004, 240–51; Hochschild 2005).

Furthermore, the emphasis on so-called racial preferences in the affirmative action debate has obscured the fact that these mandates are aimed at achieving

4. However, note that Nixon's strong support of affirmative action and other civil rights mandates was not aimed at bringing about actual deep structural change and redistribution that would call into question some of the contradictions of a free-market economy. Rather, the aim was to create the illusion of power sharing without requiring the dominant European American elite to give up control (Allen 1990, 221–31; Bonacich 1995, 138–43; Kotlowski 1998; Pauley 2001, 201–3).

gender as well as racial equity. More important, the primary beneficiaries of affirmative action policies—particularly as this relates to gains in education and white-collar employment—have been white women, especially white middle-class women, and even that within limits (Lewis 2004; Marcus 1995; Merida 1995; Washington State National Organization for Women 1998). Considering that most European American women marry European American men, one could argue that the middle-class European American family has been the biggest beneficiary of affirmative action (Ehrenreich 1995).

This backlash against compensatory racial policies like affirmative action originates in the fear of losing the entitlements and advantages that go along with whiteness and maleness (Banner-Haley 1994, 55, 70). Note that the new right has avoided overt appeals to white racism and supremacy and used "code words" instead (e.g., crime, welfare, family values, special interests, and so on) to further an implicitly racist and sexist agenda.[5] These attitudes have provided a platform for the extremist aims of the less benign far right. Groups such as the Aryan Nation, the Silent Brotherhood, and the Order, not to mention various sects of the Ku Klux Klan, have appropriated the language of egalitarianism for their own political advantage (Banner-Haley 1994, 68; Kuzenski, Bullock, and Gaddie 1995, xi–xv; Omi and Winant 1994, 113–36). This rhetorical sleight of hand (or "semantic infiltration")[6] has enabled them to exploit the current racial discourse supporting diversity and multiculturalism. Accordingly, they have sought to advance a pro-white, rather than an anti-black (and people of color generally), agenda in order to preserve European American racial, cultural, social, and political integrity—supposedly minus the element of inegalitarianism—that is to say, white racism and supremacy. Accordingly, this new right agenda is premised on the purposeful blurring of the distinction and historical relationship between the politics of difference (egalitarian pluralism) and the politics of racism (inegalitarian pluralism).

5. This was also true of earlier Republican-based politics. For example, Nixon's support of affirmative action would seem to convey an explicit endorsement of racial egalitarianism. Yet his "Southern strategy" implicitly sought to appeal to less egalitarian racial, if not racist, sentiments. His goal was to attract support from disaffected white Democrats—particularly the white working-class males and the white working class generally. These individuals objected to civil rights and other "leveling" gains enacted during the previous Democratic Kennedy-Johnson administrations. Accordingly, Nixon was able to solidify Republican rule in the South as the platform for ascendancy of the party in national politics (Flemming 2003; Pauley 2001, 201–3).

6. "Semantic infiltration" is a term coined by Daniel Patrick Moynihan. As stated by Stephen Steinberg in *Turning Back: The Retreat from Racial Justice in American Thought and Policy*, "This term refers to the appropriation of the language of one's political opponents for the purpose of blurring distinctions and molding it to one's own political position. . . . When semantic infiltration is done right, it elicits the approbation even of one's political opponents who . . . may not fully realize that a rhetorical shill game has been played upon them" (116).

The neoconservatives have been particularly successful in using this rhetorical device to further their agenda (Steinberg 1989, 116). Accordingly, they have "rearticulated" (Omi and Winant 1994, 99, 131) civil rights discourse by framing compensatory programs such as affirmative action as a betrayal of the egalitarian virtues of the civil rights movement. Furthermore, these compensatory programs are viewed as contrary to the "color-blind" premises of the American creed, which attribute success to individual merit and effort alone.[7] This was vividly illustrated in the campaign supporting California's Proposition 209. Deceptively titled the "California Civil Rights Initiative," it effectively eliminated affirmative action in public contracting, hiring, and university admissions when passed in 1996. Furthermore, these critics have questioned the purpose of collecting data on race and suggested that racial categories be abolished altogether. This would also deprive researchers and policymakers of the necessary data to monitor the social progress, or lack thereof, made by African Americans and other under-represented groups in education, jobs, income, and health—and of monitoring the harmful effects of discrimination on them (109–35).

That said, differences between neoconservatives and the new right are more a matter of degree than of kind. Both have helped undermine the gains made possible by civil rights, affirmative action, and other initiatives of the 1960s and 1970s. Many of these individuals demanded a reduction in the welfare payments, food stamps, and public housing upon which many African Americans (as do poor whites and others) rely. They also called for an end to government programs like affirmative action and antidiscrimination regulations in the schools and workplace. Opponents of these compensatory policies argue that they are detri-mental to goals of self-sufficiency by shifting the burden of responsibility to the state (Banner-Haley 1994, 46–47, 54, 68; Carter 1996, 98–123; Feagin and Feagin 1996, 253–54, 262, 266–67; Omi and Winant 1994, 109–36). Some even argue that such policies are a form of "reverse discrimination" against better-qualified

7. This was vividly borne out in the March 1988 Newsweek special report "Black and White: How Integrated is America?" which stated that only 29 percent of European Americans (in contrast to 71 percent of African Americans) believed that the federal government had not done enough to aid African Americans. More important, 53 percent of European Americans believed that affirmative action programs went too far in their attempts to equalize the scales by giving less qualified racial minorities priority over more qualified European Americans—although that was never the intent of affirmative action in any case (Gelman et al. 1988). A June 12–15, 2003, Gallup Poll showed similar results, with 70 percent of African Americans and 63 percent of Latina/os favoring affirmative action. European Americans were almost evenly divided with 44 percent approving and 49 percent disap-proving these practices. However, polling results vary significantly depending on nuances in question wording. For example, the majority of individuals say they support programs offering "assistance" to minorities in college admissions or employment. However, support decreases dramatically if the question is reworded to ask about "preferences." Polling Report.com (http://www.pollingreport.com/race.htm/); Public Agenda (http://www.publicagenda.org/press/press_release_detail.cfm?list=51/).

European Americans. Yet by framing European Americans as victims of "reverse discrimination," neoconservatives and the new right have painted themselves as the harbingers of an egalitarian society (Omi and Winant 1994, 28, 73, 116, 128).

In this climate, even white liberals (and Democratic party-based politics) were forced to distance themselves somewhat from race-specific policies that they traditionally supported. Accordingly, beginning during the Clinton administration in the 1990s, they articulated a neoliberal project that among other things downplayed, if not abandoned, the "disuniting" tendencies of racial identity politics and the politics of racial difference in favor of "unifying and universalistic politics of common culture and national identity" (Carter 1996, 98–112; Omi and Winant 1994, 149). In addition, this has been accompanied by class-reductionist discussions of race.[8]

By the mid-1980s, the declining economy and increasing inflation facilitated a shift in attitudes and the abandonment of the rhetoric of black self-determination that had characterized the previous decade. Some African Americans were simply overwhelmed by the obstacles to racial progress and psychologically paralyzed by the apparent hopelessness of achieving the fundamental political and social change that would be necessary to realize racial equality. The rising threat of unemployment within the African American community led many to focus on securing a piece of the dwindling economic pie. Idealistic goals of social transformation were relinquished for a more individualistic pursuit of the American dream (Marriott 1991; Okazawa-Rey, Robinson, and Ward 1987, 98–99).

Correspondingly, neoconservatives and the new right have been able to showcase "successful" individual African Americans and other individuals of color. These individuals have supposedly overcome significant obstacles through sheer individual effort, determination, and merit alone—thus fulfilling of the American dream and serving as a living testament to the much-vaunted color-blind tenets of the American creed. These "lift-youself-up-by-your-bootstraps" personal narratives have made it possible for neoconservatives and the new right

---

8. The new right has its counterpart in new forces on the left, which "began in the Clinton era, as previously fragmented labor, environmental, and community-based and grassroots activists cooperated to resist corporate-dominated globalization policies, with large-scale demonstrations in Seattle and other cities. Creative street action, combined with advocacy and debate (much of it web-based), fostered a new consciousness about global issues as well as a new generation of youthful organizers" (Flacks 2004). Much as the grassroots "new right" did in the Republican Party in the 1970s and 1980s, this new grassroots force on the left is articulating an agenda for social change within the Democratic Party and yet seeks to remain relatively independent of its centrist leadership. This movement's political desires and concerns express a demand for change more radical and far-reaching than the current Democratic Party agenda (as espoused by 2004 presidential candidate John Kerry) with respect to foreign policy, globalization, democratic participation, and national policies dealing with racial concerns (e.g., MoveOn.org.) (Flacks 2004).

to frame liberals (particularly European Americans) as patronizing bigots (or racist "complainers"). At the same time, these success stories have allowed neoconservatives and the new right to frame communities of color as collective self-victimizers that bemoan racial discrimination against groups, while at best significantly underestimating and at worst undermining the power of individual agency (Flanders 2004, 34–35). Neoconservatives and the new right have succeeded in not only enrolling some of these individuals in their ranks but also deploying ostensibly color-blind rhetoric that masks the continuing disproportionate representation of the masses of color in the secondary labor force and among the ranks of the underemployed and unemployed. More important, this has been effective in obscuring the selective nature of integration, in which a few individuals of color—particularly from the middle class—have been allowed to gain access to wealth, power, privilege, and prestige, provided that they do not challenge the racial status quo.[9]

The growth, prosperity, and increased integration of the African American elite do not, therefore, necessarily mean that racism has abated. On the contrary, the African American bourgeoisie, disproportionately composed of individuals who display visible European ancestry and share the sociocultural values of affluent whites because of their class status, has become a vital part of the system of oppression, serving as a double buffer between the dominant European Americans and the darker-skinned black masses. This partial integration of the black middle class into the white power structure merely furthers the illusion of power sharing without actually requiring European Americans to give up structural control. Even worse, it fosters the belief that the excluded majority of African Americans could surmount their difficulties if only they had the character and drive to do so.

Contemporary black-white relations have thus shifted away from the racial apartheid of the past, which was based principally on domination. Although this transition is uneven and truncated, formal exclusion and coercion in the manner of inegalitarian pluralism have been replaced with more informal dynamics in

9. Affirmative action has been instrumental in increasing the size of the black middle class, who because of their social and cultural capital were poised to take advantage of the increased educational and occupational opportunities made possible through such initiatives. Indeed, the black middle class is concentrated precisely in occupations where affirmative action programs have been implemented—not only in the professions and in corporate management but also in major blue-collar industries and in government. Yet affirmative action is not equipped—and perhaps was never intended—to tackle the deeper structural inequality necessary to bring about a radical redistribution that would benefit the black masses. No matter how useful, affirmative action can only bring about limited and piecemeal reform that provides occupational and educational opportunities largely for the select few (Price 1995, 43; Ringer 1983, 556–57; Steinberg 1999; Wilson 1987, 115).

a manner typified by Brazil. Moreover, these are juxtaposed with another less pervasive, yet emerging trend based on inegalitarian integration (or assimilation). Rather than ruling principally through domination (although it is not absent), this trend—which Italian public intellectual Antonio Gramsci describes as "hegemony"—allows dominant groups selectively to include its subjects and incorporate its opposition (Omi and Winant 1994, 66–69, 84, 115, 148).

Neither of these trends precludes the formation of cultures of resistance that seek to counter racial hierarchy by mounting projects in the manner of egalitarian pluralism and egalitarian integration (Scott 1990, 70–96). Yet they do not indicate that the hierarchical relationship between blackness and whiteness has been dismantled, or that the United States has actually achieved a racial democracy in which European Americans and African Americans interact in the manner of egalitarian integration. They indicate rather that the dichotomization of blackness and whiteness has been attenuated. Accordingly, the significance of the one-drop rule has decreased as the primary factor determining the social location of African-descent Americans, because of the increased currency of phenotype—particularly skin color—as a form of racial capital, working in combination with the increasing significance of culture and class (Daniel 2000, 153–78).

Similar trends among Latinas/os help support this analysis. According to the report "How Race Counts for Hispanic Americans," white and black Hispanics—as well as Hispanics who say that they are "some other race"—work different jobs, earn different levels of pay, and reside in segregated neighborhoods in terms of skin color. The report indicates that Latinas/os who identified as white on the 2000 census (nearly 50 percent) had the highest incomes and lowest rates of unemployment and poverty and tended to live near communities of non-Latina/o whites. The 2.7 percent who described themselves as black, most of them from the Caribbean, had lower incomes and higher rates of poverty than the other groups—despite having a higher level of education. Among Latinas/os who described themselves as "some other race" (47 percent), earnings and levels of poverty and unemployment fell between black and white members of their ethnic group (Arce, Murguía, and Frisbie 1987, 19–33; Fears 2003; Telles and Murguía 1990, 682–96).

As in Brazil and other parts of Latin America, African-descent Americans—and other individuals of color for that matter—who share phenotypic and sociocultural similarities with middle- and upper-class whites have achieved greater wealth, power, privilege, and prestige in the larger society. However, this illusion of power sharing disguises the fact that U.S. society is still racist to the core (Allen 1990, 2–11, 18–20; Boston 1988, 158–59; Cruse 1987, 201–3; Johnson and Farrell 1995; Wilson 1992, 108–25).

Keeping the One-Drop Rule: African American Essentialism and the Afrocentric Idea

The balance between colorism in intraracial relations among African Americans and the one-drop rule in black-white interracial relations has shifted in the direction of a more generalized societal "interracial colorism." This phenomenon originates in an inegalitarian dynamic and reflects the resurgence of the assimilationist paradigm that since the 1980s has been redefining conservative political, social, and cultural agendas. However, the new multiracial identity is not synonymous with the psychosocial pathology of colorism. Rather, it is indicative of an egalitarian dynamic that seeks to resist the hierarchical valuation of whiteness over blackness and expand both terms to include more multidimensional configurations. Given the insidious toxins in the racial ecology, opponents in the African American community contend, nevertheless, that increased interracial marriage, in conjunction with the legitimization of multiracial identity, will exacerbate the trend toward interracial colorism and lead to inegalitarian integration (column b in Figure 1). This would not result in a more inclusive transracial/transcultural commonality wherein blacks and whites would become similar to each other (column a in Figure 1), but would rather decrease the differences between blacks and whites by eliminating African American racial and cultural distinctiveness (Douglass 1988, 1–3; Jones 1994, 201–10; Njeri 1988b; Radcliffe 1988; Tourér 1988).

Generally speaking, African Americans have not sought complete de facto integration in the primary structural (or private) sphere, especially regarding intermarriage, despite having challenged both legal and informal inegalitarian pluralism in public and private spheres (Omi and Winant 1994, 113–44). What is envisioned instead is a mosaic in which African American and European American racial/cultural differences—egalitarian pluralism (column d of Figure 1)—are maintained as respectful and dissimilated, if not mutually exclusive (column c of Figure 1), groups and identities. Both whites and blacks would have equal access to all aspects of the public sphere, with the option of integrating in the private sphere—egalitarian integration (column a of Figure 1). The latter pattern would be voluntary, rather than mandated by whites, such that if and when blacks choose to integrate, they do so as equals (Davis 1991, 73–77; Yinger 1981, 249–63).

If the shift toward a more generalized "interracial colorism" indicates that European Americans have become more willing to bend the one-drop rule, many African Americans, understandably yet paradoxically, hold on to this device ever more tenaciously. The rule, by drawing boundaries to exclude African Americans from interacting with European Americans as equals, has had the unintended consequence of legitimating and forging an African American group identity. Originally a tool of oppression, the one-drop rule has become an important element of what Gayatari Spivak calls "strategic essentialism," and critical to the continuing struggle against white privilege (Jones 1994, 201–10; Landry and MacClean 1996, 7, 54–71, 159, 204, 295).

Nowhere is the power of the one-drop rule for cultural and political mobilization more obvious than in currents of Afrocentrist thought, which advance the notion of a primordial African "race" and nation. But attempts to organize based upon essentialized collectives are inherently fraught with contradiction. This is not to suggest that we should dismiss Afrocentric concerns with identity politics, considering that the pervasiveness of white racism has prevented the formation of a radical African diasporic subjectivity. The strengths of Afrocentric discourse are undeniable, especially in the fostering of group pride, solidarity, and self-respect, and the interrogation of both assimilationist ideology and the perpetuation of inequality (hooks 1995, 23–31; Marable 1995, 121–22; Nantambu 1998, 561–74; Schiele 1991, 27). The contradictions and weaknesses of radical Afrocentrism are, however, also readily apparent. Its exponents often criticize the essentialist premises that have historically underpinned scientific racism and sustained white supremacy while reinscribing essentialist notions of black identity (Asante 1980, 105–8; 1992, 17–22; Marable 1995, 122; Rattansi 1994, 57).

Eurocentric thought has used the concept of race to define historical progress or regression, and it gave rise to a historiography that deliberately "bleached out" the role of African participation in the formation of the West (Asante 1980, 105–8; 1992, 17–22; Rattansi 1994, 57). Thus, Afrocentrists are justified in pointing out that European historians have erased the African presence in Egyptian civilization and its influence on the fountainhead of Western European civilization. However, radical Afrocentrists' inclusive application of the term "black" to anyone and anything of African ancestry—no matter how remote in space or time—ignores the complex ancestral, genetic, and cultural diversity that has taken place since early humans migrated out of Africa eons ago. At best, it grossly oversimplifies prehistory and contemporary history, and at worst, distorts it. Consequently, the end result of some strains of Afrocentric revisionism—particularly its more radical variants—is very similar to the oppressive mechanism of the one-drop rule. If Eurocentrism is to be deconstructed, then the "either/or" paradigm that has served as its foundation must also be deconstructed.

The reluctance of many African-descent Americans to critique the essentialist underpinnings of radical Afrocentrism is rooted in the legitimate fear that this would cause individuals to lose sight of the African diasporic experience and the unique sensibilities and culture that have arisen from it. bell hooks proposes that we can criticize essentialism without diminishing the authority of experience. She argues there is a significant difference between rejecting the idea of an African-derived essence and rejecting an African-derived identity forged through the experience of exile and struggle (hooks 1995, 23–31).

The new multiracial identity is part of this process, but many Afrocentrists find it problematic. Some of their opposition is premised on the belief that a multiracial identity is inimical to their goal of forging African Americans into a cohesive political force (Lemert 1996, 86; Rosenau 1992, 52; Spencer 1993, 2–5). Those who support this position view multiracial identity as merely one in a series of recent attacks on the integrity of the African American community (Spencer 1993, 2–5). This criticism dismisses the potential that a multiracial identification holds for challenging from within and from without the imposition of what Victor Anderson calls a myopic and constricting "ontological blackness" (Anderson 1995, 11–19).

One factor that obscures the compatibility between Afrocentrism and the new multiracial identity is that the term "Afrocentrism" has carried different meanings, some of which obscure its deeper significance (Schiele 1991, 27). Although Afrocentrism is related to African history and has emanated from Black Nationalist thought, it is more appropriately described as a paradigm that places African-descent individuals at the center of their analyses. In addition, Afrocentrism is predicated on traditional African philosophical assumptions. Ontologically, Afrocentrism assumes that all elements of the universe are viewed as one and are seen as functionally interconnected. This rejection of clearly delineated boundaries extends to morality, temporality, and the very meaning of reality (Asante 1987, 3–18; Harris 1998, 15–26; Kershaw 1998, 27–44; Myers 1998, 1–14; Schiele 1991, 27). Afrocentrism is a human-centered orientation that values interpersonal connections more highly than material objects. Afrocentrists reject Eurocentric dichotomous thinking that divides concepts into mutually exclusive polar opposites. Afrocentricity thus provides a mode through which all individuals can liberate themselves from the restrictive dichotomization and hierarchical concepts of the modern Eurocentric model. It posits a cosmic vision that acknowledges an inheritance that all individuals share as descendants of "mitochondrial Eve" (Asante 1987, 3–18; Hochschild 1995, 137–38; Myers 1988, 1–28; Schiele 1998, 73–88).

More moderate variants of Afrocentrism *and* of the new multiracial identity criticize the pathologies of Eurocentrism and challenge rigid notions of universality and static identity within mass culture and consciousness. They thus provide the occasion for new and more inclusive constructions of self and community absent from more radical Afrocentric discourse. The new multiracial identity, rather than imploding African American identity, can potentially forge more inclusive constructions of blackness (and whiteness). This would provide the basis for varied forms of bonding and integration that would accommodate the varieties of African-derived subjectivity without simultaneously negating a larger African-derived identity (hooks 1995, 23–31). Part of the struggle for a radical African American collective subjectivity that furthers black liberation must necessarily be rooted in a process of decolonization that continually challenges and goes beyond the perpetuation of racial essentialism and the reinscription of notions of authentic identity (Collins 1993, 52–55; Connolly 1997, 65–80; hooks 1995, 23–31; Rattansi 1994, 30). This process, which George Lipsitz calls "strategic antiessentialism" (Lipsitz 2003, 32–35), should include the search for ways to oppose any reification of "the blackness that whiteness created" (Anderson 1995, 13).

A New U.S. Path: The Ternary Racial Project

The new multiracial identity resists the one-drop rule and the "commonsense" notions of the U.S. binary racial project. This resistance has taken the form of microlevel racial projects, where single actors are the agents of resistance. It has also been manifest in collective action that calls on the state to play a significant role, particularly in amending the federal standards for collecting racial and ethnic data to make possible a multiracial identification. Activists succeeded in getting officials to accept and code write-in responses of "biracial," "multiracial," and similar designations in the "other" category on the 1990 census. This was a radical departure from previous state policies.

Indeed, at no point in U.S. history have multiracial individuals been officially enumerated separately from African Americans or other traditional communities of color, although an attempt was made to count blacks and mulattoes among the African American population in each census year from 1850 to 1920 (except 1880 and 1900). In 1890, the count was further broken down into quadroon and octoroon. The methods, however, were often sloppy and the definitions of these categories varied. Considering that census takers used visual criteria, there was certainly an undercount of the number of African Americans of partial European descent. In 1900 the mulatto, quadroon, and octoroon categories were dropped. Mulatto was reintroduced in 1910 and 1920 but was never used again. Negro, Afro-American, or black became the official census terms (Davis 1991, 11–12, 57; Lee 1993, 77; Williamson 1980, 114). Furthermore, on previous censuses the enumeration of African Americans as black and multiracial (mulatto, quadroon, and octoroon) had few if any formal social implications.

The Racial State, Public Policy, and the Census

From the beginning, the state has been involved with the politics of race and coupled its system of political rule with racial classification. Historically, state officials displayed little if any uncertainty about either "the biological reality of race or the propriety of using census data to support and justify segregatory public policies." Furthermore, they had no compunction about using census data to confirm and shape the contours of racist theory. That said, the work "of past scientists, census officials, and politicians assumed and projected a veneer of (social) scientific objectivity" (Nobles 2000, 77). Scientists accepted race as something basic to human existence, census officials counted by race, and politicians utilized these data in formulating public policy. These data have provided a historical record of population diversity, changing social attitudes, health status, and policy concerns (Lee 1993, 75–77; Nobles 2000, 75–81).

Racial and ethnic data were imbued with a new significance as a result of civil rights legislation and judicial decisions of the 1960s and the 1970s, including the Civil Rights Act (1964), Voting Rights Act (1965), Fair Housing Act (1968), Equal Credit Opportunity Act (1974), and Home Mortgage Disclosure Act (1975). Federal agencies began relying on these data in monitoring and enforcing statutes relating to the equitable treatment of African Americans and other individuals of color in terms of education, employment, public accommodations, housing and mortgage lending, property insurance, health care, minority business development programs, and selecting the beneficiaries of federal grants under some four hundred programs administered by over twenty-five federal agencies (Lowry 1980, 10–11; Nobles 2000, 75).[10] This legislation also addressed African American disenfranchisement, particularly in the South, and more generally, included provisions for redistribution of the 435 seats in the U.S. House of Representatives through congressional reapportionment. They also determined the counts of voter-eligible "minorities," and the ability of such groups to mount successful voter dilution claims in order to draw a district with a voter-eligible "minority"

10. The Bureau of the Census, the Bureau of Labor Statistics, the National Center for Education Statistics, the Centers for Disease Control and Prevention, and the National Center for Health Statistics are among the various federal agencies that collect data on race and ethnicity. However, one of the driving forces for the development of the standards in Directive No. 15 was the need to monitor enforcement of civil rights legislation by agencies such as the Equal Employment Opportunity Commission (EEOC), the U.S. Commission on Civil Rights, the Civil Rights Division of the Department of Justice, the Office of Federal Contract Compliance Programs in the Department of Labor, the Office for Civil Rights in the Department of Education, and the Office for Civil Rights in the Department of Health and Human Services. State and local governments, educational institutions, and private sector employers also use the categories when providing data on race and ethnicity to meet federal reporting requirements (Fuchs 1990, 405–24; Ramirez 1996, 49–62).

population in the majority (Hill 1995, 164–71; Nobles 2000, 75–81; OMB 1997a, 36884; Parker 1995, 73–83).

Previous statutes and judicial decisions largely targeted overt discrimination against specific individuals. The 1960s, however, witnessed a reformulation of civil rights legislation in which earlier mandates were expanded to track patterns of discrimination, as indicated by "the underrepresentation of 'disadvantaged minorities' in the activity of interest" (Lowry 1980, 10). And in cases of under-representation the relevant party was required to implement "affirmative action" to rectify it, whether or not that underrepresentation was the result of deliberate discriminatory policies. The underlying principle of the "patterns of discrimi-nation" and "affirmative action" concepts is that each minority group is entitled to its "fair share" of all "openings," whether in terms of electoral ballots, employment, education, apartments in a housing development, food stamps, and so on (10–11). Activists quickly realized the practical import of the "fair share" principle, which essentially calculated each group's portion in terms of "the population at large or some relevant subset of that population" (10). The larger the official count, the greater the group's legal edge in "competing for jobs, promotions, placement in training programs, housing, education, and access to federal benefits" (12).

Previously, state officials made decisions about racial categories and "non-whites" with little intervention from the groups themselves, and without public input, review, or accountability. By the 1970s and 1980s, the racial state through the Census Bureau, along with the Office of Management and Budget (OMB)—the agency responsible for implementing changes in federal statistical surveys—increasingly had to contend with considerable federal legislation and powerful new political constituencies. Since then the concept of race and counting by race has lost the previous veneer of objectivity. Indeed, it is the very subjectivity of race and its concomitant political significance—rather than any supposed objective science upon which state officials might rely—that is now used to justify counting by race (Nobles 2000, 76–81).

OMB Statistical Directive No. 15 became the federal standard for collecting and presenting data on race and ethnicity in May 1977. The formulation of the directive was guided by the need to meet extant legislative demands and admin-istrative priorities. These included the requirements of Public Law 94-311 of June 16, 1976, mandating the collection, analysis, and publication of economic and social statistics on individuals of "Spanish origin or descent." The goal was to develop consistent terms and definitions for racial and ethnic data collected by federal agencies on a compatible and nonduplicative basis. This would make it possible to aggregate, disaggregate, or otherwise utilize and combine data col-lected by one agency in conjunction with data collected by another agency (OMB 1997a, 36874–80).

Directive No. 15 provided a minimum set of racial categories: American Indian or Alaskan Native, Asian or Pacific Islander, black, and white. It also included two ethnic categories ("Hispanic origin" and "not of Hispanic origin") when racial and ethnic data are collected separately. If a combined format was used, the minimum categories were (1) American Indian or Alaska Native; (2) Asian or Pacific Islander; (3) black, not of Hispanic origin; (4) Hispanic; and (5) white, not of Hispanic origin. In order to maintain comparability, it was recommended that data from one racial or ethnic category should not be combined with data from another category (OMB 1997a, 36876–79). Yet the directive permitted federal agencies to divide the basic categories into more detailed subgroups to meet users' needs as long as that data could be aggregated into those categories (although the Census Bureau has been one of the few agencies to exercise this option, which it has done in response to lobbying and congressional directive) (Nobles 2000, 75–81).

The racial and ethnic categories of Directive No. 15 did not, however, designate certain populations as "minority groups," and were not themselves determinative of group eligibility for participation in federal programs. Furthermore, the categories were not interpreted as scientific or anthropological in nature. Rather, they were sociopolitical constructs developed primarily on the basis of geographical origins and designed for the collection of data on major broad U.S. population groups. In addition, the directive neither established criteria (such as "blood quantum") for individuals' classification in terms of these population groups, nor specified how individuals should classify themselves. Self-identification was the preferred means of obtaining information about an individual's race and ethnicity, except in instances where this was impossible (e.g., in the case of death certificates) (Lowry 1980, 1–25; OMB 1997a, 36879).

Since 1970, responses to the race question (question no. 4) have been based primarily on self-identification when only mail-out and mail-in questionnaires are used. In cases where follow-up interviews were necessary for the 1970 census, however, enumerators were instructed to determine a person's race based on observation. In cases of uncertainty (such as reporting on persons of "mixed racial and/or ethnic origins") Directive No. 15 advised that individuals should be assigned the category that best reflected their recognition within their community. By 1980 this had changed. Enumerators were instructed to ask respondents to state their race if there was any question (Lowry 1980, 15). That said, Directive No. 15 never clarified the distinction between the concepts of race and ethnicity. Indeed, a basic and erroneous assumption of the directive was that individuals who self-identify or identify others by race and ethnicity understand what these concepts mean and see them as distinct categories of experience. Recent research indicates that many individuals consider race, ethnicity, and ancestry as one and the same (American Anthropological Association 1997).

The 1990 Census—Encountering the Racial State

The furor over the question of multiracial identity in terms of data collection first arose in response to a January 20, 1988, OMB *Federal Register* notice soliciting public comment on potential revisions of Directive No. 15. The revisions would permit individuals to identify themselves as "other" if they believed they did not fall into one of the four basic racial categories established by Directive No. 15 (OMB 1997a, 36880). Although an "other" category has been provided on each census since 1910, it is not used on all statistical surveys. In addition, write-in responses in the "other" category have been reassigned to one of the traditional racial categories (Lee 1993, 83).

Many interracial couples and multiracial-identified individuals requested that a "multiracial" or "biracial" identifier, instead of "other," be added to the existing categories. However, the OMB received overwhelmingly negative responses to that proposal from various federal agencies, as well as the public. The most significant opposition came from African American leaders and organizations (Douglass 1988, 1–3; Njeri 1988b; OMB 1997a, 36880; Radcliffe 1988; Thompson 1988; Tourér 1988, 31). Acknowledging that most, if not all, African Americans have some European and, in many cases, Native American ancestry, they feared that many individuals would designate themselves as "multiracial" in order to escape the continuing negative social stigma associated with blackness. This, in turn, would reduce the number of individuals who would be counted as black, which would impact the ability to track historical and contemporary patterns of discrimination and enforce civil rights initiatives. Representatives from other communities of color expressed similar concerns (McRae 1988; Moore 1995, 46; Morganthau et al. 1993).[11]

In April 1986 Carlos Fernández, who is of European American and Mexican American descent and was then president of I-Pride in Berkeley, joined John Brown, an interracially married African-descent American who was a member of the Interracial Family Alliance (IFA) in Atlanta, Georgia, to discuss starting an organization that would function as a national agent to coordinate strategies for gaining official recognition of multiracial-identified individuals. On November 12, 1988, the Association of MultiEthnic Americans (AMEA) was formed in Berkeley to serve this purpose (AMEA 1997a). The AMEA also sought to challenge images of interracial couples and multiracial-identified individuals as race traitors or misfits, while at the same time promoting images that

11. Many radical and liberal European American supporters of the African American struggle oppose a multiracial-identification for the same reasons, although others are unsympathetic to this identification on the grounds that racial designations should be abolished all together.

depicted them not only as stable and "normal" but also as potential "racial bridges" (Fernández 1995, 191–210).[12]

At the founding meeting and in subsequent discussions, much attention was focused on the impact a multiracial identifier would have on affirmative action and other race-based government programs. There was no general agreement on how the organization should deal with this issue, nor could consensus be reached on how to characterize multiracial individuals in this context. Furthermore, members debated whether a multiracial designator was applicable to everyone who identified as such, or whether the term should be restricted to the first-generation offspring of interracial marriages (Daniel 2002, 130–32).

The formats that might be used to collect data were also discussed. These were a separate multiracial identifier (the "pluralistic format"); checking more than one box (the "integrative format"); and a separate multiracial identifier in conjunction with some means of acknowledging more than one group, either through write-ins, fill-in blanks, or checking all applicable boxes (the "combined format"). Although there was no national consensus, the AMEA leadership recommended the combined format. The general public and the media, however, typically framed the discussion as if the movement supported only a stand-alone multiracial category (the pluralistic format), which informed later negotiations with traditional civil rights organizations (Daniel 2002, 131–32).

Prior to the founding of the AMEA, the state considered the multiracial phenomenon a marginal project located outside the normal arena of governmental activity. However, the disparity between the existing racial order organized and enforced by the state, and the growing oppositional ideology, whose proponents were the real and potential adherents of a movement comprised of multiracial-identified individuals and intermarried couples, eventually led to a "phase of crisis" (Omi and Winant 1994, 86–87).

In the months after the founding of the AMEA, support groups held public educational forums to discuss the complexities and controversy surrounding multiracial identity, particularly in relation to the upcoming 1990 census (Cheney-Rice 1988, 1–7; Douglass 1988, 1–3; Njeri 1988b, 1991). A flurry of telephone calls and correspondence between the OMB and Census Bureau officials, the AMEA leadership, and affiliated groups ultimately resulted in a small concession. This reflected a policy of "insulation" (Omi and Winant 1994, 86–87) that confined the recognition of multiracial-identified individuals to a terrain that was, if not entirely symbolic, at least not crucial to operating the racial order. Accordingly, state officials quietly notified support groups that "biracial," "multiracial," or similar designations would be acceptable write-in responses in the "other" category

---

12. Observation of public behavior at founding meeting of the AMEA, November 12, 1988.

(although they did not announce this to the general public).[13] These responses would help the OMB determine what, if any, changes should be made to include a multiracial identifier on the 2000 census.[14]

Between 1980 and 1990, the number of people who marked "other" race increased by 45 percent (from 6.8 million in 1980 to 9.8 million in 1990). Of the approximately 10 million people (close to 4 percent of the total U.S. population) who wrote in "other," 95.7 percent were Latina/o. On the 1970 census, Latina/o entries in the "other" category were reassigned to the white category unless there was a clear justification for reassigning them otherwise. On the 1980 census, which included a question concerning Hispanic "ethnicity" (question no. 7), this practice was dropped. In addition, Latina/o designators that were written in the "other" category remained in and were counted as "other" (Lee 1993, 80; OMB 1997a, 36911).[15]

The increased Latina/o presence in the United States has presented a significant challenge to the binary racial project (Morganthau et al. 1993; Skidmore 1993, 383–86). Indeed, there has been "official ambivalence" about whether Latinas/os should be considered a separate racial category. For example, the census classified Mexican Americans as "white" from 1940 to 1970 and "of any race" they chose in 1980 and 1990. By 1960, all Mexicans, Puerto Ricans, and other persons of "Latin descent" were counted as "white" unless they were specifically identified by observation as Negro, Indian, or some other race. In 1970, a separate question on "Hispanic" origin was added to the census long form (sent to one-sixth of households). In 1980 and 1990, a separate ethnicity question requesting information on "Hispanic" origins was asked of all households (U.S. Congress 1994b, 10, 25, 32, 40; Census 1970, 1980, 1990; OMB 1997a, 36909–13).

The growing number of Latinas/os reporting in the "other race" category can be explained in part by the fact that they originate in countries where terms referring to multiracial individuals (*mestizo, mulatto*) are acceptable means of

13. Much of this concession can be attributed to the efforts of the Interracial Family Circle (IFC) in Washington, D.C., which expressed frustration with the AMEA's slow progress in terms of the census. Many individuals had received delayed or no response to phone calls. Some of the AMEA's administrative inefficiency was due to financial constraints and shortage of personnel, as the AMEA, like most of the local support groups, is a nonprofit organization relying entirely on volunteer staff. In any case, in November 1989, several members of the IFC formed a splinter group that circumvented the AMEA leadership and communicated directly with officials at the OMB, the Census Bureau, and the congressional subcommittee on the census.

14. See Edwards 1989a, 1989b, 1989c, 1989d, and 1989e and McKenney 1989.

15. Evaluations of the results from the 1980 Census, the 1980 Current Population Survey, the 1990 Census, the 1990 Panel Study of Income Dynamics, and the 1991 Current Population Survey have shown that approximately 40 percent of Latinas/os select the "other" category, although the use of this category varies by group and geographical region.

self-identification. In Latin America, race is generally viewed in a way that incorporates phenotypical, social, and cultural characteristics. Consequently, racial designations are understood more as individual markers than determinants of one's reference group (OMB 1997a). In the 1990 census, just over half of Latinas/os counted themselves as racially white and 40 percent as racially "other."[16] Moreover, field tests conducted after the 1990 census to help redesign the race and ethnicity questions for the 2000 census indicated that about one-third of people who identified themselves as Hispanic on the ethnicity question also listed recognizable multiracial identifiers, such as "mestizo," "biracial," "multiracial," and so on, in the "other" category (Rodriguez and Gonzales 1996; Tilove 1991). Yet most of the responses do not appear to be expressions of a "multiracial" identity. Rather, Latinas/os view themselves as neither European American nor African American by virtue of their Latin national-cultural origins, even if they consider themselves racially black, white, mulatto, or mestizo in their respective communities (Rodriguez 1989, 49–84; 2000, 3–26, 129–52).

On the 1990 census the remaining 253,000 write-ins in the "other" category clearly indicated a multiracial identity; the largest number (56,000) coming from California (Downing 1992; Vobeja 1991). In cases where there were multiple write-ins, the data were reassigned to the first race given. For example, the 47,835 respondents who entered "black-white" were counted as black; the 27,926 who wrote in "white-black" were counted as white. Following the 1970 and 1980 census procedures (Census 1970, 1980), the 32,505 individuals who wrote in "mixed" on the 1990 census (including those who wrote in "multiracial") were left in the "other" category, as were the 17,202 respondents who wrote in "interracial" or "biracial" (Census 1990).

This change in policy on the 1990 census was an important departure from previous censuses. Yet in none of these cases were individuals officially designated as "multiracial." These figures do not, therefore, give an accurate estimate of the actual number of individuals who identify as multiracial, not to mention the vast number of people who checked one box because they were unaware of another alternative.

The 2000 Census—Reforming the Racial State

The AMEA and its affiliates failed to make "multiracial" an acceptable means of self-identification on the 1990 census and other official forms. In response to

---

16. In matters of public policy and popular culture, "Hispanic" is now treated as equivalent to a racial category, and in none of these calculations are the respondents who check this box counted as whites (Rodriguez and Gonzales 1996; Tilove 1991).

this, Susan Graham and Chris Ashe, two interracially married European American women and the parents of multiracial children, founded Project RACE (Reclassify All Children Equally). They contacted the AMEA to inquire about strategies for changing official racial categories, both on the decennial census and, more immediately, on public school forms. The AMEA, burdened by more correspondence than its volunteer staff could handle, was slow to reply, especially because Project RACE was most interested in change at the local level (particularly public schools), while the AMEA's focus was national and concerned primarily with the census.

The founders of Project RACE eventually contacted me in response to an article I had recently published in *Interrace Magazine* entitled "The Census and the Numbers Racket" (Daniel 1991, 20). Graham and Ashe wanted to know how they might implement a stand-alone identifier—the pluralistic format—on public school forms, an idea that was sure to be opposed by African Americans concerned about losing numbers, as I informed them. Since most African Americans were in fact multiracial in background (or "multigenerational"), virtually all of them could check a multiracial box if the term "multiracial" meant anyone having multiple racial ancestries.[17]

In fact, the AMEA leadership deliberately focused on the small but growing population of first-generation offspring (i.e. "biracial" individuals) as those individuals for whom these changes were being requested. They did this to sidestep the controversy surrounding multigenerational individuals. Their goal was to gain support for a multiracial identifier by appealing to concerns about children's self-esteem, as well as the symbolic importance of multiracial children as manifestations of the melting pot in action (Fernández 1995, 191–210).

As a member of the AMEA advisory board I suggested that Project RACE support the combined format that included a separate multiracial identifier in conjunction with multiple check-offs. I also recommended the inclusion of some variation on the phrase, "if you identify as multiracial" or "if you consider yourself multiracial." I argued that the focus on origins, heritages, or backgrounds without simultaneously taking self-identification into consideration would lead to unavoidable contradiction and elicit criticism from African Americans and other communities of color, who could use this contradiction to undermine the attainment of a multiracial identifier.[18]

Quite apart from the efforts of the AMEA, Project RACE began strategizing at the municipal and state levels using the combined format. In addition, the

17. Personal communication with Chris Ashe and Susan Graham, cofounders of Project RACE, September 10, 1991.
18. Personal communication with Susan Graham, executive director, Project RACE, September 10, 1991.

organization arrived at a definition of "multiracial" as someone whose "parents are of more than one race." On the surface, this seemed to focus on first-generation offspring, in keeping with the AMEA's strategy of appealing to concerns in the African American community. But the phrasing was purposely ambiguous to address first-generation and multigenerational concerns. Accordingly, "multiracial" could be interpreted as either (1) someone whose parents were themselves of more than one race (or racial background), or (2) someone who had parents that were of different racial groups.

The AMEA meanwhile continued to define "multiracial" as someone of "multiple backgrounds," "multiple heritages," "multiple origins," or "someone of more than one" of the current official categories "as indicated by the race of the parents." This continued to give the impression that the term was applicable only to first-generation offspring of interracial marriage. The AMEA switched its position only when Project RACE eventually joined forces with the organization from 1993 to 1997 to lobby for changes at the federal level. Yet the term continued to be framed in a manner that made it seem applicable to someone with more than one racial background rather than to someone who *identified* with more than one racial background (Douglass and Graham 1995; U.S. Congress 1994a, 115).

As it happened, Project RACE abandoned the combined format because of concerns expressed by state and municipal officials that it took up too much space. Yet the organization sought to politicize racial identities through lobbying state legislators, threatening legal action, and so on.[19] Project RACE eventually gained support at the state and local levels for a stand-alone multiracial identifier. This helped lay the foundation for potential conflicts within and between state agencies regarding the use of a stand-alone multiracial identifier at the state and local levels and the federal requirement demand for single-racial identifiers.

Some state and municipal agencies (particularly public schools) moved toward accommodating challenging forces; others (the OMB and the Census Bureau) remained entrenched in a protracted struggle to delay, if not prevent, changes at the federal level. Nevertheless, federal officials began a comprehensive review process (1993–97) to determine what, if any, changes could be made on the 2000 census. The AMEA and Project RACE testified at government hearings during the review. The two organizations had achieved moderate cooperation, especially after Ramona Douglass succeeded Carlos Fernández as president. Still, Project RACE continued to push for a separate identifier at the state level, hoping to use victory there to bring about changes at the federal level.

---

19. Personal communication with Susan Graham, executive director, Project RACE, December 1, 1995. One such lawsuit was filed against the OMB by Loretta Edwards—the mother of two biracial children—with the support of Project RACE.

Thanks to Project RACE, forms for the Operation Desert Shield / Desert Storm Deployment Survey included "multiracial" as a designation for the off-spring of returning veterans (Susan Graham, pers. comm., October 22, 1992).[20] In addition, Project RACE representatives succeeded in getting elected state officials to sponsor legislation that would add a multiracial category to all state forms collecting racial/ethnic data. Consequently, Georgia, Indiana, and Michigan required a stand-alone multiracial category on state forms, including health department forms, while legislation in Ohio and Illinois affected only school forms. Florida and North Carolina added a multiracial category by administrative directive to school forms (OMB 1997a, 36903).[21] At least eight other states considered legislation adding a multiracial category: California, Massachusetts, New Jersey, New York, Oklahoma, Oregon, Pennsylvania, Wisconsin, and Texas. The legislation introduced in Texas recommended the inclusion of a multiracial-identifier in combination with multiple check-offs. Other state legislation supporting a stand-alone multiracial category allowed agencies to request further data relating to the multiple backgrounds of individuals when necessary (Daniel 2002, 139).

In response to each *Federal Register* during the comprehensive review Project RACE and the AMEA mounted letter-writing campaigns recommending the combined format at the federal level (a separate multiracial identifier plus multiple check-offs).[22] Officials in Washington, as well as others in traditional communities

20. Operation Desert Shield/Desert Storm Deployment Survey, Department of Military Psychiatry, Walter Reed Army Institute of Research, Washington, D.C.

21. The ACT Testing Service (the alternative to the SAT college entrance exam) included a multiracial identifier. Williams College in Williamstown, Massachusetts, the University of Michigan's Rackham School of Graduate Studies, and several alumni associations (at, for example, UCLA and Tufts) included a multiracial identifier on official forms. Since 1989 reports prepared by the Center for Assessment and Demographic Studies at Gallaudet University in Washington, D.C., have counted individuals who indicate a multiracial background. For the most part, however, universities resisted changes in the collection of racial data on admissions forms (Daniel 2002, 138–39).

A 1994 survey of eight hundred public school districts, conducted by the Education Office for Civil Rights, found considerable variation in the classification of multiracial-identified individuals. Many districts used the mother's racial designation; others used the father's, while approximately 30 percent use a separate category (U.S. Congress 1994, 28). A similar policy for classifying the offspring of interracial unions has been used for census purposes. In 1970, they were assigned the father's racial identity; since 1980, they have been assigned the mother's (Lee 1993, 75–94). However, the use of a separate category for multiracial students conflicted with Directive No. 15 unless these data could be retrofitted at the federal level into one of the four official racial categories—black; white; Asian/Pacific Islander; and American Indian and Alaska Native (and the "Hispanic" identifier, when it is given as an option), or into the figures for each of the single-racial groups with which multiracial individuals identify—including the appropriate historically "underrepresented" racial component(s) in their background—when totaling those individual groups' respective numbers, as has been the case on admissions forms for Williams College.

22. Although the leadership of the AMEA and Project RACE supported the combined format at the federal level, data collected by Kimberly Williams indicate that 36.7 percent of the leadership of

of color, however, believed that the stand-alone identifier was the movement's only goal, perhaps in part because Project RACE gave this impression on several occasions, including congressional testimony (Graham 1996, 44–45; Sirica 1995). Yet by the time of the May 1997 congressional subcommittee hearings, the results of field-testing showed that the integrative (checking more than one box), rather than the combined format, would most likely be approved at the federal level. Shortly after the hearings, the AMEA and Project RACE called a Third Multiracial Leadership Summit to discuss the hearings and a possible compromise. The meeting was held on June 7, 1997, in Oakland, California, and sponsored by I-Pride. The summit included AMEA and Project RACE representatives, legal experts, representatives of other educational and support organizations, including Hapa Issues Forum (HIF), a national organization for individuals of partial Asian descent, and a representative of the Census Advisory Committee, who was also part of the National Coalition on the Accurate Count of Asian and Pacific Islanders.[23]

A consensus emerged that a separate multiracial box without multiple check-offs was unacceptable. Participants knew that even the combined format was unlikely to gain support from the OMB, and that traditional civil rights groups would reject it simply because of the presence of a multiracial box. Despite a preference for the combined format, the summit leadership settled instead on a revised model presented by Project RACE that recommended the integrative format. It was argued, nevertheless, that the movement's goals could be achieved in part by incorporating the word "multiracial" in the instructions to the race question, if not as one of the boxes. This compromised format was drafted after eight hours of intense and heated discussion (Daniel 2002, 140–42).

Many individuals and support groups endorsed this proposal, which has been called the Oakland Compromise (AMEA 1997b; Douglass 1997). However, there was strong opposition from individuals (including Charles Michael Byrd, the editor of *IV*) who wanted a stand-alone multiracial identifier or a multiracial identifier in which checking or writing in all the applicable single-racial groups was optional (Byrd 1997a, 1997b, 1997c, 1997d, 1997e, 1998a, 1998b; Douglas 1997a, 1997b, 1998a, 1998b). In addition, the leadership of Project RACE—perhaps under pressure from its constituents—eventually retracted support of its own revised model (Susan Graham, pers. comm., May 25, 1997; Graham 1997f). Consequently, the "Oakland Compromise" caused a rift between hard-liners, who continued to

---

various support groups preferred the integrative format and 40 percent the stand-alone multiracial identifier (K. Williams 2000).

23. Observation of public behavior at the Third Multiracial Leadership Summit, June 7, 1997, Oakland, California.

support the combined format, and moderates, who supported the integrative format. The former more or less coincided with Project RACE and its supporters and the latter with the AMEA and its affiliates.

Among other things, the leadership of Project RACE was critical of multiracial adults, who were disproportionately represented at the summit and insisted that the proposal emphatically reject a stand-alone identifier. Unlike the executive director of Project RACE, Susan Graham, who is a European American partner in an interracial marriage, these multiracial individuals saw themselves as people of color. Consequently, they rejected any format that might be interpreted as insensitive to the concerns of traditional communities of color about the potential loss of numbers.[24] However, from Project RACE's perspective, this not only dismissed but also potentially jeopardized its work at the state and municipal levels where a stand-alone multiracial identifier had been approved for use on official forms. It also jeopardized passage of H.R. 830, which supported a stand-alone identifier (Byrd 1997g, 1997h; Daniel 2002, 141–42). Introduced by Representative Thomas E. Petri (R-Wisconsin) as the "Tiger Woods" bill, H.R. 830 was intended as a last resort if the OMB failed to enact changes on its own.[25]

On July 9, 1997, the OMB announced its recommendations, unequivocally rejecting a stand-alone multiracial identifier, as well as the combined format, or any mention of the word "multiracial" in the race question. Instead, it recommended that individuals be allowed to mark one or more racial identifications (the integrative format). The recommended instructions to accompany the race question were "Mark one or more" and "Select one or more." The format on the census dress rehearsal form (and eventually on the actual census form) read: "What is this person's race? Mark [X] one or more races to indicate what this person considers herself/himself to be." This format was chosen partially in response to the various federal agencies that require racial and ethnic data. They argued that the "mark one or more" alternative—unlike the combined format—would require fewer changes on existing forms and allow for data continuity. Furthermore, the data could be retrofitted in each of the existing official single-racial categories, facilitating the continued enforcement of civil rights legislation (Daniel 2002, 141–45).

In response to these recommendations, HIF and the AMEA actively sought the support of traditional civil rights organizations such as the NAACP, Japanese

24. Observation of public behavior at the Third Multiracial Leadership Summit, June 7, 1997, Oakland, California.

25. Tiger Woods's father is of African, Chinese, and Native American descent, and his mother is of Thai, Chinese, and European (Dutch) descent. Woods is the first multiracial-identified winner of the Masters Golf Tournament in Augusta, Georgia. He is also the youngest person ever to become the Masters champion.

Americans Citizens League (JACL), which played a key role for the defense in *Loving v. Virginia*, and Mexican American Legal Defense and Education Fund (MALDEF).[26] The NAACP and various African American leaders had previously announced that they would oppose a stand-alone multiracial identifier, which they erroneously (though perhaps understandably) assumed was the only option acceptable to the multiracial movement (Daniel 2002, 145–46).

Perhaps what was most disconcerting to traditional civil rights groups and activists about the multiracial identifier was the considerable Republican support it received, whereas Democrats were either neutral or strongly opposed (undoubtedly out of fear of alienating their constituents in communities of color and black elected officials).[27] For example, Speaker of the House Newt Gingrich challenged the Democrats' lukewarm response to the multiracial identifier when he charged that "many Americans cannot fill out their census because they are an amalgam of races" (Graham 1997c, 1997d, 1997e). He also criticized Clinton's Advisory Committee on Race (Gingrich and Connerly 1997) and wrote the director of the OMB a letter supporting the multiracial identifier (Byrd 1997f; Gingrich 1997).

Though ostensibly sympathetic toward the multiracial movement's goal of challenging the oppressive rule of hypodescent, Gingrich and other prominent neoconservatives in fact seized upon this controversy to further their agenda of dismantling affirmative action and other race-conscious mandates. They argued that a multiracial category would help dilute racial consciousness, thereby undermining the obsession with race and ethnicity that fuels identity politics (Graham 1997g). They applauded the fact that a "multiracial" category did not denote a protected class under the law and thus served no statutory purpose. Consequently, gathering data on those individuals who identify as "multiracial" was viewed as a step toward dismantling what they called the racial spoils system (D'Souza 1996b; Will 1997). Thus, Republican support for a multiracial identifier led many individuals to view the multiracial movement—particularly the stand-alone identifier—as part of a right-wing "conspiracy." The movement's goals were seen as countering civil rights claims and efforts aimed at addressing social and economic inequity (Daniel 2002, 146).

26. Personal communication with Ramona Douglass, president, AMEA, June 19, 1997.
27. For example, when President Clinton was asked for his view regarding the addition of a multiracial identifier at a press conference in 1995, he gave his support, only later to equivocate (Falkerstein-Jordan 1995). At one point, however, leading Democratic Representative John Conyers of Michigan broke rank with other members of the Congressional Black Caucus by publicly supporting the "combined format" (U.S. Congress 1997, 535). Furthermore, at the state level, more Democrats sponsored legislation supporting a multiracial category than Republicans. In most cases, such legislation received bipartisan support (Williams 2003, 208–9).

Despite this guilt by association, some activists felt that the Republican majority in the House made their support essential, particularly if it became necessary to pursue this struggle through legislative channels. In other words, this move was based more on political opportunism of some activists than on actual large scale support of the neoconservative agenda by the multiracial movement (Daniel 2002, 146). In fact, when Project RACE proposed an alliance with Gingrich during the Third Multiracial Leadership Summit, none of the other representatives expressed support for this alliance (Brown and Douglass 2003, 121). However, particular segments of the multiracial movement, including APUN (A Place for Us/National), and especially Byrd of *IV*, began to actively foster ties with neoconservatives and converge with their ideological position on race, prior to and after the OMB's final decision in October 1997.

Ultimately, the lobbying efforts by the AMEA and HIF resulted in a host of traditional civil rights organizations, including the NAACP, MALDEF, the Urban League, and the National Council of La Raza, supporting the integrative format. Although they felt this format addressed questions about the loss of numbers, they voiced concerns about how the data would be tabulated for voter districting and other efforts to track and address continuing racial inequality. Meanwhile, Project RACE and its supporters, as well as Byrd and other commentators in *IV*, continued to speak out against the OMB recommendations and in support of the combined format. They also criticized the AMEA and HIF for cutting a "behind-closed-doors deal" with the NAACP (Byrd 1997a, 1997b, 1997c, 1997d, 1998a, 1998b; Douglas 1997a, 1997b, 1998a, 1998b).

The OMB's final decision on October 31, 1997, did in fact support the integrative, or check-one-or-more format, though the term "multiracial" did not appear on official forms.[28] This change was achieved in direct response to pressure from the multiracial movement. Yet this reform came about because of decay in the capacity of state policies to organize and enforce the racial status quo. Indeed, Project RACE believed it forced federal officials to capitulate to the changes it helped bring about at the state and municipal levels (Graham 1997b, 1997a, 1998; Graham and Landrith 1999).

The greatest challenge ahead was tabulating data on individuals who reported more than one race. On February 17, 1999, the OMB recommended reporting data on individuals indicating "one race" and those indicating "two or more races," but the latter category could also be broken down into various subcategories.

---

28. The title of the federal standard on racial and ethnic classification was changed from "Statistical Directive No. 15" to "Standards for Maintaining, Collecting, and Presenting Federal Data on Race and Ethnicity," but the categories themselves remain the same.

However, individuals selecting more than one race should not be listed as "multiracial" but rather, as "persons reporting two races," "three races," "four races," "five races," "six races," and so on (OMB 1999, 41–51). In each case, data on "Hispanic origin" or "not of Hispanic origin" could be reported along with the data on race. However, individuals who identify as both "Hispanic origin" and "not of Hispanic origin" (one Hispanic parent and one non-Hispanic parent), were not permitted to check both of these boxes on the ethnicity question on the 2000 census.

Data from the 2000 census indicate that nearly 7 million individuals identified with more than one race, which is about 2.6 percent of the nation's population of approximately 281.4 million. These figures are higher than what was expected based on the findings of the comprehensive review conducted between 1993 and 1997. Those findings indicated that in self-administered and interviewer-administered surveys—including the 1990 census—0.5 percent of respondents selected more than one race even when asked to select only one race. A slightly larger number—between 1 and 1.5 percent—selected a multiracial category when offered the opportunity to do so (OMB 1997a, 36906). However, the number of individuals that identified with more than one racial group on the 2000 census is still miniscule compared to those that identified with only one racial group (Census 2000).[29]

Of the 6.8 million individuals identifying with more than one race, most were in the West (40 percent), followed by the South (27.1 percent), Northeast (18 percent), and Midwest (15 percent). California had the largest number of black-white multiracial-identified individuals. However, West Virginia, Kentucky, and Ohio had the largest percentages of these individuals. Ohio and Pennsylvania were among the top ten states with both the largest number and highest percentage of black-white multiracial-identified individuals. Of the 36.4 million individuals reporting African American alone or in combination, 4.8 percent or 1.8 million reported African American as well as at least one other race (Bhattacharyya, Gabriel, and Small 2002 66–87; Jones and Smith 2001, 2–4).

On March 9, 2000, the OMB announced that individuals reporting more than one race would be tabulated as members of the "minority" background for the purpose of monitoring discrimination and enforcing civil rights laws (OMB 1999,

---

29. The most common multiracial combinations on the 2000 census were white and "some other race" (31.9 percent); white and Native American/Alaska Native (17.3 percent); white and Asian American (13 percent); and white and African American (10.9 percent). Of the sixty-three possible combinations of racial categories these four combinations alone accounted for more than 70 percent of those who selected more than one race (Jones 2005, 4; Jones and Smith 2001, 8).

41–51).[30] Employers, schools, and others must report the four expected largest multiple-race categories: American Indian and white, Asian and white, black and white, and Native American and black. They also must report any multiracial group that claims more than 1 percent of the population and include a category for any multiracial people not counted in any other group (OMB 2000).

Clearly, civil rights enforcement agencies will need to adopt common definitions for racial and ethnic categories. They must also consider the complex issues related to bridging for enforcement purposes data collected under the old standard and continuing to conduct the important business of ensuring equal employment opportunity during the transition years. Furthermore, procedures that permit meaningful comparisons of data collected under the previous standards with those collected under the new standards need to be developed. Another challenge involves getting municipal and state agencies and organizations to comply with the new federal standard, as well as providing a nationally coordinated means of monitoring that compliance. Indeed, many entities are still in the process of complying with the new OMB guidelines; others have asked for extensions beyond the January 1, 2003, deadline (OMB 1997b, 58782–88).[31] Whatever the case may be, it is clear that the United States is moving in the direction of a ternary racial project, which will socially and officially recognize three racial groups—white, black, and multiracial—as has so long been the case in Brazil.

30. Another method of tabulation would be to assign individuals to the largest or smallest "minority" group they marked. These could be ascertained from the racial composition of the surrounding population for the "relevant geography" in question (OMB 1999, 41–51).

31. Senate Bill 1615, the Ethnic Heritage Respect and Recognition Act, which is sponsored by Senator Simitian, and being considered before the California Senate Judiciary C ommittee, would make California the first state to adopt federal standards that allow multiracial individuals to identify with "one or more" racial or ethnic backgrounds on forms that ask for this information. SB 1615 would also establish standards for adopting the new 1997 OMB guidelines in order to ensure that multiracial individuals are counted in terms of civil rights and other federal actions relating to race. Indeed, with several key exceptions, many state agencies and entities are still employing outdated practices based on Directive No. 15. Personal communication with Alfredo Padilla, project manager, Mavin Foundation Campus Awareness and Compliance Initiative (CACI), April 3, 2006.

nine THE BRAZILIAN CONVERGENCE
Toward the U.S. Path

From Racial Dictatorship to Racial Democracy: Antiracism and the Color-Conscious Society

On May 11, 1988, two days before the official celebration of the centennial of the abolition of Brazilian slavery, black movement activists organized a public protest several thousand strong, who marched through downtown Rio de Janeiro chanting the slogans "Cem anos sem abolição" (One hundred years without abolition!) and "We are still enslaved! Racial democracy is a lie!" (Burdick 1992a, 23–27). This demonstration was met with the greatest display of police force since the end of the military dictatorship. These and other similar black movement activities in the 1980s attracted significant publicity and garnered support from politically and socially conscious intellectuals, the church, and workers' organizations concerned about social justice. Yet many of those seeking a more equitable society have viewed African Brazilians as part of a larger transracial working class. Thus, they believe that race-specific policies targeting African Brazilians would deviate from the main course of social reform. In addition, political organizations such as the Unified Black Movement (O Movimento Negro Unificado, MNU) have often drawn comparatively more attention from abroad than in Brazil. Consequently, they have not garnered broad backing from other sectors of the African Brazilian community (Dzidzienyo 1979, 9; Rocha 1988, 21; Skidmore 1992–93, 49–57).

The Increasing Significance of Race

Although the MNU and similar political organizations have been unsuccessful in amassing broad support for a race-specific political agenda, they are, nonetheless, part of a larger black movement encompassing a variety of social, cultural, and political organizations and activities. Prominent African Brazilians have spoken out publicly about their experiences with racial discrimination. Although it seems unlikely that large numbers of individuals will join African Brazilian political organizations, many appear willing to embrace the notion of a distinct African Brazilian culture and experience. For example, *Black People* (English title, Portuguese text), which was launched in 1993, and *Raça: A Revista dos Negros Brasileiros* (Race: The Magazine of African Brazilians), which emerged in late October 1996, have been among popular glossy magazines targeting a self-identified African Brazilian audience (Buckley 2000; Burdick 1998a, 3; Nobles 2000, 124). Beauty salons specializing in *cabelo crespo* ("kinky" hair) have sprung up in urban areas, and on city streets one finds women wearing nontraditional hairstyles, including rasta dreads, braids, and Afro permanents (Wells 2001).[1] There has also been a revitalization of African-derived religious and musical expression, as well as a growth in African Brazilian literature (Silva 1992, 12–13; Skidmore 1992–93, 49–57). Yet according to sociologist Livio Sansone, African Brazilians still display a "thin" sense of themselves as a racial collectivity while at the same time articulating a "thick" black cultural identity (which is itself to some extent part of the global flow of black cultural symbols increasingly shared by large numbers of individuals in the African diaspora, particularly the Black Atlantic) (Cornell and Hartmann 1998, 82; Sansone 2003, 5, 16, 87–92, 104).

Advertisers who have explored the market for "black" products have become aware of the financial potential of targeting an African Brazilian audience. Other advertisers have increasingly included African Brazilians in television commercials for more mainstream products (Buckley 2000; Cose 1998, 42–46; Luís 2002; Schemo 1996; Telles 2004, 155–56). Even with these gains African Brazilians are noticeably absent from the media, including television, newspapers, and magazines. The same Eurocentric bias that plagues the U.S. media, entertainment industry, and world of high fashion is perhaps even more evident in Brazil, where there are significant advantages for a more European appearance (Moore 1988, 213–26; Telles 2004, 155–56).

Women representing Brazil in international beauty pageants such as Miss Universe exemplify this phenomenon. Miss Brazil contestants of "obvious" African descent in the Miss Universe pageant have been rarer than black Miss Americas. In addition, the Brazilian public's reaction has been decidedly racist, ranging

---

1. The hairstyle called *Afro Permanente* is not a natural in the sense of wearing an Afro. It is more like the "Jheri Curl" of the 1970s and 1980s in the United States. This hairstyle turns naturally "kinky hair" into a wet curly look that is achieved with a chemical treatment similar to that used in hair straightening.

from "murmurings of distress" (Thompson 1965, 32) in the case of Vera Lúcia Couto dos Santos (who was third in 1964) to blatant scorn in the case of Deise Nunes de Souza (1986) ("Crowning" 1986, 29).[2] Despite this public outcry, the two African Brazilian women ever to wear the coveted Miss Brazil crown were multiracial, not black. Indeed, based on their phenotypes, body types, hairstyles, and attire, they represent the absorption, validation, and commodification of blackness in a form that is an acceptable reproduction of whiteness. No African Brazilian has won, or is likely in the near future to win the title of Miss Brazil displaying "strong" West African facial features or wearing an Afro, braids, or dreadlocks. Whatever moments of acceptance "black looks" may have enjoyed in the pageant, these women are anomalies; the slender white female, preferably with auburn hair and light eyes, has historically been the norm (duCille 1996, 27–28).

That said, since the 1990s the Brazilian public has become more and more aware of racism within institutions from the mass media to the university, from political parties to popular social movements, from the Catholic Church to the state (Bailey 2002, 431–35; Burdick 1998a, 3, 32; Htun 2004, 24; Reichmann 1999, 28; Rotella 1996). In June 1995 the prominent newspaper *Folha de São Paulo* published a special Sunday supplement entitled "Racismo cordial: A mais completa analise sobre preconceito de côr no Brasil" (Cordial Racism: The Most Comprehensive Analysis of Color Prejudice in Brazil). The study was based on a Datafolha survey that polled five thousand individuals on various questions, including those concerning the color terms they use in racial self-identification as well as their views on the prevalence of racism in Brazil (Nobles 2000, 124–26). The data indicated that 89 percent of white respondents agreed that African Brazilians were the targets of racism. Yet only 10 or 11 percent stated they themselves were prejudiced or behaved in discriminatory ways (Nobles 2000, 124–26; Reichmann 1999, 5).[3]

To many observers, including many black movement activists, these trends appeared promising. Yet they regarded them as "fragile and contingent" and questioned whether they were a reflection of fashion or a fundamental change in attitudes and behavior (Burdick 1998a, 3; Nobles 2000, 123–25, 127–28). Sociologist France Winddance Twine and others have noted that it is not uncommon for individuals to toe the "politically correct" line about racism yet at the same time have difficulty identifying racism in their own thoughts, behavior, or experience.

2. Jean (Gina) McPherson was a semi-finalist in 1960 but her racial designation is unclear.
3. Similar trends were indicated in research conducted by the Center for the Articulation of Marginalized Populations (Centro de Articulação de Populações Marginalizadas, CEAP), which polled 1,172 residents in Rio de Janeiro and was released in May 2000. Of the individuals surveyed 93 percent stated that racism against African Brazilians exists; 74 percent stated that there was in fact a significant amount of racism, although 87 percent stated they themselves were not racist (Buckley 2000).

They speak mainly of individual rather than structural (or institutional) racism and do nothing to interrupt either. In addition, activists argued that the achievement of long-term changes in the social and economic status of the African Brazilian masses would require major changes in the legal, educational, and health care systems (Burdick 1998a, 3; Twine 1997, 45, 53, 58–59, 61–63).

The 1988 constitution, for the first time in Brazilian history, declared racial discrimination to be a crime without bail or statute of limitation, and punishable by imprisonment (Guimarães 1999, 140; Roland 1999, 198; Skidmore 1992–93, 55). Yet the antiracist article in the 1988 constitution, like the 1951 Afonso Arinos Law, seemed more rhetoric than a societal commitment (Long 1988; Nobles 2000, 160). In addition, civil rights attorneys have found it difficult to establish a legal basis for their criminal complaints even with the passage in 1989 of the necessary constitutional enabling statute—Law 7716—commonly referred to as the Lei Caó (Caó Law) (Guimarães 1999, 140; Hasenbalg 1987, 79–96; Nobles 2000, 109; Skidmore 1992–93, 49–57).[4]

According to sociologist Antonio Sergio Guimarães these complications can be attributed in part to the fact that racism as defined by the enabling statute (and interpreted by the judiciary) is limited to acts of "segregation or exclusion based on skin color or race" (Guimarães 1999, 140), particularly in terms of public services, business establishments, and the like. Yet this type of blatant racial discrimination is rare in Brazil. When it does occur, the "racial" motive is hidden beneath a complex set of informal rules and processes and often disguised with a variety of "code words" (e.g., "good appearance," "service elevator") (Guimarães 1999, 140–41). That said, cases of racial discrimination are more frequently publicized and investigated (Long 1988).

From Racial Denial to Racial Affirmation

President Fernando Henrique Cardoso introduced important yet initially subtle changes in official racial discourse. Cardoso was one of the scholars purged from the University of São Paulo in the 1960s for his revisionist research on race relations but remained silent on the question of racism during his presidential campaign. Indeed, he reinforced the racial democracy ideology in his inaugural address. That is to say, like so many socially designated and white-identified Brazilians, he used himself as proof of the genetic and ancestral democratization that has emerged in Brazil after centuries of miscegenation. Cardoso did not say he is

---

4. The constitution also affirmed protection of African Brazilian cultural practices and granted land titles to surviving occupants of *quilombos,* communities established by runaway slaves prior to emancipation in 1888 (Htun 2005, 21).

African Brazilian, yet he publicly declared himself to have some African ancestry by referring to himself as a "mulatinho" (little mulatto or a bit mulatto) and by using the euphemism of having "um pé na cozinha" (Reichmann 1999, 8), which translates as "one foot in the kitchen." At the same time he remained silent on both the whitening ideology implied in Brazil's racial and cultural blending and the existence of socioeconomic, educational, and political inequality based on race (Nobles 2000, 123–24; Reichmann 1995, 35–42).

Yet in his presidential speech on Independence Day in 1995 Cardoso spoke openly about racism in Brazil. In addition, he acknowledged that Brazil was a racially and culturally blended society while at the same time emphasizing the value of the nation's distinct racial and cultural traditions (Nobles 2000, 124). In June 1995, the president's wife, Ruth Cardoso, remarked at a World Bank conference on Education and Development in Latin America and the Caribbean that the Brazilian education system is discriminatory and reproduces a "racist form of society" (Reichmann 1999, 21). In addition, Cardoso's 1996 National Human Rights Plan not only recognized *negros* as political subjects but for the first time in Brazilian history also officially recognized racial groups "as categories for targeting of public policies." He did not, however, commit himself to anything specific (20).

Ultimately, these discussions were signs of a shift in official racial discourse in support of affirmative action and diversity policies. Initially, this debate took place within black movement organizations and certain academic spheres. The labor movement, feminists, and state officials largely opposed such policies, even when they were familiar with the rationale underlying affirmative action. By the mid-1990s there was a noticeable about-face on this matter (Guimarães 1999, 143–53; Reichmann 1999, 20; Siss 2003, 110–97). In 1995 the Brazilian Foreign Ministry's report to the United Nations Commission on Human Rights laid the foundation for a radical reformulation of state policies to address social inequities by committing itself, in principle, to combating inequality "affirmatively." The report provided a rationale for such affirmative action as a form of positive discrimination in keeping with Brazil's constitution. This would serve as a corrective to the link between color and social inequality that disproportionately affects nonwhites. Yet the report still seemed wedded to the belief that racial inequality was attributable to class factors. Consequently, it equivocated in its support of race-based affirmative action policies (Reichmann 1999, 22–23). Indeed, the federal government's commitment seemed more rhetorical than supportive of large-scale affirmative action policies. Yet various sectors of Brazilian society began implementing a limited set of such policies. These included initiatives established by local governments, as well as "demonstration" projects by the federal government and private sector, targeting the areas of employment and education and valorizing African Brazilian culture (Reichmann 1999, 22; Telles 2004, 58–59).

Although racial concerns were not a priority for most candidates in the 2000 presidential elections, José Serra, of the government-backed Brazilian Social Democratic Party (PSDB), promised to expand the current fledgling affirmative action programs. In addition, the leftist candidate Luiz Inácio Lula da Silva (PT), promised to target African Brazilians for more occupational and educational opportunities. He also reportedly planned to promote to Cabinet level those government agencies dealing with hunger, security, and racism. At his close-of-campaign rally, Lula introduced African American activist Jesse Jackson to the crowd. Lula's triumph in the October presidential elections marked a historic shift to the left for Brazil, which has never elected a leftist president. The last leftist head of state was Vice President João Goulart, who assumed power in 1961 when the centrist president resigned.[5]

Perhaps the biggest boost to affirmative action came from the 2001 U.N. World Conference on Racism, Racial Discrimination, Xenophobia, and Related Intolerance, in Durban, South Africa. By legitimizing the discussion on racism at the global level the conference had the effect of marshaling Brazilian civil society and public opinion not only against racism in Brazil but also for affirmative action. In order to generate an official report for the conference, the Brazilian government assembled a preparatory committee of state officials, academics, and representatives of the black movement. The numerous seminars and workshops, as well as lectures and exchanges by NGOs, trade unions, and universities that took place during the year leading up to the Durban conference culminated in Brazil's first national conference on racism and intolerance. The conference was held in Rio in July 2001 and chaired by then vice governor Benedita da Silva, with some 1,700 attendees from across Brazil (Htun 2005, 20–25).

The preparatory committee's final report endorsed affirmative action programs. In the months leading up to the Durban conference, newspapers and television and radio stations across Brazil began reporting on racism and social inequalities. The op-ed pages of major newspapers covered affirmative action debates between academics, journalists, African Brazilian activists, politicians, and government officials. Later, the final document from the Durban conference reaffirmed the preparatory committee's support of affirmative action and other forms of redress. It also called for adequate representation in politics and education, adding weight to the positions adopted in Brazil's national report (Htun 2004, 60–89; 2005, 20–25).

---

5. Lula beat Serra in the first round of voting but failed to win 50 percent of the vote. Consequently, the two top candidates met in a runoff in which Lula garnered 61.5 percent as compared to Serra's 38.5 percent of the votes (Gibb 2002; Selsky 2002).

Also, one should not underestimate the impact of U.S. influence on the affirmative action debate (and racial discourse generally) in Brazil through the Ford Foundation. Since the 1970s the foundation has provided substantial funding for research and other initiatives dealing with race in Brazil (Bourdieu and Wacquant 1999, 44–48).[6] However, this was particularly the case beginning in the mid-1990s during the tenure of Edward E. Telles, a UCLA sociologist and prominent scholar on Brazilian race relations. Telles served as human rights program officer in Ford's Brazil office between 1997 and 2000. The foundation's financial support for projects dealing with racial concerns more than tripled under Telles's leadership. Ford funded academic research on racial discrimination and policy recommendations including affirmative action, as well as a network of African Brazilian attorneys and leadership training for African Brazilian politicians. More important, Ford provided African Brazilian groups with millions of dollars to prepare for, participate in, and follow-up on the Durban conference (Htun 2004, 60–89; 2005, 20–25; Telles 2003, 31–47).

Since then, state agencies began announcing affirmative action policies. Some entities, including several ministries and universities, have established percentages (or quotas) of positions that must be reserved for African Brazilians. The Foreign Ministry followed suit. This is a radical shift in policy, considering that Brazil's diplomatic corps has historically been overwhelmingly, if not totally, white. The Foreign Ministry's affirmative action program, which began in early 2003, makes annual scholarships available to twenty African Brazilian candidates to assist them in studying for the public service entrance exam (Alvin 2002; Hall 2002; Htun 2004, 60–89; 2005, 20–25).

That said, affirmative action policies have not been accompanied by the necessary federal legislation and implementation. One factor that complicates this process is that only a few agencies have historically tracked race or color. Racial identifiers have not been included on identification cards, driver's licenses, the *carteira de trabalho* (a record of employment kept by individuals and maintained by the Labor Ministry), or other personal official records. Furthermore, the absence of a clearly defined system of racial (or color) classification, along with the uneven geographical distribution of black, multiracial, and indigenous populations presents practical obstacles for implementing affirmative action (Guimarães 1999, 146–50).

---

6. Acknowledging this U.S. influence on and support for Brazilian initiatives does not dismiss the agency of Brazilian activists and scholars in developing autonomous racial discourse and strategies for tackling racial inequality (e.g., the binary racial project, one-drop rule, affirmative action, and so on) similar to those in the United States. However, there is unmistakable U.S. influence in these areas, at least since the 1970s, either directly or indirectly through the Ford and other foundations, as well as through the professional training of academic sociologists (e.g., Hasenbalg and Silva) in the United States.

Other related concerns have focused on whether affirmative action contravenes the provisions set forth in Brazil's constitution that protect the universalist and individualist principle of merit (Guimarães 1999, 146; Santos 2003, 83–126). This principle is the new democracy's primary protection against personalistic and clientelistic practices that still influence Brazilian public life. Yet there is no legal basis for the claim that affirmative action's particularistic policies contradict universalist and individualist principles set forth in the constitution. Indeed, some have argued that positive discrimination in the manner of affirmative action supporting the integration of African Brazilians and the indigenous population would further the egalitarian integration of all individuals into Brazilian society and is thus in keeping with Article 3, sections 3 and 4, of the constitution.[7]

Constitutional provisions notwithstanding, many opponents argue that race-based affirmative action has no place in a multiracial society like Brazil (Vongs et al. 2003). They believe the most egregious racial inequalities can be eradicated through universalist policies supporting improved public elementary and high-school education, basic sanitation, universal medical and dental assistance, affordable housing, improvements in basic infrastructure, increased employment, civic participation of the poor, and land reform. These would proportionally benefit more African Brazilians than whites, given that the majority of African Brazilians are poor. On the other hand, race-specific policies aimed at expanding access to university education, job promotion, preferential contracts for materials or services, and so on would primarily benefit the small African Brazilian middle class, which already has the qualifications to attend college, operate a company, or supply needed goods or services (Guimarães 1999, 147–48).

Importing the One-Drop Rule: African Brazilian Essentialism and Ontological Blackness

In the United States racial discrimination has been overt, ratified by law, and buttressed by the one-drop rule. Consequently, all individuals of African descent have been subjected to the same second-class citizenship. This in turn has stimulated the development of black organizations in the struggle for African American legal and political justice such as the NAACP, for social and economic progress such as the Urban League, as well as businesses owned and operated by African Americans for African Americans, universities for African American students,

---

7. These sections are "eradicate poverty and marginalization and reduce social and regional inequalities" (section 3) and "promote the well-being of all, without regard to origin, race, sex, color, age, or any other form of discrimination" (section 4) (Guimarães 1999, 146 n. 6).

and African American publishing houses and periodicals. These phenomena have welded African Americans into a cohesive political and social force with a sense of collective identity and history of activism despite internal tensions and cleavages based on color, culture, class, and gender. Consequently, prominent African Americans leaders who would be considered white in Brazil, such as Adam Clayton Powell, Walter White, May Street Kidd, Whitney Young, Henrietta Butler, Thurgood Marshall, Roy Wilkins, Julian Bond, Lyman Johnson, and Charlotte McGill, to mention only a few, quite possibly had more incentive to identify with the cause of the black masses than if they had been Brazilian (Toplin 1981, 9–103).

Black movement activists argue that the absence of the negative factor of legal discrimination and the one-drop rule in Brazil has undermined African Brazilian unity in the struggle against racism. Consequently, they have sought to articulate a new African Brazilian identity that borrows on the U.S. one-drop rule as a form of strategic essentialism (Bourdieu and Wacquant 1999, 47–48; Reichmann 1999, 12–13). The goal is to sensitize individuals to the idea of ethnoracial origins (that is, African ancestry) and assign positive value to the term *negro* as a replacement for both *preto* and *pardo*. In order to achieve this activists have sought to draw clear boundaries of racial identities, as well as undermine the superior valuation attached to whiteness (or more specifically, expand the boundaries of blackness and contract those of whiteness).

In practice, this has resulted in an ideological rejection of terminology referring to racially intermediate phenotypes.[8] Activists argue that such distinctions have been part of the white elite's strategy to undermine African Brazilian political unity. Contracting the boundaries of whiteness has also meant severing its connection with miscegenation and national identity. Activists argue that Brazilian society is not a homogenized, or in fact, a whiter one, but rather, is composed of distinct pluralities of racial/ethnic groups. Furthermore, these groups can rightfully lay claim to Brazilian citizenship and identity (Bernardino 2002, 247–73; Burdick 1998b, 151; Domingues 1992, 6–7; Nobles 2000, 121, 146–47, 152, 160; Oliveira 1993, 23–25).

Given the pervasiveness of white domination and hegemony in Brazil, which has sought to prevent the formation of a radical African Brazilian subjectivity, the strengths of the black movement's perspective are undeniable. The movement has fostered pride, group solidarity, and self-respect premised on egalitarian pluralism. It has also critiqued token inclusion of African Brazilians in the form of inegalitarian (or assimilationist) integration and pervasive exclusion in the manner of inegalitarian pluralism (or apartheid) (hooks 1995, 117–24; Marable

8. In fact, Burdick has noted that in black movement seminars and conferences individuals have been chastised and corrected when they inadvertently use one of the intermediate terms (e.g., *mestiço, mulato*) (Burdick 1998b, 150–52).

1995, 121–22; Schiele 1991, 27). That said, the rejection of intermediate terminology and identities may also alienate individuals who unequivocally acknowledge they are the descendents of slaves and genuinely valorize their African slave ancestry, but who cannot honestly translate these sentiments into adopting *negro* as an appropriate means of self-identification. Burdick suggests that this disconnection may originate in their awareness that their social experiences have been qualitatively different from individuals at the darker end of the color spectrum. He argues that it might be necessary to rethink whether identifying primarily as African Brazilian and calling oneself *negro* should be a precondition for involvement in the black movement. Perhaps what is most important is a genuine valorization of one's own or others' slave and African backgrounds. This could conceivably expand movement discourse to embrace the experiences of a wider group of individuals who might commit to the antiracist struggle (Burdick 1998b, 151–53).

A New Brazilian Path: The Binary Racial Project

The black movement has sought to forge a "new" African Brazilian identity that resists commonsense notions of race (or color) based on Brazil's ternary racial project. This resistance has been particularly evident in appeals to the state to replace the traditional color categories *pardo* and *preto* with the single racial designator *negro* in the collection and presentation of official data (Omi and Winant 1994, 55–56, 71–75). Indeed, the black movement has focused much attention on census and other survey data not only to emphasize that *pretos* and *pardos* have a similar socioeconomic status but also to identify its constituency as a numerical majority. Individuals who identify as *preto* on the census have never exceeded 10 percent of the population, but when this 10 percent is combined with the roughly 42 percent who identify as *pardo*, the total surpasses 50 percent. Activists have very strong feelings about this fact, and in much of movement discourse and writing they employ an expanded definition of blackness that relies on African ancestry, claiming that the percentage of African Brazilians ranges from 50 to as high as 80 percent (Burdick 1998b, 150).

That said, the Brazilian state has historically neither explicitly defined racial categories and membership nor enforced institutionalized racially discriminatory polices as has the United States. Nevertheless, from its very beginning, the Brazilian state, through the implementation of public policy, has been concerned with the politics of race and has sustained an identifiable racial order. This has linked the system of political rule to racial classification. Color terms may be flexible, and racial markers fluid, but they are not materially inconsequential. For most of the twentieth century the Brazilian racial state not only ignored pervasive racial inequities but also obscured the existence of such discrimination by deliberately promoting the ideology of racial democracy. The state's main objective in its racial policy has been repression and exclusion based on inegalitarian pluralism, or patronizing inclusion in the form of inegalitarian integration. State institutions have historically been so effective in enforcing the prevailing racial order that political channels for the expression of racial opposition and reform are a recent phenomenon. They have been achieved primarily since the democratic opening beginning in the 1970s (Nobles 2000, 122–23; Omi and Winant 1994, 77–90).

The Racial State, Public Policy, and the Census

For much of Brazil's history the racial state has gathered data on race (or color) through censuses and administrative records. These federal data collections have provided a historical record of the social, demographic, and economic character-istics of the nation's various populations. Since the first general census in 1872 six censuses have collected data on race (1890, 1940, 1950, 1960, 1980, and 1991) (Nobles 2000, 104; Piza and Rosemberg 1999, 37, 39, 41).

The significance of the color question gained momentum in the late 1970s among statisticians and analysts at the Brazilian Institute of Geography and Statistics (Instituto Brasileiro de Geografia e Estadísticas, IBGE), the government agency responsible for conducting the decennial census. The initial format of the 1980 census did not include a color question. Both academics and African Brazilian activists lobbied to have the question restored. Academics argued that the question was needed to insure consistency in research methodologies and analyses. Activists contended that it would insure that Brazil's racial composition was documented and that social stratification could be analyzed in terms of color. After intense debate the director of the IBGE announced that the color question would be restored (Andrews 1991, 250; Nobles 2000, 116–17; Skidmore 1992–93, 53).

If academics and activists welcomed the return of the color question, Gilberto Freyre expressed disappointment. In a newspaper article entitled "Brazilian—Your Color?," which appeared a month after the IBGE's announcement, Freyre stated that the color question was obsolete because individuals had transcended consciousness of their racial origin. Instead, they had become Brazilian, that is, members of a national "meta-race." He argued further, that it is impossible to capture, in four choices, the myriad colors of a "miscegenated and nationally Brazilian people" (Nobles 2000, 116). Moreover, Freyre reminded readers that at the moment the IBGE decided to restore the color question, the scientific estab-lishment was calling into question the whole notion of race and its connection to skin color. Freyre argued that reinstating the question could undermine the IBGE's own credibility. For Freyre, the term *moreno* (brown), which reflected his longstanding belief in *morenidade,* or brunettism, corresponded more closely to Brazil's metaracial reality and had the greatest salience over other designations. He concluded his article by recounting the remarks made by a Columbian observer who said Brazil represented the triumph of the multiracial individual (Andrews 1991, 252; Nobles 2000, 119–20).

Freyre skillfully shifted the terms of the debate and extolled a racialized national identity that transcends yet is the result of racial blending, even as he acknowledged that the concept of race was being challenged scientifically. Up to that point, following Freyre's reasoning, the official national discourse of racial democracy had been one of assimilation (which was framed as transculturalism/transracialism, that is, egalitarian integration). Correspondingly, the IBGE historically helped further this image. Yet the agency's reintroduction of the color question on the census could generate an alternative framing acknowledging racial discrimination (Nobles 2000, 119–20).

The controversy surrounding the 1980 census—as well as the color data from the 1976 National Household Survey (Pesquisa Nacional por Amostragem de Domicílios, PNAD)—prompted the IBGE to clarify its color terminology. This originated among a small group of statisticians and analysts within the IBGE's Department of Social Studies and Indicators (DIESO). The DIESO analysts, while working on a book about African Brazilians in the labor force, were confronted with whether "race" or "color" would be the appropriate terminology. Previously, analysts used the terms "race" and "color" interchangeably but more frequently gave "color" priority over "race." In addition, they reasoned that "racial" distinctions had been rendered insignificant by several centuries of miscegenation and the term "race" would undermine the racial democracy ideology (Nobles 2000, 119–20).

However, the DIESO researchers in their analysis of the 1980 census data, as well as the 1976 PNAD and its color supplement,[9] combined the color categories *pardo* and *preto* under the racial designator *negro.* The impetus for this quiet, seemingly matter-of-fact decision originated to some extent in their documentation of glaring disparities between whites (*brancos*) and African Brazilians (*negros*). Moreover, they argued that the term *negro* was widely used by Brazilian social scientists as well as many grassroots African Brazilian organizations seeking to emphasize that *pardos* and *pretos* have more in common than either has with *brancos* (Andrews 1991, 250; Nobles 2000, 116–20). Consequently, the DIESO analysts concluded that the term "race" captured this unity in a way that "color" did not.[10]

9. PNAD's collection of color data has been intermittent, first occurring in 1976 and becoming systematic only in 1985. Its pre-coded options, along with an open-ended questionnaire allowing for self-identification has become a standard source for analysis (Piza and Rosemberg 1999, n. 5, 38).

10. Studies have shown that Brazilians recognize a more complex and nuanced racial (or color) vocabulary than those reflected in the census color question. In the 1976 PNAD, subjects provided

The problem with the term "color," they explained, was that by emphasizing phenotype, it ignores "the cultural and historical aspects of the constitution of these social groups." "Race," on the other hand, according to the analysts, signifies "a common origin and historical trajectory" (Nobles 2000, 120) used to define African Brazilians (*pretos* and *pardos*) as descendents of Africans. Yet in arriving at their definition of "race," which would have been more appropriately defined as "ethnicity," the analysts conflated "racial" attributes with those that were cultural or behavioral in nature (Nobles 2000, 116–20; Oliveira 1993, 23–25).

The DIESO analysts' reformulation of terminology was a clear rejection of Freyre's notion of a Brazilian metarace and embraced instead the notion of an African Brazilian racial group and identity. The IBGE had previously been complicit in advancing policy decisions in the service of the national project aimed at unifying Brazil's three parent racial groups—European, African, and Native American—with the goal of projecting a whiter national image. This agency continued to use the traditional three-category concept of color—or four, if one includes the category of yellow (*amarelo*) used to designate individuals of Asian ancestry. Yet it had now moved toward a conceptualization of Brazilian race relations similar to the U.S. binary racial project (Andrews 1991, 250).

Since the inclusion of the color question on the 1980 census and on the special color supplement to the 1976 PNAD, there has been considerable growth in research using data obtained from censuses and other national surveys. Certainly, the concerns of DIESO within the IBGE and that of Brazilian academics—particularly a new generation of social scientists—have coincided well, providing activists with the necessary quantitative data to wage their struggle for social change. Historically, Brazilian scholars have not only faced the obstacles of official indifference and obstruction to releasing the data already gathered but also had to go to great expense to gain access to the data when it was made available. By the 1990s researchers had pressured for the release of future data on a timely and accessible basis and to disaggregate official socioeconomic data by race or gender (Piza and Rosemberg 1999, 40; Reichmann 1995, 26–27, 35–42; Skidmore 1992–93, 49–57).

The 1990 Census—Encountering the Racial State

Beginning in 1990, African Brazilian organizations, along with nine nongovernmental agencies (including development groups and research centers), mounted a publicity campaign directing all Brazilians to be more conscientious in filling

more than 190 terms in the open-ended question requesting self-identification (Piza and Rosemberg 1999, 38).

out the race question on the 1990 census. The campaign gained the support of the Brazilian Institute for Social and Economic Analyses (Instituto Brasileiro de Análisis Sociais e Económicas, IBASE)—Brazil's foremost leftist nongovernmental organization—and received some funding from the Ford Foundation and Terra Nuova (an Italian foundation for cooperation). The impetus behind the campaign, according to Wania Sant'Anna, the campaign's originator and first coordinator, was to produce more reliable socioeconomic data on African Brazilians. Sant'Anna frequently lacked sufficient data in this area while working at IBASE. This undermined her ability to advocate within IBASE for greater sensitivity to the racial determinant of class inequality. Thus she thought the census campaign would be a means of both getting IBASE involved in the "racial" question and awakening African Brazilians to questions of racial identity (Domingues 1992, 6–7; Nobles 2000, 150).

The campaign sought to explain the reality behind the racial democracy ideology. Its ultimate goal, however, was to sensitize African Brazilians to the concept *negro* as an affirmation of a politicized racial identity, rather than the color-coding of *preto* and *pardo* (Domingues 1992, 6–7). Furthermore, *pardo* includes all types of intermediate shades and was considered so general as to be meaningless. It also stirred controversy because of its association with *mulatto*, which reminded many individuals of the racial divisiveness of the past (Domingues 1992, 6–7; Oliveira 1993, 23–25; Valente 1986, 35–40).

The campaign's goals were captured best in its poster and brochure slogan "Não Deixe sua Côr Passar em Branco. Responda com Bom C/Senso" (Don't let your color be passed off as White. Respond with good [census] sense) (Domingues 1992, 6–7; Nobles 2000, 152). This slogan punned "census" (*censo*) and "sense" (*senso*) to address the process of racial alchemy that was attributable to self-recoding. Over time, this has led to a distortion of racial demographics. Accordingly, blacks numerically have lost a great deal and have gained little; multiracial individuals have gained more than they have lost; and whites have lost nothing and have made substantial gains (Nascimento 1979, 74–80).[11]

The year the campaign began, the IBGE announced it would include "race" and "indigenous" as new options within the color question. The color question was reformulated to ask: "What is your color or race?" and "indigenous" (or "*Indígenia*," that is, Native American) was included among the colors: *preto*,

---

11. Census figures indicate that between 1940 and 1980, *pardos* were the fastest growing racial group, rising from 21.2 percent to 38.8 percent of the national population. During the same period *brancos* declined from 63.5 percent to 54.2 percent and *pretos* from 14.6 percent to 5.9 percent. This does indicate a progressive lightening of the population. It would be less appropriately described as whitening, however, and more as a browning (Andrews 1991, 252; Hamilton 1992, 2, 13; Hasenbalg, Silva, and Barcelos 1989, 189–97; Margolis 1992, 3–7; Wood and Carvalho 1988, 135–53).

branco, pardo, and *amarelo.* Since the 1950 census, Native Americans had been classified as *pardo* (Nobles 2000, 121). In the 1990 census, however, the "race" and "indigenous" options were linked. The "race" option actually applied only to the indigenous category, although this qualification was not stated explicitly either in the census enumerator manual or on the census schedule itself. Instead, it was treated as "common sense," that is, without need of explanation (120–22, 146–62).

Political scientist Melissa Nobles has provided the most textured and insightful analysis of the unfolding of the 1990 census debate. According to Nobles the census was first scheduled to begin September 1, 1990. Nevertheless, it was postponed because of problems between the Ministry of the Economy and the Census Bureau, labor strikes, budget constraints, and the administrative reforms of then president Fernando Collor de Mello. The census was finally taken in 1991, but the campaign was launched within a climate of "uncertainty, controversy, and contention" (Nobles 1995, 150).

Considering that interpretations of census data have been used to support the racial democracy ideology as well as Brazil's whiter national image, the campaign sought to delineate clearly the boundaries of racial identities and strengthen charges of racial discrimination by contributing to the production of more accurate data. By addressing the ideologically and politically constructed nature of racial categories, as well as the politics engendered by racial enumeration, activists wanted to heighten awareness of the state's role in constituting racial groups. Yet the immediate goal of the campaign was to bring about "a more consciously black population." For campaign organizers the campaign's purpose, and thus its slogan, was to urge Brazilians to embrace their "African origins" and then select a color darker than what they would have chosen in the campaign's absence (Nobles 2000, 120–22, 146–62).

Campaign organizers expressed general dissatisfaction with the precodified census terms. They would have preferred that "race" or "ethnicity" (in substitution for "color") be included in the wording of the census question, with *negro* as the corresponding census category to replace both *preto* and *pardo*. Indeed, there was considerable support for the use of "race" and particularly "African Brazilian race" (*raça negra*). Yet according to Nobles there was no consensus on possible alternative terminology (Nobles 2000, 120–22, 146–62). Some individuals such as Januario Garcia, then president of the Research Institute for the Study of Black Cultures (Instituto de Pesquisas das Culturas Negras, IPCN), recommended the terms "white" and "nonwhite." Regina Domingues, who was now Wania Sant'Anna's successor as campaign organizer, felt there should be a more satisfactory way to accommodate the notion of "racial blending" than the term *pardo,* which she considered too vague. Father David Raimundo dos Santos thought there should be two questions: one that asked about race and another about color. That way, individuals could assume both their racial identity and "brownness" (151).

These concerns surrounding census terminology notwithstanding, the most important task was convincing Brazilians to take the campaign's appeals seriously. After all, the campaign was constrained by a limited staff and inadequate financial resources. Despite its national aspirations, most of the activities were centered in Rio de Janeiro, although there were important efforts in the cities of Salvador, Belém, São Luis, Recife, and Pernambuco and the states of Belo Horizonte and Minas Gerais (Nobles 2000, 151, 160).

Nobles observed that in 1990 the campaign received some press coverage although it had yet to mount a full-scale effort when the census was postponed. Although initially disappointed, coordinator Regina Domingues and others saw the delay as an opportunity to enlist more organizational and financial support. To that end, they approached the Italian Foundation Terra Nuova and major media outlets. Organizers selected May 12, 1991, as the date for the campaign to commence. This date was chosen in order to challenge the official celebration of the abolition of slavery scheduled for May 13, which activists considered a "farce" in light of the slavery-like living conditions that still prevailed in Brazil. Quinta da Boa Vista Park was chosen as the site for the Rio launching because it was a gathering place for many residents of Rio's North Zone (*zona norte*) and the Baixada Fluminese—which are largely composed of black and multiracial individuals. Along with such grassroots activities, the Rio operation took advantage of local and national media to convey its message. Throughout September, for example, the campaign's message was dispatched across an electronic bulletin board during soccer tournaments and read over the radio. These efforts were made possible with the support of the Bureau of Sports for the State of Rio de Janeiro (SUDERRI). Also, soccer fans were given campaign materials as they entered Maracaná Stadium (Nobles 2000, 155–56).

According to Nobles even more important was the September airing of a commercial promoting the campaign and the census on the channels of TV Globo, Brazil's most powerful media conglomerate. This commercial stressed the importance of answering the color question, and yet, to the campaign organizers' consternation, it advocated the self-selection of *pardo* (brown). Although outraged by TV Globo producers' spin on the campaign's message, campaign organizers did not reject the commercial, given that it would reach millions of Brazilians. The campaign also received international attention. The BBC's *News Hour* radio program and the *Chicago Tribune* interviewed Domingues (Nobles 1995, 155–56).

However, Nobles states that it was the August 1–6, 1991, visit of Nelson and Winnie Mandela that gave the campaign the biggest boost. The media provided extensive coverage of the Mandelas' visit. In addition, each of their public appearances attracted sizable crowds, where campaign workers were able to distribute pamphlets and buttons. The visit also set the stage for public discussion about Brazilian racial politics and African Brazilian solidarity, which were the very issues the campaign sought to raise. Yet the discussion took some unexpected turns. In his first speech in Rio de Janiero Mandela expressed his gratitude to the Brazilian government and people for their support of the anti-apartheid struggle. He then stated that Brazil, as a successful multiracial society, would serve as a model for South Africa. Furthermore, he affirmed that African Brazilians "had already reached the stage where they could use their own resources, leaders, and schools for their betterment" (Nobles 2000, 156). South African blacks on the other hand were still fighting for the right to vote (156–57).

In contrast to Mandela, a few prominent Brazilian politicians and newspaper editorials called attention to Brazil's liabilities rather than its assets. In a private meeting with Mandela Governors Leonel Brizola of Rio de Janeiro and Luiz Antonio Fleury of São Paulo reportedly discussed the existence of racism and the antiracist struggle. The newspaper *Folha de São Paulo* ran an editorial that questioned the suitability of Brazil as a model for a multiracial and nondiscriminatory society and urged Brazilians to stay the course in the antiracist struggle rather than hold onto the false image of Brazil as a racial democracy. This open repudiation of the racial democracy ideology notwithstanding, the imagery associated with it proved too compelling to resist. This was most dramatically captured in a photo op of Mandela, Brizola, and Juruna (Brazil's first Native American congressman), posing together, with the commentary "in that instant, representatives of the three races which comprise the Brazilian population were together" (Nobles 2000, 157).

In the wake of Mandela's remarks, African Brazilian activists found themselves in an unexpectedly awkward position. They were not only upstaged by mainstream politicians but also were in the position of contradicting and being contradicted by a revered champion of human rights. Thus, they charged instead, that they had been purposely prevented from meeting with him. Januario Garcia accused both the federal and Rio de Janeiro state authorities of racial discrimination in its organizing of Mr. Mandela's visit to Rio. Federal Deputy Benedita da Silva (PT) charged that party politicians "hijacked" Mandela's visit and excluded labor unions and grassroots organizations (e.g., neighborhood associations, labor unions, Native American and African Brazilian groups, and so on) (Nobles 2000, 157–58).

These circumstances ultimately made it possible for both Brazilian politicians and black movement activists to score points. For African Brazilian federal deputy and former Rio de Janeiro mayoral candidate Benedita da Silva, Winnie Mandela's appearance before the Brazilian Congress provided an opportunity to contrast racism in Brazil with that in South Africa. And as if inadvertently confirming da Silva's observation that the contrast resided in racism's subtlety in Brazil, Brazilian legislators gave her a standing ovation. Ironically, these same legislators staunchly refused to broach the issue of racism in Brazil, either rhetorically or especially programmatically (Nobles 1995, 165–66). President Collor, in contrast, took advantage of his meeting with Mandela to reaffirm Brazil's links with Africa when he commented in English, "Between Brazil and Africa there is no distance because we have the same roots" (Nobles 2000, 158).

Although displeased with Mandela's initial comments, black movement activists, according to Nobles, continued to compare Brazil and South Africa and maintained their goal of having Mandela speak about the "true" conditions of African Brazilians. Meanwhile, in later speeches, Mandela lavished considerably less praise on Brazilian race relations and the status of African Brazilians. Accordingly, he presented Brazil as a nation that had yet to confront its racial problem rather that one that already solved it. It was precisely this demystification of the racial democracy ideology that the campaign sought to achieve (Nobles 2000, 158).

Nobles states that once the census officially began on September 1, most of the campaign's work had been completed, although the nationally televised commercial and promotions at Rio soccer games lasted throughout September. In mid-September, IBASE sponsored a daylong seminar intended both to emphasize the importance of racial data and advance discussion about the new race or color questions and terms on the census. In the end, participants, drawn from the ranks of nonprofit organizations and academic institutions, appeared as divided on the issue of census categorization as the IBGE and campaign organizers themselves (Nobles 2000, 159).

Because of the one-year delay and other difficulties, demographers, statisticians, and others who utilize census data initially questioned its accuracy and reliability. Color data for the 1991 census (released in 1995) are consistent with previous ones, which indicate a progressive decline in the percentage of *pretos* and *brancos*. Yet *brancos* were still more than half of the population (52 percent), whereas *pretos* decreased slightly from 5.9 percent in 1980 to 5 percent in 1991. The percentage of *pardos* increased from 38.8 percent in 1980 to 42 percent in 1991. This is also in keeping with previous trends and is probably not attributable to the census campaign. Indeed, the data suggest that the campaign had little or no impact on racial preferences. It thus remains unknown how the Brazilian masses would have responded to the campaign's goals had they been aware of them (Nobles 2000, 122, 160).

The 2000 Census—Reforming the Racial State

The 1990 census data weakened neither the legitimacy of the black movement nor activists' resolve in continuing their goals in terms of the 2000 census. Indeed, the current open discussion about census methods within the IBGE and in the media is directly, if not completely, attributable to the campaign. Wania Sant'Anna, the campaign's originator, was appointed as an unofficial adviser to IBGE on questions relating to color data. Although activists were unsuccessful in persuading the IBGE to use *negro* as a designator in collecting data on the 1990 census, discussions for the 2000 census were ongoing. Activists made recommendations similar to those for the 1990 census. First, they suggested that the race/color question appear on both long and short forms. This would not only increase the number of responses on the race question and enhance the accuracy of the racial data but also make it possible to tabulate and release preliminary data more rapidly. Second, they asked that the term *preto* be replaced with *negro*. Third, and perhaps the most controversial, was the recommendation to add *afrodescendente* (African descent) under the *pardo* identifier. This would allow multiracial individuals to acknowledge African ancestry. Next to *afrodescendente* would also appear the option *outras* (others) for *pardo* individuals who are not of African descent (Escóssia 1997, 3; Nobles 2000, 160, 171–73; Sant'Anna 1997).

The IBGE experimented with these and other changes in the schedule for the 2000 census pilot tests conducted in 1997 and 1999. However, the agency did not include the color question on the final version of the 2000 census short form or basic schedule (Questionário básico). The color question appeared only on the long form (Questionário da Amostra). Also, the IBGE neither added *afrodescendente* as an option under the *pardo* identifier nor replaced *preto* with *negro*. Indeed, the term *negro* conveys a political orientation the state does not wish to encourage; *afrodescendente* was most likely rejected because it was thought to lack a clear definition. The pilot tests indicated that few individuals declared themselves to be an *afrodescendente* even when they self-identified as *pardo*. In many cases this lack of identification with the term *afrodescendente* could have been due to confusion about the meaning of the term rather than a desire to avoid the stigma still associated with African ancestry (Escóssia 1997, 3; Nobles 2000, 171–73; Sant'Anna 1997).

Yet President Cardoso issued a "National Program on Human Rights" in 1996 outlining his administration's goals, including a recommendation that color be included in all population statistics and registries. In addition, he called on the IBGE to continue the practice of combining *pretos* and *pardos* together as *negros* (Omi and Winant 1994, 86–87, 106). Nevertheless, this reflected a policy of "insulation" that confined activists' concerns to an area that was, if not completely symbolic, at least not central to operating the racial order. That is to say, this grouping of *pardos* with *pretos* would not appear in the actual tabulations but rather, would be used for the purposes of certain statistical work (e.g., some of the cross-tabulations) (Nobles 2000, 123, 171–72; Reichmann 1999, 13; Melissa Nobles, pers. comm., February 23, 1998).

Intent on revealing the inappropriateness of IBGE's color terms, Datafolha researchers argued that they had arrived at a more reliable means of determining Brazilians' preferences in racial identification: first, based on interviewers' own observation of the respondent; second, the respondent's self-description; and third, the respondent's choice from the list of IBGE color terms. By applying this method, the researchers found that 39 percent of the respondents identified as *branco*. The overwhelming majority of respondents rejected IBGE's term *pardo;* that is, only 6 percent self-identified as *pardo*. The number of individuals identifying as *preto* was only slightly higher, at roughly 8 percent. Interestingly, 43 percent self-identified as *moreno* (or brunette). This term can be used to describe a wide variety of "brunette" phenotypes, including those individuals who are designated as *preto, pardo,* or *branco* (if the latter have dark hair and eyes) (Nobles 2000, 125; Silva 2005, 41–42).

Accordingly, Datafolha analysts recommended that *pardo* be replaced with *moreno* on census schedules. In addition, they charged the IBGE of falsely presenting Brazil as a white nation, a portrait that was incongruous with Brazilians' own self-perceptions and perceptions of their country (Silva 2005, 41–42). In their words, "For IBGE, Brazil is a country with a white majority and a very large population of *pardos*." In contrast, "For Brazilians, a white majority does not exist in the country" (Nobles 2000, 125). Datafolha's data indicated that 51 percent of the total number of individuals identified as *moreno, negro,* or *preto*. If those who self-identified as *pardo* (6 percent), *mulato* (1 percent), and *escuro* (dark) (1 percent) are included, the final tally is 59 percent. Yet there was no indication IBGE officials were willing to adopt the term *moreno*. That said, if the IBGE should ever approve *moreno* as an official category the number of individuals identifying as "black" and "white" would decrease. This certainly would indicate that Brazil would have a nonwhite majority but would not necessarily translate into an African Brazilian majority (Nobles 2000, 125).

Nobles points out that some individuals might view the increasing support of the term *moreno,* at least in terms of the census, as the achievement of Gilberto Freyre's notion of *morenidade* (or "metaracial brunettism") and *brasilidade*

(Brazilianness). Racial blending has been uncoupled from the racial democracy ideology, and "brownness" embraced, but the notion of a nondiscriminatory Brazil does not necessarily follow from this (Nobles 2000, 126). In polite conversation the term *moreno* is often used as a euphemism to avoid more specifically racialized terminology. For some, this may be an attempt to remove social bias from color designations. For others it may an attempt at whitening. Consequently, the use of *moreno* on census forms could easily become yet another means of erasing racial distinctions and furthering the national project of unifying all individuals under an identity as Brazilians while deflecting public attention and policy away from tackling racial inequities (Piza and Rosemberg 1999, 51; Reichmann 1999, 2 n. 3).

Understandably, the term *moreno* has not met with enthusiasm among African Brazilian activists. They recognize that the vast majority of those identifying as *moreno* (and *pardo*) do not consistently view themselves or others like them as *negro*. Consequently, they most likely do not see themselves even as partners in a common cause with blacks. The census campaign sought to counter this trend by urging individuals to view African ancestry as the tie that binds *pretos* and *pardos* as constituents of the same African Brazilian group. Correspondingly, African Brazilians (or an extended "black population") would become a large plurality within, if not the majority of Brazil's national population. The term *moreno* on the census would undermine these efforts (Nobles 2000, 126–27).

That said, a comparison between the 1991 and 2000 censuses indicates that there was a slight increase in the proportion of *pretos* (5.0 percent in 1991 to 6.2 percent in 2000) and decrease in the proportion of *pardos* (42.6 percent in 1991 to 39.1 percent in 2000) (IBGE 2000; Neves 2002). In Bahia, the change was even more marked, with the proportion of *pretos* increasing from 10.2 percent in 1991 to 13.1 percent in 2000, and the proportion of *pardos* falling from 69.3 percent in 1991 to 62.5 percent in 2000. Still the 2000 census shows that *brancos* remain a majority: 53.8 percent of identified as white individuals. *Brancos* are the majority in the Southeast (62.4 percent) and South (84.2 percent). The number of *pardos* is larger in the North (63.5 percent) and Northeast (59.8 percent). The Central West displays a relative balance between *brancos* and *pretos* and *pardos* combined. Additionally, 0.5 percent of the national population was Asian and 0.4 percent was Native American (Neves 2002; Paixão 2004, 747–48).

Despite this statistical majority, President Lula has portrayed Brazil as a nation with a black majority. Yet from the racial state's perspective, this African Brazilian majority—which the black movement claims as its constituency—exists more as an abstraction than an empirical reality. Indeed, the full social, economic, and political import of regarding Brazil as a nation with an African Brazilian majority or sizable plurality has not yet registered in the public consciousness.

Nonetheless, since the 1970s and 1980s there has been a gradual yet unmistakable decline in support of the racial democracy ideology in academic circles, official discourse, and public opinion. Many Brazilians hold on tenaciously to the racial democracy ideology; some consider this ideology an unfilled potential that may be realized in the future; others have cast aside the ideology for a more critical focus on racial inequality. In addition, political discourse increasingly includes references to "racial diversity" and "multiculturalism" (egalitarian pluralism) instead of the traditional reference to "racial unity" (egalitarian integration). Correspondingly, a new statute makes the teaching of African Brazilian history and culture mandatory in the public schools (Burdick 1998a, 3; Htun 2005, 24; Nobles 2000, 123–24, 127; Reichmann 1999, 23; Telles 2004, 76–77, 238, 261).

In addition, after taking office President Lula took a number of steps, both practical and symbolic, to stress his commitment to racial equality. His cabinet included four African Brazilians, among them the minister of a newly created Secretariat for the Promotion of Racial Equality. Perhaps the most prominent African Brazilian member of the cabinet is the minister of culture, Gilberto Gil, an internationally renowned musician who is outspoken on issues of African cultural heritage. Lula appointed the first African Brazilian Supreme Court judge, Joaquim Benedito Barbosa Gomes. He created a racial equality committee and ordered three ministries to recruit African Brazilians to fill at least 20 percent of senior posts. Lula has also promised that African Brazilians will account for at least one-third of the federal government within five years (Rohter 2003).

Finally, Lula's government fully supports the Racial Equality Statute, which outlines plans and allots resources for programs that would benefit African Brazilians. If passed by Congress, this legislation would require affirmative action policies at all levels of government and even in the casting of television programs and commercials (Osava 2005). While affirmative action has come under attack in the United States, it has gained support in Brazil in terms of university admissions, government employment, and public contracts and perhaps eventually in private companies (Rohter 2003). Now, at the beginning of the twenty-first century Brazil, in an ironic about-face, appears to be heading toward nonwhiteness, if not actual blackness (Nobles 2000, 127–28). Brazilian racial discourse and to some extent public policy, if not race relations themselves, are placing increased emphasis on the black/white (or white/nonwhite) dichotomy, if not the absolute enforcement of the one-drop rule, in a manner similar to that which has historically characterized the U.S. binary racial project.

EPILOGUE

The U.S. and Brazilian Racial Orders: Changing Points of Reference

G. Reginald Daniel with Josef Castañeda-Liles

The U.S. Racial Order: Race, Multiraciality, and the Ternary Racial Project

U.S. race relations are converging with a path traditionally typified by Brazil and other parts of Latin America. This "Latin Americanization" is evident in the shift away from a binary racial project (buttressed by the one-drop rule) and a move in the direction of a ternary racial project that recognizes white, black, and multiracial identities. Furthermore, the removal of the formal mechanism supporting racial apartheid has led to discussions about the declining significance of race and the increasing importance of class and culture as factors that influence social stratification. Many individuals, in turn, have questioned the necessity of continuing affirmative action and other directives aimed at tracking and eradicating patterns of racial discrimination that supposedly no longer exist. Thus, a racial democracy ideology has been perpetuated, grounded in the notion of color-blindness.

A recent case study reflecting this shift is the debate surrounding two class-action suits filed against the University of Michigan concerning undergraduate and law school admissions. On June 23, 2003, the U.S. Supreme Court ruled that the University of Michigan's "point system" in its undergraduate admissions affirmative action program was "tantamount to a quota system" (P. Williams 2003a). This system assigned 20 points on a 150-point scale to students from underrepresented minority groups. At the same time, the court upheld the law school's admissions policy, which gave an unspecified "preference" to qualified minority applicants in an effort to assemble a diverse student body. These suits presented the Court with its most important civil rights case in twenty-five years, challenging the use of "racial preferences" in school admissions. The Court's decisions would have an impact on the future of affirmative action at public and private colleges and universities throughout the United States (P. Williams 2003a).

Affirmative Action Under Fire

The Supreme Court's last major ruling on race-based admissions was the 1978 *Regents of the University of California v. Bakke* decision. The case involved a white student named Allan Bakke who was denied admission to the University of California at Davis Medical School. Bakke claimed the university's practice of reserving 16 out of 100 spaces in the entering class for "racial minority" students prevented him from being admitted (Lane 2003; P. Williams 2003a). This denied him his rights under the Fourteenth Amendment of the Constitution, the California Constitution, and the Civil Rights Act of 1964.

The Court ruled in favor of Bakke and ordered the university to admit him, but it produced no clear holding. Lower courts have generally understood *Bakke* to mean that students' race/ethnicity may be considered in order to achieve diversity, but racial quotas are prohibited. Yet the Court did not state that diversity was a compelling justification for racial preferences in admissions (P. Williams 2003a). Justice Lewis F. Powell was the only member of the Court that endorsed this position, based on an amicus curiae brief filed by Harvard, Columbia, Stanford, and The University of Pennsylvania. In that brief, the universities underscored the benefits of diversity to the educational process. Moreover, they argued that Harvard had achieved diversity by considering race as a "plus factor" for minorities without "jeopardizing the overall competitiveness of admissions" (Lane 2003; Stohr 2004, 63–70).

Powell's pivotal opinion provided a fifth vote in a 5-4 decision permitting affirmative action to continue in some form. Although none of the other justices concurred with Powell's diversity rationale, the majority agreed that universities are not required to adopt race-blind admissions policies, citing Harvard's as an exemplary admissions program. During the past twenty-five years, companies and universities nationwide have considered Powell's opinion to be the court's holding. It became the ideological foundation of a "diversity" movement that is now a normative part of business, labor, and education (Lane 2003; Stohr 2004, 63–70; P. Williams 2003b). Accordingly, colleges and universities have sought to enroll students of different cultural, racial, ethnic, socioeconomic, and geographic backgrounds, grounded in the belief that the resulting diversity provides students with a more comprehensive and better quality education.

The University of Michigan undergraduate admissions case (*Gratz v. Bollinger*) involved Jennifer Gratz, who applied in 1995 with a grade point average of 3.8 and an ACT score of 25, and Patrick Hamacher, who applied in 1997 with a GPA of 3.0 and an ACT score of 28. Both were denied admission and enrolled in schools elsewhere. In October 1997, while attending college, Gratz and Hamacher filed a class-action lawsuit against the University of Michigan. The question before the court was whether the undergraduate affirmative action policy violated the Constitution by considering race as a favorable factor in admissions (Stohr 2004, 76–77; P. Williams 2003a).

At the time the lawsuit was filed, the university employed a two-track admissions policy that gave preference to applicants from three racial minority groups considered underrepresented on campus—African Americans, Latinas/os, and Native Americans—and admitted students from those groups at higher rates than other students with comparable grades and test scores. For example, in the 1995 entering class, 32 percent of non-minority students with scores and GPAs comparable to those of Gratz were accepted, whereas 100 percent of the minority students were admitted (Stohr 2004, 80–85; P. Williams 2003a). The plaintiff cited these statistics to argue that she suffered reverse discrimination. The university countered that grades and test scores were not "the only relevant factors" determining a student's admission. For example, in 1995, the university admitted more than 1,400 non-minority students with GPAs and test scores lower than those of Gratz and rejected more than 2,000 non-minority students with higher scores. The university argued that it admits nearly all competitive applicants from underrepresented racial minority groups because so few qualified applicants apply, noting that only 6 percent of high school students with grades of B or higher and SAT scores above 1200 are African American, Latina/o, or Native American (P. Williams 2003a).

Beginning with the 1998 entering class, the university replaced the two-track with a single-track system that assigned points on a scale of 0 to 150. In this system, up to 80 points were awarded for grades, 12 for standardized test scores, 18 for the quality of an applicant's high school and curriculum, 10 for Michigan residency, and 4 for alumni relationships. Students from underrepresented racial minority groups earned 20 points. In addition, small points were awarded for essays, personal achievement, and leadership qualities. A lower federal court declared the two-track admissions system unlawful but upheld the point system, ruling that achieving student diversity was a legitimate interest, allowing the university to factor race in its admissions practices. The students appealed, and the Supreme Court agreed to hear the case (P. Williams 2003a).

The Supreme Court also agreed to hear the law school case (*Grutter v. Bollinger*), involving Barbara Grutter, a white Michigan resident who applied in 1997. Grutter had a 3.8 GPA and scored 161 on the LSAT, ranking in the 86th percentile of students nationally but was denied admission. In response, she filed a class-action lawsuit against the university in 1997, maintaining she was a victim of reverse discrimination.

As in its undergraduate program, the law school used race as a factor in admissions, with certain preferences given to applicants from the aforementioned underrepresented minority groups. Grutter claimed that the school essentially reserved a share of each year's incoming class for minority students, ranging from 11 to 17 percent. The university stated that a student's racial background was not the main factor in its policy and there were no fixed criteria or formula for admission. Furthermore, any race-neutral policy applied to upper- and middle-range test scores would result in a class with very few minority students. The law school stated it could not increase minority enrollment by relying solely on its extensive outreach and recruiting programs. In addition, the school said it strived to admit "a critical mass" of minority students in each class to achieve "the desired diversity of interaction" and to avoid giving the impression that minority students are simply being admitted in token numbers (Stohr 2004, 76–77; P. Williams 2003a, 2003b).

The attorneys for the plaintiffs in both cases argued that the university had not met "its heavy burden of justifying" the use of racial preferences in undergraduate and law school admissions (P. Williams 2003a). They argued that the automatic awarding of points to individuals from a specified racial or ethnic group, or the focus on enrolling a "critical mass" of specified minority students, was the functional equivalent of quotas, which were deemed impermissible in *Bakke*. Furthermore, the university's assumption that selecting students based on their race would achieve a diversity of viewpoints rested on stereotypes. In other words, the admissions process assumed that students are likely to have certain experiences and display specific perspectives simply because they are members of a particular racial or ethnic group. Intellectual diversity, it was argued, could be achieved by searching for it "directly, rather than through using race as a proxy." Moreover, legally speaking, the state is permitted to make distinctions based on race and ethnicity "only when necessary to achieve a compelling interest, and then only through narrowly-tailored means" (P. Williams 2003a). The interest in diversity, tied so strongly to stereotypes, was considered to be "too indefinite, ill-defined, and lacking in objective, ascertainable standards to be fitted to narrowly-tailored measures" (P. Williams 2003b).

Attorneys representing the University of Michigan in the Gratz case argued that in the twenty-five years since *Bakke*, the nation's colleges and universities have embraced the educational value of diversity and relied on *Bakke* to design admissions policies to achieve that goal. Abandoning this practice would result in the almost complete absence of minority students in selective colleges and universities. In the past two decades, the number of minority students attending college has doubled (from 2 million to 4.3 million). Yet, according to data collected by the American Council on Education, only 40 percent of African Americans and 34 percent of Latinas/os attend college, as compared with 46 percent of whites (Dobbs 2003; P. Williams 2003a).

The university believed that part of its educational mission was to assemble a student body reflecting varied life experiences. Indeed, all too frequently, students enter college from high schools where they have had little opportunity to interact with students of different racial and ethnic backgrounds. By assembling a diverse student body, universities encourage students to identify and confront unspoken (often unconscious) stereotypes. These interactions, and the educational benefits they further, would be nonexistent without a critical mass of minority students on campus (P. Williams 2003a).

University of Michigan attorneys noted that the U.S. Justice Department argued in its amicus brief that a diverse student body could be achieved through extant race-neutral means. Examples include the "percentage plans" employed in Texas, California, and Florida, which admit a certain percentage of the highest performing graduates of each high school (ranging from 4 to 20 percent) to public universities in a state. However, the university argued that such formulas are ultimately designed to achieve some degree of racial diversity. Given that most high schools are de facto segregated along racial lines (largely because of residential patterns), the top students in predominantly minority schools would automatically be admitted along with the top students from predominantly white schools. Whatever the efficacy of these policies, they were not considered feasible for the University of Michigan because of demographic constraints. Moreover, any percentage plan would require the university to discontinue considering "a much wider and more nuanced range of academic factors" in its admissions process and dispense with its goal of assembling a broadly diverse student body (Stohr 2004, 242–45; P. Williams 2003a).

With regard to the law school admissions, the university argued that it was explicitly devised to comply with *Bakke*. The law school did not employ quotas, and race was by no means the predominant factor in admissions. In fact, the admissions practices were virtually indistinguishable from those at Harvard, which were endorsed in *Bakke*. Rather, the core of its policy was "an individualized review of the many different ways in which an applicant might contribute to the learning environment." Given the national population of college graduates, law schools like Michigan could not admit meaningful numbers of minority students without taking race into consideration. Thus, the Supreme Court would have to overrule *Bakke* in order to rule in favor of Grutter. But there was no compelling justification for such a radical break with a legal precedent. From the university's perspective, such a decision "would force most of the nation's finest institutions to choose between dramatic resegregation and completely abandoning the demanding standards" of higher education (P. Williams 2003b).

The two cases attracted a record number of amicus briefs. Those supporting the University of Michigan included several dozen Fortune 500 companies, the nation's elite private universities and colleges, the AFL-CIO, the American Bar Association, and a list of former high-ranking military officers and civilian defense officials (Lane 2003; Stohr 2004, 247–54). They did not seek to defend so much the specifics of Michigan's programs as the various race-conscious policies that could be endangered if the Court ruled against the university (Lane 2003). Though their motivations may have varied, there appeared to be a consensus among national institutions that the consideration of race (in keeping with *Bakke*) is the most meaningful way to achieve a more inclusive society. So powerful was this consensus that much of big business, a major constituent of the Republican Party's political alliance, parted company with President Bush, who supported the white students challenging Michigan's admissions programs. In his brief, Bush agreed that diversity was a "paramount" goal but stated that it should be achieved through race-neutral or color-blind means (Lane 2003; Stohr 2004, 243–44). The support for Michigan was in stark contrast to the thirteen briefs that were filed on behalf of the white students. With the exception of the briefs filed by the Bush administration, the Justice Department, the state of Florida, and its Republican governor Jeb Bush, relatively small neoconservative public-interest groups submitted the majority of these briefs. However, the latter argued that recent opinion polls indicated considerable support for their position.

In a 6-3 decision, the Supreme Court overturned the undergraduate program but upheld the law school policy by a 5-4 vote, with Chief Justice Sandra Day O'Connor aligning with the more liberal justices (Curry 2003; Stohr 2004, 229–32, 290–307). Accordingly, the Court permitted colleges to consider race as one factor in admissions but outlawed a point system favoring minorities. Yet the Court's decision also presented Michigan and other schools with a significant administrative burden: all applicants must be given individualized consideration without resorting to overt racial preferences. The court emphasized that the reason it ruled in favor of the law school admissions policy but against the undergraduate policy was that the former gave each applicant what Justice O'Connor called a "meaningful individualized review" (Curry 2003).

Writing for the majority in the law school case, O'Connor stressed that "race-conscious admissions policies must be limited in time" (Curry 2003). This stance addressed the concerns of the Justice Department that the university's pursuit of a "critical mass" of minority students would justify affirmative action policy in perpetuity (K. Williams 2003). O'Connor advised the university to develop "sunset provisions" and "periodic reviews to determine whether racial preferences are still necessary to achieve student body diversity." She also stated: "We take the law school at its word that it would 'like nothing better than to find a race-neutral admissions formula' and will terminate its race-conscious admissions program as soon as practicable. . . . We expect that 25 years from now, the use of racial preferences will no longer be necessary" (Curry 2003).

Essentially, the Court permitted the university to strive toward achieving a "critical mass" of minority students in pursuit of diversity and to monitor progress toward that goal without contravening the Constitution. It did not, however, mandate either a twenty-five-year sunset provision or a periodic review. Nevertheless, this does leave open the possibility of litigation when individuals feel these programs are no longer necessary, or when the mechanisms seem to diverge from the goal of diversity. Moreover, the Court's opinion did not provide guidelines for what constitutes racial diversity, inhibiting the determination of when such diversity has been achieved sufficiently to justify ending the use of race in admissions.

Many supporters of affirmative action applauded the Court's decision. But they also alluded to the fact that measures automatically taking race into consideration save both time and money, but a "meaningful individualized review" places a heavy burden on undergraduate admissions. Indeed, in its legal brief, the University of Michigan argued that the sheer number of undergraduate applications made it unfeasible to utilize the more individualized approach employed by the law school. Nevertheless, after the ruling, the president of the University of Michigan was confident that such a review could be given to each of the twenty-five thousand applicants (Curry 2003). To achieve this, university officials stated they would hire sixteen part-time readers and five additional full-time admissions counselors, at a projected additional cost of up to $2 million. This would not, however, lead to an increase in the university's $40 application fee (Pierre 2003). A number of other schools that previously relied on race-specific procedures, including Ohio State and the University of Massachusetts, have also pledged their support of affirmative action but have also had to employ additional staff. Many colleges have vowed to spend whatever is necessary to comply with the new rulings (Pope 2004).

The new Michigan undergraduate policy borrows from the law school's practices, replacing the point-based scheme with an approach that places a higher priority on academic achievement but subtly continues to use race as a factor (Pope 2004). This approach is similar to the University of California's "comprehensive review model" (Pierre 2003). The new procedures, affecting applicants beginning in 2004, consider a student's grades, high school curriculum, and standardized test scores, as well as personal interests, geography, alumni connections, race, family income, and educational background (Pierre 2003). Applicants are required to write more personal essays and incorporate information about their lives and family backgrounds, including parents' education and income. Two short essays have been added to the current requirement of a long essay. Applicants may select from a range of topics, including several that ask how their presence would add to campus diversity, or how cultural diversity has had an impact on their lives (Toppo 2003).

Student groups at the University of Michigan were pleased with the school's continued commitment to diversity but were withholding judgment to see whether the new policy succeeds (Pierre 2003). Meanwhile, neoconservative groups have taken a wait-and-see attitude regarding the constitutionality of the new system. If race trumps all other factors, then the new system will be as legally vulnerable as the previous system (Toppo 2003). Meanwhile, much of the debate has shifted to socioeconomic affirmative action. Many believe class-based admissions targeting the poor, regardless of race, would be a more equitable approach. Yet this would inevitably benefit larger numbers of European Americans than students of color, although the latter might benefit disproportionately because of their smaller numbers in the national population and higher levels of poverty. Some civil rights advocates are alarmed by this shift in the debate and do not believe socioeconomic affirmative action would be enough to assist African Americans and Latinas/os.

Most selective colleges would claim they have made few if any changes since the Michigan decisions because they had already ceased using race-specific policies but will continue to pursue affirmative action as aggressively as the law allows. Yet there is concern that increasingly popular colleges might conclude affirmative action is too risky and expensive—especially in an era of tight budgets and lukewarm public support (Pope 2004). In addition, there is some uncertainty whether and how the Michigan cases—which addressed only admissions—will affect scholarships, summer schools, and outreach programs for minority students, themselves increasingly important tools for colleges seeking to diversify their student bodies (Pope 2004). Admissions officers say any program that smacks of racial exclusivity is open to legal challenge (Cohen 2004; Dobbs 2003; Cohen 2004; Glater 2006). Some neoconservative organizations argue that minority outreach programs are unconstitutional if they exclude other racial groups. They have threatened legal action and, in some cases, have filed complaints with the U.S. Department of Education and the Justice Department (Clegg 2005; Dobbs 2003; Cohen 2004; Glater 2006). Since the Michigan decisions, the threat of such lawsuits has prompted a number of schools to cancel summer orientation and scholarship programs that explicitly target minorities (Pope 2004). Some universities, including Amherst, Mount Holyoke, MIT, Southern Illinois University, State University of New

York, Washington State University, and St. Louis University have altered their programs or fellowships to make them less racially exclusive. Many other colleges are expected to follow suit (Clegg 2005; Dobbs 2003; Glater 2006).

The decisions in the Michigan cases will supposedly ensure racial diversity for the most selective colleges and universities. Yet the more these institutions study these decisions, the more they realize they are navigating through a legal and political minefield (Cohen 2004; Pope 2004). Though most schools maintain a general commitment to racial diversity, they are now cautious for several reasons, including legal uncertainty, cost, and expectations that affirmative action might one day be abolished. Ultimately, many schools will probably abandon racial (and gender) preferences rather than run the risk of legal challenges. Republican domination of the executive and legislative branches of the federal government since the 2004 elections, along with the appointment of conservative judges to the nation's highest court, will almost certainly exacerbate this trend (Clegg 2005).

The Racial Privacy Initiative (RPI)

The debate surrounding the Racial Privacy Initiative (RPI)—which was placed on the October 7, 2003, California recall ballot as Proposition 54—further illustrates the "Latin Americanization" of race relations in the United States.[1] The RPI, like California's Proposition 209 and other anti–affirmative action initiatives, is a product of the liberalization of the racial order since the civil rights era and the accompanying belief that racial discrimination itself has declined. Specifically, the RPI represents an attempt by neoconservatives to frame —in a manner reminiscent of Brazil's racial democracy ideology—increased intermarriage and the growing numbers of multiracial-identified people as a reaffirmation of color-blind ideology and the realization of an egalitarian racial order. Accordingly, multiraciality is used to promote an agenda that has the progressive veneer of "dismantling" or "deconstructing" race. In actuality, this agenda seeks to eliminate race-conscious policies aimed at pursuing racial justice, and even racial categories themselves, as well as the collection of data on race. Consequently, attention is deflected away from continuing racial inequalities.

Briefly, the RPI would have banned state agencies from classifying individuals on the basis of race, ethnicity, color, or national origin (thus preventing the collection of data on race and ethnicity), effective January 1, 2005. However, the initiative identified a series of exemptions, or areas in which the collection of racial and ethnic data was perceived as necessary. These included the classification

1. The RPI was on the same ballot as the special election held on October 7, 2003, to recall Governor Gray Davis.

of medical research subjects and patients, as well as exemptions for law enforcement officers in conducting their duties, and the assignment of prisoners. The Department of Fair Employment and Housing was also exempted from the RPI, though only for ten years after the effective date of the initiative. Yet the initiative did not provide exemptions for public education, public contracting, or public employment. These were, in fact, the areas identified in the first paragraph of the initiative as subject to the ban on racial/ethnic data collection. This led many civil rights organizations to view the initiative as the "Son of 209," which would deal the final blow to any state policies oriented toward ameliorating racial inequality (Khimm 2003).[2]

The RPI arose in the aftermath of the decennial census controversy, which ultimately resulted in divisions within the multiracial movement. Once the contours of state reformism were clear, these divisions intensified, especially with regard to the format for collecting racial data. One segment of the movement, the AMEA, its affiliates, and its supporters, advocated the new state policy; its leadership was eventually incorporated into an oversight committee related to the census.[3] Meanwhile, Project RACE (Reclassify All Children Equally) and its supporters continued to pursue a stand-alone multiracial identifier (with or without multiple check-offs), or at least the inclusion of the term "multiracial" in the instructions on the race question. In addition, Project RACE and commentators on *Interracial Voice (IV)* balked at the OMB's announcement that individuals reporting more than one race would be reassigned to one racial category, rather than be counted as multiracial, for the purpose of monitoring discrimination and enforcing civil rights laws.[4] Consequently, they did not consider the new guidelines to be a significant advancement over previous methods of data collection and tabulation (Douglas 1998a, 1998b; Graham 1997a, 1997b; Graham and Landrith 1999).

Meanwhile, another segment of the movement, represented by the Multiracial Leadership Conference/Roundtable and sponsored by A Place for Us/National

2. For his part, Connerly did not deny that the RPI was designed to undermine any attempts to resurrect affirmative action policies in California under a different guise. Connerly was quoted as saying that the RPI "would be an express prohibition in the areas of public education, public contracting, and public employment, which are banned for purposes of preferential treatment anyway in California as a result of Proposition 209" (Rossomando 2001).

3. Specifically, the AMEA is a member of the Subcommittee on the Census. Ramona Douglass, president of the AMEA from 1994 to 1999, has been a key liaison between the AMEA, its constituency, and the Census Bureau (http://www.ameasite.org/).

4. The argument against the new guidelines rested on the fact that individuals who checked "black" and "white" on their employment application would be tabulated as black. Thus, they would not have grounds for redress if they tried to file a complaint with the EEOC claiming they were discriminated against because they were multiracial, as such a category is not protected under current guidelines.

(APUN), met on March 31, 2000, in Washington, D.C., and supported the elimination of official racial designations altogether ("Racial Classifications" 2000; Landrith 2001a; Sample 2000). Those attending included Steve and Ruth White of APUN, Byrd of *IV*, and another editor of an online journal, James Landrith of *The Multiracial Activist (TMA)*. Also in attendance was Ward Connerly, the conservative University of California regent who rose to prominence as one of the architects of California's Proposition 209.[5] His organization, the American Civil Rights Institute, has also criticized the OMB's rejection of a multiracial identifier (Nelson 1997). Connerly had been previously interviewed by Byrd in 1999 for *IV* (Byrd 1999) and was inducted into APUN's "Racial Harmony Hall of Fame" at the conference ("Racial Classifications" 2000).

The rift in the multiracial movement over the OMB recommendations led to a more sustained collaboration between neoconservatives and particular leaders of the movement. Particularly significant was the growing collaboration between the two website editors, Byrd and Landrith, and Connerly. Interestingly, Byrd and Landrith did not necessarily identify themselves as "conservatives." Byrd had been a registered Democrat (at least up until 1997), and while he consistently criticized black intellectuals and civil rights organizations (especially the NAACP) for what he perceived as embracing the one-drop rule and racial separatism (Byrd 1996, 1997d), he initially opposed the conservative agenda of abolishing affirmative action and other race-based programs (Byrd 1995, 1997c). Landrith has featured a "Hall of Shame" on his website, focusing on public figures and organizations across the racial and political spectrum who have "demonstrated a repugnant view of multiracial identity/interracial relationships" (Landrith 1995–2001).[6]

Byrd and Landrith were frustrated with the objections of traditional civil rights organizations to multiracial identifiers, resulting in what they perceived as the continuation of hypodescent under a different guise (Byrd 1998a, 1998b, 2000b; Landrith 2001b). Both saw as irreconcilable and hypocritical the calls of civil rights groups to dismantle racism while supporting the maintenance of racial categories, which were originally established to perpetuate racism (Byrd 2000a; Landrith 2001b). Ultimately, both editors shared a self-professed "libertarian"

5. The California State Constitution has an important but often overlooked stipulation (Article 1, section 31) specifying that "nothing can be used to prohibit any action necessary to establish or maintain eligibility for any federal or state program, where ineligibility would result in a loss of federal or state funds to the university." Universities must comply with federal mandates that still support affirmative action and other diversity-equity initiatives. Yet, in order to accomplish this in the post-209 era, universities have necessarily sought alternative means of achieving diversity without explicitly taking applicants' race into consideration, especially in light of the recent U.S. Supreme Court rulings on the University of Michigan's affirmative action programs.

6. See http://www.multiracial.com/projects/hallofshame.html/.

approach to race.[7] This approach viewed government-imposed racial classifications, along with race-based policies and, indeed, all forms of race consciousness, as not only impinging upon individual freedom and choice (particularly with regard to identity) but also perpetuating false divisions among humanity. Therefore, they perceived the elimination of racial categories as the only assured way of dismantling racism (Byrd 2000a, 2000b; Landrith 2000, 2001b).

Meanwhile, Connerly had already embarked on plans to make the elimination of racial categories a reality, at least on the state level. In a 1999 interview with Byrd for *IV*, Connerly revealed his intention to introduce a bill in the California legislature, which he anticipated would be defeated by the Democratic majority, as a way of pilot testing this legislation before submitting it to voters as a ballot measure. In later guest commentaries for *IV*, Connerly discussed the need for the United States to eliminate "those silly little boxes" (Connerly 2000, 2001a, 2001c). By April 2001, Connerly, along with his organization, the American Civil Rights Coalition, had launched a statewide campaign to place the "Racial Privacy Initiative" on the March 2002 California ballot; both Byrd and Landrith accepted invitations to participate in the steering committee for the initiative (Landrith 2001b).

Like Proposition 209, the RPI was yet another neoconservative effort to undermine race-based policies through the skilled use of color-blind rhetoric and the masterful "rearticulation" (Omi and Winant 1994, 99, 131) of civil rights discourse and iconography (such as using the image of Dr. Martin Luther King Jr. and excerpts of his "I Have a Dream" speech).[8] However, the rhetoric surrounding the RPI also selectively incorporated concerns raised by the multiracial movement throughout the previous decade. The phenomena of increasing intermarriage and growing numbers of multiracial-identified individuals (and by extension the multiracial movement itself), were co-opted as the centerpiece of the rhetorical strategy for the RPI, symbolizing the color-blind ideal that should be reflected in state policy.

This strategy is evident in Connerly's introduction to the "Reader's Guide for the RPI," featured as a guest editorial in the November/December 2001 edition of *IV*. Connerly begins this piece by referring to earlier commentaries by Byrd and other contributors about the need to "deconstruct 'race'" and offers the RPI as an opportunity to implement this goal (Connerly 2001b). Later, he cites a report that documents the substantial percentage of multiracial births (14 percent

7. Indeed, Landrith refers to his website (http://www.multiracial.com/) as a "libertarian oriented activist journal."

8. Martin Luther King Jr. was again invoked in some commentaries supporting the RPI. For instance, Shelby Steele commented that Proposition 54 was the attempt to infuse the California Constitution with the spirit of King's dream (Steele 2003).

of all births) in California in 1997 (Tafoya 2000). Engaging in a rhetorical slight of hand, Connerly then associates "the remarkable blurring of racial lines in California" with the rise in University of California applicants declining to state their race. Though Connerly could hardly have proven this association, he nevertheless concludes "the state needs to catch up and recognize that Californians increasingly no longer see themselves in racial boxes." The RPI would thus serve to "create a colorblind state for our children and grandchildren, one that is more respectful of the inherently private and complex nature of racial identity" (Connerly 2001b).

Though the logic and language of the RPI, framed within the dominant ideology of color-blindness, might have resonated with many individuals, voters across the racial spectrum rejected it by an astonishing 64-36 margin. Indeed, exit polls indicated that three-quarters of African Americans and Latinas/os, as well as a majority of European Americans, voted against the initiative (Khimm 2003; "Racial Privacy Initiative Defeated" 2003). The RPI's failure can be attributed in part to the broad spectrum of organizations and individuals that opposed it. Predictably, traditional civil rights organizations opposed it but organizations like the California Medical Association and the American Heart Association and prominent figures such as former surgeon general C. Everett Koop also came out against it. This was part of a strategy to undermine the initiative by focusing more on the ambiguous medical exemption that might have prevented physicians and other public health officials from tracking the impact of diseases on different populations. By contrast, the campaign downplayed the damage the initiative would do to efforts to address structural racial inequality in public education and other areas (Chemerinsky 2003; Khimm 2003; Sen 2003–4).[9]

Opponents of the RPI also mounted a far more visible campaign than Connerly and his coalition. They placed advertisements against it on television and radio. Student and community-based organizations mobilized against it on the grassroots level. The pro-RPI campaign, on the other hand, consisted of a few radio advertisements, and some public appearances by Connerly himself (including a few debates over the initiative). It could be that the pro-RPI coalition kept a low-profile because they hoped that voter ignorance of the initiative would work to its

9. This is not to state that the anti-RPI campaign eschewed altogether discussions about the RPI's impact on efforts to address racial inequality. In fact, online literature provided by the Coalition for an Informed California discussed the threat the RPI posed to civil rights enforcement, school reform, efforts to track racial profiling, as well as addressing public health disparities (http://www.defeat54.org/). However, television advertisements focused exclusively on health care and medical concerns. As Rinku Sen (2003–4) notes, this strategy was not only designed to appeal to voters across racial and ethnic lines, but specifically to avoid alienating European American voters by sidestepping the issue of white culpability in racial discrimination.

advantage, but it was more likely that they simply lacked the funds to do more. Between January and August 2003, the pro-RPI campaign received contributions totaling $46,640; the anti-RPI campaign received $535,801 during the same period (Sanders 2003). Democratic gubernatorial candidate Lieutenant Governor Cruz Bustamante also channeled $3.8 million from his campaign funds to defeat it (Khimm 2003; Rojas 2003).

If the RPI's message appeared tailor-made for interracial families and multi-racial individuals, the debate over it nevertheless reflected persistent cleavages within the multiracial movement. Byrd and Landrith enthusiastically promoted the RPI as the ultimate progressive step toward eliminating racism. Landrith argued that the RPI would complete the abolitionist project by eliminating those categories originally used to maintain the institution of slavery. He stated, "It is my steadfast belief that until these categories are gone, we will not be able to begin to give 'racism' the proper burial it deserves. These categories, created for the sole purpose of ensuring state political power at our nation's birth are not the solution to racism. . . . It's time to let the deconstruction begin" (Landrith 2001b). Similarly, Byrd envisioned the RPI as part of a larger "jihad" against race consciousness (Byrd 2000a), and as engaging "in the final battle of deconstructing the race notion" that traditional civil rights leaders had abandoned (Byrd 2003).

Meanwhile, various other multiracial organizations and public forums came out against the RPI. Dubbing the RPI the "Racial Ignorance Initiative," HIF argued that the RPI was "in direct opposition to the needs of the mixed-heritage Asian Pacific Islander community," as well as those of other communities of color (Hapa Issues Forum 2003). The AMEA also endorsed the anti-RPI campaign, after a discussion involving representatives from the board of directors and advisory board (including myself and Josef Castañeda-Liles). Earlier, Ramona Douglass, a former president of the AMEA and current president at large, agreed to debate Connerly on the need for census racial categories on the television program *Uncommon Knowledge,* which is sponsored by the conservative Hoover Institution at Stanford University and is aired on some PBS affiliates.[10]

In addition to HIF and the AMEA, the recently formed Mavin Foundation voiced its opposition to the RPI. The Mavin Foundation (hereafter Mavin) is a nonprofit organization founded by Matt Kelley, which began with the creation of *Mavin* magazine, a publication devoted to examining and celebrating the experiences of multiracial people. Currently Mavin also sponsors a program to increase the diversity of bone-marrow donors. This is particularly important, considering the growing complexity of backgrounds of multiracial individuals

10. The program was aired on February 22, 2002 (http://www.uncommonknowledge.org/01-02/638.html/).

and the fact that individuals are most likely to find a marrow match with someone of similar ancestry. In addition, Mavin produces the *Multiracial Child Resource Book* to educate parents and professionals about the needs of multiracial youth, among other projects.[11] Mavin issued a joint statement with HIF and the AMEA, in which the RPI was framed as rolling back the hard-won gains of the multiracial movement to implement changes in racial data collection so that multiracial people could be officially recognized (Khanna 2004).[12]

Meanwhile, Susan Graham of Project RACE expressed misgivings about the RPI but affirmed that she was "not against the spirit of Prop. 54" (Graham 2003). Her criticism focused on the ambiguous medical exemption, which she argued could have a detrimental impact on providing health care for multiracial patients. Ultimately, she felt the defeat of the RPI signaled a window of opportunity to push for a separate multiracial category, because of the lack of existing information about the medical needs of the multiracial population. Finally, Swirl, Inc., a New York-based organization founded in 2000 by Jen Chau (with chapters in seven major metropolitan areas throughout the United States and Japan), declined to take a position on the RPI. Nevertheless, the organization provided links to online resources (pro and con) discussing the initiative and advertised a number of events, including many anti-RPI rallies and forums.[13]

11. Although the support groups founded by (and essentially for) interracial couples and their first-generation offspring continue to be active, many have noticed a decline in their membership. Accordingly, many have shifted to being web-based organizations. Some of this decline in membership is attributable to the fact that interracial couples are no longer quite as anomalous as previously, thus obviating the need for social support. In addition, gains have been achieved in the primary political goal of changing official racial designators. Consequently, the focus has shifted to educational concerns (such as the AMEA's focus on the establishment of a national resource center), as well as on monitoring and procuring educational institutional compliance with the new OMB federal standard of allowing individuals to check more than one category.

The decreased interest in these support groups is also tied to the fact that young adult and adult multiracial individuals have become much more numerous and vocal. The significant growth of multiracial student groups on university campuses and other organizations (the Mavin Foundation, Swirl Inc.) founded by and primarily addressing the concerns of multiracial individuals reflects the maturation of the first-generation offspring. Many are now entering young adulthood and are able to articulate a political agenda surrounding multiracial concerns. Though multiracial individuals have typically sought avenues of expression apart from support groups, perceiving their interests as superseded by those of interracial couples, both sets of organizations have pursued similar agendas and worked together productively on a number of projects. For example, the Mavin Foundation, along with the AMEA, partnered with the MK Level Playing Field Foundation to support the Campus Multiracial Awareness and Compliance (CMAC) Project. This seeks to facilitate fuller inclusion and participation of multiracial/multiethnic students on college campuses and aid multiracial students in getting their schools to comply with OMB federal standards for the collection of racial/ethnic data.

12. See also http://www.mavin.net/pr100703.html/.

13. See http://www.swirlinc.org/.

This most recent strategic link between the multiracial phenomenon and the rhetoric of color-blindness raises questions about the role of the multiracial movement in perpetuating color-blind rhetoric, and more important, its role as part of a larger movement for racial justice. Some critics have argued that the multiracial movement is detached from the antiracist struggle. Their critique hinges on the conflation of the entire movement with the project of advocating for multiracial identifiers, particularly on the 2000 census. In part, they focus on the perceived lack of consideration among multiracial activists of how such revisions in racial categorization could impact efforts to monitor compliance with civil rights mandates and track continuing structural inequities among communities of color. These critics also focus on how some movement organizations (specifically *IV* and Project RACE) sought neoconservative support for a multiracial identifier during the 2000 census debate (Dalmage 2000, 169–72; Spencer 1999, 129–85; Texeira 2003, 30).

Indeed, the debates surrounding the 2000 census and the RPI validate, to a degree, some of these criticisms of the multiracial movement. Both controversies highlight how some movement organizations and publications (e.g., Project RACE, *IV, TMA*, and APUN) have allied themselves with neoconservatives in the pursuit of a multiracial category or the elimination of all racial categories on government forms. These same organizations have often been dismissive of, if not outright hostile to, the concerns expressed by traditional civil rights organizations about the impact such changes would have on civil rights compliance. However, these controversies also reveal how other organizations (AMEA, HIF, Mavin) have refused to ally themselves with neoconservatives and have resisted the wholesale co-optation of the multiracial movement. Clearly, the multiracial movement in its entirety cannot be characterized as complicit with the neoconservative agenda, even as the highly organized and visible coalition between *Interracial Voice, The Multiracial Activist*, and Ward Connerly may tend to overshadow other segments of the movement.

Though the multiracial movement is composed of multiple factions, each with different agendas that vary in their complicity with the neoconservative agenda, questions remain about the movement's role in the larger antiracist struggle. Indeed, critics accuse the movement of lacking an antiracist agenda, which they construct as being synonymous with a political initiative that addresses continuing structural inequalities. However, part of the struggle to dismantle racism also entails cultural initiatives that facilitate an understanding of race as a social rather than biological construction. The latter phenomenon underpinned the U.S. racial order, justifying slavery, de jure segregation, and antimiscegenation legislation.

Though biological constructions of race may now be largely discredited, they continue to shape reaction to efforts aimed at promoting greater racial integration in the primary and secondary spheres. In particular, interracial couples and multiracial individuals are still confronted with discrimination based on these "essentialist" (Frankenberg 1993, 130; Omi and Winant 1994, 187n.57) renderings of race.[14] Through cultural initiatives, multiracial organizations (regardless of their political alliance) have attempted to challenge these lingering notions by sponsoring public educational forums, organizing petition drives, providing resource materials, and providing support for interracial couples and families and multiracial individuals. While some contingents in the movement (e.g., *IV*, Project RACE, *TMA*, and APUN) may appear to be at odds with the antiracist struggle, their commentaries have nevertheless highlighted how traditional civil rights organizations, leaders, and intellectuals often uncritically embrace identities and politics that have essentialist underpinnings (e.g., the one-drop rule). Thus, it can be argued that the primary contribution of the multiracial movement as a "racial project" to the larger antiracist struggle has been challenging biological notions of race, and especially rules of hypodescent.[15]

That said, many organizations and individuals involved in the multiracial movement have failed to mount political initiatives that address lingering structural inequality. On the contrary, some organizations and leaders, particularly *IV*, *TMA*, and APUN, have endorsed a project of eliminating the collection of racial data that would undermine efforts to track (and thus address) persistent racial inequality in educational attainment, health, income, and other areas. Their advocacy, informed by an uncritical acceptance of the dominant ideology of color-blindness, reflects a naïve egalitarianism that equates all forms of race consciousness as detrimental to societal progress, thus ignoring the context of sustained racial inequality that requires racial data collection and race-based policy. Paradoxically, to the extent that these organizations reproduce color-blind ideology and support policies that would effectively perpetuate (and mask) structural inequalities, they also hinder the goals of individual and collective racial transcendence they profess to advocate.

14. One of the more notable cases in recent years involved ReVonda Bowen, a high school student in Wedowee, Alabama. The principal, Hulond Humphries, threatened to cancel the prom if interracial couples attended and told Bowen (of black/white parentage) that her parents had made a "mistake" (Byrd 1994). APUN helped organize a petition drive to get the principal fired (http://www.aplaceforus national.com/experience.html/), while Byrd and Landrith both decried the incident (Byrd 1994; http://www.multiracial.com/projects/hallofshame.html/).

15. Of course, some critics have even disagreed with this assessment, especially Rainier Spencer (see Spencer 1999, 86–96, and 2004, 357–79).

In contrast, organizations such as the AMEA and HIF have been open to addressing the concerns of traditional communities of color and civil rights organizations (especially during the census controversy), and have supported the continued enforcement of civil rights legislation and compensatory programs such as affirmative action (Daniel 2002, 141–51). Along with Mavin, the AMEA and HIF have objected to proposals (such as the RPI) that would have a detrimental impact on efforts to ameliorate structural inequality. However, it is unclear to what extent these organizations have been proactive in developing projects that address structural racism (Foster 2005, 273–309; K. Williams 2003, 92–97), notwithstanding the commitment of individual members of those organizations to such concerns. Moreover, these organizations have not been particularly adroit or especially effective in deconstructing the rhetoric of color-blindness as part of a larger agenda of dismantling racism, despite having voiced opposition to the RPI. Instead, they have focused almost exclusively on challenging dysfunctional and pathological images of interracial couples / multiracial individuals by promoting images of these individuals as stable, "normal," and potential "racial bridges." Accordingly, the rhetoric of the AMEA, HIF, and Mavin in some ways parallels that of *IV, TMA*, APUN, and Project RACE. This in turn serves to further conflate the different agendas among the various factions of the multiracial movement with the naïve egalitarianism that underpins the neoconservative agenda.

Consequently, the AMEA, HIF, and Mavin face a formidable challenge, as the coalition between *IV, TMA*, and Connerly advances a multiracial political initiative that perpetuates an association between the multiracial movement, color-blindness, and the neoconservative agenda.[16] Yet the defeat of the RPI signals an opening whereby the AMEA, HIF, and Mavin (as well as other organizations) can join forces and deploy an oppositional political initiative that is premised on an incisive critique of color-blind ideology. This would necessarily involve decoupling that ideology from its automatic association with interracial marriage and multiracial identity. It would also require demystifying the naïve egalitarianism employed by neoconservatives, in which the comparatively more fluid interpersonal dynamics in the primary structural sphere are equated with greater secondary structural (political, educational, occupational, and income) parity, where in fact significant inequality remains.

The defeat of the Racial Privacy Initiative, though a setback, hardly signifies the defeat of the neoconservative agenda, or the retreat of Connerly from the political scene. As it became apparent that the RPI would be defeated, Connerly

---

16. However, *Interracial Voice* went on hiatus in 2003–4 due in part to the founding editor's shift to "non-racialism." In the interim, Landrith has created a blog to attract interested readers (http://www.multiracial.com/blog/).

indicated that he would work with the head of the California Medical Association to draft language clarifying the Achilles' heel of the initiative—the ambiguous medical exemption (Pritchard 2003). After the RPI was defeated, Connerly shifted from advocating the elimination of racial categories to recommending the addition of a stand-alone multiracial identifier to University of California admissions and other university forms that report data on race and ethnicity (Maitre 2004). Since 1990, UC undergraduate admissions forms have allowed students to check more than one box on the racial/ethnic question (Locke 2004b; Schevitz 2004).

Though Connerly's UC proposal would seem to contradict his prior project of eliminating racial categories, it is actually a rearticulation of earlier neoconservative support for a stand-alone multiracial box on the census. This category was perceived as helping to undercut race-based policy, given that it denotes no legally protected class and thus serves no statutory purpose, by dismantling the obsession with race that fuels identity politics and the so-called racial spoils system. However, Connerly and other neoconservatives apparently have not considered that the addition of a stand-alone multiracial identifier, rather than the check-one-or-more format, might amplify rather than diminish the obsession with race consciousness and racial separatism he is supposedly seeking to remedy.

Connerly was able to garner support for his UC proposal from various segments of the multiracial movement, including Landrith of TMA, Byrd of IV, Steve and Ruth White of APUN, and Francis Wardle of the Center for the Study of Biracial Children (Landrith 2004). He was perhaps hoping to elicit support from other sectors that opposed the RPI but would support the collection of data on multiracial-identified individuals. However, the AMEA, HIF, and the Mavin voiced their opposition (Chau 2004)[17] and organized an online petition drive to be submitted to the UC Regents.[18] On November 18, 2004, the thirteen UC Regents convened a hearing (which was attended by members of Mavin, the AMEA, and HIF) at which Connerly presented his proposal. After much testimony, questioning, and clarification, the Regents strongly rejected the proposal in a 12-1 vote (Locke 2004a). Though Connerly's UC proposal was defeated, and his primary focus has shifted to dismantling affirmative action policy in Michigan with a ballot initiative similar to California's Proposition 209, he is not likely to abandon multiraciality as a cornerstone of his rhetorical strategy. Indeed, it would not be surprising if at some point he presented a ballot initiative similar

17. On September 2, 2004, the Mavin Foundation and HIF released a public statement opposing Connerly's proposed multiracial category (http://www.hapaissuesforum.org/).

18. Personal communication with Alfredo Padilla, project manager, Mavin Foundation Campus Awareness and Compliance Initiative (CACI), November 3, 2004.

to the one sponsored by APUN[19] in 1996 to implement a stand-alone multiracial category on state forms.[20]

Yet considering that the current guidelines support not a stand-alone multiracial identifier but rather the check-one-or-more format, multiracial individuals are treated as part of an "extended community" composed of members of the background(s) of color for civil rights and other purposes and claims (e.g., affirmative action). This does not preclude activists from pursuing future mandates that accord official recognition of and gain protection for the unique sets of interests and issues that crystallize around the multiracial experience. Thus far most activists have avoided pursuing such mandates in order to avoid a backlash from traditional communities of color. Such a proposal would not in and of itself be problematic. Multiracial-identified individuals are subject to racial discrimination based specifically on the fact that they are multiracial. This applies even if they are socially designated as members of single-racial groups and thus simultaneously experience discrimination based on their perceived membership in those groups. In fact, treatment as monoracial based on that perceived membership, when individuals nevertheless assert a multiracial identity, is considered by many itself to be a form of racial discrimination. In addition, antidiscrimination and civil rights claims have been extended beyond African Americans—who were the initial beneficiaries of many of these mandates—to include numerous protected racial groups, as well as women.

Recent changes on EEO forms indicate a shift in this direction in terms of multiracial-identified individuals. On November 16, 2005, technocrats in the U.S. Equal Employment Opportunity Commission (EEOC) made a seemingly routine decision to approve revisions of the racial and ethnic categories on the Employer Information Report, or EEO-1. The changes were being implemented in response to new government standards for reporting race and ethnicity

19. In December 1996, APUN filed the 1998 Multiracial/Multiethnic Children's Initiative with the state of California, seeking to place the initiative on the November 1998 ballot. The initiative was approved for circulation in February 1997, with a July 11 deadline for obtaining the necessary eight hundred thousand signatures. APUN hoped to obtain the signatures needed by the end of June in celebration of the thirtieth anniversary of *Loving v. Virginia*, but it fell short of both this goal and of the July 11 deadline. Plans to announce the success of the campaign at the Multiracial Solidarity March, held in Hollywood on August 9, had to be abandoned. The march itself had a considerably smaller turnout than the two hundred people who participated in the first Multiracial Solidarity March in July 1996 in Washington, D.C. However, both marches received enthusiastic support from those individuals who attended (Ramona Douglass, pers. comm., February 21, 1997).

20. In spring 2005, Connerly retired as UC Regent. Interestingly, he noted that the failure to gain support for his UC proposal was the low point of his term as regent (Locke 2005). At present, it seems unlikely that Connerly will continue pursuing his objective of implementing a multiracial category in California, though Michigan may become a testing ground for such an initiative. This

issued by the Office of Management and Budget in 1997. The revisions included separating "Asians" from "Pacific Islanders" and renaming certain categories, changing "Hispanic" to "Hispanic or Latino" and "Black" to "Black or African American." In total, the new form will have one ethnic category—"Hispanic or Latino"—and six "non-Hispanic or Latino" racial categories: "White," "Black or African American," "Native Hawaiian or Other Pacific Islander," "Asian," "American Indian or Alaska Native," and "Two or More Races" (OMB, 2005: 71294–71303). In addition, voluntary employee self-identification will be the "preferred method" for obtaining racial or ethnic data, and other methods, such as visual observation, will be permitted "only when employees decline to self-identify" (OMB 2005, 71294–71296).

The most controversial change on the EEO-1 Report will require reporting of data on the number of employees who identify with "two or more races." Employers will not, however, be required to report the different races with which these employees identify (Hecker 2005; OMB 2005, 71294–71296). This is a significant shift from the guidelines established with the 2000 census, which recommended that all data reported on "two or more races" be tabulated from respondents checking off more than one single race. Accordingly, the Census Bureau has published two sets of data for each race category: e.g., Black Alone (respondents who checked Black and no other race category) and Black Alone or In Combination (respondents who checked Black and one or more other race categories).

Some public commentators voiced concerns that the new EEOC guidelines supporting the tabulation of individuals who identified as "two or more races" as a separate category would lead to the subtraction of those individuals from the traditional "single-racial" categories, along with a concomitant reduction in the numbers of the latter, whereas the number of Hispanics or Latinas/os would not be effected in this way (Hecker 2005; OMB 2005, 71294–71303). Indeed, similar concerns led to the 1997 OMB guidelines that rejected the inclusion of a multiracial identifier and endorsed the check-one-or-more format in data collection, as well as the Census Bureau's guidelines for the 2000 census recommending the tabulation of two sets of data for each race category. The EEOC, however, decided to include "two or more races" in order to analyze national employment trends and also allow the Office of Federal Contract Compliance Programs (OFCCP) to

---

may depend on the success of the "Michigan Civil Rights Initiative" (MCRI), which he is currently supporting and promoting. The MCRI's executive director is Jennifer Gratz, who was a plaintiff in the 2003 University of Michigan affirmative action cases. The initiative currently has enough signatures to place a proposed constitutional amendment on the state's Novermber 7, 2006, ballot that would ban race and gender-based preferences in admissions and government hiring (Clegg 2005; Locke 2005).

count this new category as "minority" for affirmative action purposes (Hecker 2005; OMB 2005, 71294–71303).[21]

If, however, multiracial individuals become a protected group under affirmative action and other civil rights claims, this would likely raise sticky questions about the criteria used to determine who "qualifies" as a "real" multiracial person. Currently, self-identification as multiracial is the criterion, which is largely indicative of individuals who reference their sense of "we-ness" in more than one community, directly in response to the multiple racial/cultural backgrounds in their genealogy. Yet considering that modern science has not produced empirical data confirming the existence of clearly delineated biophysical racial boundaries, along with the fact that a "multiracial" lineage or background is normative among humans, there is a real possibility of abuse in this area—particularly if the legal stakes rise in being designated as multiracial. Indeed, there is the risk that interpretations of physical appearance, or ancestral fractions and percentages, could gain in significance over self-identification in defining who is multiracial and safeguarding against potential "multiracial imposters and opportunists." Therefore, the recognition of a category of "multiracial" individuals with legally protected group rights—quite apart from what format might be used to collect data on these individuals—should give cause for serious reflection.

Whatever the case may be, it is clear that the controversy surrounding the decennial census and the Racial Privacy Initiative have highlighted the role of interracial families and multiracial individuals in shaping the future of race relations in the United States. As traditional binary (and biological) constructions of race become discredited, multiracial-identified people will increasingly play a central role in reifying or deconstructing the racial status quo. The challenge facing advocates of racial justice involves subverting the seductive and persuasive ideology of color-blindness as part of the antiracist struggle; multiracial organizations and individuals can and must play a central role in dismantling this ideology.

Furthermore, it remains to be seen whether a greater coalition can be built between multiracial and traditional civil rights organizations. Such a coalition could combine a cultural initiative that seeks to dismantle rigid, essentialist, and socially imposed group boundaries with a political initiative that addresses inequalities of opportunity and life chances (Foster 2006, 273–309). However, it is clear that the achievement of a genuinely "color-blind" social order in which race would not determine the distribution of wealth, power, privilege, and prestige will necessarily require a unified and concerted effort to address the myriad ways

---

21. The OFCCP is part of the U.S. Department of Labor's Employment Standards Administration and is responsible for ensuring that employers doing business with the federal government comply with the laws and regulations requiring nondiscrimination.

in which racial essentialism, hierarchy, and inequality are maintained. More important, it is imperative that all advocates of racial justice be self-reflective in regard to their potential role in reproducing these phenomena.

A "New" Multiracial Identity

The multiracial movement has sought to affirm a "new" multiracial identity that dismantles the one-drop rule inherited from the colonial past by deconstructing not only the dichotomization of blackness and whiteness as mutually exclusive categories of experience but also the hierarchical relationship between these two categories. The growing numbers of individuals who display this identity seek to embrace their European American background and European Americans but without diminishing their affinity with the experience of African Americans. The 1980s and 1990s were marked by successful political and social efforts to gain recognition of this growing population of multiracial-identified people, particularly on the decennial census. In the first decade of this century, we are already witnessing the implications of this milestone, as contemporary generations of multiracial individuals are increasingly assuming a biracial or multiracial identity as a normative part of their experience (Maria P.P. Root, pers. comm., September 10, 2004).

As long as public policy requires the collection of data on race and ethnicity—particularly as a means of tracking the nation's progress in achieving social equity—the inclusion of a multiracial identifier, regardless of the format, will not only provide a more accurate picture of contemporary demographics. It will also help alleviate the psychological oppression embedded in methods of data collection that support and are supported by the binary racial project. In addition, a multiracial identifier is a logical step in the progression of civil rights, with the potential to change social attitudes. Correspondingly, it helps deconstruct the notion of racial purity by encouraging people to question the artificially fixed, static, and mutually exclusive nature of racial/ethnic categories, which are central to perpetuating racist ideology and racial privilege in the United States. Ultimately, multiracial identity can initiate a long overdue national conversation about the shared ancestral connections that have been obscured by centuries of racism.

Yet many African Americans have expressed opposition to this new multiracial identity. They fear that many individuals will designate themselves as "multiracial" rather than as African American in order to escape the social stigma associated with blackness, perpetuating a divisive and pernicious "colorism" between multiracial individuals and blacks that privileges the former. Some critics maintain that multiracial individuals would be granted a structurally intermediate status subordinate to dominant whites but also superior to that of African

Americans in a manner similar to Brazil. In addition, those who physically approximate European Americans would be co-opted into the mainstream of society as provisional whites.

It is still not a normative and sanctioned pattern in the U.S. racial order, however, for individuals to identify as racially white while simultaneously acknowledging African American ancestry, as has historically been the case with Native American and other ancestries of color. Nevertheless, recent research on first-generation or biracial young adults indicates that a small yet increasing number of individuals of partial African American descent—particularly those who more closely approximate a European Amerian phenotype—embrace a white racial identity. More important, this identity has been validated through social interaction, particularly with European American peers ("White Girl" 2000; Rockquemore and Brunsma 2002, 45–47; Rockquemore and Laszloffy 2005, 7, 20–22, 118–21). Such an identity does not necessarily originate in discomfort with or rejection of their background(s) of color. Rather, it can reflect the preponderance of European Americans in their social milieu and/or relative lack of contact with family members and other individuals from their background(s) of color (Root 2003, 16).

Further indications of new trend may have been reflected in the public response to recent DNA evidence confirming the long-disputed contention that Thomas Jefferson—one of the founding fathers and third President of the United States—fathered several children with a slave mistress, Sally Hemings, who was of partial African descent. The DNA evidence indicates that Jefferson most likely fathered at least one of Sally Hemings's sons (Eston). Eston and some of his descendants apparently passed as European American. The contemporary descendants of this individual were socialized as white and had no knowledge of their African American ancestry. Although widely publicized, at no time in the public discussion of these findings was there any suggestion that these ostensibly European American individuals were now black, either legally or informally (Curtis 1998; Ellis 1998, 67–69; Murray 1997, 54–56; Murray and Duffy 1998, 59–64; Rosellini 1998, 66; Truscott 1999, 82–84).

It is possible that these individuals—and the many others who will likely emerge if more European Americans explore their genealogy—may reconsider the appropriateness of their racial socialization and designation as whites (Sim 1999, 68–78). What is crucial is that they did not conceal their African ancestry but instead allowed it to become public knowledge in the national media without any interrogation whether this ancestry now discredited them as bona fide whites. In the past, the potentially negative ramifications would have prevented most individuals from making such a disclosure.

More recently, theatrical legend Carol Channing, who is perhaps best known for her Broadway performances in *Gentlemen Prefer Blondes* (1949) and *Hello! Dolly*

(1963), acknowledges in her recent autobiography *Just Lucky I Guess* (2002) that she is of partial African American descent. This information was revealed to Channing the day she was headed off to Bennington College when her mother informed her that her father, George Channing, was the offspring of a German American mother and an African American father. While he was still quite young, George's mother, who worked as a domestic, moved him and his sister from his birthplace in Augusta, Georgia, to Providence, Rhode Island, where she felt people would not notice his "full features" (Channing 2002, 8). Revealing this information early on in her career would have presented serious obstacles to Channing becoming the toast of Broadway and achieving her five decades of prominence in entertainment.

Conversely, it is not clear whether or to what extent a white racial designation might be extended to individuals who have been socialized as African American (or even as multiracial) but select a white racial identity, while at the same time being aware of (or acknowledging) African American ancestry and/or displaying some African American phenotypical traits. Yet a shift in this direction may have been indicated by audience response on a segment of *The Maury Povich Show* involving two African American identified women ("Black Women Who Look White," Paramount Domestic Television, July 27, 1993). Both were phenotypically indistinguishable from European Americans but had been socialized as African American, as had several generations of antecedents who had lived in the same community at least since 1840. Many whites and some blacks in the audience chastised the women for not embracing both their African American and European American backgrounds, considering their phenotypical whiteness. Some individuals, including some African Americans, even argued that the women were actually white, despite their socialization and self-identification as African Americans.

It is difficult to determine to what extent this more inclusive whiteness is representative of a larger societal trend. Indeed, some have argued that African Americans will continue to be marked as the ultimate racial outsiders, whereas many of those now defined as nonwhite (e.g., Asian-descent and Latina/o-descent individuals, and so on) are likely to be included as racial insiders as the definition of whiteness expands. According to this scenario, the black/nonblack dynamic will replace the extant white/nonwhite dynamic as the new primary racial divide in the United States (Bonilla-Silva 2004, 224–39; Warren and Twine 1997, 200–218; Yancey 2005, 86–111). Yet these analyses do not taken into consideration the current decline in the rigid enforcement of the one-drop rule and the increasing significance of physical appearance working in combination with culture and class as determinants in social stratification.

Indeed, current trends indicate that select African-descent Americans who more closely approximate the dominant psychosomatic norm image in terms of phenotype and culture may very well be extended the status of racial insiders as the boundaries of whiteness continue to expand. If the one-drop rule has historically been an unquestioned and almost sacred social concept (Bourdieu 1977, 159), which has acquired the force of nature in the U.S. racial order, these trends indicate that European Americans may have become more willing to bend this rule. Meanwhile, African Americans generally have held onto this rule ever more tenaciously. This cannot be reduced simply to an uncritical acceptance and internalization among African Americans of an externally imposed definition. The one-drop rule, by excluding African Americans from interacting with European Americans as equals, paradoxically and unintentionally resulted in forging and legitimating group identity. This in turn provided the foundation for collective action against the very forces that created this rule. Though originally oppressive, the rule is viewed as an essential mechanism of maintaining a distinct, but equal, African American racial and cultural identity, which continues to mobilize blacks in the struggle against white privilege (Daniel 1992a, 333–41; Jones 1994, 201–10).

Consequently, if it is true that the denial of the legitimate right to identify with the fullness of one's racial background is a constant reminder to multiracial individuals that they do not fit in, or even exist—a situation certainly not supportive of healthy identity development in children—any discussion on this topic must necessarily consider its wide-ranging and long-term consequences. We especially should be concerned about any half-hearted attack on the Eurocentric paradigm (e.g., "interracial" colorism) that merely attenuates the dichotomization of blackness and whiteness, while leaving intact the hierarchical relationship between these two categories of experience that maintains white privilege.

Although embodied in individuals, the new multiracial identity is perhaps best characterized as a cluster of new possibilities in the U.S. collective racial consciousness that seeks to transform traditional racial categories and boundaries by expanding definitions of blackness and whiteness. While the new multiracial identity is a flagship for this alternative consciousness, it should not be viewed as the solution, in and of itself, to racism and racial inequality. It remains to be seen how many individuals will actually live out the promise of the new multiracial identity and help create a more egalitarian racial order in the United States. There is no single multiracial voice but many different voices, including those of reactionaries and radical visionaries. Some individuals will reinscribe racial hierarchies associated with previous multiracial identity projects. Those who display the new multiracial identity, however, resist pressures to conform to the existing racial order, with its inequitable power relations. Many will devote their energies to developing institutions that address the needs and interests of multiracial individuals in the manner of egalitarian pluralism. At the same time, they will seek to build bridges across the racial divide in the manner of egalitarian integration. In the process, these individuals will become part of the larger antiracist struggle for human liberation.

The Brazilian Racial Order: Race, Multiraciality, and the Binary Racial Project

The trajectory of Brazilian race relations has moved closer to a binary racial project that places greater emphasis on the *negro/branco* (or black/white) dichotomy, if not strictly enforcing the one-drop rule. In addition, the public and political debate has converged on race, not class and culture, as a determinant of social stratification—a focus more typical of the United States. This "Anglo-Americanization" of Brazilian race relations has been accompanied by recommendations for implementing affirmative action and other initiatives similar to those aimed at monitoring and eradicating patterns of racial discrimination in the United States.

One recent case study reflecting this shift is the current debate surrounding affirmative action in public university admissions. In the wake of the U.N. World Conference on Racism, held in Durban, South Africa (August–September 2001), state officials openly acknowledged that the primary source of persistent inequality in Brazil is racial discrimination. Indeed, inequality between African Brazilians and whites has actually increased, despite overall social and economic gains during the past few decades. The educational gap between whites and African Brazilians has remained unchanged during the last decade, although general access to education has improved. These statistics helped bolster support for specific government policies targeting African Brazilians, including explicit quotas in universities (Galdino and Pereira 2003, 157–72; Guimarães 2003, 75–82; Queiroz 2003, 137–56; Toni 2004).

Affirmative Action Under Construction

Following the Durban Conference, Rio de Janeiro State University (UERJ) and the Northern Fluminense State University (UENF), two of Brazil's largest and most prestigious centers of higher learning, became the first public institutions to comply with October 2, 2001, legislation in the state of Rio de Janiero requiring universities to observe a 40 percent quota for African Brazilians in its 2003 entering class.[22] This figure corresponded to the fact that approximately 45 percent

---

22. The State University of Bahia instituted similar measures, followed in 2003 by the Federal University of Brasília, the Federal University of Alagoas, and the State University of Mato Grosso do

of Brazil's 175 million people consider themselves African Brazilian (black and mulatto). In addition, the legislation mandated a 50 percent quota for graduates from public secondary schools (as well as 10 percent for students with physical disabilities or special needs). The average Brazilian attends the public secondary schools. They are overcrowded, underfunded, and significantly inferior to the private schools, where middle class, wealthy (and overwhelmingly white) Brazilians send their children. Brazil's government-operated universities are among the most prestigious in Latin America and are the training ground for the corporate and political elite. They are also the bastion of the white and affluent: less than one student in five is African Brazilian (Dias 2004; Jeter 2003; Margolis 2003; Martins, Medeiros, and Nascimento 2004, 806–11; "Race in Brazil, Out of Eden" 2003; Rochetti 2004; Villardi 2004, 3).

College admission is highly competitive, with many more applicants than places available, especially for the prominent public universities. Consequently, the notorious *vestibular,* or college entrance exam, has become the arbiter for admission. According to some, this exam is a "democratic victory" that represents a noteworthy exception to the pervasive habit of gaining entry into the elite through one's social connections. Yet critics consider the *vestibular* to be a "game played with marked cards" ("Race in Brazil, Out of Eden" 2003). Students who attend private schools have an unfair advantage because they are better prepared to score well. In order to level the playing field, the Rio-based group Educafro and other similar grassroots organizations throughout Brazil, has sponsored pre-*vestibular* tutorials for poor and African Brazilian students (Margolis 2003; Martins, Medeiros, and Nascimento 2004, 806–11; "Race in Brazil, Out of Eden" 2003; Telles 2004, 159).

Of the 1.4 million students admitted to universities each year, only 3 percent have typically identified as African Brazilian and only 18 percent have come from public schools, where most African Brazilians are enrolled (Jeter 2003; Rohter 2003). The implementation of affirmative action has effectively doubled (and in some cases tripled) the enrollment of black and multiracial students in elite professional schools such as law, engineering, and medicine at UERJ (Jeter 2003). Although these policies have stimulated a national debate about racial inequality and encouraged more working-class students to apply, it has had ambiguous results and is proving to be an awkward solution to a complex problem.

One caveat is that affluent African Brazilians and graduates of the few elite state high schools have been the primary beneficiaries of affirmative action. For example, only 243 (or 5 percent) of Rio de Janeiro State University's entering

---

Sul, which already had a quota for indigenous individuals (Martins, Medeiros, and Nascimento 2003, 806–11).

class of 4,970 black and multiracial students were admitted solely to meet racial quotas. The majority of African Brazilians had the test scores to be admitted anyway (Astor 2004). These individuals were able to pay for private high schools. In fact, one-third of the African Brazilians admitted had household incomes of about 2,000 *reais* (or roughly US$800) a month—at least ten times the minimum wage ("Race in Brazil, Out of Eden" 2003). In order to rectify this problem and address the concerns of poor African Brazilians, state legislators are recommending that students who benefit from racial quotas also be required to prove their families earn no more than 300 *reais* a month—about US$100 (Astor 2004; Villardi 2004, 3).

The Ministry of Education, together with the Special Secretariat for the Promotion of Racial Equality, has been preparing guidelines on affirmative action for all public universities. Although the prospects for affirmative action in higher education appear promising, African Brazilian leaders acknowledge that other obstacles remain. Helping African Brazilians complete their educations is the next challenge. Many students admitted to universities through quotas soon withdraw because they live far away from campus and must rely on precarious public transportation systems. Those who work are often too exhausted to maintain their studies. In addition, many cannot afford the costs of travel, books, computers, and other expenses, although tuition is free (Martins, Medeiros, and Nascimento 2004, 806–11). Several Brazilian grantees of the Ford Foundation are working with universities and higher education officials to establish scholarships and special courses to ease the transition for these students. State legislators also addressed this problem by approving a modest monthly stipend of approximately US$65 for economically disadvantaged students admitted to UERJ through the quota system (Tobar 2003).

In addition, some critics have expressed concerns about the noticeable change in student test scores since the implementation of affirmative action. The average score for individuals admitted into UERJ law school in 2002 was nearly 81 percent. According to university admissions officials, the average score was 64 percent under the quota system, which many interpret as a lowering of academic standards. Supporters of affirmative action counter that racial quotas are not the problem. Rather, the focus should be on improving the schools at every level and increasing employment opportunities (Jeter 2003).

The affirmative action debate has also focused on the percentage that should be designated for African Brazilians. The quotas at UERJ were themselves controversial in that some critics argued that the 40 percent for African Brazilian students overlapped with the 50 percent for students from public secondary schools where African Brazilians are the majority. Many argue that the ceiling should be set at 20 percent, at least for the moment. Others contend that quotas should vary from state to state and be based on the percentage of the population that is black or multiracial (Rohter 2003).

By 2003, Brazil's nascent affirmative action programs, much like those in the United States, had provoked a backlash from white students who worked hard and prepared themselves for college admissions, only to be rejected despite scoring higher on the entrance examination (Astor 2004; Jeter 2003; Margolis 2003). As in the United States, they have challenged affirmative action in the courts. Brazil's racial quotas have brought a flurry of lawsuits from some three hundred white students who won injunctions (Martins, Medeiros, and Nascimento 2004, 806–11; Telles 2004, 74), claiming they were being discriminated against and denied "equality of access to schooling guaranteed by Brazil's 1988 Constitution" (Rohter 2003). The controversy surrounding the quotas culminated in a constitutional challenge that reached Brazil's federal Supreme Court ("Brazil: Affirmative Action in Higher Education" 2003–2004, 3).[23]

Civil rights advocates predict that the debate is likely to intensify and become more acrimonious if the sweeping Racial Equality Statute now before Congress is passed. This legislation, which is being met with resistance in the Senate (Osava 2005), recommends a 20 percent quota for African Brazilians in government jobs and public universities, enterprises with more than twenty employees, and actors in television programming, including soap operas and commercials. In addition, 30 percent of political party candidates must be African Brazilians (Margolis 2003; "Race in Brazil, Out of Eden" 2003). Critics argue, however, that affirmative action is a solution imported from the United States—where racial definitions and relations are quite different—and therefore will exacerbate rather than ameliorate the situation in Brazil. Other opponents argue that conditions for African Brazilians will improve as poverty is gradually eliminated. Supporters respond that racial quotas are a legitimate means of expanding educational and other opportunities for African Brazilians, despite the imperfections (Dias 2004; Jeter 2003; Rochetti 2004; Rohter 2003; Vongs et al. 2003).

Many observers believed the Brazilian Supreme Court, which began deliberating the constitutionality of racial quotas and a dispute by preparatory schools that the university quotas favor public schools, would determine the ultimate outcome of these developments. Supporters of affirmative action viewed President Lula's recent appointment of Joaquim Barbosa Gomes, the first African Brazilian to sit on the highest court, as portending a strong ruling in their favor. Yet considering its reputation for caution and middle-of-the-road approaches, the high court was expected to give a moderate endorsement to preferences

---

23. However, some of these white students would still not have gained admission if the quota system were not in place (Martins, Medeiros, and Nascimento 2003, 806–11).

(Margolis 2003; Martins, Medeiros, and Nascimento 2004, 806–11). Notably, some critics of racial quotas have evoked the U.S. Supreme Court's rulings in *Bakke* and the University of Michigan cases, which permitted race to be considered as one factor in the admissions process but prohibited explicit quotas and point systems (Vongs et al. 2003). Indeed, affirmative action has been the most contested aspect of racial (and gender) politics because it has frequently been interpreted to mean quotas rather than target goals (Reichmann 1999, 21). In Brazil, this interpretation can be attributed in part to the U.S. and global media, as well as public perceptions that often erroneously frame U.S. affirmative action policies as quotas.

That said, the history of the U.S. Supreme Court's affirmative rulings could provide Brazilians with a template for their own programs. Seeking to take advantage of U.S. expertise in affirmative action, the Ford Foundation in August 2003 arranged for a group of U.S. attorneys to visit Brazil. These lawyers, who were associated with the International Human Rights Law Group (IHRLG) and also involved in the Michigan cases, joined with a number of African Brazilian leaders to form an affirmative action affinity group. This group was charged with forging a partnership between Brazil and the United States in order to generate political and media support for affirmative action in university admissions. To further these goals, the committee met with the dean of UERJ, African Brazilian attorneys, the recently created Special Secretariat for the Promotion of Racial Equality, officials in the Ministry of Education, and others. The IHRLG delegation was hosted by the Institute of Racial and Environmental Action (IARA), which is composed of the attorneys that argued the affirmative action case before Brazil's Federal Supreme Court. The visit by U.S. attorneys not only advanced substantially the cause of Brazilian antidiscrimination groups but also resulted in the formation of the Affirmative Action Expert Group, which is an international network of attorneys seeking to combat discrimination throughout Latin America (Toni 2004).

The possibility of a Supreme Court decision in the State University of Rio de Janeiro cases that would set a strong precedent supporting affirmative action was circumvented, however, by the university itself. It proposed a new law to the Rio de Janeiro State Assembly that was approved in August 2003, in time to be implemented for the 2004 entrance exam. This statute halved the university's quotas to 20 percent for African Brazilians, 20 percent for public-school students, and 5 percent for students with physical disabilities as well as students of indigenous background. These changes in state law at least rendered the initial challenges null and void, although the reduced quotas have also been challenged in the state court ("Brazil: Affirmative Action in Higher Education" 2003–2004, 3; Margolis 2003; Martins, Medeiros, and Nascimento 2004, 806–11; Telles 2004, 74–75; Toni 2004; Villardi 2004, 3).

Nevertheless, educators remain undaunted in their support of affirmative action. The Federal University of Brasília has adopted a 20 percent quota for African Brazilians (Davies 2003; "Race in Brazil, Out of Eden" 2003; Margolis 2003; Martins, Medeiros, and Nascimento 2004, 806–11; Toni 2004; Villardi 2004, 3). The State University of Minas Gerais and Federal University of Bahia (UFBA) have also supported racial quotas. The University Council at UFBA, which is composed of administration, faculty, and students, voted to reserve 45 percent of the openings in various fields of study for students from Bahia's public schools, which are attended by the majority of the state's overwhelmingly African Brazilian population. Though whites make up only 20 percent of Bahia's population, they compose more than 65 percent of the students in UFBA's medical program, almost 60 percent of the dental program, and more than 70 percent of the industrial chemistry program. In the academic year ending in 2000, nearly 86 percent of the dentistry degrees were awarded to whites, and less than 1 percent to African Brazilians. According to the UFBA plan, 36 percent of slots would be reserved for African Brazilians, 2 percent for Native Americans, and the remaining 7 percent for other nonblacks who attend public schools (Kane 2004).

Various African Brazilian activist groups, including the Unified Black Movement (MNU), the Domestic Workers Union, the Steve Biko Cultural Institute, and Union of Blacks for Equality (União de Negros pela Igualdade, UNEGRO), have supported the UFBA plan. Yet many have noted that even with affirmative action in university admissions, private schools, which are largely attended by whites, are still better equipped to prepare their students for the college entrance exam than the overwhelmingly African Brazilian public schools. Consequently, the Steve Biko Cultural Institute has organized a postsecondary program that seeks to prepare African Brazilians to pass the university's entrance examination. Its volunteer teachers instruct students in math, chemistry, and physics, which are lacking in their public high schools. This is largely attributable to the lack of teachers for these subjects. Moreover, public school teachers are significantly underpaid ("Brazil's Unfinished Battle" 2000; Kane 2004; Margolis 2003).

Although affirmative action is not yet normative as social policy, support for these practices has grown considerably since Brazil's former president Cardoso introduced goals for the development and implementation of such policies. Indeed, African Brazilian leaders now consider affirmative action an indispensable corrective to racial discrimination. Three federal ministries recently introduced quotas of 20 percent for African Brazilians in senior jobs. A few cities in the state of São Paulo have introduced racial quotas in the past several years. The city of São Paulo has recommended holding 30 percent of city jobs for *pretos* and *pardos* (Margolis 2003; Martins, Medeiros, and Nascimento 2004, 806–11).

As the idea of affirmative action has spread, some sympathetic whites have grown uneasy. Accordingly, some propose a broader affirmative action program, including scholarships and subsidized pre-*vestibular* courses for African Brazilians and poor whites (Jeter 2003; "Race in Brazil, Out of Eden" 2003). What is transpiring in Brazil, however, is not simply a dialogue about the merits of affirmative action. Rather, the current debate is reflective of a broader discourse on inequality, race, and what social debt, if any, the nation owes to African Brazilians. More important, it is indicative of a rearticulation of African Brazilian collective identity (as well as Brazilian national identity) grounded in a positive valuation of blackness (Bernardino 2002, 262–70; Jeter 2003). Indeed, the ideology of whitening and the aesthetic bias attached to European physical appearance, although challenged and somewhat attenuated by the black movement, continues to permeate Brazilian mass culture and holds sway over the public imagination in determining an individual's perceived worth (Telles 2004, 76–77).

That said, Brazil is reexamining its image as a racial democracy. For many Brazilians, the nation's history of racial and cultural blending, which has sustained the racial democracy ideology, continues to be held in high esteem. Moreover, it serves as a point of contrast with the racial history of the United States and South Africa. Nevertheless, the debate over affirmative action has forced the nation to acknowledge the existence of racism, discrimination, and social exclusion. Indeed, many supporters of affirmative action believe that Brazil is a living refutation of any notion that increased racial intermarriage and multiracial offspring decreases or eliminates racism (Jeter 2003; Telles 2004, 76–77). If the Brazilian experience could be a harbinger of challenges for the United States as its multiracial population increases, similarly the U.S. experience could signal challenges for Brazil (Vongs et al. 2003). In some ways, legal challenges to the State University of Rio de Janeiro's race-conscious admissions policy raise the same fundamental questions as those in the University of Michigan cases. But the debate in Brazil is also markedly different from that in the United States. The question of who is African American has long been settled in the United States (although U.S. definitions of racial categories are now also being challenged). By contrast, Brazilians are now being forced to grapple formally with defining who is African Brazilian (Jeter 2003; Rohter 2003).

For example, the State University of Rio de Janeiro targeted all applicants declaring themselves to be "of African descent" (*Afrodescendentes*) on admission forms (Cristaldo 2003; Rohter 2003). Yet the potential for abuse in this area is very real, considering that large numbers, if not the majority, of white Brazilians have varying degrees of African ancestry. Technically speaking, the term "African Brazilian" can include anyone who identifies as such. Indeed, some candidates who were typically white-designated and white-identified stated they were African

Brazilians on the admissions form, which significantly increased their chances of admission (Astor 2004; Cristaldo 2003; Jeter 2003; Martins, Medeiros, and Nascimento 2004, 806–11; Rochetti 2004).[24] Some recommend that the solution in doubtful cases would be to establish a commission to verify students' racial identities, putting an end to any idea that race is strictly a matter of self-identification ("Race in Brazil, Out of Eden" 2003). Whatever the case may be, the question of formulating precise definitions of racial categories, which is pivotal to affirmative action, has been perplexing for Brazilian policymakers. Such a question challenges Brazilian racial thinking, considering that the overwhelming majority of Brazil's population of 175 million has some African ancestry—whether or not they acknowledge or identify with it (Jeter 2003; Margolis 2003).

A "New" African Brazilian Identity

The black movement has sought to forge a "new" African Brazilian identity that overcomes the secondary color divide between *pardos* and *pretos* associated with Brazil's colonial past. The goal has been to integrate them into a racial group as *negros* by reinforcing the primary racial divide between *negros* and *brancos*. Accordingly, this new identity rearticulates the dichotomization of blackness and whiteness as distinct categories of experience in order to dismantle the hierarchical relationship of whiteness over blackness.

As long as public policy deems it necessary to collect racial data—particularly as a means of tracking Brazil's progress in achieving social equity—combining *pretos* and *pardos* into a single statistical category such as *negro* will provide a more accurate picture of continuing patterns of racial discrimination. Whether for the purposes of public presentation and certain statistical work, or in actual tabulations, this would alleviate the social oppression imbedded in traditional methods of data collection, which have supported the ternary racial project and the mulatto escape hatch. Ultimately, an African Brazilian identifier, however formatted, is a logical step in the pursuit of genuine racial democracy, with the potential to change social attitudes. This identifier could initiate a long overdue and "honest" national conversation about the African ancestry shared by the majority of Brazilians, which has been obscured by the whitening ideal. This ideal is the very means by which racist ideology and racial privilege have been perpetuated in Brazil (Conceição 2004; Vianna 2004).

24. Apparently about 14 percent of the students who listed themselves as black or multiracial before the introduction of affirmative action quotas changed their racial designation to white so as not to qualify under the new guidelines. This was supposedly due to concerns about possible charges of reverse discrimination, along with the potential stigma attached to being admitted to college based on quotas rather than based on merit alone (Astor 2004).

Yet any definition of *negro* that relies on ancestry poses series logistical problems in Brazil (Reichmann 1999, 11–13). African ancestry (not to mention African phenotypical traits) is widespread throughout the entire population, including among large numbers of self-identified and socially designated whites. Indeed, the question remains whether the term *negro* can include individuals who typically would be considered "phenotypically white" in Brazilian terms but who identify as African Brazilian. It also remains to be seen whether individuals who previously self-identified and were designated as mulattoes or whites are fully welcomed as newly self-identified or "assumed blacks" (*negros assumidos*). Although self-definition is supposedly used to determine racial identification, some tension has arisen over who is "authentically" *negro* or African Brazilian.[25]

However, opposition to the perpetuation of a multiracial identity, or rather, opposition to acknowledging the potentially legitimate differences between the experience, and therefore, identities of black and multiracial individuals, is premised on the erroneous belief that these differences are automatically and inherently invidious distinctions. Consequently, a multiracial identity is viewed as being not only antithetical but inimical to the goal of forging African Brazilians into a cohesive political force. By focusing primarily on eradicating a multiracial identification, or absorbing it into a singular egalitarian African Brazilian identity, activists have overlooked, or outright rejected, the possibility of a multiracial identity formulated on egalitarian or antiracist premises (Conceição 2004; Daniel 2002, 72–179; Vianna 2004). This precludes the exploration of new possibilities for critiquing the pathologies of racism, which originated in the Eurocentric master racial project and have sustained Brazil's ternary racial project as much as the binary racial project of the United States.

Part of the struggle for a radical black subjectivity should include finding ways of constructing self and identity that oppose reifying "the blackness that whiteness created" (Anderson 1995, 13). This struggle must be rooted in a decolonization process that challenges the perpetuation of racial essentialism and the reinscription of notions of authentic identity. In addition, it requires the recognition of the multiple experiences of African-descent identity rooted in the lived conditions that make diverse identities and cultural productions possible (hooks 1995, 23–31). A "new" multiracial identity, rather than imploding African Brazilian identity, could potentially forge a more inclusive blackness and whiteness. This in turn would provide the basis for forms of bonding and integration that would

---

25. For example, journalist Nilza Iraci identifies as African Brazilian (*negro*) but could easily be seen as white. In a conference on racism in the early 1990s she heard an activist comment, "I didn't know our organization is already accepting whites." When defending the rights of African Brazilian women in another meeting. Ms. Iraci was questioned by a white colleague, who stated, "But why are you saying all these things when you aren't even black?" (Neves 2002).

accommodate the varieties of African Brazilian subjectivity without negating a larger African Brazilian group, or recreating that group as the complete antithesis of whiteness (Conceição 2004; Daniel 2002, 172–79; hooks 1995, 23–31; Vianna 2004).

Notwithstanding the fact that the new African Brazilian identity at times seems to perpetuate the racial essentialism and some of the attendant pathologies that underpin the one-drop rule, it nevertheless rearticulates a black identity typified by the U.S. binary project without the hierarchical valuation that was historically attached to African and European racial/cultural differences. This new identity challenges the mulatto escape hatch by promoting solidarity among all Brazilians of African descent. It remains to be seen whether activists will eventually question their racial essentialism and reconsider a new multiracial identity formulated on egalitarian premises.

From "Either/Or" to "Both/Neither": The Law of the Included Middle

Part of the struggle for achieving fully participatory racial democracies involves deconstructing the very racial categories and identities inherited from colonialism that have served as the basis of racism and racial hierarchy in Brazil and the United States (Spickard, Fong, and Ewalt 1995, 581–84). Yet any comparison that does not take into consideration the differences between the historical, as well as contemporary sociological contexts of the two countries risks providing an analysis that is inconclusive at best and distorted at worse. Just as the new African Brazilian identity cannot be equated with the articulation of black identity in the United States, the new multiracial identity in the United States cannot be equated with multiracial identity in Brazil. Multiracial identity in Brazil originated in a colonial system of exclusion that sought to control the threat of nonwhites to white dominance by allowing multiracial individuals to avoid the full brunt of discriminatory policies. Consequently, multiraciality became a means by which individuals distanced themselves from the stigma of non-whiteness, even if this identity has not conferred upon them white racial privilege.

In contrast, the new multiracial identity in the United States is not a means by which individuals seek to avoid racial stigma or gain racial privilege. As a racial project, the new multiracial identity in the United States rearticulates the ternary racial project typified by Brazil but without the hierarchical valuation of blackness and whiteness that historically gave rise to that identity. Rather, it is indicative of an egalitarian dynamic that challenges racial hierarchy and the whole notion of racial privilege. This new identity is part of a fundamental shift that is also seeking to dismantle the dominant "either/or" mode of racial thinking inherited by both nations from their colonial and Eurocentric pasts. Instead, it seeks to affirm a more inclusive racial identity premised on the "Law of the Included Middle," which incorporates concepts of "partly," "mostly," or "both/neither," and acknowledges shades of gray.

Yet the new African Brazilian and multiracial identities are not inherently immune to larger social forces. Thus the inegalitarian pluralism typified by the U.S. one-drop rule could be rearticulated in Brazil and the inegalitarian integration typified by the Brazilian mulatto escape hatch could be rearticulated in the United States. Accordingly, multiracial individuals would be impelled to renounce their European backgrounds for the sake of African Brazilian unity in the struggle against white privilege in Brazil, and to surrender the African aspect of their identity in the United States in order to achieve the first-class citizenship of whites. If Brazil and the United States are to create genuinely "new" racial orders out of these "new" racial projects, then both nations would do well to learn from each other's colonial pasts as their paths converge in the twenty-first century.

Discussion on this topic, however, should not center on multiracial identity as being inherently problematic. Being multiracial in a hierarchical system, whether pluralist or integrationist or both, can mean being a little less black, and thus a little less subordinate but does not assure equality with whites. Indeed, even the best-intentioned efforts to eradicate racial inequality will be continually thwarted as long as whites in Brazil and the United States refuse to confront and eradicate notions of white privilege, however subtle this phenomenon may be. The critical challenge is to dismantle completely the Eurocentric underpinnings of the racial order in both nations by deconstructing the dichotomous and hierarchical relationship between blackness and whiteness. Such a development would hold promise for moving race relations in both countries toward a new multiracial synthesis. In such a model, African and European heritage—likened to that liminal dimension between day and night—would become relative and complementary rather than absolute and antithetical. Black and white identities would be extremes on a continuum of blended grays that absorbs all colors, as does black, while at the same time reflecting them all, as does white, with no one color or heritage being superior or inferior to another. As multiracial-identified individuals climb over the walls, cross the borders, erase and redraw the boundaries that separate them, everyone will be reminded that they actually live most of their lives in the liminal gray space between the extremes of black and white, whether or not they are conscious of that fact.

The goal should be to affirm the equality of differences in the manner of egalitarian pluralism, while at the same time nurturing new kinds of inclusion based on equality in the manner of egalitarian integration. This in turn would not only acknowledge the complementary and simultaneous nature of pluralistic and integrative dynamics but also challenge the inegalitarian modalities of both pluralism and integration, which turn these differences into inequalities. This transformative consciousness would seek to achieve equality of similarity without advocating assimilation, to encourage unity without perpetuating uniformity, and to build new kinds of community without promoting conformity (Higham 1975, 242–46). Yet this integrative pluralism (or "pluralistic integration") is greater than the sum of its parts in that it exists at a deeper level of organization than either pluralism or integration alone (Wilber 1996, 188–90; Ken Wilber, pers. comm., December 2, 1998). Differences become the basis upon which to forge a web of interdependent, yet flexibly integrated, racial and cultural pluralities that not only maintain relatively permanent centers of reference but allow optimal autonomy for their individual constituents (Laszlo 1987, 133–49). These dynamics acknowledge the reality of black-white differentiation but maintain porous boundaries that are easily crossed. Group pluralism functions in tandem with individual pluralism that is integrated under a larger national consciousness and identity (Chesler 1981, 217–43; Higham 1975, 242–46; Merelman 1995, 284–99; Thomas 1996, 195–211). Increased contact would result in a better understanding and appreciation of differences and commonalities and lead to a broader basis for cooperation and collaboration.

By now, the lessons of history should have taught both Brazil and the United States that neither political reform nor appeals to conscience alone can solve issues of racial inequality. Yet a new racial contract, as well as a new national consciousness and identity, based on integrative pluralism, would help coordinate political action and public policy. This in turn would facilitate building other issue-based coalitions, regardless of racial and ethnic group differences, to work toward an inclusive politics that recognizes the complexity of various types of oppression and how each feeds on the others in order to thrive (Hutchins and Kaahumanu 1991, xxii–xxiv). This kind of politics would create a constructive and beneficial relationship between the different groups, one marked by mutual respect, interdependence, a balance of power, and a shared commitment to community and nation (and ultimately to the larger human community).

Yet genuine integrative pluralism is unlikely to be achieved on a large scale until both Brazil and the United States are willing to commit to the "social engineering, constant vigilance, government authority, official attention to racial behavior" and sacrifice necessary to achieve it (Steinhorn and Diggs-Brown 1999, 222–23). It also requires a more honest assessment of the factors that keep individuals of African descent in a disadvantaged position, and those of European descent in an advantaged one, not to mention a more accurate rendering of the historical and cultural forces that put them there in the first place. Moreover, it necessitates an open discussion of how systems of racial oppression not only deprive subordinate groups of basic human amenities but also deprive dominant groups of their own humanity by preventing them from embracing the humanity of racialized "Others" (Thomas 1996, 195–211).

Forging this consciousness will require both Brazil and the United States to disabuse their citizens of the illusions and falsehoods spawned by history. There must be a genuine commitment to undermining hierarchical and dichotomous thinking, particularly in the media and the classroom. The current trend toward multiculturalism in the United States and that proposed by many activists in Brazil, however—which tends to emphasize differences in the manner of group pluralism—are not likely to nurture an integrative pluralism. Multiculturalism without a simultaneous commitment to transculturalism could easily harden into a pernicious isolationism, despite its egalitarian premises and goals (Siss 2003, 86–109). Instead, what is needed are comprehensive and nationally coordinated curricula that explore and validate not only racial and cultural diversity (egalitarian pluralism) but also shared racial and cultural commonalities (egalitarian integration). A comprehensive anti-bias curriculum and a program that teaches skills in conflict mediation must buttress this agenda (Allis, Bonfante, and Booth 1991, 12–17; Derman-Sparks 1989, ix–10, 31–38; Finn 1990; Ravitch 1990; Schlesinger 1991, 1–3, 20–57).

The acceptance of integrative pluralism should in time generate in the minds and hearts of whites greater sensitivity to the experience of people of color, or what sociologist Jon Cruz has called ethnosympathy (Cruz 1999, 3–4, 68). Ultimately whites and people of color would develop a greater level of identification with and appreciation of each other's experiences in the manner of ethnoempathy. This would enable both whites and people of color in Brazil and the United States acknowledge the historical ramifications of these designations (without internalizing respectively any sense of "white guilt" and "victimization"), and take collective responsibility for their future socioeconomic and political implications (Helms 1990a, 1990b; Steele 1990, 48–49, 77–109). Taken to its logical conclusion, this would ensure that wealth, power, privilege, and prestige are more equitably distributed among citizenry in the United States and Brazil in the political, socioeconomic, and educational spheres. Such a transformation in thought and behavior would move the United States closer to its ideal as the land of equal opportunity for all and Brazil to its ideal of a racial democracy.

REFERENCES

Adler, Peter S. 1974. "Beyond Cultural Identity: Reflections on Cultural and Multicultural Man." In *Topics in Cultural Learning*, ed. Richard W. Brislin, 2:23–40. Honolulu: East-West Center.

Adorno, Sérgio. 1999. "Racial Discrimination and Criminal Justice in São Paulo." In *Race Relations in Contemporary Brazil: From Indifference to Equality*, ed. Rebecca Reichmann, 123–38. University Park: Pennsylvania State University Press.

Alden, Dauril. 1963. "The Population of Brazil in the Late Eighteenth Century: A Preliminary Study." *Hispanic American Historical Review* 43 (May): 173–205.

Algeo, John. 2003. "The Origins of Southern American English." In *English in the Southern United States*, ed. Stephen J. Nagle and Sara L. Sanders, 6–16. New York: Cambridge University Press.

Allahar, Anton L. 1993. "When Black First Became Worth Less." *International Journal of Comparative Sociology* 34, no. 1–2:39–55.

Allen, Robert L. 1990. *Black Awakening in Capitalist America: An Analytic History*. Trenton, N.J.: Africa World Press.

Allen, Theodore W. 1994. *The Invention of the White Race: Racial Oppression and Social Control*. Vol. 2. New York: Verso.

Allis, Sam, Jordan Bonfante, and Cathy Booth. 1991. "Whose America? A Growing Emphasis on the Nation's 'Multicultural' Heritage Exalts Racial and Ethnic Pride at the Expense of Social Cohesion." *Time*, July 8, 12–17.

Almaguer, Tomás. 1994. *Racial Fault Lines: The Historical Origins of White Supremacy in California*. Berkeley and Los Angeles: University of California Press.

Almeida, Bira. 1986. *Capoeira, a Brazilian Art Form: History, Philosophy, and Practice*. 2nd edition. Berkeley, Calif.: North Atlantic Books.

Alvin, Marta. 2002. "Mixed Race, Mixed Up Feelings." *Brazzil*, March. http://www.brazzil.com/pages/cvro2.htm/.

American Anthropological Association. 1997. Response to OMB Directive 15: Race and Ethnic Standards for Federal Statistics and Administrative Reporting (September 1997). http://www.aaanet.org/gvt/ombdraft.htm (accessed June 10, 2005).

AMEA. *See* Association of MultiEthnic Americans.

Amin, Samir. 1989. *Eurocentrism*. New York: Monthly Review Press.

Anderson, Benedict. 1983. *Imagined Communities: Reflections on the Origin and Spread of Nationalism.* New York: Verso.

Anderson, Victor. 1995. *Beyond Ontological Blackness: An Essay on African American Religious Criticism.* New York: Continuum.

Andrews, George Reid. 1991. *Blacks and White in São Paulo, Brazil, 1888–1988.* Madison: University of Wisconsin Press.

Anthony, Arthé A. 1995. "Collective Memory and Ethnicity: The Black Creole Community in Los Angeles, 1940s–1990s." Paper presented at the Conference on Ethnicity and Multiethnicity: The Construction and Deconstruction of Identity, Division of Social Sciences and the Institute of Polynesian Studies, Brigham Young University, Laie, Hawaii, May 10–13.

Antonil, João André. [1711] 1967. *Cultura e Opulencia do Brasil por suas Drogas e Minas.* São Paulo: Companhia Editora Nacional.

Antonovsky, Aaron. 1956. "Toward a Refinement of the 'Marginal Man' Concept." *Social Forces* 35 (October): 57–67.

Anzaldúa, Gloria. 1987. *Borderlands: La Frontera—The New Mestiza.* San Francisco: Spinsters/Aunt Lute.

Arce, Carlos, Edward Murguía, and W. Parker Frisbie. 1987. "Phenotype and Life Chances Among Chicanos." *Hispanic Journal of Behavioral Sciences* 9, no. 1:19–33.

Arnold, Marvin C. 1984. "The Effects of Racial Identity on Self-Concept in Interracial Children." Ph.D. diss., Saint Louis University.

Asante, Molefi. 1980. *Afrocentricity: The Theory of Social Change.* Buffalo: Amulefi.

———. 1987. *The Afrocentric Idea.* Philadelphia: Temple University Press.

———. 1992. *Kemet, Afrocentricity, and Knowledge.* Trenton, N.J.: Africa World Press.

Association of MultiEthnic Americans. 1997a. "AMEA's History." http://ameasite.org/history.asp/.

———. 1997b. "Statement of the Third Multiracial Leadership Summit, June 7, 1997, Oakland, California." http://www.ameasite.org/classification/mlss6797.asp/.

Astor, Michael. 2004. "Brazil Tries Quotas to Get Racial Equality." *Los Angeles Times,* February 29, A3.

Azoulay, Kathya Gimbel. 1997. *Black, Jewish and Interracial: It's Not the Color of Your Skin, But the Race of Your Kin.* Durham: Duke University Press.

Bailey, Stanley R. 2002. "The Race Construct and Public Opinion: Understanding Brazilian Beliefs About Racial Inequality and Their Determinants." *American Journal of Sociology* 108, no. 2 (September): 406–39.

Banet-Weiser, Sarah. 1999. *The Most Beautiful Girl in the World: Beauty Pageants and National Identity.* Berkeley and Los Angeles: University of California Press.

Banks, William M. 1996. *Black Intellectuals.* New York: W. W. Norton.

Banner-Haley, Charles T. 1994. *The Fruits of Integration: Black Middle-Class Ideology and Culture, 1960–1990.* Jackson: University Press of Mississippi.

Banton, Michael. 1979. "The Idea of Race and the Concept of Race." In *Race, Education, and Identity,* ed. Gajendra K. Verma and Christopher Bagley, 15–30. New York: St. Martin's Press.

Barbosa, Márcio. 1998. *Frente Negra Brasileira: Depoimentos, Entrevistas e Textos.* São Paulo: Quilombhoje.

Barcelos, Luiz Claudio. 1999. "Struggling in Paradise: Racial Mobilization and the Contemporary Black Movement in Brazil." In *Race Relations in Contemporary Brazil:*

From Indifference to Equality, ed. Rebecca Reichmann, 155–66. University Park: Pennsylvania State University Press.

Beato, Lucila Bandera. 2004. "Inequality and Human Rights of African Descendants in Brazil." *Journal of Black Studies* 34, no. 6 (July): 766–86.

Bell, Caryn Cosé. 1997. *Revolution, Romanticism, and the Afro-Creole Protest Tradition in Louisiana, 1718–1868*. Baton Rouge: Louisiana State University Press.

Bender, Gerald. 1978. *Angola Under the Portuguese*. Berkeley and Los Angeles: University of California Press.

Berlin, Ira. 1974. *Slaves Without Masters: The Free Negro in the Ante-bellum South*. New York: Random House Books.

———. 1998. *Many Thousands Gone: The First Two Centuries of Slavery in North America*. Cambridge: Harvard University Press.

Berman, Morris. 1989. *Coming to Our Senses: Body and Spirit in the Hidden History of the West*. New York: Bantam Books.

Bernal, Martin, 1987. *Black Athena: The Afroasiatic Roots of Classical Civilization*. Vol. 1. New Brunswick: Rutgers University Press.

Bernardino, Joaze. 2002. "Ação Afirmativa e a Rediscussão da Democracia Racial no Brasil." *Estudos Afro-Asiáticos* 24, no. 2:247–73.

Berquó, Elza. 1999. "Sterilization and Race in São Paulo." In *Race Relations in Contemporary Brazil: From Indifference to Equality*, ed. Rebecca Reichmann, 207–15. University Park: Pennsylvania State University Press.

Berry, Brewton. 1963. *Almost White: A Study of Certain Racial Hybrids in the Eastern United States*. New York: Macmillan.

Berzon, Judith. 1978. *Neither White nor Black: The Mulatto Character in American Fiction*. New York: New York University Press.

Bhattacharyya, Gargi, John Gabriel, and Stephen Small. 2002. *Race and Power: Global Racism in the Twenty-First Century*. New York: Routledge.

"Biracial Children of Interracial Divorce." 1994. *Oprah Winfrey Show*, ABC, October 7.

Bloom, Jack M. 1987. *Class, Race, and the Civil Rights Movement*. Bloomington: Indiana University Press.

Blu, Karen I. 1980. *The Lumbee People: The Making of an American Indian People*. New York: Cambridge University Press.

Boadi-Siaw, S. Y. 1982. "Brazilian Returnees of West Africa." In *Global Dimensions of the African Diaspora*, ed. Joseph Harris, 291–308. Washington, D.C.: Howard University Press.

Bobo, Lawrence, James R. Kluegel, and Ryan A. Smith. 1997. "Laissez-Faire Racism: The Crystallization of a 'Kindler, Gentler' Anti-Black Ideology." In *Racial Attitudes in the 1990s: Continuity and Change*, ed. Steven A. Tuch and Jack K. Martin, 15–42. Westport, Conn.: Praeger Publishers.

Bonacich, Edna. 1995. "Inequality in America: The Failure of the American System for People of Color." In *Sources: Notable Selections in Race and Ethnicity*, ed. Adalberto Aguirre Jr. and David V. Baker, 138–43. Guilford, Conn.: The Duskin Publishing Group.

Bond, Selena, and Thomas F. Cash. 1992. "Black Beauty: Skin Color and Body Images Among African-American College Women." *Journal of Applied Psychology* 22, no. 11:874–88.

Bone, Robert. 1965. *The Negro Novel in America*. Revised edition. New Haven: Yale University Press.

Bonilla-Silva, Eduardo. 2001. *White Supremacy and Racism in the Post-Civil Rights Era.* Boulder, Colo.: Lynne Rienner Publishers.

———. 2003. *Racism Without Racists: Color-blind Racism and the Persistence of Racial Inequality in the United States.* New York: Rowman and Littlefield.

———. 2004. "From Biracial to Triracial: The Emergence of a New Racial Stratification in the United States." In *Skin Deep: How Race and Complexion Matter in the "Color-Blind" Era,* ed. Cedric Herring, Verna M. Keith, and Derrick Horton, 224–38. Urbana: University of Illinois Press.

Bontemps, Arna. 1969. "Introduction." In *Cane,* by Jean Toomer, vii–xvi. New York: Perennial Classic, Harper and Row.

Borowich, Fergus M. 1996. *Killing the White Man's Indian: Reinventing Native Americans at the End of the Twentieth Century.* New York: Doubleday.

Boston, Thomas D. 1988. *Race, Class, and Conservatism.* Boston: Unwin Hyman.

Bourdieu, Pierre. 1977. *Outline of a Theory of Practice.* Translated by R. Nice. New York: Cambridge University Press.

Bourdieu, Pierre, and Loïc Wacquant. 1999. "On the Cunning of Imperialist Reason." *Theory, Culture, and Society* 16, no. 1:41–58.

Bowser, Frederick P. 1972. "Colonial Spanish America." In *Neither Slave nor Free: The Freemen of African Descent in the Slave Societies of the New World,* ed. David. W. Cohen and Jack P. Greene, 19–58. Baltimore: Johns Hopkins University Press.

Boxall, Bettina, and Ray F. Herndon. 2000. "Far from Urban Gateways, Racial Lines Blur in Suburbs." *Los Angeles Times,* August 15, A1, A25.

Bradshaw, Carla. 1992. "Beauty and the Beast." In *Racially Mixed People in America,* ed. Maria P.P. Root, 77–90. Thousand Oaks, Calif.: Sage Publications.

"Brazil: Affirmative Action in Higher Education." 2003–2004. Global Rights. http://www .globalrights.org/site/DocServer/LA_Fact_Sheets_AffirmActionBrazil.pdf?docID=3623

"Brazil's Unfinished Battle for Racial Democracy." 2000. *Economist,* April 22, 31.

Breen, T. H. 1987. "The 'Giddy Multitude': Race and Class in Early Virginia." In *From Different Shores: Perspectives on Race and Ethnicity in America,* ed. Ronald Takaki, 109–19. New York: Oxford University Press.

Brooks, Dalton B. 1998a. "Cultural and Historical Information of the Lumbee Tribe." Official Home Page of the Lumbee Tribe. http://www.lumbee.org/.

———. 1998b. "The Lumbee Tribe of North Carolina." Society of Native American Cultures (SNAC) Home Page—Lumbee Tribe. http://www.ncsu.edu/ncsu/stud_orgs/native_american/nctribes_orgs/lumbee.html/.

Brookshaw, David. 1986. *Race and Color in Brazilian Literature.* Metuchen, N.J.: The Scarecrow Press.

———. 1988. *Paradise Betrayed: Brazilian Literature of the Indian.* Amsterdam: Centrum voor Studie en Documentatie van Latijns America.

Brown, Nancy, and Ramona Douglass. 1996. "Making the Invisible Visible: The Growth of Community Network Organizations." In *The Multiracial Experience: Racial Borders as the New Frontier,* ed. Maria P.P. Root, 323–40. Thousand Oaks, Calif.: Sage Publications.

Brown, Philip M. 1990. "Biracial Identity and Social Marginality." *Child Adolescent Social Work* 7, no. 4 (August): 319–37.

Brown, Ursula M. 2000. *The Interracial Experience: Growing Up Black/White Racially Mixed in the United States.* Westport, Conn.: Praeger Publishers.

Buckley, Stephen. 2000. "Brazil's Racial Awakening: Multihued Nation Takes a New Look at Prejudice and Inequalities." *World News*, June 12, A12.

Bueno, Wagner. 1996. "Capoeira." Capoeira of San José. http://www.capoeirasj.com/history/.

Burdick, John. 1992a. "Brazil's Black Consciousness Movement." *North American Congress on Latin America Report on the Americas* 25, no. 4 (February): 23–27.

———. 1992b. "The Myth of Racial Democracy." *North American Congress on Latin America Report on the Americas* 25, no. 4 (February): 40–42.

———. 1998a. *Blessed Anastácia: Women, Race, and Popular Christianity in Brazil*. New York: Routledge.

———. 1998b. "The Lost Constituency of Brazil's Black Movement." *Latin American Perspectives* 25, no. 1 (January): 136–55.

Burma, John H. 1946. "The Measurement of Negro 'Passing.'" *American Journal of Sociology* 52 (July): 18–20.

Burns, E. Bradford. 1970. *Latin America: A Concise Interpretive History*. Englewood Cliffs, N.J.: Prentice-Hall.

———. 1993. *A History of Brazil*. 3rd edition. New York: Columbia University Press.

Butler, Kim. 1998. *Freedoms Given, Freedoms Won: Afro-Brazilians in Post-Abolition São Paulo and Salvador*. New Brunswick: Rutgers University Press.

Byrd, Charles Michael. 1994. "Wedowee: Opportunity Missed!" *Interracial Voice*, September. http://www.webcom.com/intvoice/editor94.html/.

———. 1995. "About Race: The Census' One-Drop Rule." *Interracial Voice*, September/October. http://www.webcom.com/intvoice/editor2.html/. (This article appeared as an Op-Ed piece in the June 14, 1995, issue of *New York Newsday*.)

———. 1996. "Kwesi Mfume: Perpetuating White 'Racial Purity.'" *Interracial Voice*, March/April. http://www.interracial voice.com/editor4html/.

———. 1997a. "Government Officially Nixes Multiracial Category." *Interracial Voice*, October 30. http://www.webcom.com/intvoice/this_in3.html/.

———. 1997b. "Interracial Voice Will Not Oppose or Support." E-mail from Charles Michael Byrd to Multiracial Community, June 18.

———. 1997c. "Leftist Socialism or Multiracial Libertarianism: Our Community's Two Choices?" *Interracial Voice*, November/December. http://www.interracialvoice.com/editorial13.html/.

———. 1997d. "OMB's Preliminary Recommendations and an IV Commentary." *Interracial Voice*, July 12. http://www.interracialvoice.com/omb_iv.html/.

———. 1997e. "The Political Color Continuum." *Interracial Voice*, July/August. http://www.interracialvoice.com/editor12.html/.

———. 1997f. "The Speaker's Apparent Endorsement of a Multiracial Classification." *Interracial Voice*, June 20. http://www.webcom.com/intvoice/this_in3.html/.

———. 1997g. "Update on HR 830, OMB and the Newtmeister." *Interracial Voice*, June 16. http://www.webcom.com/~intvoice/this_in3.html/.

———. 1997h. "Wisconsin Congressman Introduces Multiracial Legislation in House of Representatives." *Interracial Voice*, March 10. http://www.webcom.com/~intvoice/this_in3.html/.

———. 1998a. "Compensation's Secret." *Interracial Voice*, December 26. http://www.webcom.com/~intvoice/editor7.html/.

———. 1998b. "Census 2000 Protest: Check American Indian." *Interracial Voice*, January 7. http://www.webcom.com/~intvoice/protest.html/.

————. 1999. "An Interview with Ward Connerly." *Interracial Voice*, April 24. http://www.webcom.com/intvoice/interv6.html/.

————. 2000a. "From the Editor—The Political Realignment: A *Jihad* Against 'Race'-consciousness." *Interracial Voice*, September/October. http://www.interracialvoice.com/jihad.html/.

————. 2000b. "The Third Wave: Meditations on a New-era Synthesis." *Interracial Voice*, January/February. http://www.interracialvoice.com/editor26.html/.

————. 2003. "Racial Privacy Initiative and Religion's Failure." *Interracial Voice*, September/October. http://www.interracialvoice.com/editor35.html/.

Carneiro, Sueli. 1999. "Black Women's Identity in Brazil." In *Race Relations in Contemporary Brazil: From Indifference to Equality*, ed. Rebecca Reichmann, 217–38. University Park: Pennsylvania State University Press.

Carnoy, Martin. 1994. *Faded Dreams: The Politics and Economics of Race in America*. New York: Cambridge University Press.

Carter, Dan T. 1996. *From George Wallace to Newt Gingrich: Race in the Conservative Counterrevolution, 1963–1994*. Baton Rouge: Louisiana State University Press.

Castro, Nadya Araúj, and António Alfredo Guimarães. 1991. "Racial Inequalities in the Labor Market and the Workplace." In *Race Relations in Contemporary Brazil: From Indifference to Equality*, ed. Rebecca Reichmann, 83–108. University Park: Pennsylvania State University Press.

Census. *See* U.S. Bureau of the Census.

Channing, Carol. 2002. *Just Lucky I Guess: A Memoir of Sorts*. New York: Simon and Schuster.

Chau, Jen. 2004. "The UC Board of Regents Meets Today to Discuss Ward Connerly's Proposal." *Mixed Media Watch*, November 17. http://www.xanga.com/item.aspx?tab=weblogs&user=mixedmediawatch&uid=158805491/.

Cheers, D. Michael. 1978. "Seattle's Interracial Children, A Question of Choice and Pride." *Jet*, September 7, 14–16.

Chemerinsky, Erwin. 2003. "Why California's Racial Privacy Initiative Is Unconstitutional." August 22. http://www.cnn.com/2003/LAW/08/22/findlaw.analysis.chemerinsky.race/.

Cheney-Rice, Steven. 1988. "Kaleidoscope: Annual Conference of MASC (Multiracial Americans of Southern California)." *Spectrum: Newsletter of (MASC) Multiracial Americans of Southern California* (Los Angeles), November-December, 1–7.

Chesler, Mark A. 1981. "Creating and Maintaining Interracial Coalitions." In *The Impacts of Racism on White Americans*, ed. Benjamin P. Bowser and Raymond G. Hunt, 217–43. Thousand Oaks, Calif.: Sage Publications.

Chirot, Daniel. 1994. *How Societies Change*. Thousand Oaks, Calif.: Pine Forge Press.

Clegg, Roger. 2005. "Time Has Not Favored Racial Preferences." *Chronicle of Higher Education*, January 14. http://chronicle.com/weekley/w51/i19/19b01001.htm/.

Cohen, David W., and Jack P. Greene. 1972. "Introduction." In *Neither Slave nor Free: The Freemen of African Descent in the Slave Societies of the New World*, ed. David. W. Cohen and Jack P. Greene, 1–23. Baltimore: Johns Hopkins University Press.

Cohen, Jodi S. 2004. "Minority Programs Eroding on Campus." *Chicago Tribune*, September 29. http://www.chicagotribune.com/news/printedition/chi-0409290190sep29,1,2715710.story/.

Collins, Patricia Hill. 1990. *Black Feminist Thought: Knowledge, Consciousness, and the Politics of Empowerment*. Boston: Unwin Hyman.

———. 1993. "Setting Our Own Agenda." *Black Scholar* 23, no. 3-4:52–55.

Comas-Diaz, Lillian. 1996. "Latinegra: Mental Health Issues of African Latinas." In *The Multiracial Experience: Racial Borders as the New Frontier*, ed. Maria P.P. Root, 167–90. Thousand Oaks, Calif.: Sage Publications.

Conceição, Fernando. 2004. "As Cotas Contra o Apocalipse." *Folha de São Paulo Caderno Mais*, June 27.

Conley, Dalton. 1999. *Being Black, Living in the Red*. Berkeley and Los Angeles: University of California Press.

Connerly, W. 2000. "A Homecoming with Too Much Color." *Interracial Voice*, May/June. http://www.interracialvoice.com/connerly.html/.

———. 2001a. "Let's Rid Ourselves of Those Silly Race Boxes." *Abolitionist Examiner*, August/September. http://www.multiracial.com/abolitionist/word/connerly.html/.

———. 2001b. "The Racial Privacy Initiative." *Interracial Voice*, November/December. http://www.interracialvoice.com/connerly5.html/.

———. 2001c. "Towards a Twenty-First Century Vision of Race: Why We Should Get Rid of the Boxes Altogether." *Interracial Voice*, May/June. http://www.interracialvoice.com/connerly3.html/.

Connolly, Paul. 1997. "Racism and Postmodernism: Towards a Theory of Practice." In *Sociology After Postmodernism*, ed. David Owen, 65–80. Thousand Oaks, Calif.: Sage Publications.

Conrad, Robert. 1972. *The Destruction of Brazilian Slavery, 1850–1888*. Berkeley and Los Angeles: University of California Press.

Conselho Nacional de Estatística (CNE). 1961. *Contribuições para o Estudo da Demografia no Brasil*. Rio de Janeiro: CNE.

Coon, Carlton S. 1965. *The Living Races of Man*. New York: Alfred A. Knopf.

Cornell, Stephen, and Douglas Hartmann. 1998. *Ethnicity and Race: Making Identities in a Changing World*. Thousand Oaks, Calif.: Pine Forge Press.

Cose, Ellis. 1998. "Shaking Up 'Paradise': Brazil's Vocal Black-Identity Movement Creates a New Politics of Race." *Newsweek*, March 9, 42–46.

Costa, Emilia Viotti da. 1985. *The Brazilian Empire: Myths and Histories*. Chicago: University of Chicago Press.

Coutinho, A. 1989. "El fenómeno de Machado de Assis." *Brasil Kultura* 14, no. 63:8–12.

Covin, David. 1996. "The Role of Culture in Brazil's Unified Black Movement, Bahia in 1992." *Journal of Black Studies* 27, no. 1 (September): 39–55.

Cozart, Forrest. 1909. *The Manasseh: A Story of Mixed Marriages*. Atlantic City, N.J.: State Register Publishing Company.

Cristaldo, Janer. 2003. "Spare Me Quotas." *Brazzil*, March. http://www.brazil-brasil.com/p112mar03.htm/.

Crowe, Charles. 1975. "Indians and Blacks in White America." In *Four Centuries of Southern Indians*, ed. Charles M. Hudson, 148–69. Athens: University of Georgia Press.

"Crowning of Country's 1st Black Miss Brazil." 1986. *Jet*, August, 29.

Cruse, Harold. 1987. *Plural But Equal: A Critical Study of Blacks and Minorities in America's Plural Society*. New York: William Morrow.

Cruz, Jon. 1999. *Culture on the Margins: The Black Spiritual and the Rise of American Cultural Interpretation*. Princeton: Princeton University Press.

Cunningham, George E. 1965. "The Italian, A Hindrance to White Solidarity in Louisiana, 1890–1898." *Journal of Negro History* 50, no. 3 (July): 22–36.

Curry, Tom. 2003. "Split Decision on Racial Preferences: Court Backs Weighing Race in College Admissions, with Limits." *MSNBC*, October 23. http://msnbc.msn.com/id/3339980/.

Curtis, Emory. 1998. "Technology Uncovers Jefferson." *Interracial Voice*, November 2. http://www.webcom.com/~intvoice/curtis2.html/.

Dalmage, Heather. 2000. *Tripping on the Color Line: Black-white Multiracial Families in a Racially Divided World.* New Brunswick: Rutgers University Press.

Daniel, G. Reginald. 1989. "Converging Paths: Race Relations in Brazil and the U.S." Paper presented at Winter Colloquium Series, University of California, Los Angeles, Center for African American Studies, March 2.

———. 1991. "The Census and the Numbers Racket." *Interrace*, September/October, 20.

———. 1992a. "Beyond Black and White: The New Multiracial Consciousness." In *Racially Mixed People in America*, ed. Maria P.P. Root, 333–41. Thousand Oaks, Calif.: Sage Publications.

———. 1992b. "Passers and Pluralists: Subverting the Racial Divide." In *Racially Mixed People in America*, ed. Maria P.P. Root, 91–107. Thousand Oaks, Calif.: Sage Publications.

———. 1996. "Black and White Identity in the New Millennium: Unsevering the Ties That Bind." In *The Multiracial Experience: Racial Borders as the New Frontier*, ed. Maria P.P. Root, 121–39. Thousand Oaks, Calif.: Sage Publications.

———. 2000. "Multiracial Identity in Brazil and the United States." In *We Are a People: Narrative and Multiplicity in Constructing Ethnic Identity*, ed. Jeffrey Burroughs and Paul R. Spickard, 153–78. Philadelphia: Temple University Press.

———. 2002. *More Than Black? Multiracial Identity and the New Racial Order.* Philadelphia: Temple University Press.

Darden, Joe T. "African-American Residential Segregation: An Examination of Race and Class in Metropolitan Detroit." In *Residential Apartheid: The American Legacy*, ed. R. Bullard, C. Lee, and J. E. Grigsby, 85–90. Los Angeles: UCLA Center for African-American Studies.

Darnovsky, Marcy, Barbara Epstein, and Richard Flacks. 1995. "Introduction." In *Cultural Politics and Social Movements*, ed. Darnovsky, Epstein, and Flacks, xii–xv. Philadelphia: Temple University Press.

Davies, Rodrigo. 2003. "Brazil Takes Affirmative Action in HE." *Guardian*, August 4. http://education.guardian.co.uk/higher/worldwide/story/0%2C9959%2C1012157%2C00.html/.

Dávila, Jerry. 2003. *Diploma of Whiteness: Race and Social Policy in Brazil, 1917–1945.* Durham: Duke University Press.

Davis, Darien. 1999. *Avoiding the Dark: Race and the Forging of National Culture in Modern Brazil.* Aldershot: Ashgate.

Davis, David Brian. 1967. *The Problem of Slavery in Western Culture.* Ithaca: Cornell University Press.

Davis, F. James. 1991. *Who Is Black? One Nation's Definition.* University Park: Pennsylvania State University Press.

———. 2001. *Who Is Black? One Nation's Definition.* Tenth anniversary edition. University Park: Pennsylvania State University Press.

Day, Caroline Bond. 1932. *A Study of Some Negro-White Families in the United States.* Cambridge: Harvard University Press.

Decaro, Lou. 1992. "Mixed Relations: The Italian African-American Dis-Connection." *Interrace*, May/June, 17–19.

Degler, Carl N. 1971. *Neither Black nor White: Slavery and Race Relations in Brazil and the United States*. Madison: University of Wisconsin Press.

Denton, Nancy A. 1994. "Are African-Americans Still Hypersegregated in 1990?" In *Residential Apartheid: The American Legacy*, ed. R. Bullard, C. Lee, and J. E. Grigsby, 49–81. Los Angeles: UCLA Center for African-American Studies.

Derman-Sparks, Louise. 1989. *Anti-Bias Curriculum: Tools for Empowering Young Children*. Washington, D.C.: National Association of the Education of Young Children.

Devisse, Jean, and Michel Mollat. 1979. "Africans in the Christian Ordinance of the World (Fourteenth to Sixteenth Century)." Translated by William Granger Ryan. In "From the Early Christian Era to the 'Age of Discovery,'" vol. 2, pt. 2, pp. 154–60, of *The Image of the Black in Western Art*, ed. Ladislas Bugner. New York: William Morrow.

Dias, Maria Clara. 2004. "Affirmative Action and Social Justice." *Connecticut Law Review* 36, no. 871 (spring). http://web.lexis-nexis.com/universe/document?_m=1106436f c4604e1c657008681a5d586d&_docnum=3&wchp=dGLbVlb-zSkVb&_md5 =b39fc162a951dfa9830c64ad83e3a115/.

Dillion, Glaucio Ary, and Nelson do Valle Silva. 1987. "Urbanization, Race, and Class in Brazilian Politics." *Latin American Research Review* 22, no. 2:155–76.

Dobbs, Michael. 2003. "At Colleges, an Affirmative Reaction: After Rulings, Recruiters Take More Inclusive Diversity Approach." *Washington Post*, November 14. http:// www. msnbc.com.news/993930.asp?odm=C21DN/.

Domingues, Petrônio. 2004. *Uma História Não Contada: Negro, Racismo, e Branqueamento em São Paulo no Pós-Abolição*. São Paulo: Editora Senac.

Domingues, Regina. 1992. "The Color of a Majority Without Citizenship." *Conexões: African Diaspora Research Project, Michigan State University* 4, no. 2 (November 1992): 6–7.

Domínguez, Virginia R. 1986. *White By Definition: Social Classification in Creole Louisiana*. New Brunswick: Rutgers University Press.

Dorman, James H. 1992. "Louisiana's 'Creoles of Color': Ethnicity, Marginality, and Identity." *Social Science Quarterly* 73, no. 3 (September): 615–26.

———. 1996. "Ethnicity and Identity: Creoles of Color in Twentieth Century South Louisiana." In *Creoles of Color of the Gulf South*, ed. James H. Dorman, 166–79. Knoxville: University of Tennessee Press.

Douglas, Nathan. 1997a. "I Solemnly Swear." *Interracial Voice*, May 22. http://www.inter racialvoice.com/natdoug3.html/.

———. 1997b. "Leaving the Scene of a Crime." *Interracial Voice*, July 12. http://www .interracialvoice.com/natdoug4.html/.

———. 1998a. "The Kinky Hair Machine." Project RACE. January 5. http://www.projec-trace.com/zcommentary/archive/commentary-002.php/.

———. 1998b. "What We're Up Against." *Interracial Voice*, March/April. http://www .interracialvoice.com/natdoug2.html/.

Douglass, Ramona. 1988. "Socio-political Consequences of Racial Classification in the U.S." *Interracial/Intercultural Connection. The Newsletter of the Biracial Family Network* (Chicago), November/December, 1–3.

———. 1997. "Endorsements of the Multiracial Leadership Summit." AMEA (Association of MultiEthnic Americans). July 9. http://www.ameasite.org/classification/mlss6797.asp/.

Douglass, Ramona (AMEA), and Susan Graham (Project RACE). 1995. Letter to Katherine Wallman, Office of Regulatory Affairs, OMB, September 29.

Downing, Karen E. 1992. "1990 Census Statistics 'Other' Category." Multiracial/Multicultural Group of the University of Michigan. October.

Drake, St. Claire. 1987. *Black Folk Here and There.* 2 vols. Los Angeles: UCLA Center for African American Studies.

Drake, St. Clair, and Horace Cayton, 1962. *Black Metropolis: A Study of Negro Life in a Northern City.* Revised edition. Vol. 1. New York: Harper Torchbooks.

D'Souza, Dinesh. 1996a. *The End of Racism: Principles for a Multiracial Society.* New York: Free Press.

———. 1996b. "The One-Drop-of-Blood-Rule." *Forbes Today,* December 2.

———. 2002. *What's So Great About America.* Lanham, Md.: Regnery Publishing.

duCille, Ann. 1996. *The Skin Trade.* Cambridge: Harvard University Press.

Dyer, K. F. 1976. "Patterns of Gene Flow Between Negroes and Whites in the U.S." *Journal of Biosocial Science,* 8, no. 4 (October): 309–33.

Dzidzienyo, Anani. 1979. *The Position of Blacks in Brazilian and Cuban Society.* Minority Group Rights Reports, no. 7. London: Minority Rights Group.

———. 1987. "Brazil." In *International Handbook on Race and Race Relations,* ed. Jay A. Sigler, 23–42. New York: Greenwood Press.

Easlea, Brian. 1980. *Witch-hunting, Magic, and the New Philosophy.* Brighton: Harvester Press.

Edwards, Pat. 1989a. "Open Forum." *Interrace,* March/April, 20.

———. 1989b. IFC (Interracial Family Circle), Washington, D.C. Letter to Edna Paisano, acting chief, Racial Statistics Branch, Population Division, Bureau of the Census, November 27.

———. 1989c. IFC (Interracial Family Circle), Washington, D.C. Letter to MASC (Multiracial Americans of Southern California), November 28.

———. 1989d. IFC (Interracial Family Circle), Washington, D.C. Letter to MASC (Multiracial Americans of Southern California), December 18.

———. 1989e. IFC (Interracial Family Circle), Washington, D.C. Letter to Darlene Y. Willoth, IFC, Atlanta, Ga., December 18.

Ehrenreich, Barbara. 1995. "Planet of the White Guys." *Time,* March 13, 114.

Elbashir, Ahmed E. 1983. *The United States, Slavery, and the Slave Trade in the Nile.* Lanham, Md.: University Press of America.

Ellis, Joseph J. 1998. "When a Saint Becomes a Sinner." *U.S. News and World Report,* November 9, 67–69.

Escóssia, Fernanda da. 1997. "Cores e Nomes: IBGE Etuda Alterações no Questionário Levantamento de 2000." *Folha de São Paulo,* November 2, 3.

Falkerstein-Jordan, Kristina. 1995. "Clinton Needs to Hear From You." *Spectrum: The Newsletter of (MASC) Multiracial Americans of Southern California* (Los Angeles), June, 4.

Feagin, Joe R. 2000. *Racist America: Roots, Current Realities and Future Reparations.* New York: Routledge.

Feagin, Joe R., and Clairece Booher Feagin. 1996. *Racial and Ethnic Relations.* 5th edition. Upper Saddle River, N.J.: Prentice-Hall.

Feagin, Joe R., and Melvin P. Sikes. 1994. *Living with Racism: The Black Middle-class Experience.* Boston: Beacon Press.

Fears, Darryl. 2003. "Race Divides Hispanics, Report Says Integration and Income Vary with Skin Color." *Washington Post*, July 14, A03. http://www.washingtonpost.com/ac2/wp-dyn/A51282- 2003Jul13?language=printer/.

Fears, Darryl, and Claudia Deane. 2001. "Biracial Couples Report Tolerance: Survey Finds Most Are Accepted by Families." *Washington Post*, July 5, A01.

Fernandes, Florestan. 1969. *The Negro in Brazilian Society*. Translated by Jacqueline D. Skiles, A. Brunel, and Arthur Rothwell. Edited by Phyllis B. Eveleth. New York: Columbia University Press.

Fernández, Carlos A. 1995. "Testimony of the Association of Multiethnic Americans Before the Subcommittee on Census, Statistics, and Postal Personnel of the U.S. House of Representatives." In *American Mixed Race: The Culture of Microdiversity*, ed. Naomi Zack, 191–210. New York: Rowman and Littlefield.

Field, Lynda. 1996. "Piecing Together the Puzzle: Self-Concept and Group Identity in Biracial Black/White Youth." In *The Multiracial Experience: Racial Borders as the New Frontier*, ed. Maria P.P. Root, 211–26. Thousand Oaks, Calif.: Sage Publications.

Finkelman, Paul. 1987. "Slavery and the Constitutional Convention: Making a Covenant with Death." In *Beyond Confederation: Origins of the Constitution and American National Identity*, ed. Richard Beeman, Stephen Botein, and Edward C. Carter II, 188–225. Chapel Hill: University of North Carolina Press.

Finn, Chester E., Jr. 1990. "Why Can't Colleges Convey Our Diverse Culture's Unifying Themes?" *Chronicle of Higher Education*, June 13, A40.

"First Americans in the Arts Awards to Be Presented." 1999. *OCB Tracker*, February.

Flacks, Dick. 2004. "The Protests: Peaceful But Potent." *Newsday*, Opinion Section, September 5. http://www.nynewsday.com/news/opinion/nyc-vpfla053955278sep05,0, 7911465.story?coll=nyc-viewpoints-headlines./

Flemming, Erik. 2003. "Southern White Male Democrats, Where Ya At?" *Alternet*, November 19. http://www.alternet.org/story/17221/.

Flory, Thomas. 1977. "Race and Social Control in Independent Brazil." *Latin American Studies* 9, no. 2 (November): 199–224.

Fogel, Robert William. 1989. *Without Consent or Contract: The Rise and Fall of American Slavery*. New York: W. W. Norton.

Foner, Laura. 1970. "The Free People of Color in Louisiana and St. Domingue: A Comparative Portrait of Two Three-Caste Slave Societies." *Journal of Social History* 3, no. 4:406–30.

Foner, Philip S. 1975. *History of Black Americans: From Africa to the Emergence of the Cotton Kingdom*. Vol. 1. Westport, Conn.: Greenwood Press.

Fontaine, Pierre-Michel. 1981. "Transnational Relations and Racial Mobilization: Emerging Black Movements." In *Ethnic Identities in a Transnational World*, ed. John F. Stack, 141–62. Westport, Conn.: Greenwood Press.

Foran, John. 1997a. "A Comparative-Historical Sociology of Third World Social Revolutions: Why a Few Succeed, Why Most Fail." In *Theorizing Revolutions: New Approaches from Across the Disciplines*, ed. John Foran, 227–68. New York: Routledge.

———. 1997b. "Introduction." In *Theorizing Revolutions: New Approaches from Across the Disciplines*, ed. John Foran, 1–10. New York: Routledge.

Forbes, Jack D. 1971. "Black Pioneers: The Spanish-Speaking Afro-Americans of the Southwest." In *Minorities in California History*, ed. George E. Frakes and Curtis B. Solberg, 20–33. New York: Random House.

———. 1988. *Black Africans and Native Americans: Color, Race and Caste in the Evolution of Red-Black Peoples.* Oxford: Blackwell.

———. 1990. "The Manipulation of Race, Caste, and Identity: Classifying Afro-Americans, Native Americans, and Red-Black People." *Journal of Ethnic Studies* 17, no. 4:37–38.

Fosten, Nikitta A. 2003. "Miss America Takes a Stand on Abstinence and Bullying—Erika Harold." *Ebony*, March. http://www.findarticles.com/p/articles/mi_m1077/is_5_58/ai_97874234#continue/.

Foster, Johanna. 2006. "Defining Racism to Achieve Goals: The Multiracial and Black Reparations Movements." In *Mixed Messages: Multiracial Identities in the "Color-Blind" Era*, ed. David Brunsma, 273–309. Boulder, Colo.: Lynne Rienner Publishers.

Fowler, David H. 1963. "Northern Attitudes Towards Interracial Marriage: A Study of Legislation and Public Opinion in the Middle Atlantic States and the States of the Old Northwest." Ph.D. diss., Yale University.

Frank, Thomas. 2004. *What's the Matter with Kansas? How Conservatives Won the Heart of America.* New York: Metropolitan Books.

Frankenberg, Ruth. 1993. *White Women, Race Matters: The Social Construction of Whiteness.* Minneapolis: University of Minnesota Press.

Fredrickson, George. 1981. *White Supremacy: A Comparative Study in American and South African History.* New York: Oxford University Press.

Freeland, Gregory. 1992. "The Changing Black Political Movement in Brazil: The Goulart Period (1961–64) vs. Democratization (1985–1990)." Paper presented at the Seventeenth International Congress on Latin American Studies, Los Angeles, September 24–27.

Frey, William H. 2003. "Charticle." *Milken Institute Review*, 3rd quarter: 8–10.

Freyre, Gilberto. 1963a. *The Mansions and the Shanties.* Translated by Harriet de Onís. New York: Alfred A. Knopf.

———. 1963b. *The Masters and the Slaves.* Translated by Harriet de Onís. New York: Alfred A. Knopf.

———. 1970. *Order and Progress.* Translated and edited by Rod W. Horton. New York: Alfred A. Knopf.

Fuchs, Lawrence H. 1990. *The American Kaleidoscope: Race, Ethnicity and the Civic Culture.* Hanover: University Press of New England.

Funderburg, Lise. 1994. *Black, White, Other: Biracial Americans Speak About Race and Identity.* New York: William Morrow.

Gaines, Kevin K. 1996. *Uplifting the Race: Black Leadership, Politics, and Culture in the Twentieth Century.* Chapel Hill: University of North Carolina Press.

Galdino, Daniela, and Larissa Santos Pereira. 2003. "Acesso à Universidade: Condições de Produção de um Discurso Facioso." In *Levando a Raça a Sério: Ação Afirmativa e Universidade*, ed. Joaze Bernardino and Daniela Galdino, 157–72. Rio de Janeiro: DP&A Editora.

Gann, Lewis H., and Peter Duignan. 1972. *Africa and the World: An Introduction to the History of sub-Saharan Africa from Antiquity to 1840.* San Francisco: Chandler Publishing.

Garvin, Russell. 1967. "The Free Negro in Florida Before the Civil War." *Florida Historical Quarterly* 46, no. 1 (July): 1–17.

Gates, Henry Louis, Jr., and Cornell West. 1996. *The Future of the Race.* New York: Alfred A. Knopf.

Gatewood, Willard B. 1990. *Aristocrats of Color: The Black Elite, 1880–1920.* Bloomington: Indiana University Press.

Gayle, Addison. 1976. *The Way of the New World: The Black Novel in America.* New York: Anchor Press.

Gelman, David, Karen Springen, Karen Brailsford, and Mark Miller. 1988. "Black and White in America." *Newsweek,* March 7, 18–23.

George, Lynell 1992. *No Crystal Stair: African Americans in the City of Angels.* New York: Verso.

———. 1999. "Guessing Game," *Los Angeles Times Magazine,* (February 21): 18–21, 34, 36.

Gerber, Raquel. 1989. *Orí* (Videorecording). New York: Third World Newsreel / Camera News.

Gibb, Tom. 2002. "Brazil's Black-and-White Poll." *BBC News World Edition,* October 6. http://bbc.co.uk/2/hi/Americas/2303059.stm/.

Gingrich, Newt. 1997. Letter from Speaker of the U.S. House of Representatives to Franklin D. Raines, director of the OMB, July 1.

Gingrich, Newt, and Ward Connerly. 1997. "Face the Failure of Racial Preferences." *New York Times,* June 15, sec. 4, p. 5.

Ginsberg, Elaine K. 1996. "The Politics of Passing." In *Passing and the Fictions of Identity,* ed. Elaine Ginsberg, 1–18. Durham: Duke University Press.

Gist, Noel P. 1967. "Cultural Versus Social Marginality: The Anglo-Indian Case." *Phylon* 28, no. 4:361–65.

Glater, Jonathan D. 2006. "Colleges Open Minority Aid to All Comers." *The New York Times,* March 14. http://www.nytimes.com/2006/03/14/education/14minority.html?ex=1143090000&en=c9490162797b5344&ei=5070&emc=etal

Gold, Russell. 2000. "The New Melting Pot: Texans, Americans Are Increasingly Mestizo." *San Antonio Express-News,* October 9, A, 1A.

Goldberg, Milton M. 1941. "A Qualification of the Marginal Man Theory." *American Sociological Review* 6, no. 1:52–58.

Goldoni, Ana Maria. 1999. "Racial Inequality in the Lives of Brazilian Women." In *Race Relations in Contemporary Brazil: From Indifference to Equality,* ed. Rebecca Reichmann, 181–93. University Park: Pennsylvania State University Press.

Goldstein, Thomas. 1980. *The Dawn of Modern Science: From the Arabs to Leonardo da Vinci.* Boston: Houghton Mifflin.

González, Lelia. 1985. "The Unified Black Movement: A New Stage in Black Mobilization." In *Race, Class and Power in Brazil,* ed. Pierre-Michel Fontaine, 120–34. Los Angeles: UCLA Center for African American Studies.

Gossett, Thomas F. 1963. *Race: The History of an Idea in America.* New York: Oxford University Press.

Gould, Virginia Meachum. 1996. "The Free Creoles of Color of the Antebellum Gulf Ports of Mobile and Pensacola: A Struggle for the Common Ground." In *Creoles of Color of the Gulf South,* ed. James H. Dorman, 28–50. Nashville: University of Tennessee Press.

Graham, Lawrence Otis. 1999. *Our Kind of People: Inside America's Black Upper Class.* Philadelphia: HarperCollins.

Graham, Susan. 1996. "The Real World." In *The Multiracial Experience: Racial Borders as the New Frontier,* ed. Maria P.P. Root, 37–48. Thousand Oaks, Calif.: Sage Publications.

———. 1997a. "Advocates to Continue to Fight for Multiracial Classification." Project RACE. July 25. http://www.projectrace.com/hotnews/archive/hotnews-072597.php/.

———. 1997b. "From the Executive Director." Project RACE. October 29. http://www
.projectrace.com/hotnews/archive/hotnews-102997.php/.

———. 1997c. "From the Speaker." Project RACE. July 1. http://www.projectrace.com/
hotnews/archive/hotnews-070197.php/.

———. 1997d. "Newt Confirms." Project RACE. July 15. http://www.projectrace.com/
hotnews/archive/hotnews-061597.php/.

———. 1997e. "Newt Said It." Project RACE. January 7. http://www.projectrace.com/
hotnews/archive/hotnews-010797.php/.

———. 1997f. E-mail to Multiracial Community Leaders and Activists, June 14.

———. 1997g. "The Speaker Says." Project RACE. July 19. http://www.projectrace.com/
hotnews/archive/hotnews-061997.php/.

———. 1998. "The Illegitimate Birth of 'Multiple Race People.'" Project RACE. January 5.
http://www.projectrace.com/.

———. 2003. "May the RPI (Racial Privacy Initiative) RIP (Rest in Peace)." Project RACE.
October 17. http://www.projectrace.com/hotnews/archive/hotnews-101703.php/.

Graham, Susan, and James Landrith. 1999. "Blood Pressure." Project RACE. April 21.
http://www.projectrace.com/hotnews/archive/hotnews-02un99.php/.

Green, Arnold W. 1947. "A Re-examination of the Marginal Man Concept." *Social Forces*
26 (December): 167–71.

Grosz, Gabe. 1989. "From Sea to Shining . . . : A Current Listing of Interracial Organizations and Support Groups Across the Nation." *Interrace*, November/December, 24–29.

Gubar, Susan. 1997. *Racechanges: White Skin, Black Face in American Culture*. New York:
Oxford University Press.

Guimarães, Antonio Sérgio Alfredo. 1999. "Measures to Combat Discrimination and
Racial Inequality in Brazil." In *Race Relations in Contemporary Brazil: From Indif-
ference to Equality*, ed. Rebecca Reichmann, 143–53. University Park: Pennsylvania
State University Press.

———. 2003. "Ações Afirmativas para a População Negra nas Universidades Brasileiras."
In *Ações Afirmativas: Políticas Públicas Contra as Desigualdades Raciais*, ed. Renato
Emerson dos Santos and Fátima Lobato, 75–82. Rio de Janeiro: DP&A Editora.

Haberly, David T. 1972. "Abolitionism in Brazil: Anti-slavery and Anti-slave." *Luso-
Brazilian Review* 9, no. 2:30–46.

———. 1983. *Three Sad Races: Racial Identity and National Consciousness in Brazilian
Literature*. New York: Cambridge University Press.

Hacker, Andrew. 1992. *Two Nations: Black and White, Separate, Hostile, Unequal*. New
York: Charles Scribner's.

Hall, Christine C. Iijima. 1980. "The Ethnic Identity of Racially Mixed People: A Study of
Black-Japanese." Ph.D. diss., University of California, Los Angeles.

———. 1992. "Please Choose One: Ethnic Identity Choices for Biracial Individuals." In
Racially Mixed People in America, ed. Maria P.P. Root, 250–64. Thousand Oaks,
Calif.: Sage Publications.

Hall, Gwendolyn Midlo. 1992a. *Africans in Colonial Louisiana: The Development of Afro-
Creole Culture in the Eighteenth Century*. Baton Rouge: Louisiana State University
Press.

———. 1992b. "The Formation of Afro-Creole Culture." In *Creole New Orleans: Race and
Americanization*, ed. Arnold R. Horsch and Joseph Logsdon, 58–90. Baton Rouge:
Louisiana State University Press.

Hall, Kevin G. 2002. "Brazil Program Will Set Aside Jobs for Blacks: Government Plans to Address Inequities." *Detroit Free Press*, June 21. http://www.freep.com/news/nw/nbrazil11_20011001/.

Hall, Ronald. 1995. "The Color Complex: The Bleaching Syndrome." *Race, Class, and Gender* 2, no. 2 (winter): 99–109.

Haller, John S., Jr. 1971. *Outcasts from Evolution: Scientific Attitudes of Racial Inferiority, 1859–1900.* Urbana: University of Illinois Press.

Hamilton, Charles V., Lynn Huntley, Neville Alexander, Antonio Sergio Alfredo Guimarães, and Wilmot James, eds. 2001. *Beyond Racism: Race and Inequality in Brazil, South Africa, and the United States.* Boulder, Colo.: Lynne Rienner Publishers.

Hanchard, Michael George. 1994. *Orpheus and Power: The Movimento Negro of Rio de Janeiro and São Paulo, Brazil, 1945–1988.* Princeton: Princeton University Press.

———. 1999. *Racial Politics in Contemporary Brazil.* Durham: Duke University Press.

Hanger, Kimberly S. 1997. *Bounded Lives, Bounded Places: Free Black Society in Colonial New Orleans, 1769–1803.* Durham: Duke University Press.

Hapa Issues Forum. 2003. "Vote No on Prop. 54. HIF Joins Coalition to Defeat Racial Privacy Initiative Better Known as the Racial Ignorance Initiative (Prop. 54)." Hapa Issues Forum Website. http://www.hapaissuesforum.org/community/pr_rpi.html/.

Harris, Cheryl. 1995. "Whiteness as Property." In *Critical Race Theory: The Key Writings That Formed the Movement*, ed. Kimberlé Crehshaw, Neil Gotanda, Gary Peller, and Kendall Thomas, 276–91. New York: New Press.

Harris, Marvin. 1964. *Patters of Race in the Americas.* New York: Walker.

Harris, Norman. 1998. "A Philosophical Basis for an Afrocentric Orientation." In *Afrocentric Visions: Studies in Culture and Communication*, ed. Janice D. Hamlet, 15–26. Thousand Oaks, Calif.: Sage Publications.

Hasenbalg, Carlos. 1979. *Discriminação e Desigualdades Raciais no Brasil.* Rio de Janeiro: Graal. Translation of "Race Relations in Post-Abolition Brazil: The Smooth Preservation of Racial Inequalities." Ph.D. diss., University of California, Berkeley, 1978.

———. 1985. "Race and Socioeconomic Inequalities in Brazil." In *Race, Class and Power in Brazil*, ed. Pierre-Michel Fontaine, 25–41. Los Angeles: UCLA Center for African American Studies.

———. 1987. "O Negro nas Vésperas do Centenário." *Estudos Afro-Asiáticos* 13 (March): 79–86.

———. 1999. "Perspectives on Race and Class in Brazil." In *Black Brazil: Culture, Identity, and Social Mobilization*, ed. Larry Crook and Randal Johnson, 61–84. Los Angeles: UCLA Latin American Center.

Hasenbalg, Carlos A., Nelson do Valle Silva, and Luiz Claudio Barcelos. 1989. "Notas Sobre Miscegenação no Brasil." *Estudos Afro-Asiáticos* 16, no. 3:189–97.

Haskins, James. 1975. *The Creoles of Color of New Orleans.* New York: Thomas Y. Crowell.

Hazzard-Gordon, Katrina. 1989. "The Interaction of Sexism and Racism in the Old South: The New Orleans Bals Du Cordon Bleu." *Minority Voices*, 2d series, 6, no. 1 (fall): 14–25.

Hecker, Stinson Morrison. 2005. "EEO Reporting on Race/Ethnicity to Change in 2007." Law at Work. Employment and Labor Law, Employee Benefits Group. December 4. http://www.lawatwork.com/news2005/12/04/eeo_reporting_on_raceethnicity_to_change_in_2007.html

Hellwig, David J. 1990. "Racial Paradise or Run-around? Afro-American Views of Race Relations in Brazil." *American Studies* 31 (fall): 4–59.

———. 1992. "Introduction." In *African-American Reflections on Brazil's Racial Paradise*, ed. Hellwig, 3–13. Philadelphia: Temple University Press.

Helms, Janet E. 1990a. "An Overview of Black Racial Identity Theory." In *Black and White Identity: Theory, Research, and Practice*, ed. Helms, 9–32. Westport, Conn.: Greenwood Press.

———. 1990b. "Toward a White Racial Identity Development." In *Black and White Identity: Theory, Research, and Practice*, ed. Helms, 49–66. Westport, Conn.: Greenwood Press.

Hemming, John. 1987. *Amazon Frontier: The Defeat of the Brazilian Indians*. London: Macmillan.

Henig, Robin Marantz. 2004. "The Genome in Black and White (and Gray)." *New York Times Magazine*, October 10. http://www.nytimes.com/2004/10/10/magazine/10GENETIC.html/.

Higginbotham, A. Leon, Jr. 1978. *In The Matter of Color: Race and the American Legal Process: The Colonial Period*. New York: Oxford University Press.

Higham, John. 1975. *Send These to Me: Jews and Other Immigrants in Urban America*. New York: Atheneum.

Hill, Walter. 1995. "Redistricting in the 1990s: Opportunities and Risks for African Americans." In *From Exclusion to Inclusion: The Long Struggle for African American Political Power*, ed. Ralph C. Gomes and Linda Faye Williams, 164–71. Westport, Conn.: Praeger Publishers.

Hirsch, Arnold. 1992. "Simply a Matter of Black and White: The Transformation of Race and Politics in Twentieth-Century New Orleans." In *Creole New Orleans: Race and Americanization*, ed. Arnold R. Hirsch and Joseph Logsdon, 262–319. Baton Rouge: Louisiana State University Press.

Hodes, Martha. 1997. *White Women, Black Men: Illicit Sex in the Nineteenth-Century South*. New Haven: Yale University Press.

Hoetink, Hartimus. 1967. *Caribbean Race Relations: A Study of Two Variants*. London: Oxford University Press.

———. 1973. *Slavery and Race Relations in the Americas: Comparative Notes on Their Nature and Nexus*. New York: Harper and Row.

Hochschild, Arlie. 2005. "The Chauffeur's Dilemma." *TomDispatch*, June 25. http://www.tomdispatch.com/.

Hochschild, Jennifer L. 1995. *Facing Up to the American Dream: Race, Class, and the Soul of the Nation*. Princeton: Princeton University Press.

Hoogvelt, Ankie M.M. 1978. *The Sociology of Developing Societies*. 2nd edition. London: Macmillan.

hooks, bell. 1995. *Yearning: Race, Gender, and Cultural Politics*. Boston: South End Press.

Htun, Mala. 2004. "From 'Racial Democracy' to Affirmative Action: Changing State Policy on Race in Brazil." *Latin American Research Review* 39, no. 1:60–89.

———. 2005. "Racial Quotas for a Racial Democracy." *NACLA Report on the Americas* 38, no. 4:20–25.

Hughes, Michael, and Bradley R. Hertel. 1990. "The Significance of Color Remains: A Study of Life Chances, Mate Selection, and Ethnic Consciousness Among Black Americans." *Social Forces* 68, no. 4 (1990): 1105–20.

Hunter, Allen. 1995. "Rethinking Revolution in Light of the New Social Movements." In *Cultural Politics and Social Movements,* ed. Marcy Darnovsky, Barbara Epstein, and Richard Flacks, 320–46. Philadelphia: Temple University Press.

Hutchins, Loriane, and Lani Kaahumanu. 1991. "Bicoastal Introduction." In *Bi Any Other Name: Bisexual People Speak Out,* xxii–xxiv. Boston: Alyson Publications.

Hutchinson, George. 1993. "Jean Toomer and American Racial Discourse." *Texas Studies in Literature and Language* 35 (summer): 226–50.

———. 1995. *The Harlem Renaissance in Black and White.* Cambridge: Harvard University Press.

IBGE. *See* Instituto Brasileiro de Geografia e Estadísticas.

Ignatiev, Noel. 1995. *How The Irish Became White.* New York: Routledge.

Instituto Brasileiro de Geografia e Estadísticas (IBGE). 1996. *Anuário Estatístico do Brasil.* Vol. 56. Rio de Janeiro: Fundação IBGE.

———. 2000. *Censo Demográfico 2000. Características Gerais da População. Resultados da Amostra. Tabelas de Resultados.* Rio de Janeiro: Fundação IBGE.

James, Joy. 1997. *Transcending the Talented Tenth: Black Leaders and American Intellectuals.* New York: Routledge.

Jeter, Jon. 2003. "Affirmative Action Debate Forces Brazil to Take Look in the Mirror." *Washington Post,* June 16.

Johnson, Deborah. 1992. "Developmental Pathways: Toward an Ecological Theoretical Formulation of Race Identity in Black-White Biracial Children." In *Racially Mixed People in America,* ed. Maria P.P. Root, 37–49. Thousand Oaks, Calif.: Sage Publications.

Johnson, James H., Jr., and Walter C. Farrell Jr. 1995. "Race Still Matters." *Chronicle of Higher Education,* July 7, A48.

Johnson, Jerah. 1992. "Colonial New Orleans: A Fragment of the Eighteenth-Century French Ethos." In *Creole New Orleans: Race and Americanization,* ed. Arnold R. Horsch and Joseph Logsdon, 12–57. Baton Rouge: Louisiana State University Press.

Johnson, Ollie A., III. 1998. "Racial Representation and Brazilian Politics: Black Members of the National Congress, 1983–1999." *Journal of Interamerican Studies and World Affairs* 40, no. 4 (winter): 97–117.

Johnson, Randal, and Larry Crook, eds. 1999. *Black Brazil: Culture, Identity and Social Mobilization.* Los Angeles: UCLA Latin American Center.

Johnston, Hank, Enrique Laraña, and Joseph R. Gusfield. 1994. "Identities, Grievances, and Social Movements." In *New Social Movements: From Ideology to Identity,* ed. Johnston, Laraña, and Gusfield, 3–35. Philadelphia: Temple University Press.

Jones, Nicholas A. 2005. *We the People of More Than One Race.* U.S. Census Bureau, Census 2000 Brief, CENSR-22. http://www.census.gov/prod/2005pubs/censr%2D22.pdf/.

Jones, Nicholas A., and Amy Symens Smith. 2001. *The Two or More Races Population: 2000.* U.S. Census Bureau, Census 2000 Brief, C2KBR/01-6. http://www.census .gov/prod/2001pubs/c2kbr01-6.pdf/.

Jones, Patrice M. 2001. "Brazil Debates Affirmative Action: Many Lawmakers Push Racial Quotas." *Chicago Tribune,* December 27, sec. 1, p. 9.

Jones, Rhett S. 1994. "The End of Africanity? The Bi-Racial Assault on Blackness." *Western Journal of Black Studies* 18, no. 4:201–10.

Jordan, Winthrop D. 1962. "American Chiaroscuro: The Status and Definition of Mulattoes in British Colonies." *William and Mary Quarterly* 19, no. 2 (April): 183–200.

————. 1968. *White Over Black: American Attitudes Toward the Negro, 1550–1812*. Chapel Hill: University of North Carolina Press.

Kane, Gregory. 2004. "In Bahia, University Council Votes in Favor of Quotas." Blackamericaweb.com. http://blackamericaweb.com/site.aspx/bawnews/diaspora/brazil3/.

Kaplan, Erin Aubry. 2003. "Black Like I Thought I Was." *Alternet*, October 7. http://www.alternet.org/story.html?StoryID=16917/.

Karasch, Mary. 1975. "From Portage to Proprietorship: African Occupations in Rio de Janeiro, 1808–1850." In *Race and Slavery in the Western Hemisphere: Quantitative Studies*, ed. Stanley L. Engerman and Eugene D. Genovese, 369–94. Princeton: Princeton University Press.

————. 1987. *Slave Life in Rio de Janeiro, 1808–1850*. Princeton: Princeton University Press.

Keith, Verna M., and Cedric Herring. 1991. "Skin Tone and Stratification in the Black Community." *American Journal of Sociology* 97, no. 3 (1991): 760–78.

Kelley, Matt. 1999. "Transracial Adoptees: Creating an "Other" Identity." *Mavin: The Mixed Race Experience* 3 (fall): 12–19.

Kellner, Bruce. 1987. "Introduction." In *The Harlem Renaissance: A Historical Dictionary of the Era*, ed. Kellner, xiii–xxvii. New York: Routledge and Kegan Paul.

Kennedy, James H. 1974. "Luiz Gama: Pioneer of Abolition in Brazil." *Journal of Negro History* 59, no. 3 (July): 255–57.

————. 1986. "Political Liberalization, Black Consciousness, and Recent Afro-Brazilian Literature." *Phylon* 47, no. 3: 199–209.

Kennedy, N. Brent. 2002. "The Melungeons: A New Path." *Interracial Voice*, July/August. http://www.interracialvoice.com/kennedy.html/.

Kennedy, N. Brent, and Robyn Vaughan Kennedy. 1997. *The Melungeons: The Resurrection of a Proud People. An Untold Story of Ethnic Cleansing in America*. Second, revised, and corrected edition. Macon: Mercer University Press, 1997.

Kerckhoff, Alan C., and Thomas. C. McCormick. 1995. "Marginal Status and Marginal Personality." *Social Forces* 34, no. 1 (October): 48–55.

Kerman, Cynthia Earl, and Richard Eldridge. 1987. *The Lives of Jean Toomer: A Hunger for Wholeness*. Baton Rouge: Louisiana State University Press.

Kershaw, Terry. 1998. "Afrocentrism and the Afrocentric Method." In *Afrocentric Visions: Studies in Culture and Communication*, ed. Janice D. Hamlet, 27–44. Thousand Oaks, Calif.: Sage Publications.

Khanna, Nikki. 2004. "Mavin, HIF, AMEA Joint Statement." Mavin Foundation, August. http://www.mavin.net/pr100703.html/.

Khimm, Suzy. 2003. "Avalanche Against Prop." 54. *Alternet*, October 17. http://www.alternet.org/story.html?StoryID=16972/.

Kich, George Kitahara. 1996. "In the Margins of Sex and Race: Difference, Marginality, and Flexibility." In *The Multiracial Experience: Racial Borders as the New Frontier*, ed. Maria P.P. Root, 263–76. Thousand Oaks, Calif.: Sage Publications.

Kilson, Marion. 2000. *Claiming Place: Biracial Young Adults of the Post-Civil Rights Era*. Westport, Conn.: Bergin and Garvey.

Klein, Herbert S. 1972. "Nineteenth-Century Brazil." In *Neither Slave nor Free: The Freemen of African Descent in the Slave Societies of the New World*, ed. David. W. Cohen and Jack P. Greene, 309–34. Baltimore: Johns Hopkins University Press.

————. 1986. *African Slavery in Latin America and the Caribbean.* New York: Oxford University Press.

Knight, Franklin W. 1974. *The African Dimension in Latin American Societies.* New York: Macmillan.

Korgen, Kathleen Odell. 1998. *From Black to Biracial: Transforming Racial Identity Among Americans.* Westport, Conn.: Praeger Publishers.

Kotlowski, Dean J. 1998. "Richard Nixon and the Origins of Affirmative Action." *Looksmart,* spring. http://www.findarticles.com/p/articles/mi_m2082/is_n3_v60/ai_20649393/.

Kovel, Joel. 1970. *White Racism: A Psychohistory.* New York: Columbia University Press.

Kreb, Nina Boyd. 2000. *Edgewalkers: Defusing Cultural Boundaries on the New Global Frontier.* Far Hills, N.J.: New Horizon Press.

Kuzenski, John C., Charles S. Bullock III, and Ronald Keith Gaddie. 1995. "Introduction." In *David Duke and the Politics of Race in the South,* ed. Kuzenski, Bullock, and Gaddie, xi–xv. Nashville: Vanderbilt University Press.

Lacayo, Richard. 1989. "Between Two Worlds: The Black Middle Class Has Everything the White Middle Class Has, Except a Feeling That It Really Fits In." *Newsweek,* March 13, 58–68.

Laham, Nicholas. 1998. *The Reagan Presidency and the Politics of Race: In Pursuit of Color-blind Justice and Limited Government.* Westport, Conn.: Praeger Publishers.

Landers, Jane. 1999. *Black Society in Spanish Florida.* Urbana: University of Illinois Press.

Landrith, James. 1995–2001. "Hall of Shame." *The Multiracial Activist.* http://multiracial .com/content/category/1/17/2/.

————. 2000. "Free Will (or The Right Not to Decide)." *Abolitionist Examiner,* October/ November. http://www.multiracial.com/abolitionist/word/landrith.html/.

————. 2001a. "Drama Overload." *Interracial Voice,* May/June. http://www.interracialvoice .com/landrith5.html/.

————. 2001b. "Statement on the Racial Privacy Initiative." *Abolitionist Examiner,* October/ November. http://www.multiracial.com/abolitionist/word/landrith3.html/.

————. 2004. "Stand Up and Sound Off, Joint Letter to University of California Board of Regents." *Multiracial Activist,* November 16. http://www.multiracial.com/letters/ 2004-11-16.html/.

Landry, Bart. 1987. *The New Black Middle Class.* Berkeley and Los Angeles: University of California Press.

Landry, Donna, and Gerald Maclean, ed. 1995. *The Spivak Reader: Selected Works of Gayatri Chakravorty Spivak.* New York: Routledge.

Lane, Charles. 2003. "U-Michigan Gets Broad Support on Using Race." *Washington Post,* February 11, A01.

Laszlo, Ervin. 1987. *Evolution: The Grand Synthesis.* Boston: Shambhala, New Science Library.

Lay, Kenneth James. 1993. "Sexual Racism: A Legacy of Slavery." *National Black Law Journal* 13, no. 1–2 (spring): 165–83.

Lee, Jennifer, and Frank D. Bean. 2004. "America's Changing Color Lines: Immigration, Race/Ethnicity, and Multiracial Identification." *Annual Review of Sociology* 30:221–41.

Lee, Sharon M. 1993. "Racial Classification in the U.S. Census: 1890–1990." *Ethnic and Racial Studies* 16, no. 1:75–94.

Lefkowitz, Mary. 1996. *Not Out of Africa: How Afrocentrism Became an Excuse to Teach Myth as History.* New York: Basic Books.

Lemert, Charles. 1996. *Sociology After the Crisis.* Boulder, Colo.: Westview Press.

Lemke, Sieglinde. 1998. *Primitivist Modernism: Black Culture and the Origins of Transatlantic Modernism.* New York: Oxford University Press.

Lempel, Leonard Richard. 1979. "The Mulatto in United States Race Relations: Changing Status and Attitudes." Ph.D. diss., Syracuse University.

Leslie, Connie, Regina Elam, and Allison Samuels. 1995. "The Loving Generation: Biracial Children Seek Their Own Place." *Newsweek,* February 13, 72.

Lesser, Jeffrey. 1999. *Negotiating National Identity: Immigrants, Minorities, and the Struggle for Ethnicity in Brazil.* Durham: Duke University Press.

Lewis, Diane E. 2004. "Inequality Among Women Explored." *Boston Globe,* May 7. http://www.boston.com/business/articles/2004/05/07/inequality_among_women_explored?mode=PF/.

Lichter, Daniel T. 1988. "Racial Difference in Underemployment in American Cities." *American Journal of Sociology* 93, no. 4:771–92.

Lieberson, Stanley, and Mary C. Waters. 1988. *From These Strands: Ethnic and Racial Groups in Contemporary America.* The Population of the United States in the 1980s, a Census Monograph Series. New York: Russell Sage Foundation.

"Light and Dark." 1997. *Nightline,* ABC, February 28.

Lipsitz, George. 1998. *The Possessive Investment in Whiteness: How White People Profit from Identity Politics.* Philadelphia: Temple University Press.

———. 2003. "Noise in the Blood: Culture, Conflict, and Mixed Race Identities." In *Crossing Lines: Race and Mixed Race Across the Geohistorical Divide,* ed. Marc Coronado, Rudy P. Guevarra Jr., Jeffrey Moniz, and Laura Furlan Szanto, 32–35. Santa Barbara, Calif.: Multiethnic Student Outreach, in collaboration with the Center for Chicano Studies, University of California, Santa Barbara.

Little, Bryce. 1989. "Pluralism and Integration." Manuscript.

Locke, Michelle. 2004a. "Regents Vote Against Adding 'Multiracial' Box." *San Francisco Chronicle,* November 16. http://www.sfgate.com/cgibin/article.cgi?file=/news/archive/2004/11/17/state2105EST0163.DTL/.

———. 2004b. "UC Regent Ward Connerly Pushes For Multiracial Category." Press Center, *Equal Justice Society,* March 17. http://www.equaljusticesociety.org/pres_ap_2004_03_17.html/.

———. 2005. "Controversial Regent Retires." *Daily Breeze,* January 16, A6.

Lockhart, James, and Stuart B. Schwartz. 1987. *Early Latin America: A History of Colonial Spanish America and Brazil.* New York: Cambridge University Press.

Logsdon, Joseph, and Caryn Cosé Bell. 1992. "The Americanization of Black New Orleans, 1850–1900." In *Creole New Orleans,* ed. Arnold R. Hirsch and Joseph Logsdon, 201–61. Baton Rouge: Louisiana State University Press.

Long, William R. 1988. "Brazil: No Equality for Blacks Yet." *Los Angeles Times,* April 9, 1, 16.

Longo, James McMurtry. 2001. "Princess Isabel and the Emperor Pedro II: Imperial Power in the Hands of the Abolitionist Regent of Brazil, 1888." Paper presented at the Twenty-Third International Congress on Latin American Studies, Washington, D.C., September 6,

López, Ian F. Haney. 1996. *White by Law: The Legal Construction of Race.* New York: New York University Press.

Lovell, Peggy A., and Charles H. Wood. 1998. "Skin Color, Racial Inequality, and Life Chances in Brazil." *Latin American Perspectives* 25, no. 3 (May): 90–109.

Lovell-Webster, Peggy. 1987. "The Myth of Racial Equality: A Study of Race and Mortality in Northeast Brazil." *Latinamericanist,* (May): 1–6.

Lowry, Ira. 1980. "The Science and Politics of Ethnic Enumeration." Paper presented at the annual meeting of the American Association for the Advancement of Science in San Francisco, January 3–8.

Lugaila, Terry, and Julia Overturf. 2004. *Children and the Households They Live In: 2000.* U.S. Census Bureau, Census 2000 Special Reports, CENSR-14, February. http://www.census.gov/prod/2004pubs/censr-14.pdf/.

Luís, Émerson. 2002. "Up and Coming." *Brazzil,* August 1. http://www.brazzil.com/content/view/7432/74/.

Luna, Francisco Vidal, and Herbert S. Klein. 2003. *Slavery and the Economy of São Paulo, 1750–1850.* Stanford: Stanford University Press.

Luna, Luiz. 1976. *O Negro na Luta Contra Abolicão.* Rio de Janeiro: Editora Leitura.

Lynell, George. 1999. "Guessing Game." *Los Angeles Times Magazine,* February 21, 18–21, 34, 36.

Maitre, Michele. 2004. "Connerly Sets New Tack on UC Forms." *Oakland Tribune.* March 11.

Marable, Manning. 1995. *Beyond Black and White: Transforming African-American Politics.* New York: Verso.

Marcílio, Maria Luisa. 1984. "The Population of Colonial Brazil." In *Colonial Latin America,* vol. 2 of *The Cambridge History of Latin America,* ed. Leslie Bethell, 37–63. New York: Cambridge University Press.

Marcus, Ruth. 1995. "Affirmative Action Supporters Hope Women Play Key Role in Debate." *Washington Post,* May 31, A16.

Marger, Martin N. 1991. *Race and Ethnic Relations: American and Global Perspectives.* Belmont, Calif.: Wadsworth.

Margolis, Mac. 1992. "The Invisible Issue: Race in Brazil." *Ford Foundation Report* 23, no. 2 (summer): 3–7.

———. 2003. "Brazil's Racial Revolution: Affirmative Action Has Finally Come of Age. And Latin America's Most Diverse Society May Change in Ways Few Had Ever Imagined." *Newsweek International,* November 3, 46.

Marriott, Michelle. 1991. "Colorstruck." *Essence,* November, 93.

Martins, Sérgio da Silva, Carlos Alberto Medeiros, and Elisa Larkin Nascimento. 2004. "Paving Paradise: The Road from 'Racial Democracy' to Affirmative Action in Brazil." *Journal of Black Studies* 34, no. 6 (July): 787–816.

Marx, Anthony W. 1995. "Contested Citizenship: The Dynamics of Racial Identity and Social Movements." *International Review of Social History* 40, no. 3:159–83.

———. 1998. *Making Race and Nation: A Comparison of the United States, South Africa, and Brazil.* New York: Cambridge University Press.

Massey, Douglas S., and Nancy A. Denton. 1993. *American Apartheid: Segregation and the Making of the Underclass.* Cambridge: Harvard University Press.

Mathews, Thomas G. 1974. "The Question of Color in Puerto Rico." In *Slavery and Race Relations in Latin America,* ed. Robert Brent Toplin, 299–323. Westport, Conn.: Greenwood Press.

Mattoso, Katia M. de. 1986. *To Be A Slave in Brazil, 1550–1888.* New Brunswick: Rutgers University Press.

Mazlish, Bruce. 1989. *A New Science: The Breakdown of Connections and the Birth of Sociology.* New York: Oxford University Press.

McDaniel, Antonio. 1996. "The Dynamic Racial Composition of the United States." In *An American Dilemma Revisited: Race Relations in a Changing World*, ed. Obie Clayton Jr., 269–87. New York: Russell Sage Foundation.

McIntosh, Peggy. 1992. "White Privilege and Male Privilege: A Personal Account of Coming to See Correspondence Through Work in Women Studies." In *Race, Class, and Gender: An Anthology*, ed. Margaret Anderson and Patricia Hill Collins, 70–81. Belmont, Calif.: Wadsworth.

McKay, Ruth G., and Christine C. Hijima Hall. 1996. "Transracial Adoptions: In Whose Best Interest?" In *The Multiracial Experience: Racial Borders as the New Frontier*, ed. Maria P.P. Root, 63–78. Thousand Oaks, Calif.: Sage Publications.

McKenney, Nampeo R. 1989. Nampeo McKenney, Assistant Division Chief, Special Population Statistics, Population Division, U. S. Census Bureau. Letter to Ms. Darlene Y. Willoth, Interracial Family Circle, Atlanta, Georgia, December 18, 1989.

McRae, F. Finley. 1988. "Watson Fears Use of 'Mixed Race' on Census Forms." *Los Angeles Sentinel*, September 22, A12.

Mencke, John G. 1979. *Mulattoes and Race Mixture: American Attitudes and Images, 1865–1918*. Ann Arbor: University of Michigan Institute of Research.

Mendonça, Renato. 1973. *A Influência Africana no Portuguêse do Brazil*. Rio de Janiero: Civilização Brasileira.

Merelman, Richard. 1995. *Representing Black Culture: Racial Conflict and Cultural Politics in the United States*. New York: Routledge.

Merida, Kevin. 1995. "Rights Debate: Both Sides Uneasy; Review for Dole Finds Affirmative Action Usually Doesn't Mean Quota." *Washington Post*, February 23, A13.

Miller, Robin. 1992. "The Human Ecology of Multiracial Identity." In *Racially Mixed People in America*, ed. Maria P.P. Root, 24–36. Thousand Oaks, Calif.: Sage Publications.

Miller, William Lee. 1996. *Arguing About Slavery: The Great Battle in the United States Congress*. New York: Alfred A. Knopf.

Mills, Gary B. 1977. *Forgotten People: Cane River's Creoles of Color*. Baton Rouge: Louisiana State University Press.

Mitchell, Michael. 1985. "Blacks and the Abertura Democrática." In *Race, Class and Power in Brazil*, ed. Pierre-Michel Fontaine, 120–34. Los Angeles: UCLA Center for African American Studies.

Monroe, Sylvestre. 1990. "Love in Black and White: The Last Racial Taboo." *Los Angeles Times Magazine*, December 9, 14–22, 58–62.

Moore, Trudy S. 1995. "Black Lawmakers Oppose Michigan Bill That Makes New Multiracial Class." *Jet*, June, 46.

Moore, Zelbert. 1988. "Reflections on Blacks in Contemporary Brazilian Popular Culture in the 1980s." *Studies in Latin American Popular Culture* 7:213–26.

Morganthau, Tom, Susan Miller, Gregory Beals, and Regina Elam. 1993. "What Color Is Black." *Newsweek*, February 13, 63–65.

Morrison, Ken. 1995. *Marx, Durkheim, Weber: Formations of Modern Social Thought*. Thousand Oaks, Calif.: Sage Publications.

Morse, Richard M. 1974. *From Community to Metropolis: A Biography of São Paulo, Brazil*. New York: Farrar, Straus and Giroux.

Moulthrop, David. 2001. "Capoeira's History." Capoeira IC Homepage. October 16. http://www.ithaca.edu/capoeira/pages/history.html/.

MSNBC. 2003. "Racial Privacy Initiative Defeated." October 7. http://www.msnbc.com/news/976981.asp?cp1=1/.

Murray, Barbara. 1997. "Clearing the Heirs: We May Soon Know If Jefferson Had Black Children." *U.S. News and World Report,* December 22, 54–56.

Murray, Barbara, and Brian Duffy. 1998. "Did the Author of the Declaration of Independence Take a Slave for His Mistress / DNA Tests Say Yes." *U.S. News and World Report,* November 9, 59–64.

Muwakkil, Salim. 2005. "Black Men: Missing?" *Alternet,* June 23. http://www.alternet.org/rights/22283/.

Myers, Linda James. 1988. *Understanding an Afrocentric World View: Introduction to an Optimal Psychology.* Dubuque, Iowa: Kendall/Hunt Publishing.

Myers, Samuel L. 1997. "Preface." In *Civil Rights and Race Relations in the Post Reagan-Bush Era,* ed. Samuel L. Myers, viii–xiii. Westport, Conn.: Praeger Publishers.

Myrdal, Gunnar. 1944. *An American Dilemma: The Negro Problem and Modern Democracy.* New York: Harper and Brothers.

Nantambu, Kwame. 1998. "Pan-Africanism Versus Pan-African Nationalism: An Afrocentric Analysis." *Journal of Black Studies* 28 (May): 561–74.

Nascimento, Abdias do. 1967. "The Negro Theater in Brazil." *African Forum* 2, no. 4:35–53.

———. 1979. *Mixture or Massacre? Essays on the Genocide of a Black People.* Translated by Elisa Larkin Nascimento. Buffalo: Puerto Rican Studies and Research Center, State University of New York at Buffalo.

———. 2004. "Teatro Experimental do Negro: Trajetória e Reflexões." *Estudos Avançados* 18, no. 50 (April): 209–24.

Nascimento, Abdias do, and Elisa Larkins do Nascimento. 1992. *Africans in Brazil: A Pan-African Perpsective.* Trenton, N.J.: Africa World Press.

Nash, Gary B. 1982. *Red, White and Black: The Peoples of Early America.* 2nd edition. Englewood Cliffs, N.J.: Prentice-Hall.

———. 1990. *Race and Revolution.* Madison, Wis.: Madison House.

———. 1999. *Forbidden Love: The Secret History of Mixed-Race America.* New York: Henry Holt.

Nelson, Jennifer. 1997. "ACRI Criticizes Federal Government's Rejection of a Multiracial Census Box." American Civil Rights Institute, ACRI News, News Release. July 9. http://www.acri.org/news/070997.html/.

Neves, Francisco. 2002. "Two Brazils." *Brazzil,* May 1. http://www.brazzil.com/content/view/2562/68/.

Nishida, Meiko. 1998. "From Ethnicity to Race and Gender: Transformations of Black Lay Sodalities in Salvador, Brazil." *Journal of Social History* 32, no. 2 (winter): 329–48.

Njeri, Itabari. 1988a. "Colorism: In American Society Are Light-skinned Blacks Better Off?" *Los Angeles Times,* April 24, F1, F10, F12–F13.

———. 1988b. "A Sense of Identity." *Los Angeles Times,* June 5, F1, F8–F9

———. 1991. "Call for Census Category Creates Interracial Debate." *Los Angeles Times,* January 13, E1, E9–E11.

Nobles, Melissa. 1995. "Responding With Good Sense: The Politics of Race and Censuses in Contemporary Brazil." Ph.D. diss., Yale University.

———. 2000. *Shades of Citizenship: Race and the Census in Modern Politics.* Stanford: Stanford University Press.

Nunes, Maria Luisa. 1979. *Lima Barreto: Bibliography and Translations*. Boston: G. K. Hall.

Okazawa-Rey, Margo, Tracy Robinson, and Janie V. Ward. 1987. "Black Women and the Politics of Skin Color and Hair." In *Women, Power, and Therapy*, ed. Marjorie Braude, 89–102. New York: Haworth Press.

Oliveira, Cloves Luiz Pereira. 1999. "Struggling for a Place: Race, Gender, and Class in Political Elections in Brazil." In *Race Relations in Contemporary Brazil: From Indifference to Equality*, ed. Rebecca Reichmann, 167–77. University Park: Pennsylvania State University Press.

Oliveira, Elvira. 1993. "Dia Nacional da Consciencia Negra." *Nova Escola*, November, 23–25.

Oliver, Melvin L., and Thomas M. Shapiro. 1995. *Black Wealth, White Wealth: A New Perspective on Racial Inequality*. New York: Routledge.

Olsen, Otto H. 1967. *The Thin Disguise: The Turning Point in Negro History—Plessy v. Ferguson, A Documentary Presentation (1864–1896)*. New York: Humanities Press.

OMB. *See* U.S. Office of Management and Budget.

Omi, Michael, and Howard Winant. 1994. *Racial Formation in the United States: From the 1960s to the 1990s*. 2nd edition. New York: Routledge.

Ortiz, Fernando. 1947. *Cuban Counterpoint*. Translated by Harriet de Onís. New York: Alfred A. Knopf.

Osava, Mario. 2005. "Rights—Brazil: Blacks Demand Adoption of Promised Measures." Inter-Press Service News Agency, November 16. http://www.ipsnews.net/news.asp?idnews=31051/.

Otten, Allen L. 1991. "Interracial Marriages Increase, But Still Rare." *Wall Street Journal*, May 9, B1.

Paixão, Marcelo. 2004. "Waiting for the Sun: Account of the (Precarious) Social Situation of the African Descendant Population in Contemporary Brazil." *Journal of Black Studies* 34, no. 6 (July): 743–65.

Park, Robert E. 1928. "Human Migration and the Marginal Man." *American Journal of Sociology* 33 (May): 881–93.

Parker, Frank. 1995. "Eradicating the Continuing Barriers to Effective Minority Voter Participation." In *From Exclusion to Inclusion: The Long Struggle for African American Political Power*, ed. Ralph C. Gomes and Linda Faye Williams, 73–83. Westport, Conn.: Praeger Publishers.

Parker, Richard. 1991. *Bodies, Pleasures, and Passions: Sexual Culture in Contemporary Brazil*. Boston: Beacon Press.

Pauley, Garth E. 2001. *Modern Presidency and Civil Rights: Rhetoric on Race from Roosevelt to Nixon*. Presidential Rhetoric Series, no. 3. College Station: Texas A&M University Press.

Penha-Lopes, Vânia. 1996. "What Next? On Race and Assimilation in the United States and Brazil." *Journal of Black Studies* 26, no. 6 (July): 809–26.

Pierre, Robert E. 2003. "U-Michigan Reveals New Policy: Provost Says Diversity Will Remain a Priority in Admissions." *Washington Post*, August 29, A02.

Piersen, William D. 1993. *Black Legacy: America's Hidden Heritage*. Amherst: University of Massachusetts Press.

Pierson, Donald. 1967. *Negroes in Brazil: A Study of Race Contact at Bahia*. Carbondale: Southern Illinois University Press.

Pinkney, Alphonso. 1984. *The Myth of Black Progress*. New York: Cambridge University Press.

Pinto, Regina Pahim. 1996. "A Frente Negra Brasileira." *Cultura Vozes* 4 (July–August): 45–59.

Piper, Adrienne. 1992. "Passing for White, Passing for Black." *Transition* 58, no. 4:13–15.

Piza, Edith, and Fúlvia Rosemberg. 1999. "Color in the Brazilian Census." In *Race Relations in Contemporary Brazil: From Indifference to Equality*, ed. Rebecca Reichmann, 37–52. University Park: Pennsylvania State University Press.

Pope, Justin. 2004. "Colleges Find Affirmative Action Isn't Easy: Lawsuit Threats Cause Schools to Drop Programs Aimed at Minorities." Associated Press, June 21. http://www.msnbc.com/id/5256459/.

Poppino, Rollie E. 1961. *Brazil: The Land and the People*. Oxford: Oxford University Press.

Poston, W.S. Carlos. 1990. "The Biracial Identity Model: A Needed Addition." *Journal of Counseling and Development* 69 (November/December): 152–55.

Prado, Caio, Jr. 1969. *The Colonial Background of Modern Brazil*. Translated by Suzette Macedo. Berkeley and Los Angeles: University of California Press.

Pritchard, J. 2003. "Debate Highlights Health Care's Role as Prop. 54 Issue." *Santa Barbara News-Press*, September 30, A9.

Qian, Zhenchao. 1997. "Breaking the Racial Barriers: Variations in Interracial Marriage Between 1980 and 1990." *Demography* 34, no. 2 (May): 263–376.

Queiroz, Delcele Mascarenhas. 2003. "A Negro, Seu Acesso ao Ensino Superior e as Ações Afirmativas." In *Levando a Raça a Sério: Ação Afirmativa e Universidade*, ed. Joaze Bernardino and Daniela Galdino, 137–56. Rio de Janeiro: DP&A Editora.

"Race in Brazil, Out of Eden." 2003. *The Economist Print Edition*, July 3. http://www.economist.com/world/la/displayStory.cfm?story_id=1897546/.

"Racial Classifications on Census Forms." 2000. C-SPAN. Program ID: 156340-1, March 31, News Conference, Washington, D. C.

"Racial Privacy Initiative Defeated." 2003. MSNBC. October 7. http://www.msnbc.com/news/976981.asp?cp1=1/.

Radcliffe, Elizabeth. 1988. "Round One Lost." *The Communiqué: Newspaper of the Interracial Family Alliance* (Houston), fall, 1–2.

Ramirez, Deborah A. 1996. "Multiracial Identity in a Color Conscious World." In *The Multiracial Experience: Racial Borders as the New Frontier*, ed. Maria P.P. Root, 49–62. Thousand Oaks, Calif.: Sage Publications.

Ramirez, Manuel, III. 1983. *Psychology of the Americas: Mestizo Perspectives on Personality and Mental Health*. New York: Pergamon Press.

Randolph, Laura B. 1989. "Black Women/White Men: What's Goin' On?" *Ebony*, March, 154, 156–62.

Rankin, David C. 1977–78. "The Impact of the Civil War on the Free Colored Community of New Orleans." *Perspectives in American History* 11 (August): 379–416.

Raphael, Allison. 1990. "From Popular Culture to Microenterprise: The History of Brazilian Samba Schools." *Latin American Music Review* 11, no. 1 (June): 73–78.

Rattansi, Ali. 1994. "'Western' Racisms, Ethnicities and Identities in a 'Postmodern' Frame." In *Racism, Modernity and Identity: On the Western Front*, ed. Ali Rattansi and Sallie Westwood, 15–86. Cambridge, Mass.: Polity Press.

Ravitch, Diane. 1990. "Multiculturalism Yes, Particularism No." *Chronicle of Higher Education*, October 24, A44.

Reichmann, Rebecca. 1995. "Brazil's Denial of Race." *North American Congress on Latin America Report on the Americas* 28, no. 6:35–42.

———. 1999. "Introduction." In *Race Relations in Contemporary Brazil: From Indifference to Equality*, ed. Reichmann, 1–35. University Park: Pennsylvania State University Press.

Renn, Kristen A. 2004. *Mixed Race Students in College: The Ecology of Race, Identity, and Community on Campus*. Albany: State University of New York Press.

Riencourt, Amaury de. 1974. *Sex and Power in History*. New York: David McKay.

Rifkin, Jeremy. 1991. *Biosphere Politics: A Cultural Odyssey from the Middle Ages to the New Age*. San Francisco: HarperCollins.

Riggs, Marlon. 1986. *Ethnic Notions*. VHS. San Francisco: California Newsreel.

Ringer, Benjamin B. 1983. *We the People and Others: Duality and America's Treatment of Its Racial Minorities*. New York: Routledge.

Ritzer, George. 2000. *Sociological Theory*. 5th edition. New York: McGraw Hill.

Roberts, Robert E.T. 1994. "Black-White Intermarriage in the United States." In *Inside the Mixed Marriage: Accounts of Changing Attitudes, Patterns, and Perceptions of Cross-Cultural and Interracial Marriages*, ed. Walton R. Johnson and Michael D. Warren, 25–79. Lanham, Md.: University Press of America.

Robinson, Cedric. 1983. *Black Marxism: The Making of the Black Radical Tradition*. Totowa, N.J.: Zed Books.

Robinson, Lori S. 1994. "The Two Faces of Brazil; A Black Movement Gives Voice to an Invisible Majority." *Emerge*, October, 38–42.

Rocha, Jan. 1988. "A Hundred Years of Servitude." *South*, August, 21–25.

Rochetti, Ricardo. 2004. "Not as Easy as Black and White: The Implications of the University of Rio de Janeiro's Quota-Based Admissions Policy on Affirmative Action." *Vanderbilt Journal of Transnational Law* 37, no. 1423 (November). http://web .lexis-nexis.com/universe/document?_m=5eb66ec1eb9aff3afe64e92c41a1df60 &_docnum=3&wchp=dGLbVlb-zSkVb&_md5=0571753367a1a6b0fa45e78 41eee1b9b/.

Rockquemore, Kerry A., and David L. Brunsma. 2002. *Beyond Black: Biracial Identity in America*. Thousand Oaks, Calif.: Sage Publications.

Rockquemore, Kerry Ann and Tracey Laszloffy. 2005. *Raising Biracial Children*. Altamira Press. A Division of Rowman and Littlefield. Laham, Md.

Rodrigues, Ana Maria. 1984. *Samba Negro Espoilação Branca: Um Estudo das Escolas de Samba do Rio de Janeiro*. São Paulo: Editora Hucitec.

Rodriguez, Clara E. 1989. *Puerto Ricans Born in the U.S.A.* Boston: Unwin Hyman.

———. 2000. *Changing Race: Latinos, the Census, and the History of Ethnicity in the United States*. New York: New York University Press.

Rodriguez, Roberto, and Patricia Gonzales. 1996. "Census Bureau Paints the U.S. White." *Chronicle Features*, January 14.

Roediger, David. 1991. *The Wages of Whiteness: Race and the Making of the American Working Class*. London: Verso.

Rogin, Michael. 1996. *Blackface, White Noise: Jewish Immigrants in the Hollywood Melting Pot*. Berkeley and Los Angeles: University of California Press.

Rohter, Larry. 2002. "From Maid to Rio Governor, and Still Fighting." *New York Times*, August 1. http://www.nytimes.com/2002/08/17/international/americas/17FPRO.html ?ex=1117425600&en=9573ae6e6cb18052&ei=5070&oref=login/.

———. 2003. "Racial Quotas in Brazil Touch Off Fierce Debate." *New York Times*, April 5. http://www.nytimes.com/2003/04/05/international/Americas/05BRAZ.html/.

Rojas, Armando. 2003. "Bustamante to Shift Disputed Donations: The $3.8 Million Move to Fight Prop. 54 Aims to Quiet His Critics." *Sacramento Bee,* September 7, A1.

Roland, Edna. 1999. "The Soda Cracker Dilemma." In *Race Relations in Contemporary Brazil: From Indifference to Equality,* ed. Rebecca Reichmann, 195–206. University Park: Pennsylvania State University Press.

Root, Maria P. P. 1990. "Resolving 'Other' Status: Identity Development of Biracial Individuals." In *Complexity and Diversity in Feminist Theory and Therapy,* ed. Laura S. Brown and Maria P. P. Root, 185–205. New York: Haworth Press.

———. 1992. "Within, Between and Beyond Race." In *Racially Mixed People in America,* ed. Maria P.P. Root, 3–11. Thousand Oaks, Calif.: Sage Publications.

———. 2001. *Love's Revolution: Interracial Marriage.* Philadelphia: Temple University Press.

———. 2003. "Five Mixed-Race Identities: From Relic to Revolution." In *New Faces in a Changing America: Multiracial Identity in the 21st Century,* ed. Loretta I. Winters and Herman L. DeBose, 3–20. Thousand Oaks, Calif.: Sage Publications.

Rosellini, Lynn. 1998. "Cutting the Great Man Down to Size." *U.S. News and World Report,* November 9, 66.

Rosenau, Pauline Marie. 1992. *Postmodernism and the Social Sciences: Insights, Inroads, and Intrusions.* Princeton: Princeton University Press.

Rosenblatt, Paul C., Terri A. Karis, and Richard D. Powell. 1995. *Multiracial Couples: Black and White Voices.* Thousand Oaks, Calif.: Sage Publications.

Rossomando, John. 2001. "California Initiative Seeks to End Racial Classifications." *CNS News,* December 31. http://www.cnsnews.com/Politics/Archive/200112/POL20011231a .html

Rotella, Sebastian. 1996. "Singer Finds Race Issue No Laughing Matter in Brazil." *Los Angeles Times,* September 5, A1, A15.

Rothman, Joshua D. 1999. "James Callender and Social Knowledge of Interracial Sex in Antebellum Virginia." In *Sally Hemings and Thomas Jefferson: History, Memory, and Civic Culture,* ed. Jan Ellen Lewis and Peter S. Onuf, 87–113. Charlottesville: University Press of Virginia.

Russell, James W. 1994. *After the Fifth Sun: Class and Race in North America.* Englewood Cliffs, N.J.: Prentice-Hall.

Russell, Kathy Y., Midge Wilson, and Ronald Hall. 1992. *The Color Complex: The Politics of Skin Color Among African Americans.* New York: Harcourt Brace Jovanovich.

Russell-Wood, A.J.R. 1972. "Colonial Brazil." In *Neither Slave nor Free: The Freemen of African Descent in the Slave Societies of the New World,* ed. David. W. Cohen and Jack P. Greene, 84–133. Baltimore: Johns Hopkins University Press.

Sacks, Karen. 1994. "How Did Jews Become White Folks?" In *Race,* ed. Steven Gregory and Roger Sanjek, 78–102. New Brunswick: Rutgers University Press.

Sample, Herbert. A. 2000. "Connerly Joins Foes of 'Silly' Queries on Census Forms: He Weighs Ballot Drive to Limit Race Data," *Capitol Alert, The Sacramento Bee News,* April 1. http://www.capitolalert.com/news/capalert02_20000401.html/.

Sanders, Edith. 1969. "The Hamitic Hypothesis: Its Origin and Function in Time Perspective." *Journal of African History* 10, no. 4:521–32.

Sanders, Jim. 2003. "Prop. 54 Funding Is Questioned: Most Comes from a Nonprofit That Doesn't Identify Donors." *Sacramento Bee,* August 18, A3.

Sanjek, Roger. 1994. "Intermarriage and the Future of Races." In *Race,* ed. Steven Gregory and Roger Sanjek, 103–30. New Brunswick: Rutgers University Press.

Sansone, Livio. 2003. *Blackness Without Ethnicity: Constructing Race in Brazil.* New York: Palgrave Macmillan.

Sant'Anna, Wania. 1997. "Informe e Comentários sobre a 'Reunião Temática—Contéudo do Questionário Censo Demográfico do Ano 2000.'" Unpublished circular.

Santos, Sales Augusto dos. 2003. "Ação Afirmativa e Mérito Individual." In *Ações Afirmativas: Políticas Contra as Desigualidades Raciais,* ed. Renato Emerson dos Santos and Fátima Lobato, 83–126. Rio de Janeiro: DP&A Editora.

Saunders, A. C. de C. M. 1982. *A Social History of Black Slaves and Freedmen in Portugal, 1441–1555.* Cambridge: Cambridge University Press.

Saxton, Alexander. 1990. *The Rise and Fall of the White Republic: Class Politics and Mass Culture in Nineteenth Century America.* London: Verso.

Sayers, Raymond. 1956. *The Negro in Brazilian Literature.* New York: Hispanic Institute in the United States.

Schemo, Diana Jean. 1996. "Among Glossy Blondes, A Showcase for Brazil's Black Faces." *New York Times,* October 18, A13.

Schevitz, Tanya. 2004. "UC Regents Connerly Wants Multi-race Box on University Admissions Applications." *San Francisco Chronicle,* November 15. http://www.sfgate.com/cgi-bin/article.cgi?file=/chronicle/archive/2004/11/15/BAGGI9RF7D1.DTL/.

Schiele, Jerome H. 1991. "Afrocentricity for All." *Black Issues in Higher Education,* September 26, 27.

———. 1998. "Rethinking Organizations from an Afrocentric Viewpoint." In *Afrocentric Visions: Studies in Culture and Communication,* ed. Janice D. Hamlet, 73–88. Thousand Oaks, Calif.: Sage Publications.

Schlesinger, Arthur, Jr. 1991. *The Disuniting of America: Reflections on a Multicultural Society.* Knoxville, Tenn.: Whittle Direct Books.

Schwartz, Stuart. 1987a. "Formation of Colonial Identity in Brazil." In *Colonial Identity in the Atlantic World, 1500–1800,* ed. Nicholas Canny and Anthony Pagden, 15–50. Princeton: Princeton University Press.

———. 1987b. "Plantations and Peripheries, c.1580–c.1750." In *Colonial Brazil,* ed. Leslie Bethell, 67–44. New York: Cambridge University Press.

Scott, James. 1990. *Domination and the Arts of Resistance: Hidden Transcripts.* New Haven: Yale University Press.

Scott, Walter. 1998. "Walter Scott's Personality Parade." *Parade Magazine,* August 23, 2.

Segura, Denise. 1986. "Chicanas and Triple Oppression in the Labor Force." In *Chicana Voices: Intersections of Class, Race, and Gender,* ed. Teresa Córdova, Norma Cantu, Gilberto Cardenas, Juan Garcia, and Christine M. Sierra, 46–65. Austin, Tex.: Center for Mexican American Studies.

Selsky, Andrew. 2002. "Brazil Elects Silva as President." Associated Press, October 28, 1.

Sen, Rinku. 2003–4. "Winning Race." *Colorlines* 6, no. 4 (winter): 7–8.

Sertima, Ivan Van. 1976. *They Came Before Columbus: The African Presence in Ancient America.* New York: Random House.

Shellenbarger, Sue. 1993. "Work-force Study Finds Loyalty Is Weak, Divisions of Race and Gender Are Deep." *Wall Street Journal,* September 3, B1.

Sheriff, Robin E. 1999. "The Theft of *Carnival:* National Spectacle and Racial Politics in Rio de Janeiro." *Cultural Anthropology* 14, no. 1:3–28.

———. 2001. *Dreaming of Equality: Color, Race, and Racism in Urban Brazil.* New Brunswick: Rutgers University Press.

Shohat, Ella, and Robert Stam. 1994. *Unthinking Eurocentrism: Multiculturalism and the Media*. New York: Routledge.

Silva, Denise Ferreira da. 1989. "Revisiting Racial Democracy: Race and National Identity in Brazilian Thought." *Estudos Afro-Asiáticos* 16, no. 3:157–70.

Silva, Luiz. 1989. "Luiz Gama: Uma Trajetória Além do Seu Tempo." *Estudos Afro-Asiáticos* 16, no. 2:59–69.

———. 1992. "The Black Stream in Brazilian Literature." *Conexões: African Diaspora Research Project, Michigan State University* 4, no. 2:12–13.

Silva, Maria Palmira da. 2005. "Identidade Racial Brasileira." In *Racismo no Brasil: Percepções da Discriminação e do Preconceito Racial no Século XXI*, ed. Gevanilda Santos and Maria Palmira da Silva, 37–44. São Paulo: Editora Fundação Perseu Abramo.

Silva, Nelson do Valle. 1978. "White-NonWhite Income Differentials: Brazil." Ph.D. diss., University of Michigan.

———. 1985. "Updating the Cost of Not Being White in Brazil." In *Race, Class, and Power in Brazil*, ed. Pierre-Michel Fontaine, 42–55. Los Angeles: UCLA Center for African American Studies.

———. 1999. "Racial Differences in Income in Brazil." In *Race Relations in Contemporary Brazil: From Indifference to Inequality*, ed. Rebecca Reichmann, 67–82. University Park: Pennsylvania State University Press.

Silva, Nelson do Valle, and Carlos A. Hasenbalg. 1999. "Race and Educational Opportunity in Brazil." In *Race Relations in Contemporary Brazil: From Indifference to Equality*, ed. Rebecca Reichmann, 53–66. University Park: Pennsylvania State University Press.

Sim, Jillian A. 1999. "Fading to White: One Woman's Journey into Her Family's Past Uncovers a Story That Affects Every American." *American Heritage*, February/March, 68–78.

Simmons, Tavia, and Martin O'Connell. 2003. *Married-Couple and Unmarried-Partner Households: 2000*. U.S. Census Bureau, Census 2000 Special Reports, CENSR-5, February. http://www.census.gov/prod/2003pubs/censr-5.pdf/.

Simon, Rita J., and Howard Alstein. 1987. *Transracial Adoptees and Their Families: A Study of Identity and Commitment*. New York: Praeger.

Sirica, Jack. 1995. "The Race Question: Five Years Before the Next Forms Go Out, a Fight Is Breaking Out Over Census Question 4." *Newsday*, January 16, B4–5.

Siss, Ahyas. 2003. *Afro-Brasileiros, Cotas, e Ação Afirmativa: Razões Históricas*. Rio de Janeiro: Quartet Editora.

Skidmore, Thomas A. 1974. *Black into White: Race and Nationality in Brazilian Thought*. New York: Oxford University Press.

———. 1985. "Race and Class in Brazil: A Historical Perspective." In *Race, Class and Power in Brazil*, ed. Pierre-Michel Fontaine, 11–24. Los Angeles: UCLA Center for African American Studies.

———. 1992–93. "Race Relations in Brazil." *Camões Center Quarterly* 4, no. 3-4:49–57.

———. 1993. "Bi-racial U.S.A. vs. Multi-racial Brazil: Is the Contrast Still Valid?" *Journal of Latin American Studies* 25, no. 2 (May): 383–86.

Slater, David. 1994. "Exploring Other Zones of the Postmodern: Problems of Ethnocentrism and Difference Across the North-South Divide." In *Racism, Modernity, and Identity: On the Western Front*, ed. Ali Rattansi and Sallie Westwood, 87–126. Cambridge, Mass.: Polity Press.

Small, Stephen. 1994. *Racialized Barriers: The Black Experience in the United States and England in the 1980s*. New York: Routledge.

Smedley, Audrey. 1993. *Race in North America: Origin and Evolution of a Worldview*. Boulder, Colo.: Westview Press.

Snipp, C. Matthew. 1986. "Who Are American Indians? Some Observations About the Perils and Pitfalls of Data for Race and Ethnicity." *Population Research and Policy Review* 5, no. 3:247–51.

Sobel, Michel. 1987. *The World They Made Together: Black and White Values in Eighteenth-century Virginia*. Princeton: Princeton University Press.

Sorokin, Pitirim. 1957. *Social and Cultural Dynamics: The Study of Change in Major Systems of Art, Truth, Ethics, Law and Social Relationships*. Revised and abridged. Boston: Porter Sargent Books.

Sowell, Thomas. 1975. *Race and Economics*. New York: D. McKay.

———. 1981. *Ethnic America: A History*. New York: Basic Books.

———. 1982. *The Economics and Politics of Race: An International Perspective*. New York: William Morrow.

———. 1984. *Civil Rights: Rhetoric or Reality?* New York: William Morrow.

Spencer, Jon Michael. 1993. "Trends of Opposition to Multiculturalism." *Black Scholar* 23, no. 2:2–5.

———. 1997. *The New Colored People: The Mixed-Race Movement in America*. New York: New York University Press.

Spencer, Rainier. 1999. *Spurious Issues: Race and Multiracial Identity Politics in the United States*. Boulder, Colo.: Westview Press.

———. 2004. "Assessing Multiracial Identity Theory and Politics." *Ethnicities* 4, no. 3:357–79.

Spickard, Paul R. 1989. *Mixed Blood: Intermarriage and Ethnic Identity in Twentieth-Century America*. Madison: University of Wisconsin Press.

———. 1992. "The Illogic of American Racial Categories." In *Racially Mixed People in America*, ed. Maria P.P. Root, 12–23. Thousand Oaks, Calif.: Sage Publications.

Spickard, Paul R., Rowena Fong, and Patricia L. Ewalt. 1995. "Undermining the Very Basis of Racism—Its Categories." *Social Work* 40, no. 5:581–84.

Spitzer, Leo. 1989. *Lives In Between: Assimilation and Marginality in Austria, Brazil, and West Africa, 1780–1945*. Cambridge: Cambridge University Press.

Stanton, Lucia, and Diane Swann-Right. 1999. "Bonds of Memory: Identity and the Hemings Family." In *Sally Hemings and Thomas Jefferson: History, Memory, and Civic Culture*, ed. Jan Ellen Lewis and Peter S. Onuf, 161–86. Charlottesville: University Press of Virginia.

Staples, Robert. 1988. "An Overview of Race and Marital Status." In *Black Families*, ed. Harriet Pipes McAdoo, 187–190. Thousand Oaks, Calif.: Sage Publications.

Starr, Paul. 1992. "Civil Reconstruction: What to Do Without Affirmative Action." *American Prospect*, winter, 7–16.

Steele, James D., and Rick Reese. 1989. *We Do Not Begin—We Continue (Afro-Brazilians in the Year of the Abolition)*. VHS. Washington, D.C: Reunion Communications.

Steele, Shelby. 1990. *The Content of Our Character: A New Vision of Race in America*. New York: St. Martin's Press.

———. 2003. "Race Card Is the Sign of a Losing Hand. *Los Angeles Times*, September 18. http://www.latimes.com/la-oe-steele18sep18,1,2511763.story/.

Steinberg, Stephen. 1989. *The Ethnic Myth: Race, Ethnicity and Class in America*. Boston: Beacon Press.

————. 1999. "Confronting the Misuse of Class-Based Affirmative Action." *New Politics* 7, no. 2 (new series), no. 26 (winter).

Steinhorn, Leonard, and Barbara Diggs-Brown. 1999. *By the Color of Our Skin: The Illusion of Integration and the Reality of Race.* New York: Dutton.

Sterkx, H. E. 1972. *The Free Negro in Antebellum Louisiana.* Rutherford: Farleigh Dickinson University Press.

Stohr, Greg. 2004. *A Black and White Case: How Affirmative Action Survived Its Greatest Legal Challenge.* Princeton, N.J.: Bloomberg Press.

Stonequist, Everett V. 1937. *The Marginal Man: A Study in Personality and Culture Conflict.* New York: Russell and Russell.

Stromberg, Roland N. 1975. *An Intellectual History of Modern Europe.* 2nd edition. Englewood Cliffs, N.J.: Prentice-Hall.

Sundiata, I. K. 1987. "Late Twentieth-Century Patterns of Race Relations in Brazil and United States." *Phylon* 48, no. 1 (March): 62–76.

Tafoya, Sonya. 2000. "Check One or More . . . Mixed Race and Ethnicity in California." *California Counts: Population Trends and Profiles* 1, no. 2 (January): 1–15.

Talalay, Kathryn. 1995. *Composition in Black and White: The Tragic Saga of Harlem's Biracial Prodigy.* New York: Oxford University Press.

Taylor, Quintard. 1978. "Frente Negra Brasileira: The Afro-Brazilian Civil Rights Movement, 1924–1937." *Umoja* 2, no. 1:30.

Taylor-Gibbs, Jewelle. 1989. "Biracial Adolescents." In *Children of Color: Psychological Interventions with Minority Youth,* 322–50. San Francisco: Jossey-Bass.

Taylor-Gibbs, Jewelle, and Alice Hines. 1992. "Negotiating Ethnic Identity." In *Racially Mixed People in America,* ed. Maria P.P. Root, 223–38. Thousand Oaks, Calif.: Sage Publications.

Telles, Edward. E. 1992. "Residential Segregation by Skin Color in Brazil." *American Sociological Review* 57, no. 2 (April): 186–98.

————. 1993. "Racial Distance and Region in Brazil: Intermarriage in Brazilian Urban Areas." *Latin American Research Review* 28, no. 2:141–62.

————. 2003. "U.S. Foundations and Racial Reasoning in Brazil." *Theory, Culture, and Society* 20, no. 4:31–47.

————. 2004. *Race in Another America: The Significance of Skin Color in Brazil.* Princeton: Princeton University Press.

Telles, Edward E., and Edward Murguia. 1990. "Phenotypic Discrimination and Income Differences Among Mexican Americans." *Social Science Quarterly* 7, no. 4 (December): 682–96.

Tenzer, Laurence R. 1990. *A Completely New Look at Interracial Sexuality: Public Opinions and Select Commentaries.* Manahawkin, N.J.: Scholar's Publishing House.

Texeira, Mary Thierry. 2003. "The New Multiracialism: An Affirmation of or an End to Race as We Know It?" In *New Faces in a Changing America: Multiracial Identity in the 21st Century,* ed. Loretta Winters and Herman Dubose, 21–73. Thousand Oaks, Calif.: Sage Publications.

Thernstrom, Stephen, and Abigail Thernstrom. 1997. *America in Black and White: One Nation, Indivisible.* New York: Simon and Schuster.

————, eds. 2002. *Beyond the Colorline: New Perspectives on Race and Ethnicity in America.* Stanford, Calif.: Hoover Institution Press.

Thomas, David Y. 1911. "The Free Negro in Florida Before 1865." *South Atlantic Quarterly* 10, no. 4 (October): 335–37.

Thomas, Richard W. 1996. *Understanding Interracial Unity: A Study of Race Relations.* Thousand Oaks, Calif.: Sage Publications.

Thompson, Era Bell. 1965. "Does Amalgamation Work in Brazil?" *Ebony*, August, 27–30, 32–34, 41.

Thompson, Evelyn. 1988. "From the Editor." *Spectrum: The Newsletter of MASC (Multiracial Americans of Southern California)*, May, 1, 4.

Thompson, Maxine S., and Verna M. Keith. 2001. "The Blacker the Berry: Gender, Skin Tone, Self-Esteem, and Self-Efficacy." *Gender & Society* 15, no. 3 (June): 336–57.

Thornton, Michael. 1992. "Is Multiracial Status Unique? The Personal and Social Experience." In *Racially Mixed People in America*, ed. Maria P.P. Root, 321–25. Thousand Oaks, Calif.: Sage Publications.

Thornton, Russell. 1987. *American Indian Holocaust and Survival: A Population History Since 1492.* Norman: University of Oklahoma Press.

Tiffin, Helen. 1990. "Introduction" In *Past the Last Post: Theorizing Post-Colonialism and Post-Modernism*, ed. Ian Adam and Helen Tiffin, vii–xvi. Calgary: University of Calgary Press.

Tilove, Jonathan. 1991. "Talking about Race, National Identity." Newhouse News Service. *MSNBC News*, July 3.

Tizard, Barbara, and Ann Phoenix. 1993. *Black, White, or Mixed-Race: Race and Racism in the Lives of Young People of Mixed Parentage.* London: Routledge.

Tobar, Héctor. 2003. "A Racial Quake in Brazil." *Los Angeles Times*, October 1, column 1.

Tobias, Philip V. 1972. "The Meaning of Race." In *Race and Social Difference*, ed. Paul Baxter and Basil Sansom, 19–43. Penguin Modern Sociology Series. London: Penguin Books.

Toni, Ana. 2004. "For Brazil, First Steps Toward Affirmative Action." Ford Foundation Report, winter. http://www.fordfound.org/publications/ff_report/view_ff_report_detail.cfm?report_index=478/.

Toplin, Robert Brent. 1981. "Reinterpreting Comparative Race Relations: The United States and Brazil." In *Freedom and Prejudice: The Legacy of Slavery in the United States and Brazil*, ed. Robert Brent Toplin, 9–103. Westport, Conn.: Greenwood Press.

Toppo, Greg. 2003. "Michigan Unveils Admissions Standards, University Alters Policy on Race Following Ruling." *USA Today*, August 29, A4.

Torres, João Camilo de Oliveira. 1969. *Interpretação da Realidade Brasileira.* Rio de Janeiro: Livraria José Olímpio Editôra.

Tourér, Yemi. 1988. "Census Bureau Stopped in Its Tracks." *Challenger* (Buffalo, N.Y.), August 31, 10.

Trochim, Michael R. 1988. "The Black Guard: Racial Conflict in Post-Abolition Brazil." *Americas* 44, no. 3 (January): 287–88.

Trubshaw, Bob. 1995. "The Metaphors and Rituals of Place and Time: An Introduction to Liminality, or Why Christopher Robin Wouldn't Walk on the Cracks." *Mercian Mysteries* 22 (February): 1–8.

Truscott, Lucian K., IV. 1999. "Tom and Sally and Frank and Me: A Jefferson Descendent on Luck, Ancestry, and the Meaning of the DNA Findings." *American Heritage*, February/March, 82–84.

Tsui, Anne S., Terri D. Egan, and Charles A. O'Reilly III. 1992. "Being Different: Relational Demography and Organizational Attachment." *Administrative Science Quarterly* 37:549–79.

Tucker, Belinda M., and Claudia Mitchell-Kernan. 1990. "New Trends in Black American Interracial Marriage: The Social Structural Context." *Journal of Marriage and the Family* 52 (February): 209–19.

Turner, Doris. 1992. "The *Teatro Experimental do Negro* and Its Black Beauty Contests." *Afro-Hispanic Review* 11, no. 1–3 (1992): 76–81.

Turner, J. Michael. 1985. "Brown into Black: Changing Racial Attitudes of Afro-Brazilian University Students." In *Race, Class and Power in Brazil*, ed. Pierre-Michel Fontaine, 73–94. Los Angeles: UCLA Center for African American Studies.

Turner, Victor Witter. 1969. *The Ritual Process: Structure and Anti-Structure*. Chicago: Aldine.

Twine, France Winddance. 1997. *Racism in a Racial Democracy: The Maintenance of White Supremacy in Brazil*. New Brunswick: Rutgers University Press.

U.S. Bureau of the Census. 1918. *Negro Population, 1790–1915*. Washington, D.C.: Government Printing Office.

———. 1970. *1970 Census. General Coding Procedures III-III-A-Attachment C-1*. Washington, D.C.: Government Printing Office.

———. 1980. *Questionnaire Reference Book. 20th Decennial Census—1980*. Form D-561 (May) Washington, D.C.: Government Printing Office.

———. 1992. *1990 Census Alphabetical Race and American Indian Tribe Code List (Outside data Users)*. (April). Washington, D.C.: Government Printing Office.

———. 2003. *Census 2000 Special Tabulation. Census 2000 PHC-T-19. Hispanic Origin and Race of Coupled Households: 2000*. Table 1. Hispanic Origin and Race of Wife and Husband in Married-Couple Households for the United States:2000. (March 13). http://www.census.gov/population/cen2000/phc-t19/tab01.pdf/.

———. 2005. *Census 2001c*. Table FG4. Married Couple Family Groups, by Presence of Own children/1 In Specific Age Groups, and Age, Earnings, Education, and Race and Hispanic Origin/2 of Both Spouses: 2003. (January 25). http://www.census.gov/population/socdemo/hh-fam/cps2001/tabFG4.pdf/.

U.S. Congress. 1994a. House. "Testimony of Project RACE Before House Subcommittee on Census, Statistics, and Postal Personnel, Committee on Post Office and Civil Service." *Hearings on the Review of Federal Measurements of Race and Ethnicity*. 103rd Cong., 1st sess., June 30, 115. Washington, D.C.: Government Printing Office.

———. 1994b. House. Subcommittee on Census, Statistics and Postal Personnel. *Review of Federal Measurements of Race and Ethnicity*. 103rd Cong., 1st sess., Serial No. 103-7 (April 14; June 30; July 29; November 3, 1993). Washington, D.C.: Government Printing Office.

———. 1997. House. Subcommittee on Government Management, Information and Technology of the House Committee on Government Reform and Oversight. "Statement of Congressman John Conyers." *Hearing on Federal Measures of Race and Ethnicity and the Implications for the 2000 Census*. 105th Cong., 1st sess., July 25, 535. Washington, D.C.: Government Printing Office.

U.S. Office of Management and Budget. 1997a. "Recommendations from the Interagency Committee for Review of the Racial and Ethnic Standards to the Office of

Management and Budget Concerning Changes to the Standards for the Classification of Federal Data on Race and Ethnicity; Notice." *Federal Register* 62, no. 131 (July 9).

———. 1997b. "Revisions to the Standards for the Classification of Federal Data on Race and Ethnicity." *Federal Register* 62, no. 210 (October 30).

———. 1999. Tabulation Working Group Interagency Committee for the Review of Standards for Data on Race and Ethnicity. "Draft Provisional Guidance on the Implementation of the 1997 Standards for Federal Data on Race and Ethnicity." February 17.

———. 2000. *Guidance on Aggregation and Allocation of Data on Race for Use in Civil Rights Monitoring and Enforcement,* omb Bulletin no. 00-02, March 9. http://www.whitehouse.gov/omb/bulletins/boo-02.html/.

———. 2005. "Equal Opportunity Commission." *Federal Register* 70, no. 227 (November 28).

Usdansky, Margaret L. 1992. "For Interracial Kids, Growth Spurt." *USA Today,* December 11, 7A.

Valente, Ana Lúcia E.F. 1986. *Política e Relações Raciais: Os Negros e As Eleições Paulistas de 1982.* São Paulo: Fundação de Amparo a Pesquisa do Estado de São Paulo.

Vianna, Hermano. 2004. "Mestiçagem Fora de Lugar." *Folha de São Paulo Caderno Mais,* June 27.

Vianna, Hermano, and John C. Chasteen. 1999. *The Mystery of Samba: Popular Music and National Identity in Brazil.* Chapel Hill: University of North Carolina Press.

Villardi, Raquel. 2004. "Acesso à Universiadade pro Meio de Ações Afirmativas: Estudo da Situação dos Estudantes com Matrícula em 2003 e 2004 (Junho)." uerj (Universidade do Estado do Rio de Janeiro) Report.

Vobeja, Barbara. 1991. "Categorizing the Nation's Millions of 'Other Race.'" *Washington Post,* April 29, A9.

Vongs, Pueng, J. Prakash, Marcelo Ballve, and Sandip Roy. 2003. "Around the World, Countries Grapple with Affirmative Action." *Pacific News Service,* July 11. http://news.pacificnews.org/news/view_article.html?article_id=3e26118fcdf4fba57da467da3e eb43do/.

Waldinger, Roger, and Tom Bailey. 1991 "The Continuing Significance of Race: Racial Conflict and Racial Discrimination in Construction." *Politics & Society* 19, no. 3:291–323.

Walker, Sheila S. 1989. "Africanity Versus Blackness: The Afro-Brazilian/Afro-American Identity Conundrum." In *Introspectives: Contemporary Art by Americans and Brazilians of African Descent,* ed. Nancy McKinney, 17–21. Los Angeles: California Afro-American Museum.

Wallace, Kendra R. 2001. *Relative/Outsider: The Art and Politics of Identity Among Mixed Heritage Students.* Westport, Conn.: Agathon.

Wardle, Francis. 1987. "Are You Sensitive to Interracial Children's Special Identity Needs." *Young Children* 43, no. 2 (January): 53–59.

Warger, W. Warren. 1977. *World Views: A Study of Comparative History.* Hinsdale, Ill.: Dryden Press.

Warren, Jonathan W., and France Winddance Twine. 1997. "White Americans, The New Minority? Non-Blacks and the Ever-Expanding Boundaries of Whiteness." *Journal of Black Studies* 28, no. 2 (November): 200–218.

Washington, Robert E. 2003. *The Ideologies of African-American Literature: From the Harlem Renaissance to the Black Nationalist Revolt.* New York: Rowman and Littlefield.

Washington State National Organization for Women. 1998. "Washington State National Organization for Women Position Paper on Affirmative Action." January. http://www.wanow.org/pp/affirmative_action.html/.

Waters, Mary. 2000. "Multiple Ethnicities and Identity Choices: Some Implications for Race and Ethnic Relations in the United States." In *We Are a People: Narrative and Multiplicity in Ethnic Identity*, ed. Paul R. Spickard and Jeffrey Burroughs, 30–31. Philadelphia: Temple University Press.

Wells, Mark. 2001. "Down in Black Bahia." *Brazzil*, June. http://www.brazzil.com/pages/blajuno1.htm/.

West, Candace, and Sarah Fenstermaker. 1995. "Doing Difference." *Gender and Society* 9, no. 1 (February): 8–37.

"White Girl." 2000. *Nightline*, ABC, May 9.

Whitlaw, Roger. 1974. *Black American Literature: A Critical History*. Totowa, N.J.: Littlefield, Amas.

Wilber, Ken. 1996. *A Brief History of Everything*. 2nd edition. Boston: Shambhala.

Wilkerson, Isabel. 1992. "Middle-Class Blacks Try to Grip a Ladder While Lending a Hand." In *Race, Class, and Gender in the United States*, 2nd edition, ed. Paula Rothenberg, 113–20. New York: St. Martins Press.

Wilkes, Rima and John Iceland. 2004. "Hypersegregation in the Twenty-First Century." *Demography* 41, no. 1 (February): 23–36.

Wilkins, Mariah. 1989. "The Triracial Isolates." Manuscript.

Will, George. 1997. "Melding in America." *Washington Post*, October 5, C07.

Williams, Kimberly M. 2000. "Multiracial Organizing: Updating You on My Dissertation Research." Personal journal. April, issue no.4, p. 4.

———. 2003. "Parties, Movements, and Constituencies in Categorizing Race: State Level Outcomes of Multiracial Category Legislation." In *States, Parties, and Social Movements: Pushing the Boundaries of Institutionalized Politics*, ed. Jack A. Goldstone, 197–225. Cambridge: Cambridge University Press.

———. 2005. "Multiracialism and the Civil Rights Future." *Daedelus* 134, no. 1 (winter): 53–60.

Williams, Patrick, and Laura Chrisman. 1994. "Colonial Discourse and Post-Colonial Theory: An Introduction." In *Colonial Discourse and Post-Colonial Theory: A Reader*, ed. Williams and Chrisman, 1–19. New York: Columbia University Press.

Williams, Pete. 2003a. "Gratz v. Michigan Undergraduate affirmative action program struck down." *NBC News*, June 9. http://msnbc.msn.com/id/3071007/.

———. 2003b. "Grutter v. Michigan Law School affirmative action program upheld." *NBC News*, June 9. http://msnbc.msn.com/id/3071004/.

Williams, Richard. 1990. *Hierarchical Structures and Social Value: The Creation of Black and Irish Identities*. Cambridge: Cambridge University Press.

Williams-León, Teresa K. 2001. "The Convergence of Passing Zones: Multiracial Gays, Lesbians, and Bisexuals of Asian Descent." In *The Sum of Our Parts: Mixed Heritage Asian Americans*, ed. Williams-León and Nakashima, 146–61. Philadelphia: Temple University Press.

Williams-León, Teresa K., and Cynthia L. Nakashima. 2001. "Introduction—Reconfiguring Race, Rearticulating Ethnicity." In *The Sum of Our Parts: Mixed Heritage Asian Americans*, ed. Williams-León and Nakashima, 3–12. Philadelphia: Temple University Press.

Williamson, Joel. 1980. *New People: Mulattoes and Miscegenation in the United States*. New York: New York University Press.

Wilson, Carter A. 1996. *Racism: From Slavery to Advanced Capitalism*. Thousand Oaks, Calif.: Sage Publications.

Wilson, Terry. 1992. "Blood Quantum: Native-American Mixed Bloods." In *Racially Mixed People in America*, ed. Maria P.P. Root, 108–25. Thousand Oaks, Calif.: Sage Publications.

Wilson, William Julius. 1980. *The Declining Significance of Race*. 2nd edition. Chicago: University of Chicago Press.

———. 1987. *The Truly Disadvantaged: The Inner City, the Underclass, and Public Policy*. Chicago: University of Chicago Press.

Wiltz, Teresa. 1995. "Can We Tell Who Is White or Black? Generations After Slavery, Issues of Identity Are Confusing, Complex." *Chicago Tribune*, February 26, 1, 4.

Winant, Howard. 1994. *Racial Conditions: Politics, Theory, Comparisons*. Minneapolis: University of Minnesota Press.

———. 2001. *The World Is a Ghetto: Race and Democracy Since World War II*. New York: Basic Books.

Winters, Loretta, and Herman DeBose, eds. 2003. *New Faces in a Changing America: Multiracial Identity in the Twenty-First Century*. Thousand Oaks, Calif.: Sage Publications.

Wintz, Cary D. 1988. *Black Culture and the Harlem Renaissance*. Houston: Rice University Press.

Wood, Charles H., and José Alberto Magno de Carvalho. 1988. *The Demography of Inequality in Brazil*. New York: Cambridge University Press.

Woodson, Jon. 1999. *To Make a New Race: Gurdjieff, Toomer, and the Harlem Renaissance*. Jackson: University of Mississippi Press.

Wright, George C. 1985. *Life Behind a Veil: Blacks in Louisville, Kentucky, 1865–1930*. Baton Rouge: Louisiana State University Press.

Wright, Roy Dean, and Susan W. Wright. 1972. "A Plea for a Further Refinement of the Marginal Man Theory." *Phylon* 33 (winter): 361–68.

Yancey, George. 2006. "Racial Justice in a Black/Nonblack Society." In *Mixed Messages: Multiracial Identities in the "Color-Blind" Era*, ed. David Brunsma, 86–111. Boulder, Colo.: Lynne Rienner Publishers.

Yinger, Milton J. 1981. "Toward a Theory of Assimilation and Dissimilation." *Ethnic and Racial Studies* 4, no. 3 (July): 249–63.

Young, Robert. 1994. "Egypt in America." In *Racism, Modernity, and Identity: On the Western Front*, ed. Ali Rattansi and Sallie Westwood, 150–70. Cambridge, Mass.: Polity Press.

———. 1995. *Colonial Desire: Hybridity in Theory, Culture, and Race*. New York: Routledge.

Zack, Naomi. 1994. *Race and Mixed Race*. Philadelphia: Temple University Press.

———, ed. 1995. *American Mixed Race: The Culture of Microdiversity*. Lanham, Md.: Rowman and Littlefield.

INDEX

abolition
    in Brazil: African Brazilians on, 43, 54, 56;
        anniversary celebrations of, 70–71, 237,
        252; Black Guard on, 57–58;
        brotherhoods and, 43; Free Coloreds on,
        33, 53; Gama and, 54–55, 77; gradualist
        approach to, 54–55, 54 n. 1; law enacting,
        56; racial resistance in, 76–77; ternary
        racial project after, 40–51
    in U.S.: binary racial project after, 104–18;
        Free Coloreds after, status of, 92–93;
        Thirteenth Amendment on, 105, 105 n. 11
Academy of Letters, Brazilian, 60
ACT Testing Service, 229 n. 21
Adams-Onís Treaty (1819), 109, 110
adoption, transracial, 163, 168
advertising
    in Brazil: African Brazilians targeted by, 238;
        in 1990 census campaign, 252
    in U.S., on Racial Privacy Initiative, 271
Advisory Committee on Race, 232
affirmation, racial, in Brazil, 240–44
affirmative action
    in Brazil: backlash against, 288; opposition
        to, 244, 288–89; problems with
        implementation of, 243–44; support for,
        241–43, 258, 290; Supreme Court on,
        288–89; at universities, 285–92; U.S.
        influence on, 243, 243 n. 6, 288–89
    in U.S.: backlash against, 210–13; Black
        Experimental Theater and, 73; and black
        middle class, 214 n. 9; and Brazilian race
        relations, 178; class-based, 266;

        dismantling of, 210; gender-based, 211;
        multiracial identifier and, 224; for
        patterns of discrimination, 221;
        pluralism of, 147; political right on,
        210–12, 264, 266; public opinion of, 212
        n. 7, 264; Supreme Court on, 259–67,
        289; at universities, 259–67
Affirmative Action Expert Group, 289
Afonso Arinos Law (Brazil, 1951), 74, 177, 240
Africa. *See also* South Africa; West Africa
    art of, 60
    culture of: in Brazil, 36–37, 49, 74; in U.S.,
        87–88
    decolonization of, 185
    Egypt as part of, 23–24, 103, 217
    freed slaves emigrating to, 42–43
    origin of humans in, xi, 21, 103
African(s)
    African Americans as, 88
    humanity of, 19, 21
    Muslim, as slaves, 17
    symbology of blackness of, 19–20
African Americans
    after abolition, 104–18
    African influences on, 87–88
    American *vs.* racial creed and, 103, 106–8
    as Americans *vs.* Africans, 88
    and amnesia, racial, 210–15
    Black Experimental Theater on, 73–74
    in bourgeoisie, 206–9, 214, 214 n. 9
    Brazilian culture influenced by, 60, 185
    Brazilian race relations and, 175–76
    in census, 96–97, 219, 222

Áurea, Lei (1888), 56
avant-garde, 59–61
awareness, racial
    in Brazil, 239–40
    colonialism and, 16
    religion and, 16–17
Azeredo, Albuíno, 196 n. 9
Azevedo, Thales de, 179–80

backlash, against affirmative action and civil
    rights
    in Brazil, 288
    in U.S., 210–13
Bacon's Rebellion (1676), 87
Bahia (state)
    Black Front in, 79
    demographics of, 42, 257
    home-grown whites in, 45
    racial order in, 42–45
    social change in, research on, 179–80
Bahia, State University of (UFBA), 285 n. 22, 290
Bahian School, 179–80
Baker, Josephine, 74
Bakke, Allan, 260
Bakke, Regents of University of California v., 260,
    262, 263–64
Barreto, Afonso Henriques de Lima, 2, 55–56,
    77
Bastide, Roger, 179
BBC, 184, 252
beauty contests
    African Americans in, 204
    African Brazilians in, 74–75, 75 n. 6, 83,
    238–39
behavior, race and, 26
Berkeley (California), 157–58
Bernal, Martin, 21–22, 22 n. 5
BFN. See Biracial Family Network
Bible
    and Egyptians, 23
    and human origins, 21
    and slavery, 19, 20
binary racial project
    Brazilian: affirmative action and, 285–92;
    census data collection and, 246–58;
    movement toward, 258, 285; new
    African Brazilian identity and, 292–94
    U.S., 85–118; after abolition, 104–18; in
    Anglo vs. Latin North America, 92–98;
    Brazilian mobilization inspired by, 192;
    Creoles of color and, 130–33;
    dismantling of, 154–63; Latinas/os and,

225; multiracial elite and, 123–26;
    multiracial identity and, 172–73, 219;
    multiracial movement and, 154–63; one-
    drop rule in, viii, 91–98; opponents
    contesting, 119–37; origin of, 85–91;
    passing and, 119–23; racial resistance to,
    133–37; triracial isolates and, 126–30;
    white domination and, 91–98; white
    supremacy and, 98–104
biological concept of race, xii–xiii
    vs. ancestral notions, 165 n. 12
    definition of, 165 n. 12
    multiracial identity and, 165
    multiracial movement on, 274–75
    passing as challenge to, 135
    rise of, 24
Biracial Family Network (BFN), 158
biracial individuals
    in census, 223
    first-generation individuals as, 160
    use of term, xi
black Americans. See African Americans
black Brazilians. See African Brazilians; pretos
Black Club for Social Culture, 67, 70–71
Black codes, colonial, 91
Black Doll, 75
black Egyptians, 23–24, 103
Black Experimental Theater, 72–75
    on democracy ideology, 73–74, 83–84
    establishment of, 72
    political mobilization by, 72–75, 82
    racial resistance by, 81–84
Black Front, 61–67
    anti-immigrant sentiments in, 66–67
    Black Experimental Theater and, 73, 74
    decline of, 67
    establishment of, 62
    on Integralist movement, 67
    leadership of, 62, 66, 67, 80
    membership of, 62–63
    as political party, 62, 67
    racial resistance by, 78–81, 83–84
    reorganization of, 70–71
    tactics of, 65–66
    under Vargas, 63–65, 68, 81
Black Guard, 57–59
    in abolitionist movement, 57–58
    establishment of, 57
    mission of, 57
    racial resistance by, 77–78, 83–84
    reforms advocated by, 57–59, 77–78
    violence by, 58–59, 77, 78

INDEX 347

France, Free Coloreds under, 95, 96
Franco, Afonso Arinos de Mello, 74
Franklin, Aretha, 185
fraternities, 125
Frazier, E. Franklin, 176
Free Coloreds
    in Brazil: in civilian militia, 32; in colonial
        period, 30–34; in labor force, 31–32;
        mulattoes as, 30; number of, 30–31, 42;
        on slavery, 32, 33, 53; social status of,
        33–34
    in U.S.: in Anglo North America, 92–93,
        96–98; Europeanization of, 95; in labor
        force, 97–98; in Latin North America,
        94–98, 109–10; lifestyles of, 98;
        mulattoes *vs.* blacks as, 96–97; number
        of, 92, 95, 96–97; passing among, 121;
        from Saint-Domingue, 96; status of,
        91–98
free market, and discrimination, 206 n. 3
Free Womb, Law of the (Brazil, 1871), 54, 54 n. 1
Freeland, Gregory, 182
Frente Negra Brasileira (FNB). *See* Black Front
Frente Negra Socialistas, 67
Freud, Sigmund, 59, 60
Frey, William, 152, 152 n. 6
Freyre, Gilberto
    Casa Grande e Senzala, 69, 73
    on census, color in, 247–48, 256
    on national identity, 69–70
    on portraits, retouching of, 37
    on Portuguese colonizers, 27, 69
    in *Quilombo*, 73
    on race relations, 1, 177
    on racial democracy, 1, 178
    on ternary racial project, 27
    Vargas and, 69
fugitive slaves, 101
futurists, 60

Gallaudet University, 229 n. 21
Gama, Luís Gonzaga de Pinto da, 2, 53–55, 77
gangs, *capoeira*, 58 n. 2
Garcia, Januario, 251, 253
Garotinho, Anthony, 196 n. 10
Garvey, Marcus, 115
Gay Heads, 127
Geledés (organization), 188
gender. *See* women
genealogies, European Brazilian, 35, 37
General Assembly (Virginia), 99
genetics, xi–xii

genotypes, xi–xii
Georgia
    legal definition of blackness in, 93
    multiracial identifier in, 229
German immigration
    to Brazil, 37, 59
    to U.S., 118 n. 15
Getting Interracial Families Together (GIFT),
    158 n. 10
Gil, Gilberto, 258
Gingrich, Newt, 232, 233
glass ceilings, 208
Gliddon, George, 24
Golden Law (Brazil, 1888), 56
Goldoni, Ana Maria, 191
Gomes, Joaquim Benedito Barbosa, 258, 288
Goulart, João, 181–83, 194, 242
government. *See* state
Graham, Susan, 227, 231, 273
Gramsci, Antonio, 215
grandfather clauses, 110, 110 n. 13
Gratz, Jennifer, 260–61, 279 n. 20
Gratz v. Bollinger, 260–67
Great Britain. *See* Britain
Great Chain of Being, 10–11
Great Migration, 142, 157
Greece, ancient
    Ancient *vs.* Aryan Model of, 21–22, 22 n. 5
    Egyptian influence on, 21–23, 22 n. 6
    sensate sociocultural mode in, 13
group formation
    identity formation and, 167, 199
    among multiracial individuals, 169
    one-drop rule and, 217
Grupo Cultural Afro-Reggae, 186
Grupo Evolução, 185
Grupo Negro, 185
Grutter, Barbara, 261–62
Grutter v. Bollinger, 261–67
Guadalupe Hidalgo, Treaty of (1848), 110
Guarda Negra. *See* Black Guard
Guimarães, Antonio Sergio, 240
Guinea-Bissau, 185
Guineas, 127
Gurdjieff, George, 155

hairstyles, 238, 238 n. 1
Haliwas, 127
Ham, curse of, 19–20, 19 n. 4, 23
Hamacher, Patrick, 261
Hapa Issues Forum (HIF)
    in antiracist struggle, 276